# The Cottage Bible

# THE Cottage Bible

Gerry Mackie & Laura Elise Taylor

*The* BOSTON MILLS PRESS

**A BOSTON MILLS PRESS BOOK**

First Printing

**Library and Archives Canada Cataloguing in Publication**
Mackie, Gerald L., author
The Cottage Bible / Gerry Mackie & Laura Elise Taylor.
Second edition.
Includes bibliographical references and index.
ISBN 978-1-77085-706-3 (paperback)
1. Vacation homes—Handbooks, manuals, etc.  I. Taylor,
Laura Elise, 1975-, author  II. Title.
GV191.6.M22 2016          643'.25          C2015-906912-2

**Publisher Cataloging-in-Publication Data (U.S.)**
Gerry L. | Taylor, Laura Elise, 1975-
The Cottage Bible / Gerry Mackie & Laura Elise Taylor.
Second edition.
Includes bibliographical references and index.
Summary: Contains everything you need to know about
cottage living, from maintaining the systems in your
cottage to dealing with wildlife.
Identifiers: 978-1-77085-706-3 (pbk.)
LCSH: Vacation homes—Handbooks, manuals, etc. | Outdoor
recreation—Handbooks, manuals, etc. | Lakes—Recreational use.
Classification: LCC GV191.6M335 |DDC 643.25 – dc23

Published by Boston Mills Press, 2016

In Canada:
Distributed by Firefly Books Ltd.
50 Staples Avenue, Unit 1
Richmond Hill, Ontario, Canada L4B 0A7

In the United States:
Distributed by Firefly Books (U.S.) Inc.
P.O. Box 1338, Ellicott Station
Buffalo, New York, USA 14205

Cover and interior design: Kathe Gray / electric pear
Printed in China

The publisher gratefully acknowledges the financial support for our
publishing program by the Government of Canada through the Canada
Book Fund as administered by the Department of Canadian Heritage.

FRONT COVER, TOP: J.P. Holecka / Powershifter Media Corp.
FRONT COVER, BOTTOM ROW, LEFT TO RIGHT: Laura E. Taylor, Laura E. Taylor, Laura E. Taylor, Ryan McVay
BACK COVER, TOP ROW, LEFT TO RIGHT: Yanik Chauvin, Keith Levit, Tomo Jesenicnik, Nancy Louie; BOTTOM: Trevor Allen
FRONT INSIDE FLAP: Michael Gomez; SPINE: Denis Pepin; TITLE PAGE: Sebastien Windal
ILLUSTRATIONS ON COVER, HALF-TITLE AND CONTENTS: Ryan Price

# Contents

CHAPTER 1    Getting to Know Your Lake    13

CHAPTER 2    Boating    43

## CHAPTER 3 Swimming 89

## CHAPTER 4 Fishing 109

## CHAPTER 5 Living with Wildlife 133

CHAPTER **6** Cottage Operations **215**

## Acknowledgments **271**

## Bibliography **273**

## Credits **276**

## Index **277**

# Introduction

Owning your own cottage, camp or cabin can mean weeks, summers or even a year-round lifetime of enjoyment and pleasure.

SOME OF US HAVE A PLACE TO RETREAT to on weekends, on holiday, maybe even all the time. It is a place on a lake where we can relax and get outdoors and feel a special connection with nature. When we're on our way from the city to this special place, we say we're going up to the lake. We've called it a cottage, but to you it could be a camp or a cabin, a lodge or a chalet. What we are thinking about is a getaway place in the form of a dwelling that is generally small, simple and close to or on the water—and a source of great pleasure and enjoyment. It may be a place you have known since childhood, or it may be a place you are still dreaming of.

We begin in **Getting to Know Your Lake** by providing information on how to determine the origin of your lake, its anatomy, nutrient base, physical attributes and how to assess its water quality using some simple physical and chemical measurements, as well as the plants and animals that live in the lake.

In **Swimming**, we explore phenomena that dog-paddlers and endurance swimmers alike may experience while in the water—hot and cold spots, swimmer's itch and even beaver fever. For those who are wary of snapping turtles, leeches, bloodsuckers, and tangled mats of weedy plants, we've tried to lessen fears by showing the whole underwater picture.

Rain or shine, a cottage is a place to relax and reconnect with family, friends and nature.

Relaxing at the cottage (*left*) and on the lake (*right*).

The excitement of that first big catch.

For tips on how to predict weather from cloud formations, wind patterns, sky colors and more, look to the **Boating** and **Fishing** chapters, where weather predictions are highly relevant. We've done our best to dispel some common myths (snapping turtles snap only when you bug them enough, pike do lose their teeth regularly), and provide some useful guidance (for instance, on how to remove a fish hook from yourself).

Our intent in this book has been especially to consider the importance of the natural world around us as it relates to life at the cottage. We do not go to our cottages simply to swim, boat and fish. We like to commune with the plant and animal life that surrounds us, to enjoy it and, occasionally, to challenge it if it creeps into our cottage. In **Living with Wildlife** you'll meet an eclectic assemblage of plants and animals that can enhance or aggravate your life at the cottage. Learn how to remove porcupine quills and how to get rid of skunk odors. Find answers to other questions. Is it true that birds do not have blue pigments? How big an opening do mice need to enter a cottage? Do bats control mosquito populations?

Nearly all cottagers make at least three annual sojourns to the lake, one to open the cottage, one to close it and one of longer duration for a vacation. We've added advice for people who are looking to purchase property, with or without a dwelling, in the **Cottage Operations** chapter. We also deal with plumbing, septic systems, energy sources, how to cut and pile wood, how to build a sauna, the best woods for burning, building and making furniture, and even building a raft to get to your haven away from home by water. If you have zebra mussels in your plumbing system, here is where you'll find out how to deal with them.

We end with helpful tips for first aid kits, plant remedies, what to do if you're lost in the woods and campfire safety. Checklists are also provided for opening and closing a cottage.

We have tried to include many aspects of cottage life. Our coverage of plants and animals is eclectic because there are simply too many organisms in North America to describe them all in a book of this kind. If you cannot find what you are looking for here, go to any one of numerous books that deal exclusively with, for instance, birds of North America, or mammals, weeds, trees, or mushrooms of your part of North America. If you want to learn how to sail, canoe, or build a cottage, look for specialized books or courses on those subjects. See the **Bibliography** at the end of this book for some resources we have found useful.

Most cottagers have had to deal with minor and major disasters (from mouse dirt in the cupboards to a tree splitting the cottage roof), and in the remote wilderness we have to be especially innovative, but few if any have had one ounce of regret.

A cottage — and cottage living — is a legacy that can be passed down through generations.

In many cases, our offspring will inherit the cottage, as some of us did from our parents. Especially rewarding are the times spent doing things at the cottage with our children and their children — not only the fun activities such as swimming and fishing and toasting marshmallows over a campfire, but also the onerous chores that need to be done every year, hooking up the water, splitting and piling wood, putting away the boats. These are great times for bonding. It's especially gratifying when your children leave the cottage as they found it, wood box filled, enough gasoline for all generators and outboards, and a tidy cottage. Teach your children early to respect nature in the water and on the land; it soon becomes second nature and cottaging becomes a blissful family tradition.

Happy cottaging and camping!

*Left* Sharing cottage country with wildlife.

# CHAPTER 1

# *Getting to Know Your Lake*

It's up to each of us to become active stewards of the lakes we live on.

G IVEN THE SEEMINGLY ENDLESS network of lakes we enjoy, cottagers in the temperate zone of North America have a very special thing going for them. Where else in the world can you find water bodies as pristine, beautiful and accessible?

Long-time cottagers know where the deep spots are, where the fish hang out, where the rocks, the reeds and the weeds are. But newcomers — and veterans who want to separate lake lore from reality — would do well to get acquainted with the physical characteristics of their lake. Making a bathymetric map of the lake bottom is a great excuse for buying a fish finder, and knowing the type of lake you live on will help determine which fish might live there.

Each lake is connected to a broader watershed, the mineral characteristics of which influence the quality of the lake water, as well as its hardness and vulnerability to acid rain. Within each watershed, and often on cottage property, are wetlands teeming with life and vital to the health of the lakes they feed. The color, clarity and temperature of the lake water can indicate whether the lake is healthy or polluted, and how it has been affected by either natural enrichment as plants very slowly fill in and take over, or by human pollution.

Countless hours can be whiled away getting to know your lake.

# Lake origins

## Centuries of secrets: meromictic lakes

Some kettle lakes have steep sides surrounded by high hills. These meromictic lakes are so sheltered that wind never completely mixes the waters, leaving the bottom undisturbed and devoid of oxygen for centuries. Scientists have used core samples from the settled layers of pollen and algae to learn about the history of local plant populations, climate, and human activities.

In the slow march of geological time, glaciers grow and retreat, volcanoes erupt, and water wears away the landscape, creating and molding lakes. The origins of a lake will tell you much about the lake's water quality, how deep it is, how steep the drop-off is, and which fish and other species you're likely to find in it. Many different forces can create a lake.

## Glacial forces

Glacial activity is by far the most common lake-creating force. About 10,000 years ago, when the glaciers melted and retreated, they gouged huge cavities in the earth, and the melting ice filled the cavities. Because of the massive sizes of glaciers, there are huge areas such as the Great Lakes region filled with thousands of glacier-carved lakes. Most lakes formed by glacial scouring have an elongated shape, and because the ice in a particular area retreated in one direction, the lakes in that area are all oriented in the same direction. Several types of glacial lakes have been formed by ice-scouring action.

> Look on topographic maps of scale 1:100,000, 1:250,000 or larger to see the glacier-origin lakes all lined up like the claw marks of a retreating beast.

**Kettle lakes**  The most common glacial lakes are kettle lakes. They are plentiful in the most northern states, particularly New York, Michigan and Minnesota, and in Ontario, Quebec and Manitoba. Kettle lakes form when blocks of ice become trapped in glacial debris, called moraine. As the ice melts, the moraine is deposited around the edges, and the melt-water fills the depression.

**Cirques**  In mountainous areas, cirques evolve in rocky cliff basins where the slow downhill movement of ice and the continual freezing and thawing activity erodes and fractures the rock. Cirque lakes are usually deepest near the cliff and shallowest near the outlet.

**Paternoster lakes**  A chain of cirque lakes will form as a river flows down the mountainside, much like a string of beads, to form paternoster lakes. Many cottages in the Rocky Mountains are located on cirques and paternoster lakes.

**Fjord lakes and piedmont lakes**  Many cottages in mountainous coastal areas, especially Newfoundland, are on fjord and piedmont lakes. Fjord lakes occur along glaciated coastlines, and piedmont lakes occur at the foot of

cirque lake

piedmont lake

paternoster lakes

ice margin

cryogenic lake in permafrost

continental glacier

moraine lake in outwash plain

sea

fjord

permafrost

ground moraine

kettle lake in ground moraine

---

Thousands of years ago the ice-scouring action of glaciers retreating formed countless lakes of various types.

A chalet looks out over a chain of pasternoster lakes (*left*), and a fjord on the Newfoundland coast (*right*).

mountains in inland alpine areas. Because of the proximity of fjord lakes to oceans, they are often saltier than piedmont lakes.

**Moraine lakes, cryogenic or thaw lakes, glacial hydraulic lakes** In some cases, moraines trapped meltwater as the ice retreated to create moraine lakes. Cryogenic or thaw lakes occur when frozen ground or permafrost thaws, leaving the meltwater to fill the depression. The mere weight of some glaciers was sufficient to create depressions in the Earth's surface that filled with meltwater to create glacial hydraulic lakes.

## Tectonic forces

Earthquake! When the Earth's shell warps and buckles along its fault lines, lakes can form. Most tectonic lakes are very deep and tend to be rectangular. A few lakes on the west coast of the United States and Canada are graben or rift lakes.

**Graben and rift lakes** Graben lakes—such as Lake Tahoe, California, and Lake Baikal in Russia—form as a result of large, depressed areas located between adjacent faults. Where the fault block is not tilted, it forms a flat bottom in a trough. Rift lakes also form because of a single earthquake, with the depression (lake floor) caused by tilting.

## Volcanic forces

Erupting volcanoes spew lava that forms craters. The lava cools, forming a huge bathtub with no drain, which with years of rainwater forms a lake. The lava's basaltic minerals, which are low in nutrients and dissolved minerals, make the water clear and largely uninhabitable.

**Maars and calderas** Maars are circular depressions with diameters of less than a mile (1.6 km); although small, they can be extremely deep. Sometimes the rim of the volcano remains after the eruption, creating walls around a basin, called a caldera. Crater Lake in Oregon (1,969 feet / 600 m deep!) is a spectacular caldera that was formed by the collapse of the center of the volcanic cone.

### Extraterrestrial forces

The few meteoric crater lakes in North America, such as Coon Butte Crater Lake, Arizona, have dried up. The only evidence of the visitor from outer space is the crater.

The Mistaya River valley in Banff National Park.

Rivers entering the quiet waters of a lake may deposit large amounts of sediments to form deltas. Within these deltas can be long, narrow lakes called deltaic lakes. Some rivers, such as the Vermillion River in central Ontario, contain series of lakes that are just large bulges carved out by the erosional forces of the river, in places aided by glacial scouring. These lakes can be very deep, some exceeding 200 feet (61 m), and make ideal lake trout habitat.

## Solution lakes

In areas where rock is predominately limestone (calcium carbonate), rock salt (sodium chloride), or gypsum (calcium sulphate), water percolating through the ground slowly dissolves away the rock to form solution lakes. Generally circular and conically shaped, solution lakes are also known as sinks, dolines, or swallow holes.

**Karsts, false karsts and pipes** Lakes formed within limestone bedrock are called karsts. They are common in areas with hot springs, especially in the Rocky Mountains. The hot water increases the solubility of calcium carbonate, making the water very hard and alkaline (see **Acid rain** in this chapter). These amazing natural hot tubs have unique fauna and flora and are typically protected by federal and provincial and state laws. Solution lakes that form within sandstone are called false karsts or pipes.

## Erosional forces

Give water enough time and it will wear anything away, even rock. When rivers carve the land, lakes form.

**Plunge pools, deltaic lakes and "river bulges"** Plunge pool lakes are formed by the erosional forces of water at the base of a waterfall, often creating a favorite spot for trout and minnows.

**Oxbow lakes and levees** Oxbow lakes form on large, meandering rivers when one of the loops is cut off by the deposition of silt. Silt deposits at the edges of rivers can also isolate the main stream from an adjacent levee lake. Levees and oxbow lakes are refilled when floodwaters spill over the silt banks. Some can be destroyed by spring floods, while others have become more permanent. Most oxbow lakes fill up, creating first a marsh.

Over time an isolated loop of an oxbow river (like the U-shaped wood that fits under the neck of an ox) can become an oxbow lake.

The dam at the bottom left is a saddle dam built to confine the reservoir created by a primary dam, either to permit a higher water elevation and storage or to limit the extent of a reservoir for increased efficiency.

# Impoundments and reservoirs

We build dams, impoundments and reservoirs to meet our insatiable need for hydroelectric power, to control flow and prevent flooding, and for recreational use. The deepest area is always near the dam. There are many of these artificial lakes on the Missouri and Mississippi Rivers and in southern Ontario, their shores lined with cottages.

If you cottage on a lake or reservoir where the water is at times controlled by other than natural forces, you would be wise to be aware of what is going on in your part of the world. Year-round locals might know when the water levels are going to artificially rise or fall because they've received notice or know it happens every year, but new or occasional cottagers might not be aware and leave things (boats, docks or water lines, for instance) that could be swamped or left high and dry.

Reservoirs usually have three mandates: flood control, low-flow augmentation and recreation. Water levels are generally lowered every fall to accommodate spring runoff. Some controlled lakes allow no outboards; others allow them. Stay away from the dam itself, where the fast-flowing water can suck you under. New cottagers need to know the purposes of any dam that is connected to their lake, to figure out rises and falls in water level and to be aware of any possible dangers or problems.

Reservoirs created to generate hydroelectric power are generally much larger than those used for flood control.

> Not all dams are bad, nor are they all the result of human activity. Flooding caused by beaver dams is part of the natural cycle of change and renewal.

## Dam advantages

- Clean hydroelectric power
- Easier distribution of irrigation water
- Flood control

## Dam drawbacks

- Block the migration of fish such as trout (modern dams have fish ladders)
- Unnaturally shift river ecosystems to lake ecosystems, disrupting aquatic habitat
- Flood huge areas, disrupting land habitat
- Produce rotting vegetation that reduces oxygen levels at the bottom
- Poison fish and humans with methyl mercury

# Lake anatomy

**Quashing fears**

Scared that the monster at the bottom of the lake will someday rise up and take a bite out of your swimming body? Understanding what lives in the profundal zone can help dispel this common lake phobia.

In a eutrophic lake, most of the life is in the limnetic, littoral and sublittoral zones.

There's much more to your lake than the meets the eye. Unless you live on a boat full-time, you are likely most familiar with the shoreline—the sandy beach, the rocks, the reeds, the beat of the water as it laps or slams into the dock—but as you head out into open water and the bottom falls away into cold darkness, you are venturing into the unknown.

Most deep lakes can be divided into two zones. The deep open-water zone is called the *limnetic* zone. The sun warms the upper layer of the limnetic zone in the summer, while the lower layer remains cold and dark. The shallow water at the edge of the lake is called the *littoral* zone. Here, light penetrates to the bottom, and all sorts of aquatic plants grow, including those that bury their roots in the soil and lift their "heads" above water, such as cattails and bulrushes. As the land drops away, aquatic plants such as pondweed grow on the lake bottom, under the water. This is the *sublittoral* zone.

As the lake gets deeper, and light no longer reaches the bottom, plant life drops off. This cold, deep, dark, plantless bottom is called the *profundal* zone. In the summer, species such as lake trout that need cool, well-oxygenated water take refuge from the surface heat by hanging out above the profundal zone of oligo-trophic lakes. In shallower, nutrient-enriched lakes, bacteria decomposing organic material use up a lot, sometimes all, of the oxygen in the profundal zone. The oxygen is replenished in the spring and fall, when surface waters mix with the lower layers.

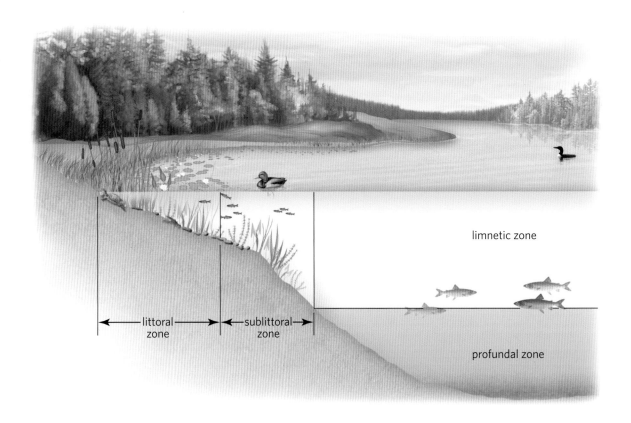

littoral zone — sublittoral zone — limnetic zone — profundal zone

# Important features of your lake

If you want to know where the fish hang out, where you can dive without bashing into rocks, how far out you can swim and still touch bottom, where the boating hazards are and how high the waves can get, you need to figure out the physical features of your lake. We recommend you use both of these time-tested methods: (1) Ask the neighbors (more than one, since consensus is rare); and (2) do a little measuring.

The features to measure are lake surface area, maximum length, maximum width, mean width and depth. A little knowledge of these features, together with information on the lake's origin and its watershed characteristics, such as bedrock types, can also help you determine the water quality of a lake.

## Surface area, length, width and depth

It isn't hard to measure your lake. It's a lot like measuring a room for a carpet. To do the measurements, you'll need

- a ruler, or a map measurer, available where you buy topographical maps, and
- an aerial or topographical map of your lake, usually 1:25,000 scale or less. If you have to use a 1:50,000 scale topographic map, enlarge it (using a photocopier) to a size large enough to draw depth contours at 3-foot (1 m) intervals and still fit it on a standard 8.5-by-11-inch sheet of paper. Make sure some grid lines show on the photocopy because they provide the scale and the true or magnetic north orientation of the lake.

Map measurers. The top one has a digital read-out and smaller wheel, making it more accurate and easier to use than the bottom one, which has a tape read-out.

The grid lines are separated by 2 cm, or 1 km (or 1 cm = 0.5 km) on a 1:50,000 scale map, regardless of whether the contours are given in feet or meters. So if a lake on a 1:50,000 topographic map is enlarged eight times, the scale should be 1 cm = 0.5 km / 8 = 0.0625 km.

- To see how this works, follow along on the hypothetical Golf Lake, on the next page. The Golf Lake topographic map is 1:50,000 scale. The magnetic north and true north lines are determined by the grid north lines using the declination shown on the right side of the map.

**Surface area** An easy way to measure the surface area is to trace the lake's outline from the map onto squared graph paper. Figure out how much area is represented by one square. Count the squares. The surface area of Golf Lake is 8.4 km² (3.2 square miles), using the squared paper method.

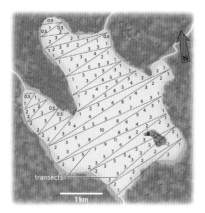

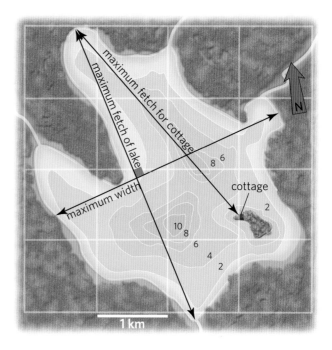

Golf Lake.  At left: Numbers are depths recorded by a fish finder.  At right: Lines (contours) are drawn through depths at 2, 4, 8 and 10 meters to show bathymetry of the lake.  Lengths and widths of the lake are measured with a ruler using a 1-kilometer scale.

**Maximum length** The maximum length is the longest straight-line distance across the water from one shoreline to the next, regardless of whether it passes through an island or one or more points of the lake. The longer the lake, the higher and stronger the waves can get, which will affect shoreline erosion and water safety. See the **Boating** chapter to determine maximum wave height for your lake. Use your ruler or map measurer and the topographic map to measure maximum length. The maximum length of Golf Lake is 4.4 km, or approximately 2.7 miles.

**Maximum width** The maximum width affects the same factors as maximum length. At right angles to the axis of the maximum length, measure the line that connects the greatest distance between two points on opposite shores. Golf Lake has a maximum length of 3.51 km (about 2.2 miles).

**Mean width** Mean width can affect the recreational potential of the lake — try windsurfing on a narrow lake! Divide the surface area of the lake by its maxi-

mum length to determine the mean width. Golf Lake has a mean width of 8.4 km² / 4.4 km, which equals 1.9 km (3.2 square miles / 2.2 miles = ½ miles).

**Lake bathymetry (where the deep spots are)**
Lake bathymetry details the depth contours of your lake to show you where the shallow and hazardous areas are and tell you how quickly the land drops off close to shore. If you can't get a bathymetric map for your lake and want to create one, you have to measure the depths, using a depth recorder (sounder). Fish finders are excellent for sounding lakes.

Draw several transects across the map of your lake. Use markers on the shores to follow a straight path with your boat. Record the depths at regular intervals (for instance, every ten to twenty seconds on each transect). Once you've recorded all the points, connect the dots in rings of depth around the lake, starting at the shore. Depth contours can be at any interval but 2- to 4-foot (0.5–1 m) intervals work best for shore areas and 15- to 30-foot (5–10 m) intervals are good for deeper areas.

# Watersheds

We all live in a watershed. Watersheds, also called drainage basins, are made up of all the streams and rivers that drain into a body of water, such as a lake. That lake belongs to a larger watershed, which in turn drains into the ocean. Hills or mountains divide watersheds, directing the paths of rainwater, streams and rivers from headwaters to outflows.

Just as children inherit many of their parents' and grandparents' qualities, lakes inherit the qualities of their watershed. Climate, geology, flora and fauna, topography and human activity (pollution) all affect the mineral and nutrient composition of water, making each watershed unique. The larger the watershed, the more physical and chemical influence it has on its streams and lakes. The shape of the watershed determines the number and size of the streams that drain the watershed. For example, in elongated watersheds, lakes are fed by a large number of small streams; in rounded watersheds, lakes are fed by several sizes of streams, with small ones draining into larger ones and larger ones draining into very large ones.

You can determine the size and shape of your lake's watershed from a topographical map. Moving outward from your lake, find the highest contour points all around it, and connect the dots.

## Back to bedrock

The geology of the watershed allows you to predict the mineral content of the streams and lakes within the watershed. Groundwater that flows over limestone (calcium carbonate) will contain more calcium carbonate than groundwater that flows over granite or quartz (mostly silica). Most parts of northern and central Ontario, northern Manitoba and Saskatchewan, Minnesota, Michigan and the Adirondack area in New York have granite

### Diamonds in the Great Lakes?

Diamonds originate in metamorphic rocks known as peridotite and eclogite. Some diamonds have been mined in metamorphic rock in the Great Lakes basin. But don't get out the pick and shovel yet — the rocks originated at depths of more than 93 miles (150 km) and are probably more than 2,500 million years old.

---

Divide line (in red) marks the extent of the watershed for Pedro Lake. The dots are on high points (see top right for details) and through saddles (see bottom right for details).

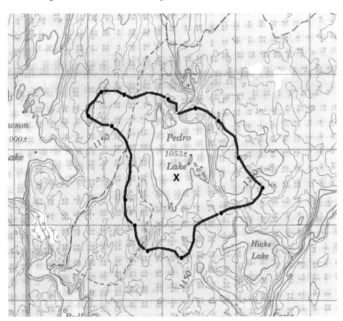

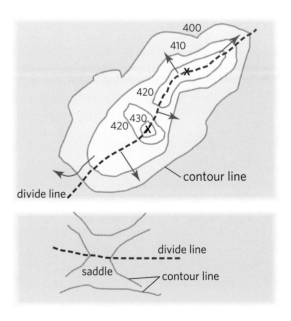

# Rock origins

Rocks are classified into three main groups based on their origin.

Basalt is a common volcanic rock.

**Igneous rocks** are formed by the cooling and crystallization of molten rock magma. Igneous rocks include granite, composed principally of quartz and feldspars. Such rocks contain some potassium and sodium ions, along with a little bit of calcium, but not much is leached from the rock to the watershed.

Sandstone is composed of grains of both quartz and feldspar.

**Sedimentary rocks** are formed by the deposition of mineral and rock particles by wind, water and ice in layers. The contributing rock particles may be igneous, sedimentary or metamorphic. For example, sandstone is compressed quartz and feldspar sand; limestone is composed mainly of calcite or dolomite. Coal is also a sedimentary mineral, composed of organic material compressed over time.

Slate forms from shale, a sedimentary rock.

**Metamorphic rocks** are igneous and sedimentary rocks that have been transformed by great heat and pressure within the Earth's crust. Common metamorphic rocks include gneiss, composed of crystalline grains of quartz and feldspars; shale, changed to slate, a rock that splits easily into thin sheets; quartzite, transformed into quartz sandstone; and marble, a recrystallization of limestone.

bedrock. Most parts of southern Ontario, southern Quebec, the Maritimes and northern parts of New York State have limestone or dolomite bedrock.

Streams and lakes with high calcium carbonate content from limestone tend to be more nutrient rich and support larger fisheries than lakes lying over granite bedrock. Lakes in granite have so few minerals that they are essentially "beakers" with glass (quartz) walls that contribute no chemistry to the water.

## The Canadian Shield

The Canadian Shield contains some of the oldest igneous rocks in the world, dating back to the Precambrian period, a mere one billion years ago. The Shield is generally quite flat and exposed, interrupted by a few mountain ranges such as the Laurentians in southern Quebec, the Otish Mountains in central Quebec and the Torngat Mountains near Ungava Bay. The geology of the Canadian Shield, Appalachians, Laurentians and the St. Lawrence Plain (also known as Lowlands) was influenced by the last ice age, which ended over 10,000 years ago. The Shield also has an extensive aquatic network with over a million lakes, peat bogs, rivers and streams, all shaped by glaciers. The retreating sheets of ice left glacial deposits of boulders, gravel and sand, and postglacial seawater and lakes left thick clay deposits on some parts of the Shield.

## The Appalachians

The Appalachian mountains run from Alabama north to Newfoundland. The rocks of this range are sedimentary, dating back to the Paleozoic era 250 to 500 million years ago. The mean elevation is about 1,650 feet (500 m), but some rise above 3,300 feet (1000 m). Intense folding raised the Laurentians during the Precambrian era and caused the Champlain Sea, to recede from the Canadian Shield, exposing the region to erosion for a long period of time. When the folding forces diminished and the region subsided adequately for the sea to flood the region once again, all the former peaks had been worn down to mere hills. The St. Lawrence Plain is almost entirely flat because of the clay deposits left behind by the Champlain Sea, which extended northward covering all of Montreal. The relief is broken only by the weathered Monteregian Hills.

# Flooding

We each have our own criteria for choosing a cottage location: a nice beach or a rock shelf, a warm south- or east-facing slope, a mix of trees, an absence of mosquitoes... But what about flooding? Is the dock going to disappear every spring? Will the basement become a wading pool? Understanding how rivers work, and reading a topographical map of the area will help you choose the best and safest spot.

All rivers flood and this flooding affects any connected lakes. It's a natural thing for waters to jump the banks each spring, and after heavy rains. Flooding brings nutrients to the lands adjacent to the river, creating river valleys with rich soils. Where there are forests and wetlands that use up and store a lot of water, flooding is naturally controlled, and seldom reaches devastating, cottage-obliterating levels. Human activity such as clear-cutting forests, draining wetlands, paving parking lots and building dams increases the size and frequency of flooding.

## Assessing the danger zone

Scientists can fairly accurately predict the size of a flood from one year to the next, but find it difficult to predict the timing and extent

Planning the location of your cottage wisely can save you money and heartache.

of the highest of floods. For most of us, the average high-water mark on a river is warning enough. You can determine the average high-water mark by measuring the height of debris hanging from the branches of shrubs in the area adjacent to the river (the riparian zone). Between 3 to 7 feet (1–2 m) is an average high-water height. Triple or quadruple this number for a 1-in-50-year flood!

## Predicting floods

Some flooding can be expected every year, so watch that high-water mark. Somewhat higher levels can be expected every ten years, and abnormally high levels can be expected every 50 years. Scientists measure the highest flow each year and chart the results over time. If you are wondering when your river is due for the next big flood, contact either the U.S. Geological Survey or Environment Canada.

*Left* Historic highs and lows.

## Setback

There is a minimum distance, called setback, that a cottage can be located from a lake or river. The setback is regulated by local authorities, but cottagers should also be concerned with flood levels. If there is little slope to the land, build the cottage beyond the 50-year flood level.

## Septic beds and run-off

Every district or municipality has guidelines on minimum setbacks and clearances for septic system absorption area, septic or holding tanks, privies and wells. In general, septic systems should be a minimum of 150 feet (45 m) from wells or water bodies and privies at least 100 feet (30 m) from a well or water body, but be sure to check with your local authority for your septic system and well. See the **Cottage Operations** chapter for septic system details.

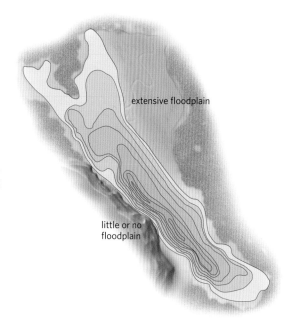

extensive floodplain

little or no floodplain

Tower Lake bathymetry indicates the surrounding floodplains. You would not be wise to build a cottage close to or on the floodplain.

# Floodplains: don't build here!

Floodplains are the flat, barren or vegetated areas at the edge of streams, rivers and lakes that tend to get flooded regularly. Some support grasses; others have shrubs or trees. They are frequently at or near the same elevation as the top of the stream banks.

Measure the extent of the floodplain by doubling the distance of the highest-water mark. For example, if the river rises 5 feet (1.5 m), the landward edge of the floodplain is 10 feet (3 m) from the river's edge. The highest-water mark can be very high, often 7 to 10 feet (2–4 m) above the normal water level!

Two people fish along the riparian zone of a river.

# River and lake buffers: the riparian zone

The land adjacent to the normal high-water line in a stream, river, lake or pond is called the riparian zone. It extends 100 feet (30 m) from the water's edge plus another 100 feet to allow for wind-fallen trees or shrubs, for a total of 200 feet (60 m). This important buffer strip absorbs chemical and physical extremes:

- The roots of plants absorb nutrients and contaminants such as phosphates, nitrates and pesticides from runoff before they enter the stream.
- Some riparian zones have trees that shade the stream and prevent water temperatures from rising too high.
- The soils, roots and organisms in the riparian zones filter the water. As water flows through vegetation, the current is slowed and silt settles out, clarifying the water.
- All components of the riparian zones are essential for maintaining the integrity of the shoreline and helping prevent shore erosion.

To protect the water system and prevent erosion, leave your shoreline as natural as possible. If you want to remove vegetation—cut down trees, build a retaining wall—always check with your local conservation authority.

# Lake health and water quality

What is a healthy lake? We have varying interpretations of human health. If someone never catches colds but needs a hip replacement, is he unhealthy?

It's the same for lakes. Lake health looks at the overall well-being of the lake and all the creatures that live in and around it—humans included. Some people consider a clear, pristine, oligotrophic lake healthier than a cloudy, nutrient-enriched eutrophic one. However, while oligotrophic lakes have oxygen at all depths and are nice to swim in, they are nutrient-poor and lack the species diversity that you find in lakes with more nutrients. (See **Nutrient level: trophic status** for further explanation.)

If you define health as water quality, then nutrient enrichment may not be an issue at all. It's possible to have a polluted oligotrophic lake if someone dumps sewage into it, or acid rain lowers the pH and kills some fish, or everyone uses two-stroke outboards that dump fuel and oil into the water. Water quality refers to all the characteristics of your lake water, from color and clarity to bacteria and toxins. Water quality falls somewhere between clean and polluted for most lakes and rivers.

There are many factors to consider in determining lake health and water quality. First we can look at nutrient enrichment (trophic status), and how the level of enrichment can be determined by assessing the physical characteristics of color, clarity and temperature. Then we can consider the chemical characteristics of oxygen, nitrogen and phosphorus levels as they relate to nutrient enrichment. Finally, there are the harmful bacteria, algae, and chemical pollutants that might be present in your lake.

## Muddy bottoms and nutrient enrichment

Hate mucky bottoms? Avoid nutrient-rich lakes. Nutrient enrichment refers to the algae and other living and dying organic material in the lake. Generally speaking, the more nutrients, the more algal life; the more algal life, the more organic material at the bottom; and the more organic material, the more muck.

A eutrophic lake (*left*) and an oligotrophic one (*right*).

# Environmentally friendly cleaners

Protect your lake. Choose products that are labeled "phosphate free" or, better still, check out our homemade environmentally friendly cleaners.

### Non-streaking glass cleaner:
Mix ¼ cup (59 mL) of white vinegar, 1 tablespoon (15 mL) of cornstarch, and 2 cups (472 mL) of warm water in a 34-fluid ounce (1 L) spray bottle. Shake until cornstarch dissolves. Spray liberally on glass then wipe with a clean cloth.

### All-purpose cleaner and disinfectant:
In a 34-fluid ounce (1 L) spray bottle combine 1 teaspoon (5 ml) of borax, ½ teaspoon (2.5 mL) of washing soda, and 2 tablespoons (30 ml) of lemon juice. Add 1 cup (236 mL) of very hot water and shake and mix well until dry ingredients dissolve. It stores indefinitely. To use, just spray and wipe.

### Nontoxic toilet bowl cleaner:
Flush the toilet to wet the sides. Sprinkle 1 cup (236 mL) of borax along the sides of the inside of the bowl. Spray ½ cup of vinegar over the borax and leave overnight. Scrub with a toilet brush and flush.

### Septic toilet activator:
If there is an odor from the septic tank and to beef up the sewage-digesting bacteria count, try this. Dissolve 1 pound (454 grams) of brown sugar in 1 quart (0.95 L) of hot water and allow to cool to lukewarm. Stir in 2 teaspoons (10 mL) of dried yeast, and immediately flush the mixture down the toilet.

### Dishwashing liquid:
In a bowl combine ¼ cup (59 mL) of soap flakes and 2 cups (472 mL) of hot water and stir until the soap is dissolved. Cool to lukewarm. Stir in ¼ cup (59 mL) of glycerin and ½ teaspoon (2.5 mL) of lemon essential oil and let it cool. As it cools a loose gel will form; stir with a fork to break up the gel and then pour into an empty 34-fluid ounce (1 L) shampoo or ketchup bottle. To use, squirt 3 teaspoonfuls into hot running water. Do not use this in automatic dishwashers.

### Lemon-scent furniture oil:
Mix 1 cup (236 mL) of olive oil or vegetable oil and 1 teaspoon (5 mL) of lemon essential oil. Apply mixture with a soft rag then wipe and buff to a glassy shine.

### Oven cleaner:
Mix the 16 ounces (453 g) of baking soda and ¼ cup (59 mL) of washing soda in a 17-fluid ounce coverable plastic container. Wet the floor and walls of the oven with water using a rag or paper towel. Generously sprinkle the walls and floor with the oven cleaner mixture and leave overnight. Next day, wipe all the grease and film away using an old rag. Rinse well. Use an abrasive pad and some salt on stubborn stains.

### Hard water clothes washer gel soap:
In a medium pot, stir together 2 cups (472 ml) of soap flakes, 1½ cups (354 ml) of borax, and 6 cups (1.4 L) of water. Heat slowly and stir until the mixture is clear. Add ½ cup (118 mL) of glycerin and set aside to cool. When cool, add 2 teaspoons (10 ml) of essential oil, lavender, lemon, or eucalyptus and stir thoroughly. Store in a Mason jar or other container and cover. To use, add 1 cup (236 mL) of gel soap per load of clothes. Make sure the soap is dissolved before adding clothes to the water. Works best in warm or hot water.

### Fabric softener:
Fill the washing machine or basin with water. Add ¼ cup (59 mL) of baking soda, stir it to dissolve, then add the clothes. After rinsing the clothes, make a final rinse with ½ cup (118 mL) of vinegar.

### Steel wool scouring pads:
To prevent soap-filled pads from rusting, put them in the freezer.

### Paint brushes:
If you are going to use the same color of paint again, put the brushes in the freezer between uses so you don't have to rinse them out.

### The magic of baking soda:
- leave an open box in the fridge to combat odors
- use it to brush your teeth
- combine with water and use as a stain remover
- combine with a little detergent to clean greasy surfaces
- use it with borax to bleach

### Soaps and shampoos:
Although soaps and shampoos don't contain phosphates, that doesn't mean you should use your lake as a bathtub. Many shampoos have ingredients derived from petrochemicals such as ammonium laureth sulfate, which can be harmful to animals. (And we use it on our heads!)

# Nutrient level: trophic status

There are three commonly used terms to describe the nutrient level, or "trophic status," of a lake: eutrophic, mesotrophic and oligotrophic.

♦ *Eutrophic* lakes are shallow, reedy and rich in nutrients, not the greatest for swimming but good for fish that like the reeds and don't mind the warmish, turbid water, such as carp. These lakes may sit on limestone bedrock. The nutrients come from the natural process of plant growth and decay, but can be raised to alarming levels by human activities.

♦ Pristine, *oligotrophic* lakes have clear, deep, well-oxygenated waters, potentially teeming with lake trout. Many oligotrophic lakes are surrounded by granite and quartz bedrock, which don't release many minerals into the water.

♦ Many cottage lakes are moderately enriched, or *mesotrophic*. Shorelines may have reedy patches and a diversity of aquatic life, but open-water zones are still clear, perhaps slightly colored, and deep.

# Eutrophication

All lakes started out as oligotrophic and are naturally progressing to a eutrophic state in an enrichment process called eutrophication. Over time, run-off from the surrounding area adds nutrients to the lake. Plants grow, die and accumulate at the bottom of the lake. Eventually (eons later), so much decomposing plant and animal matter builds up that the lake fills in, no water remains, and land species move in.

# Cultural eutrophication

Humans have accelerated the eutrophication process in many lakes by adding nutrients, such as phosphorous in detergents and fertilizers, excrement and garbage to the water. Although cultural eutrophication remains a serious problem in cottage country, the good news is that the reduction of phosphate and fertilizer use and the improvements at sewage facilities have allowed lakes that were suffering in the 1970s to recover slightly. Lake Erie, for example, is less eutrophic now than it was 30 years ago.

## Go phosphate-free: nitrogen and phosphorus pollution

Plants need nitrogen and phosphorus to survive. Problems arise when the levels of soluble nitrogen and phosphorus in the environment are much higher than needed. Algae feed off the excess phosphorus and nitrogen, choking waterways with massive blooms. Bacteria decomposing the dead algae reduce the amount of oxygen available for other aquatic life. Most phosphorus falls to the bottom in particle form. In oligotrophic lakes, it stays there. In eutrophic lakes, the lack of oxygen at the bottom releases the phosphate from the sediments into the water, making it available to the algae.

| TROPHIC STATUS | NUTRIENT LEVEL | PHYSICAL CHARACTERISTICS | COLOR | SECCHI DEPTH | INDICATOR SPECIES |
|---|---|---|---|---|---|
| Oligotrophic (known to some as pristine) | no organic enrichment | deep, clear, firm bottom often quartz and granite bedrock U-shaped lake basin | black or blueish | greater than 16.4 feet (5 m) | trout, whitefish, burbot, sculpins, mayflies, caddisflies, freshwater shrimp |
| Mesotrophic | moderate enrichment | deep and clear with some reedy, muddy shallows between V-U shaped lake basin | | 6.6–16.4 feet (2–5 m) | walleye, yellow perch |
| Eutrophic | organically enriched | shallow, reedy, muddy bottom, loon poop limestone bedrock V-shaped lake basin | greenish to brownish | Less than 6.6 feet (2 m) | white sucker, brown bullhead, red midgefly larvae, tubificid worms |

# Assessing water quality, part 1:
# Physical characteristics

### Red

The red wavelengths heat the lake. Only the upper layer of lake water heats up in the summer, because the red light does not penetrate the depths.

### Aquamarine

The color of death: a beautiful, clear aquamarine-blue lake may be suffering from acid rain pollution. See later in this chapter for more on acid rain.

### Orange

That orange water pouring from your tap is not necessarily orange because of iron in the lake or well water. The culprits are probably your ancient cast-iron pipes or water tank. Modern stainless steel, copper and plastic pipes have eliminated this problem.

Most of us covet a blue lake with clear water, but want warm swimming water in the summer. Lake color, clarity and temperature can give us an idea of the trophic status of the lake. *Color, clarity* and *temperature* are related. Light waves give color to water, but the kinds of materials dissolved and suspended in the water will modify the color. Also, light (red and infrared rays) creates heat. The amount of heat and rate of heating also depends on the materials dissolved and suspended in the water.

## Lake color

A lake's color is more than just a sign of beauty. It can often inform us about the health of a lake.

Most lakes appear blue for the same reasons that the sky appears blue; the color that we perceive in lakes is the scattered or reflected light. Just as in the atmosphere, light is scattered and absorbed or refracted by particles in the water. The light that enters the water has the same colors as the rainbow: at the left end of the light spectrum are blue and ultraviolet rays that have short wavelengths and high frequencies, and at the right end are red and infrared rays that have long wavelengths and short frequencies.

As light penetrates lake water, some wavelengths of light are absorbed. The reds and infrareds are absorbed first and penetrate the least, only to the 3- to 4-foot (1 m) depth. Only blue and violet light remains in deep lake water. In pure water, blue penetrates the deepest, followed by green, UV, red and infrared.

The order of absorption changes if there is dissolved material in the water. The more sus-

pended materials, the less blue and green light penetrate, and the more UV penetrates. The type of material suspended in the water affects the transmission of certain light waves. For example, lakes with lots of blue-green algae will appear green or turquoise-color. Blue-green algae absorb red and orange light, and transmit green and blue-green colors, which are then reflected upward to our eyes.

Lakes with lots of blue-green algae will appear green, as this one does.

## Color and trophic status

Is your lake blue or brown?

Pristine, clear, oligotrophic lakes should appear bluish or black because there are few particles to absorb the light. The blue wavelengths also penetrate the deepest in clear lakes. This explains why blue light is the dominant color scattered back to the surface in clear lakes. Of course, reflection of a blue sky also helps.

Nutrient-rich, cloudy, eutrophic lakes contain considerable amounts of reddish brown

organic materials that absorb blue light and transmit red light. This explains why these lakes appear brownish.

### True vs. apparent color

Because the color of the lake bottom and the color of the sky affect our perception, what we see is *apparent color*. To see the *true color* of water, we need to eliminate the lake bottom color, the sky and suspended particles. Comparing a water sample that has been filtered or centrifuged to remove suspended particles to a series of color standards shows the true color, influenced by the minerals and other substances dissolved in it. Scientists use true color to determine water quality.

# Transparency and the Secchi disc

Some water is so murky that when you step into it your feet disappear. The amount of material in the water affects the clarity, or transparency, of the water. The greater the amounts of suspended materials, such as algae, silt and microorganisms, the lower the transparency. Since algae are usually the dominant organisms, and the amount of algae is related to the level of enrichment, water clarity gives us some idea of the lake's health.

The Secchi disc measures the depth that light penetrates the water. It is a disc, usually 8 inches (20 cm) in diameter, with black and white quadrants. An eye bolt fastened to the center of the disc has a rope attached that is clearly marked off in feet or meters or half meters. The black and white quadrants are painted on with good-quality marine paints.

### Using a Secchi disc

This is a very easy procedure. Lower the disc into the water until the white quadrants disappear from view. Note the depth on the rope. Lower the disc a bit further, then raise the disc until it reappears. Note the depth again. The depth at which it disappeared will probably be different from the depth at which it reappeared. Repeat the procedure until the depth is the same. This is the Secchi depth.

The Secchi depth is a measure of the relative depth of light penetration. It is a "relative" measurement because the readings usually vary from one individual to the next, from one day to the next, and even from one hour to the next. Factors such as cloud cover, surface water conditions, and whether you take the measurement from the shaded or the sunlit side of the boat may affect the measurement. Normally, the measurement is taken at the same time every day from the shaded side of the boat.

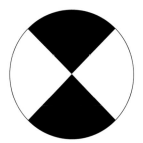

Overhead view of a Secchi disc with its white and black quadrants.

### Secchi depth and trophic status

In spite of all the variables involved, there is an excellent relationship between Secchi depth and trophic status of a lake. The Secchi depths for oligotrophic lakes are greater than 16 feet (5 m); eutrophic lakes are less than 7 feet (2 m); mesotrophic lakes are between 7 and 16 feet (2–5 m).

# Temperature zones and fish finding

If you're an angler, you'll want to know where the deep, cold zone of the lake begins. The division between the sun-warmed upper layer (the epilimnion) and the cold, dark lower layer (the hypolimnion) is called the thermocline (some refer to it as the metalimnion). Since sport fish such as trout hang out in the hypolimnion, you need to know where this zone begins. Many fish finders will indicate where the thermocline is.

### Temperature and trophic status

Have you ever floated in a lake with your body in warm water and your toes dangling in the cold water beneath? The depth of the warm, epilimnion layer, the layer that has been warmed by the sun, can help you determine the enrichment level of your lake.

Using a Secchi disc to measure the clarity of the water. The disc is lowered into the water until the white quadrants disappear, then, noting the measurement on the rope, raised until they reappear.

Because the water of enriched, eutrophic lakes is more colored and clouded with organic materials, light (especially heating reds and infrareds) cannot penetrate as deeply as in clear, oligotrophic lakes, so the warm epilimnion layer of eutrophic lakes should be shallower. However, winds can mix the warm water deeper into shallow lakes than in deeper lakes. So, while still colder than the surface waters, the deeper water of eutrophic lakes will be warmer than the deeper water of most oligotrophic lakes. If the warm epilimnion waters don't mix with the cold, deep waters, the temperature of the hypolimnion will always be near 39° F (4° C), even in the summer.

The illustration at left shows an oligotrophic lake with a narrow epilimnion and deep hypolimnion at 39° F (4° C). At right is a eutrophic lake with a deeper epilimnion (because organic matter absorbs more heat energy) and a narrow hypolimnion (because lake bottom fills up with ooze) at 45° to 50° (7–10° C), because winds can mix warm water to deeper levels in spring and summer.

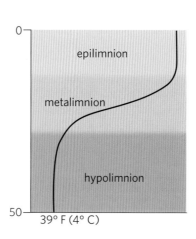

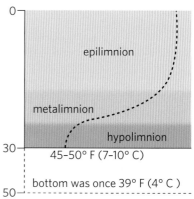

# Assessing water quality, part 2:
# Chemical characteristics

## Oxygen content

Like terrestrial life, all aquatic life (except the anaerobic bacteria) requires oxygen to survive. Most aquatic organisms use oxygen dissolved in the water, but a few can use atmospheric oxygen, such as mosquito larvae. Lakes that have high levels of oxygen at all depths all year round are *oligotrophic*. Lakes that have used up their oxygen in the lower depths by the end of the summer are enriched, *eutrophic* lakes.

Lakes are considered oligotrophic as long as there is at least 75 percent oxygen saturation throughout the deep hypolimnion zone. Eutrophic lakes have less than 25 percent oxygen saturation in the hypolimnion. *Mesotrophic* lakes have oxygen saturation between 25 percent and 75 percent in the hypolimnion.

The bottoms of eutrophic and mesotrophic lakes have loads of organic material and bacteria, which use up all the oxygen during the summer to reduce the organic matter to carbon dioxide. Many eutrophic lakes have no oxygen at the bottom, and have the rotten-egg smell of hydrogen sulfide and or methane gas.

## Phosphate and nitrate levels

Phosphates and nitrates are the most important nutrients to plants, including algae. Spring turnover concentrations of total phosphorous and total nitrogen are excellent criteria for assessing lake health. Spring values are used because algae begin to use nutrients as the water warms up and the values fall throughout the summer.

A healthy lake like this one will have high levels of oxygen and low levels of both phosphorus and nitrogen.

Because phosphorous and nitrogen are such important variables in water quality assessments, your local cottager's association may regularly sample your lake. Here are the criteria for trophic status for spring values of total phosphorous and nitrogen ("µg" is a microgram: 1000 µg = 1 milligram):

| TROPHIC STATUS | TOTAL PHOSPHOROUS | TOTAL NITROGEN |
|---|---|---|
| Oligotrophic | < 10 µg/l | < 300 µg/l |
| Mesotrophic | 10-30 µg/l | 300-650 µg/l |
| Eutrophic | > 30 µg/l | > 650 µg/l |

# Assessing water quality, part 3:
# Creature characteristics

## Red tide

Sometimes masses of dead fish will wash up on sea shores and the water looks red. The fish have eaten blooms of *Gonyaulax* and *Gymnodinium* algae, which cause serious illness in humans and kill fish and other marine animals. In freshwater, a massive bloom of *Euglena* algae will look red, because the algae have red eye-spots.

## Gut feelings: bacterial contamination

Many bacteria—including the infamous *Escherichia coli*, the bacterium that lives in the colons of all vertebrates, including humans—cause serious health problems. (See the **Swimming** chapter.) Most municipalities have a local health unit that will do a bacteria count for a nominal fee or even for free. All have a specific protocol you need to follow if they are to analyze your samples. For example, you need to submit five water samples weekly during the summer period. The health unit usually supplies the sample bottles free and provides an average number of total coliforms and fecal coliforms per hundred millileters of water. Beaches are closed if the levels exceed state or provincial standards for two consecutive weeks.

**The bad guys**: Several kinds of bacteria can be used to diagnose fecal contamination. Positive indications of human waste or fecal contamination are the presence in large numbers of any one of the following bacteria: *Escherichia coli, Pseudomonas aeruginosa, Salmonella, Shigella, Leptospira, Pasturella, Vibrio.*

**The good guys:** Not all bacteria are harmful! Many species are needed to maintain good water quality. In fact, the sludge of septic tanks and sewage treatment plants relies on bacteria to decompose organic matter. Certain bacteria are crucial for transforming nutrients such as nitrogen and sulfur into forms that plants can use. These bacterial communities prevent the buildup of ammonia, nitrite and hydrogen sulfide, and are indicators of a healthy aquatic environment.

## Testing your water

### What to test for
Test your supply of potable water for total coliform bacteria and fecal coliform bacteria on an annual basis. Also test annually for nitrates, high levels of which can cause infant cyanosis (blue baby) in pregnant women, and is an indicator of the potential presence of other contaminants. Nitrates are present in foods, water, atmosphere and soil. A good time to test the water is two days after opening in the spring. Most testing authorities require three different water samples taken over a three-week period, but check to make sure what the sampling protocol is in your area.

### What else to test for and when
Unless you detect something unusual (for example, in odor, taste, color), test your drinking water every three to five years. Also test the water if your well-head is flooded or submerged in the spring, if your neighbor's well has contamination, or if a chemical spill has occurred within 500 feet (152 m) of your well. Test for hardness, pH, iron, sulfates and chlorides every three to five years.

A Hach kit. This kit measures total alkalinity and calcium and total hardness. Other Hach kits measure dissolved oxygen and pH. Find them where swimming pool products are supplied or go to www.hach.com.

# Toxic algae

Some algae produce toxins that can be lethal to animals, including humans. In fresh waters, nearly all the toxic algae are blue-greens. One kind is known to produce toxins that can be fatal to cattle and chickens and cause a contact type of dermatitis in humans. Others produce toxins that induce symptoms of hayfever. The disintegration of large amounts of blue-green algae on sand filters of water treatment plants and the passage of their toxic products into the distribution system can cause gastro-intestinal upset.

The factors that cause concentrated blooms of blue-green algae are poorly understood, except that they always occur in eutrophic waters during warm, sunny weather. Depending on the species, algae either excrete their toxins or released them into the water when the algae decompose. Many algae give off distinct odors. (See the **Swimming** chapter.)

# The human element

Poisons and pollutants enter our watersheds and lakes from major industries as well as from our own homes and cottages. The more we learn about the serious, long-lasting effects of pollutants, the more stringent environmental regulations for industries become. But when it comes to household pollutants, we have to educate and police ourselves if we want to play in and drink from the lakes we love without killing ourselves.

Some of the most harmful industrial pollutants are the chlorine-based organic compounds, such as polychlorinated biphenyls (PCBS), which accumulate in fatty tissues. Another long-lived pollutant is DDT, a widely used pesticide. Although it was banned in the United States and Canada in the 1970s, residues are found in animal tissues to this day, and DDT continues to be used in other parts of the world. Heavy metals from mines and

Some household pollutants that should never make it to the lake are batteries, oil-based and latex paints, stains and paint thinners.

factories, among them mercury, lead and cadmium, stay in the environment for ages and are stored in muscle and even brain tissue.

# Effects of pollutants

Have you ever poured paint thinner down the drain? Maybe you thought, oh, it's just this once. Unfortunately, your neighbors did the same thing. Eventually, those toxic chemicals made it into your lake and into the food chain. Microscopic phytoplankton organisms accumulated the pollutants from the water. Larger organisms fed off the phytoplankton, which in turn were eaten by small fish. A large fish ate many of the smaller fish, accumulating the pollutants from all of them. Sometime later, along you come and catch the fish...

The higher up the food chain you go, the greater the concentration of pollutants — a process called biomagnification. Creatures at the top of their food chains — for instance, birds of prey (and humans) — are most harmed by the effects of pollutants.

When concentrations of environmental toxins peaked in the 1950s and 1960s, populations of fish-eating birds were devastated. The effects on humans who ate a lot of contaminated fish are still being assessed. As a species, we can be rather shortsighted.

## Household toxic chemicals

Pollutants can be found in many common materials and substances.

- Dry cell batteries
- Marine and car batteries
- Gasoline
- Motor oils
- Herbicides
- Insecticides
- Plastics
- Clothes
- Paints

# Assessing water quality, part 4:
# Animal indicators

Some aquatic creatures have very little tolerance for change in their environments, preferring that everything remain "just so." The presence or absence of these species indicates the level of nutrient enrichment in a lake.

The habits of aquatic creatures have evolved slowly over eons, especially in the deep, dark, profundal zones of lakes. Organisms that live in the profundal zone of oligotrophic lakes have developed a penchant for cold, clear, well-oxygenated water. All oligotrophic lakes are pretty much dominated by the same group of organisms, so much so that they are called *oligotrophic indicator organisms*. They are intolerant of eutrophic conditions.

Similarly, the dominant organisms of eutrophic lakes are pretty much the same in the deep, profundal zones. They have developed a tolerance of low-oxygen, turbid, warmer waters and are called *eutrophic indicator organisms*.

## Insect indicators

Biologists often count mayflies, stoneflies and caddisflies to measure the level of water quality in streams that feed lakes. A biotic index called EPT (short for Ephemeroptera, Plecoptera, Trichoptera) is calculated by summing up all the different families present in each order in a random sample of 100 bottom organisms. The water is considered unpolluted if the sample has more than 10 families, slightly polluted if there are 6 to 9 families, moderately polluted if there are 3 to 5 families and severely polluted if there are 2 or fewer families.

## Mayflies

The disappearance of mayfly species is an excellent early warning indicator of environmental stress. They are intolerant of low oxygen levels, low pH and nutrient enrichment. None survive in acidic environments.

Mayfly species live in a variety of habitats, including ponds, streams and lakes. In lakes, most mayflies are found in plant-laden areas. Some are found in large numbers only in deep, cold, well-oxygenated water. They are reliable indicators of oligotrophic lakes and are a favorite food of lake trout and deep-water sculpins.

Mayfly nymphs are aquatic, and have three tail filaments. Nearly all feed on small bits of organic matter or algae in their months or years at the bottom of the lake or stream. When the time comes to emerge, mayflies have a unique, short, sub-adult stage. The metamorphosis or hatch into adults takes only a few seconds to minutes. Sometimes large numbers hatch at the same time and the water surface boils with wriggling adults trying to shed their sub-adult skin.

Adult mayflies are elegant fliers but cannot cope with wind. Most don't feed, mating being their sole adult purpose. After a graceful dance, mayflies mate in the air, and die. In many species, hatching, mating, egg laying and death take place within a few hours, often in May. Paved roadways can be slippery and treacherous to drive on when masses die at once. Mayflies are also known as shadflies, drakes, spinners, Canadian soldiers, willowflies and fishflies.

Adult mayfly.

## Stoneflies

Stoneflies are related to cockroaches. The nymphs of most species seek shelter among stones or leaves in streams, shredding leaf litter. Stoneflies are almost entirely stream dwellers, preferring cold, clear, well-oxygenated water in headwater areas, and are reliable indicators of ultra-clean waters.

All stonefly nymphs have two tail filaments. Their antennae are very long, sometimes as long as their body. Adult stoneflies run well but fly awkwardly, with their abdomen dangling down. When disturbed, they would rather run than fly, and when in flight, fly in a straight line, unable to navigate turns. They fly only in good weather, at sunup or sundown. Many adult stoneflies feed on lichen; others, like mayflies, do not feed at all.

Stoneflies fall into two main groups, the summer stoneflies and the winter and spring stoneflies. Winter and spring stonefly nymphs are generally less than half an inch (10 mm) long. The adults emerge in the fall, winter or spring. Summer stoneflies tend to be larger, emerging in spring, summer or fall.

The adults of slender winter stoneflies emerge in the winter and can be seen as little "flies" walking on snow and ice near streams.

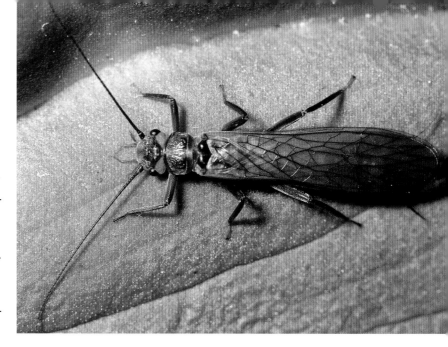

Adult stonefly.

## Caddisflies

Almost all caddisfly larvae are indicators of good water quality. Caddisfly larvae caddy their portable homes around their aquatic habitats. They construct cases entirely or mostly of plant material, sand or gravel particles, or silk they secrete. Some make tortoise-like cases, snail-shaped cases, or hood-like cases; micro-caddisflies have purse-like cases made of silk or silk and bottom materials. Of the non-portable cases, fingernet caddisflies have finger-like cases; trumpetnet and tubemaking caddisflies live in silken tubes that are trumpet-shaped or tube-shaped; and netspinners live behind catch-net retreats made of silken nets, collecting and eating food trapped by the net as it filters food from the water flowing through it.

All larvae have legs with stout claws for holding themselves within the case or to surfaces of rocks and twigs when outside their shelters. Although trout and sculpins will eat the larvae with its case, the cases and retreats are generally well adapted for hiding the caddisflies and protecting them from predators.

The larvae modify their cases into sealed cocoon. After two to four weeks, the adult insect cits itself free, floats to the surface and flies off quickly. Most are noctural and are attracted to lights.

It is the larval (nymphal) stages of insects such as this caddisfly larvae in its case that are useful indicators of nutrient enrichment and environmental change.

# Tolerance scores

Trout.

Burbot.

Water sculpin.

North American scientists have provided tolerance scores from 0 to 10 for most of the invertebrate species that live in freshwaters; they indicate how much change these creatures can handle.

The most sensitive species have a score of 0; the most tolerant species have a score of 10. For example, red blood worms have a score of 10. They can live in the worst levels of enrichment where there is almost no oxygen. Most stoneflies and mayflies score a 0. Even the slightest change in water quality will kill them.

Fish species are scored as intolerant (oligotrophic indicators), tolerant (eutrophic indicators) or moderately tolerant (mesotrophic indicators). Below is a list of the most sensitive and most tolerant species that indicate trophic status. We are interested only in the species that live in the deep, dark profundal zone in the summer.

Finding the fish is easy: just ask any angler on the lake what they are catching. For the invertebrates, you need a bottom sampler to catch them alive. As it happens, the best samplers are the fish — open a few stomachs and see what they are eating.

| | Oligotrophic indicators | Eutrophic indicators |
|---|---|---|
| **Fish in hypolimnion** | Lake trout, burbot, deep water sculpin | Few to none; no oxygen, no fish |
| **Invertebrates in hypolimnion** | Pill clam, fingernail clam, opossum shrimp | No clams nor shrimps |
| | Crustaceans: mysids and scuds | Aquatic worms |
| | Insects: mayflies | Insects: red midgefly larvae |

## Midges: red bloodworms

The larvae of this group are probably the most important of all flies, perhaps all insects. The large, common family called *Chironmidae* is the most widely adapted to a variety of aquatic habitats. Some species have very specific environmental requirements and for that reason are considered good indicators of environmental conditions. Other species are relatively tolerant of pollution, and biologists rely heavily on them for assessing the level of pollution in different aquatic environments.

Red bloodworms, genus *Chironomus*, named because they have hemoglobin for blood, are especially tolerant of low oxygen levels. They store oxygen obtained through their gills in the hemoglobin. Since very few organisms can tolerate low oxygen levels, the bloodworms have no competition for food or space and usually occur in enormous numbers, sometimes more than 50,000 individuals per square meter. Most feed on detritus, others are predators, herbivores or even parasitic. Red bloodworm larvae, which can grow to more than 1 inch (30 mm), are so efficient at consuming detritus that, in massive numbers, they are vital to the efficient operation of sewage oxidation ponds, feeding on and preventing the accumulation of dead algae.

Adult males generally "dance" in swarms that may be so dense that they look like clouds. Any ripe female that enters the "cloud" is immediately captured and fertilized by a male.

## Rattailed maggots

The presence of rattailed maggot larvae (for example, *Eristalis* species) is bad news for water quality. They live in highly organically enriched waters that lack dissolved oxygen, such as sewage ponds, and in shallow edges of ponds, streams and lakes. The larvae use a breathing tube (rattail) that can be extended to the surface of the water like a snorkel. Including the extended tube, they can be up to 3 inches (75 mm) long. The body is wrinkled, semi-transparent and maggot-like but has legs on most segments. The adults, called "drone flies," are brightly colored and patterned, somewhat like honeybee drones.

# Acid rain

When acid rain falls on lakes and on land, the results can be devastating. Especially discouraging to those of us who love the natural world is the fact that acid rain is caused by humans and is totally preventable.

Rain becomes more acidic than normal when there is excess sulfur and nitrogen gas in the atmosphere. The air pollutants—carbon dioxide, sulfur dioxide, nitrogen oxide—react with water vapor to create acid rain, snow or sleet.

The acidity of precipitation varies from one region to another. Areas with industries that burn fossil fuels (such as coal) and smelt metals, and cities that have large populations of commuters whose cars belch carbon dioxide, sulfur dioxide and nitrous oxide in their exhaust emissions, have highly acidic precipitation, between 4 and 5. The precipitation in areas that have no industries and small populations has a normal pH of near 5.6. Regions downwind from major industries are also affected by the deadly, acidic wind.

Most animals cannot tolerate pH levels of less than 6.5. When the pH drops below 6, all fish are killed and only the most tolerant invertebrates can survive. At pH 5 all aquatic life disappears, except a few bacteria. Particularly in foggy regions, trees suffer from the acidity in the air and soil.

## Dead lakes

That crystal-clear aquamarine lake contained in granite bedrock looks beautiful, but it might be dead. As the pH drops, aquatic animals begin to disappear. The offspring of fish don't survive, invertebrates such as crayfish die, algae die and the lake becomes much too clear. There is growing evidence that if the acid rain stops (as industries curb their dirty emissions), the lakes can come to life again—very slowly.

## Why do some lakes acidify while others don't?

If your lake sits in limestone, you're probably wondering what the fuss is about. The composition of the rock and soils of a region can help to buffer the effects of acid rain. It's the ability of lake water to neutralize the acidity of precipitation that determines the pH.

Lakes with limestone or dolomite bedrock in their watershed or lake basin can neutralize

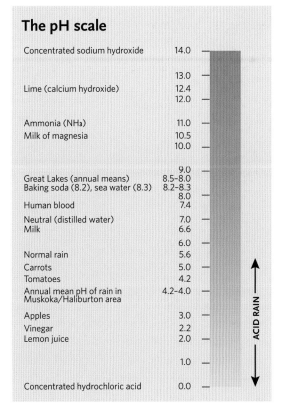

### The pH scale

| | |
|---|---|
| Concentrated sodium hydroxide | 14.0 |
| | 13.0 |
| Lime (calcium hydroxide) | 12.4 |
| | 12.0 |
| Ammonia (NH₃) | 11.0 |
| Milk of magnesia | 10.5 |
| | 10.0 |
| | 9.0 |
| Great Lakes (annual means) | 8.5–8.0 |
| Baking soda (8.2), sea water (8.3) | 8.2–8.3 |
| | 8.0 |
| Human blood | 7.4 |
| Neutral (distilled water) | 7.0 |
| Milk | 6.6 |
| | 6.0 |
| Normal rain | 5.6 |
| Carrots | 5.0 |
| Tomatoes | 4.2 |
| Annual mean pH of rain in Muskoka/Haliburton area | 4.2–4.0 |
| Apples | 3.0 |
| Vinegar | 2.2 |
| Lemon juice | 2.0 |
| | 1.0 |
| Concentrated hydrochloric acid | 0.0 |

ACID RAIN

### "Normal" rain

Normal precipitation—in equilibrium with the natural carbon dioxide in the atmosphere—is essentially carbonic acid. Rain is a naturally acidic pH 5.6, so when it lands on the surface of a lake it tends to acidify the water, unless the water has carbonates or bicarbonates from limestone and dolomite to neutralize the acidic effects.

The pH scale is a measure of the acidity (the hydrogen ion content) of water. On the scale of 0 to 14, 7 is neutral. Waters with pH less than 7 are acidic (like vinegar) and waters with pH greater than 7 are alkaline (like baking soda).

Juvenile red-spotted newt.

The ability of water
to neutralize acids
is called alkalinity,
which is a measure
of the bicarbonate
(for example, calcium
bicarbonate) and
carbonate (as in calcium
carbonate) content of
water. There are kits
available to measure
the total alkalinity of the
water. Most swimming
pool suppliers can
measure it for you.

the carbonic acid in rainwater and will have
a pH between 7 and about 8.5. Lakes with
quartz and granite bedrock lack the ability to
neutralize the carbonic acid and have a pH
between 4 and 7.

## The opposite problem: lake whitening

Some lakes look white. The particles suspended in the water column are essentially
chalk—calcium carbonate—called marl. Marl
occurs in very alkaline lakes (with pH greater
than 8.2) with dolomite bedrock and algal
blooms.

When algae photosynthesize, they use up
carbon dioxide, which increases the alkalinity
of the water. In the process, calcium carbonate
precipitates out of the water, causing the lake
to look white. The resulting cloudiness of the
lake is exacerbated by turbulent waters that
prevent the particles from settling.

## Spring acid shock and amphibian indicators

If you don't hear frogs singing in the spring,
your region may be in trouble. Meltwater pools
where environmentally sensitive amphibians
such as frogs, toads and salamanders breed
can be devastated by acid precipitation. When
the acidic snow melts, a winter's worth of
accumulated acid is released at once, killing
eggs and harming larvae.

Amphibians breathe through their skin,
gills, lungs, or a combination of these. Like
fish and reptiles, they are cold-blooded;
their body temperature is maintained by
external sources instead of being internally
controlled, as in birds and mammals. Most
amphibians lay small eggs surrounded by
a jellylike layer that swells when in contact
with water. Amphibians live in or near moist
places because of their skin and eggs, and
their development usually includes a free-
swimming aquatic larval stage after hatching.

Larval salamanders have external gills that disappear during metamorphosis. Larval frogs, called tadpoles, lack visible external gills and have a horny beak. Both types of larvae have a tail for swimming, but in frogs the tail is later reabsorbed into the body.

# Salamanders

**The mudpuppy** (10–12 in / 25–30 cm) has feathery, red external gills, is reddish-brown on the back with black spots scattered over the body. Mudpuppies live their whole lives in permanent bodies of water ranging from static, turbid, weed-choked ditches to clear, fast-moving streams. They need abundant bottom debris and moving water during spawning. Mudpuppies struggle against habitat loss and water pollution. Some populations have also been reduced by the use of lampricides in rivers and streams for lamprey control.

**The yellow-spotted salamander** (6–12 in / 15–30 cm) is black with yellow spots beginning at the head and extending to the tail. In spring they breed in temporary and permanent woodland ponds, while in summer and winter they live in deciduous and mixed forests with fallen logs and moist, soft soils needed for tunneling. They have migration corridors between the spring breeding ponds and the forest habitat. Yellow-spotteds larvae are a favorite food of many fish species. Their numbers have also been reduced by pesticide use.

**The blue spotted salamander** (3–5 in / 8–13 cm) is black with several bluish flecks and spots along the sides and extending on to the tail. They breed in temporary and permanent ponds but can be found under logs and rocks near ponds in spring and fall.

**The Eastern newt / red-spotted newt** (3–4 in / 8–10 cm) is yellowish to greenish brown with black-bordered red spots on the back and solid black dots present on the back and belly in aquatic adults. The terrestrial stage, called an eft, is orange to reddish brown with black-bordered red spots down the back. The aquatic adults live in ponds, lakes, backwaters of rivers and swamps among an abundance of submerged plants. The efts prefer moist woodlands where they feed on spiders, worms, caterpillars and other invertebrates.

## Tadpoles: tiny wonders

Tadpoles are among the tiny wonders of a pond in spring. The amazing metamorphosis from tiny egg to tadpole to full-grown frog takes about 12 weeks. Female frogs lay the eggs, which hatch into small tadpoles that have tails and breathe with gills. As they grow, tadpoles feed on algae, other plants and insects. Hind legs develop between 6 and 9 weeks, and front legs are fully developed after about 11 weeks. The gills are gradually replaced by lungs, at which time they must swim to the surface to breathe. The tail begins to be absorbed by the developing tadpole, and by 12 weeks it resembles a young frog. At this stage the tadpoles are less dependent on water and seek refuge among plants in and around the pond.

Northern leopard frog.

# Toads and frogs

Frogs are excellent indicators of environmental changes on land and in water. They have a permeable skin, which allows substances to move relatively freely into their body and concentrate many poisonous substances in their fatty tissues. This makes frogs susceptible to chemical contamination and excess uv radiation on land and in water, making their disappearance a good early-warning indicator of localized problems in marshes, ponds and lakes.

**The Northern leopard frog** (2–3 ½ in / 5–9 cm) is green to light brown with large, dark, circular black spots with light outlines on its back. The species is very common in lakes, ponds, marshes, and backwaters with emergent vegetation and grasses, and will move to moist, grassy fields in summer to forage. Acid precipitation and uv light exposure are among the stressors being blamed for declines in leopard frog numbers.

Bullfrog.

**The wood frog** (1–2 in / 3–5 cm) is tan or brown with a distinctive black mask that extends across the face and behind the eardrums and a white stripe on the upper jaw. They are most common in moist woodlands near ponds that have emergent vegetation for egg attachment. Populations are declining in some areas because of the loss of forests and wetlands.

**The green frog** (2–4 in / 6–10 cm) is green to dark brown, often with small black dots, and prominent ridges running down the back on each side of the body. Males have a yellow throat in the breeding season. It is most common in permanent bodies of water such as ponds, lakes, streams and marshes. Tadpoles of the green frog overwinter.

**The American toad** (2–4 in / 5–10 cm) has a body covered with brown "warts," one or two of which are contained within numerous dark blotches. Behind each eye is a kidney-shaped poison gland. The American toad is the most terrestrial of the temperate zone's amphibians and is found in a variety of habitats, in cottage gardens, ditches, and heavily forested areas. They seek shallow, warm water ponds for breeding.

**The tetraploid gray tree frog** (1–2 in / 3–5 cm) can change its mottled and warty skin from greenish-gray to gray-black according to its surroundings. Tree frogs climb trees using their toe discs, which look like suction cups. In the spring, look for them in trees and shrubs close to temporary or permanent bodies of water. After breeding they move away from the wetlands and into the forest.

**The bullfrog** (4–6 in / 10–15 cm) is the largest frog in the temperate zone. It is green to greenish-brown, and has a fold that extends from the rear edge of the eye to the eardrum. The shorelines of lakes, bays and ponds abound with bullfrog tadpoles with one or more generations often present. The tadpoles need two or more years to transform and must overwinter in the water. Some populations are in decline, perhaps because of over-harvesting and habitat loss.

# Water hardness

If it's difficult to form lather with water at your cottage and your kettle is caked with scale, hard water—water with lots of calcium and magnesium in it—is the culprit. The concept of hardness originated in the early 1900s to express the "soap-consuming" power of water; the harder the water, the greater its ability to eat up soap before it can do its cleaning job. The term makes sense when you think of how impossible it is to form lather with hard water. The calcium and magnesium ions cause the soap to precipitate instead of foaming, leaving a scum line, the "ring-around-the-tub."

The concentration of calcium and magnesium, along with carbonates and bicarbonates, is known as *temporary hardness* because it can be removed from the water by boiling. The concentration of calcium and magnesium combined with non-carbonates such as sulfates, chlorides and phosphates can't be removed by boiling and is known as *permanent hardness*. Add the two together to get the *total hardness*. Kits are available to measure water hardness. Swimming pool suppliers can measure it for you as well.

## Scale and vinegar

Since the white, flaky scale formed by hard water is a carbonate, any acid will dissolve it. Household vinegar is a cheap, effective cleaner that won't harm the environment or the walls of your kettle. Scale forms on any container where water is heated to boiling, such as dishwashers, car radiators and water heaters.

## Water softeners

If you have hard water, consider installing a water softener to save appliances such as water heaters and dishwashers from ruin. Water softeners "soften" the water by replacing calcium and magnesium with either sodium or potassium. If iron and manganese are present, they are also removed. The most common water softeners are ion exchangers. They have a pressure tank that is partially filled with ion exchange resin that contains "exchange sites" that remove calcium and magnesium, or "hard" ions, and replace them with sodium or potassium, or "soft" ions. The softener system also includes a brine tank to provide a source of sodium or potassium for regenerating the resin.

## Hard water indicators

**Common duckweed** is an indicator of hard water. It has a single root below each leaf, reproduces by budding, proliferates rapidly and becomes a nuisance.

**Stonewort** (because of the lime deposits on the "leaves") or musk grass (because of its skunky smell) of the genus *Chara*, is a large alga. Being an alga, the whorled "leaves" are really filaments with columnar cells that contain chlorophyll. The plant is an indicator of very hard water.

### How hard is hard?

The concentration of calcium and magnesium in water is measured in milligrams of calcium carbonate ($CaCO_3$) per liter:

◆ Soft waters
  less than 60 mg
◆ Medium-hard waters
  60–120 mg
◆ Hard waters
  120–240 mg
◆ Very hard waters
  more than 240 mg

Well water in limestone regions can have over 1000 mg per liter!

The presence of duckweed is usually not good news. It prevents light from penetrating the water, light that algae need to produce oxygen for the aquatic life below. All life below the pond surface, except anaerobic bacteria, die, and rotten egg-smelling hydrogen sulfide forms.

# CHAPTER 2

# Boating

At the lake, boats mean freedom to come and go as you please. With basic skill, caution and common sense, your lake can be the most liberating playground imaginable.

GETTING OUT ON THE WATER IS one of the best things about life at the lake. Whether you prefer the tranquility of an early-morning paddle in a cedar-strip canoe or the hair-whipping exhilaration of zipping around in a sleek motorboat, you will probably have a boat.

In this chapter we'll explore the venerable art of canoeing and the independence of kayaking big water. We offer tips for learning to stay on your sailboard, and as much information about outboard motors — types, operation, repair — as you'll need to avoid major difficulties. We also go over how to winterize your boat and motor so that they're ready to go again when the ice has melted.

The wrong combination of wind, waves and weather can turn any three-hour tour into a wild ride. Understanding weather-predicting cloud formations and knowing the power of wind and waves can save you from white-knuckle lake crossings, mishaps and even injury or death. Finally, when you make it safely home, you'll need a sturdy dock. You can build a dock that suits your needs, be they boating, swimming, fishing or sunbathing, and has minimal impact on the sensitive ecology of the shoreline. Happy boating!

A tranquil paddle on a calm lake: breathe in the fresh air, soak up the sun.

In deep wilderness, canoes are king. If you are planning to do any kind of portaging, remember that a canoe is much easier to carry than a kayak. Lightweight Kevlar canoes (*above*) are a particularly good choice when portaging is an inevitability.

# Canoes

The first canoe was probably developed in the early 1500s. The term is apparently derived from "canoa," which was a boat the Cariban Indians of Haiti used for traveling across water. The boats were made from a single large tree, hollowed out with a sharp stone and propelled with paddles. Some canoes used by the natives could hold up to forty people, especially war canoes. Imagine portaging one of those monsters! Today, canoes are made from a variety of lightweight materials. It is amazing to think that there still is no other human-powered vessel so transportable, sturdy, maneuverable and swift for travel in shallow and narrow waters.

Nothing is as tranquil as paddling across a glassy lake just after sunrise on a fresh spring day in a canoe. Especially exhilarating is shooting a stretch of whitewater rapids in a canoe. And knowing you have all the right gear and safety equipment makes for more relaxing trips. Have this checklist in mind before pushing off each time you canoe: at least two paddles; two lines, a bow line and stern line plus an extra throw rope for emergencies stored safely and neatly (loose ropes can be deadly); a pea-less whistle attached to your lifejacket; a first-aid kit and a quick-repair kit (each stored inside a waterproof covering). And don't forget to visit your local bookstore and library for even more information on canoeing—there are canoeing guidebooks covering almost every subject you can think of, from how to paddle to what to pack for daytrips, and sometimes even including a history and maps of the very lake you cottage on.

# Choosing the best canoe for you

With all of the options out there these days, choosing a canoe has never been a more overwhelming experience. Start by deciding what exactly you want the canoe for. Are you and the kids going to take it out on the lake a few times a season? Do you want to shoot river rapids? Venture out on overnight canoe trips? Use it as a dock ornament? There are as many types of canoes as there are activities, and real canoeheads usually have more than one boat. However, if you are looking for an all-around canoe that will keep you and your family safe and happy on flat water, there are some factors to consider.

Aluminum canoes: inexpensive and sturdy.

## Material

**Wood** Traditionalists say that if it's not made of wood, it's not a canoe. Cedar-strip canoes are very beautiful, paddle well and make great winter handyman projects. However, they require are heavy when wet, and cost a lot.

**Aluminum** Aluminum canoes are built like tanks, look like tanks and can take just as much of a beating. They also weigh a ton. And forget about sneaking up on wildlife or friends snoozing on the dock: paddles hitting the sides sound like a pot-lid symphony. They are cheap, though.

**Fiberglass** Not too heavy, quite tough, and not that expensive. There are lots of used fiberglass canoes around for reasonable prices. If you have a cottage and want the requisite red canoe, this is your boat.

**Kevlar** Kevlar is a lighter, sturdier and more expensive material than fiberglass. Kevlar canoes are a dream to portage, and are the typical canoetripper's choice.

**Plastic** Royalex is a durable, flexible and resilient plastic composite, making these canoes ideally suited for running rapids. These rugged, low-maintenance boats frequently come with expensive price tags.

Ultra-light and resilient, plastic canoes are well-suited to whitewater canoeing, particularly when outfitted with a spraydeck to prevent water from spilling into the boat.

### Tips for not tipping

Keep your head over the boat at all times. This will keep your center of gravity firmly in the boat. If you feel as if the boat is going to tip, crouch low in the canoe.

Traditional and romantic, wooden canoes also require a lot of maintenance.

## Extra passengers

Don't sit on the center thwart; it keeps the gunwales from spreading apart and is not a seat. The third passenger usually sits in front of or behind it. Although those in the middle like to think they are helping out by paddling, they usually just get in the way of the main paddlers and should relax and enjoy the scenery instead.

## Shape and stability

Canoes with wide, flat bottoms feel very stable when you first push off the dock onto calm water. However, if the waves happen to build, you are better off in a canoe with a rounder bottom. While rounder-bottomed boats may initially feel more tippy (and if you are a complete novice, they can be), they are safer in waves, and easier to move across the water.

## Size

Canoes range in length from 15 to 18 feet. If the boat will usually be carrying two people, a 16-foot canoe is fine. If the whole family, including the dog, will be coming along, choose a 17- or 18-foot boat. The smaller canoes are slower but much easier to maneuver than the longer ones.

# Selecting a paddle

Like canoes, paddles are manufactured from wood, metal and synthetics. Select the material according to your preferences for weight, strnegth and flexibillity. Other important factors to consider are blade shape and size, grip shape, shaft straighness, and paddle length.

To size your paddle, kneel on the floor as you would in a canoe, approximating the distance you would be away from the water. Hold your paddle vertically, with the grip end on the floor and the tip pointing up. The throat of the paddle (where the shaft meets the blade) should be at about your nose height. Double-check the paddle length when you are in the canoe: put the paddle blade into the water up to the throat. The grip should be at your nose height.

# Know your canoe

A recreational canoe with a fiberglass hull and basket seats.

You can tell the difference between the bow and stern of a canoe by looking at the distance between the seat and the end of the canoe. The bow has more space for you to put your legs.

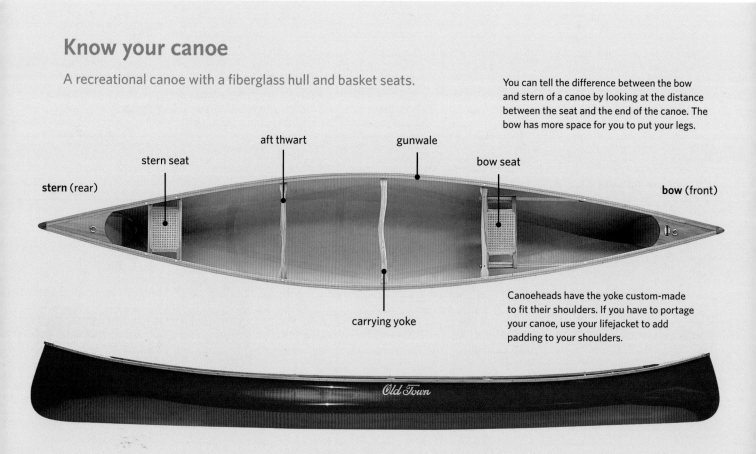

stern seat

aft thwart

gunwale

bow seat

stern (rear)

bow (front)

carrying yoke

Canoeheads have the yoke custom-made to fit their shoulders. If you have to portage your canoe, use your lifejacket to add padding to your shoulders.

# Canoe paddling tips

Learning to paddle a canoe is an incredibly liberating experience. It gets even better when you stop going round in circles and learn to paddle in a straight line. One of the most common myths about steering is that the person in the front, the bow paddler, doesn't have to know how. While the major adjustments tend to be made by the stern paddler (the person in the back), the bow paddler can and should contribute to the venture.

A word on paddling sides: everyone will have a preferred paddling side, but it's wise to get used to using all strokes on both sides, so you can switch when you or your partner get tired.

## How to hold the paddle

If you want to paddle all day and not be tired and miserable, it is important to hold the paddle correctly. Keep one hand on top of the grip, and the other hand firmly at the throat, where the shaft meets the paddle. If this is uncomfortable, let the lower hand come further up the shaft.

Holding the paddle properly.

Choose your paddling partner wisely and you will have many pleasant memories of time spent out on the water.

## Basic forward stroke

This is the power stroke that will take you places. Keep the paddle as near vertical as possible (close to the side of the canoe). Your upper hand should be at about eye level. Reach out with your lower hand as far as possible, arm fully extended. Dip the blade in the water and push forward with your upper hand, drawing the paddle toward you. Don't waste your energy by letting the stroke continue past your hip. To make the stroke more efficient, use a twist of your upper body and torso instead of your arm strength to move the paddle through the water.

If neither paddling partner knows any steering strokes yet, switch sides every five to six strokes to keep a sort-of straight course.

## Reverse or back stroke

This stroke uses the same movement as the forward stroke, but in the opposite direction. It is employed to stop the canoe, slow your approach, give you time to decide which way to go, or to back up the boat.

## Couples therapy: paddling together

The keys to paddling with a partner are communication and consistency. The bow paddler sets the pace. Try not to be erratic, and speak up about rocks and other obstacles while there is still a chance to avoid them. Shrieking at the last second does not indicate confidence in the abilities of your partner. Stern paddler: don't stop paddling and think your partner won't notice. If the bow paddler is "lilydipping" (the paddle is going in and out but accomplishing nothing), gently ask them to step it up. "Accidentally" splashing your partner is allowed in warm weather.

The back stroke.

A solo canoeist nearing a waterfall would do well to have mastered his J-stroke (*left*) and his draw stroke (*right*) but especially his back stroke (*see previous page*) before he gets anywhere close to the falls.

### The goon stroke

If you think you are doing a J-stroke, but always seem to trail the other canoes, you may be finishing your J in a way that puts on the brakes. Look at your grip hand at the end of the stroke: if your thumb is pointing toward you, you are pushing out with the wrong side of the paddle, arresting forward movement. A proper J-stroke uses the same side of the paddle throughout the motion.

### The J-stroke

The J-stroke is used by the stern paddler to correct for the natural tendency of the canoe to turn slightly away from the paddling side. The stroke begins like the forward stroke, and ends with a hook, so that the paddle draws a J in the water. As your paddle approaches your hip, turn your grip hand forward and down as you move the paddle perpendicular to the boat, correcting your path. Use the J-stroke only as needed to correct your path. You'll probably use it more often when alone in the canoe. If you are paddling backward, the bow person can use a "reverse" J-stroke to rudder the canoe.

### Draw stroke

Use the draw stroke to change your direction quickly. Place the paddle on the side you want to move toward. Reach out, plunge the blade into the water and draw it in toward you. The motion is perpendicular to the direction of the canoe. When the paddle reaches the canoe, pull it out and repeat, or rotate the blade 90 degrees and slice outward through the water with the paddle. If both paddlers draw on the same side at the same time, the boat will move sideways to the paddling side. This is a great stroke for avoiding obstacles such as rocks and deadheads.

## Personal flotation devices

When choosing a personal flotation device (PFD) for boating, especially canoeing or kayaking, make sure that it doesn't ride too high or chafe under your arms. If it fits comfortably, you're more likely to wear it, as you absolutely should. No matter how good a swimmer you are, you need a PFD to keep you afloat. You could end up in the water with a head injury or some other problem over which you have no control. Make sure that the vest is designed for your size and weight.

There are four types: Type I, Offshore Life Jacket; Type II, Near-Shore Buoyant Vest; Type III, Flotation Aid; and Type IV, Throwable Device. Type I is best for all waters; the other three are good for calm, inland water, or where there is a good chance of quick rescue. PFDs for kayakers tend to be shorter so as not to interfere with getting into and paddling the kayak.

Kayaks rule the open water. With the proper kayak, you can manage waves and whitewater that canoeists would cower at.

# Kayaks

Kayaks were invented by indigenous people of the Arctic, who used the boats to hunt on lakes, rivers and the coastal waters of the Arctic, Atlantic and Pacific oceans. The word "kayak" means "hunter's boat" or "man's boat." They were very personal crafts, built by the man who would use them and covered by animal hides, measured, fitted and sewn by his wife for maximum maneuverability and action. A jacket was sewn to the opening to provide the kayaker with a waterproof seal so he could perform "Eskimo" rolls without getting water in the kayak. The rolls were a necessity rather than a fun exercise since few kayakers could swim and most journeys were in very cold waters, often with big waves.

If you can convince someone to let you use it, you can practice your kayak rolls and wet exits in your local pool before the summer cottage season begins. Explore the recreation section of your bookstore or library for books on kayaking how-to and adventuring.

A long and slender sea kayak with two deck hatches.

# Choosing a kayak

When choosing a kayak, first consider what you'll use it for. Are you planning to mess about on a quiet lake? Go on an overnight adventure? Shoot some rapids? There are kayaks designed specifically for each activity.

## Types of kayaks

**Recreational** If you are a beginner, you probably want to stick with this versatile kayak. Stable, easy to paddle, and good for calm waters, this kayak is a great way to introduce the whole family to the sport. The short, wide kayaks that you sit on top of (not inside of) are also recreational kayaks.

**Whitewater** Whitewater kayaks are stubby, plastic boats that can turn on a dime. They are designed for playing in the rapids, not for going straight.

**Day touring** Day touring kayaks are a bit longer and sleeker than the general recreational models, have modest storage capacity (for your lunch and so on), and better tracking ability.

**Sea kayaks** Touring or sea kayaks are the longest, most slender kayaks, designed for overnight trips across open water. Beginners find them tippy at first, but they are extremely stable in big waves, and have lots of storage capacity.

## Know your kayak

A day touring kayak: this one lacks a skeg and rudder.

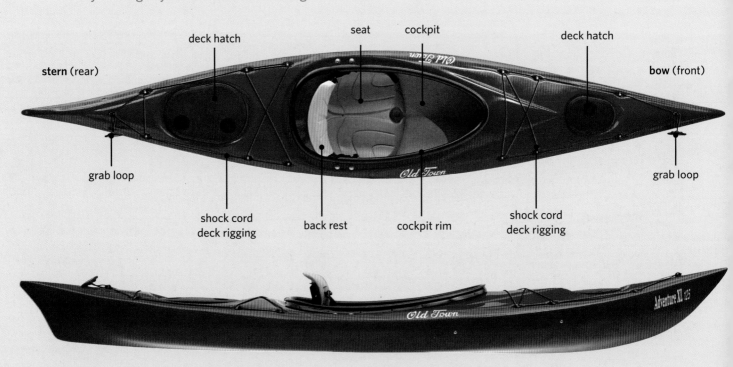

stern (rear)   deck hatch   seat   cockpit   deck hatch   bow (front)

grab loop   shock cord deck rigging   back rest   cockpit rim   shock cord deck rigging   grab loop

### Kayak characteristics

- A short kayak is easy to turn but will be slower than a long kayak, which is faster and easier to keep straight.
- The wider the boat, the more stable it is, particularly for beginners.
- The stability of the kayak in rough water depends on the hull shape. The more flat it is, the more stable it will feel initially. The more banana-shaped, the better it will fare in waves.

### Kayak materials

Wooden kayaks are the most beautiful and most fun to paddle, but require the most maintenance. Plastic kayaks are great for whitewater, and can take a lot of abuse. Fiberglass and Kevlar boats are very easy to paddle, but fiberglass in particular is very heavy.

> Always test-drive a kayak before you buy. Make sure that the seat is comfortable, and that the back rest and thigh brace position suit you (long-legged folk need to be particularly careful).

# Kayak paddling tips

While propelling and steering a kayak are not difficult, paddling inefficiently can wear you out quickly, particularly until you master going straight. Most touring or sea kayaks have a rudder that you control with foot pedals. You can steer all kayaks using a few basic strokes.

### The forward stroke

Grasp the paddle with both hands, shoulder width apart. Lean forward, place one blade into the water close to the boat, and bring it through the water until it almost reaches your hip. Then do the same with the other blade on the other side. If you think of punching your top hand forward instead of focusing on pulling back with the lower hand, you will be able to use your torso muscles more than your arms. Your arms always stay in front of your body, and move as though you are hand-pedaling a bicycle. Keep your grip loose to avoid blisters and unnecessary strain.

### The reverse stroke

Use this stroke to go backward, and to break or stop. It is the opposite of the forward stroke.

### The forward sweep

Use this stroke to turn the boat away from the stroke side (if you do the sweep on the left, you will turn right). Start as in the forward stroke but then sweep the blade out in a wide arc that ends behind your body. Rotate your torso through the stroke, and tilt the kayak slightly into the turn.

### The back sweep

The back sweep is the reverse of the forward sweep. The boat will turn toward the sweep side. (Back sweep on the left for the boat to turn left.)

**What is a Skeg?**

No, a skeg doesn't come from your local Swedish furniture store. A skeg is a type of rudder built into the hull and is used to "trim" the boat when conditions affect its performance. When the skeg is up, the kayak weathercocks; when the skeg is down, the kayak turns downwind; and when the skeg is halfway down the kayak turns crosswind.

*Left* Recreational kayaks are a great way to introduce novices to watersports.

Performing an "Eskimo" roll.

## Wet exits

Most beginners are extremely apprehensive about capsizing. However, getting out of a kayak that has flipped is much easier than it would seem; when the boat is upside down, you basically fall out. If your spray skirt is on, pull the grab loop as you somersault forward. If you miss the loop, your forward motion should be enough to release it anyway. It's a good idea to practice a "wet exit" in a safe environment until you are confident enough to head into deep water.

## The draw

Use this stroke if you want to go sideways to raft up with another kayak. Turn your torso to the side, hold the paddle vertical to the water, reach out (not too far), plunge the blade into the water and pull it in toward you. You will move sideways in the direction of your stroke side. (Draw right to go right.)

## Going straight

Most paddlers rely on the forward stroke, making slight adjustments from side to side, to keep them straight. If you have to correct your course, rudder by holding the blade in the water alongside the stern. Although this will slow you down, it will turn the boat in the direction of the rudder side. (Rudder right to go right.)

## Rolling

Wet exiting is not the usual option for the avid kayaker. Rolling is the way to go—and it becomes not only a means of survival, but also an art. The experienced roller may have a repertoire of six or more techniques, depending on circumstances and water conditions, but one of the simplest and easiest is the Eskimo roll. The basic idea is to pull the body to the surface and back over the boat using the waist, knees and hips and then use the paddle to stop the body from sinking after the "hip flick." The safest and best way to learn a kayak roll is with a friend, preferably an experienced kayaker. It is a good idea to wear a nose plug and snorkeling mask when practicing the roll the first few times.

The roll can be performed with or without the paddle but it is best to start without the paddle. It's not used anyway to help you roll. Have your friend stand waist deep in the water, holding your torso out to the side while your head remains just above the water's surface and your forearms are resting on the sides of the boat. Rotate the kayak through the full 180 degrees by curving your torso to the surface of the water as you end up on the opposite side. The main idea is to shift pressure from one side of your bottom to the other. Use only your knees, never your arms, to right the boat. Use your torso to help float yourself near the surface of the water and rotate the kayak up with your knees and torso. Only one knee does the work of righting the kayak; the other knee relaxes, barely even touching the kayak's side. Hanging onto the kayak with both knees will only defeat the hip action.

After a good summer of hard play, your canoe or kayak will need some maintenance, including an application of finish restorer to scratched and faded hulls.

# Maintaining canoes and kayaks

No matter how much you baby your craft, life on the water and rocks of cottage country will take its toll. When the paddling season is over, you owe it to your faithful vessel to properly repair and store it for the winter. Luckily, the procedures for keeping your ship shipshape are relatively simple:

1. Tighten any hardware (seats, gunwales, and so on) that may have come loose.

2. Clean debris from hatches, and rudder or skeg systems on your kayak. Sand can get in the rudder system and foot peg rails.

3. Lubricate rudder, hatch gaskets and any other moving parts on your kayak.

4. Oil (or repaint if painted) any exposed wood. Oil will stop water from penetrating exposed wood on gunwales, caned seats and so on.

5. Treat your boat with a hull finish restorer if it has faded from uv exposure or is scratched.

6. Store the boat upside down on a rack or suspended by ropes from the ceiling in a shed or garage, out of the elements. To suspend the canoe or kayak, hook a piece of rope suspended from the rafters to one end of the canoe. For the other end, hang a small pulley on a short length of rope from the rafters. Run a rope through a hook or handle on the canoe, back through the pulley and then to a cleat on the wall. This will make it easy to lower the front end of the canoe to the ground.

7. Inspect paddles for any damage, especially the tip of the blade for any splitting. If splitting has occurred, use a good quality epoxy and clamp the glued joint. If the paddle shows signs of discoloring, use a wood stain remover or bleaching agent, such as is used for decks. If the paddle has an oil finish, apply a generous coat, let sit for 30 minutes then wipe dry; repeat several times. If the paddle has a hard finish (varnish or polyurethane), sand the paddle to remove all the old finish. Otherwise, areas where the finish is cracked will allow moisture to penetrate. To refinish the paddle, hang it from the top grip and varnish all sides working your way down to the blade. Apply a minimum of three coats.

What looks like a pair of tiny florescent shorts on this windsurfer is actually a harness, so he can hook himself to his rig when a really big wind comes along.

# Windsurfers

### Board and boat words

**Stern**  Back end of the board

**Bow**  Front end of the board

**Port**  When facing the bow, the left side.

**Starboard**  When facing the bow, the right side.

A windsurfer rides a board much like a surfboard, only with a sail attached. And a windsurfer generally has much greater control than a surfboarder! When you are windsurfing, you use your body to steer the sailboard to catch the wind. The wind pushes the sailboard along in directions you choose to go.

## Know your windsurfer

A complete windsurfing rig includes a board (with a fin or skeg and daggerboard on the bottom, and on top, footstraps and a base to hold the mast), a mast, a sail (usually with battens, little sticks that help keep the sail stiff) and a boom onto which is attached a rope called an uphaul. Masts, often made of lightweight aluminum or composite, can be as tall as 16 feet (5 meters), but a shorter mast is usually best for beginners. The boom is the U-shaped handle that attaches to the mast and wraps around the sail—the boom is what you hang on to, and it plays a big role when you are changing direction. To help you hang on, you may want to acquire slip-proof boots and gloves and, eventually, a special harness for riding big winds.

# Types of boards and sails

Call it windsurfing or sail boarding or board-sailing—they all mean the same thing—but boards and sails come in different sizes and styles, depending on own your size and ability, where you are windsurfing, and what you are using the board for. For instance, if you and your family of young children want a board for recreational play on a fairly quiet, calm lake, you won't likely use the same rig as your daredevil brother-in-law who likes riding the waves and racing in big wind out on the Great Lakes.

A smaller sail and bigger, more stable board is easier for learners and those without a lot of upper-body strength. Most beginners start with a standard flat board about 9 feet (3 m) long. Boards have different degrees of rocker (curvature from nose to tail); a board with less rocker rides faster but turns less easily than one with a lot of rocker. There are boards for different kinds of races, including slalom, wave and speed boards. Sailors may choose a different size sail (from 9 to 20 square feet/ 3 to 6 m²) depending on the speed they expect to sail, and a different shape sail, depending on the conditions and kind of sailing. Wave sails are for windsurfing on waves and slalom sails are for racing on flat water. Convertible sails can be used for both kinds of sailing. There are hard sails and soft sails; hard sails provide better power and speed, but soft sails are easier to control. Most windsurfing specialty stores offer package deals or kits that include everything you need to get you started.

# Learning to windsurf

If you are yearning to windsurf, do yourself a favor and take a lesson or two before you invest in a board. There is nothing like experience with someone who knows how to do it, particularly a qualified instructor. You don't

You don't need a whole lot of upper-body strength to hold a sail and you don't need to be heavy to stay on the board. You just need to have the right equipment and know how to use it!

have to be very strong, big or even especially athletic to windsurf. But you'll need to practice. It may take you ages before you stay on long enough to go for a ride, but once you've got it, you're halfway there. Windsurfing is a fabulous sport, best learned out on the water, but it also helps if you spend some time learning a few sailing words and principles. Once you understand how the wind works, you can really have fun. For more on how to windsurf, and general sailing terms, we suggest you consult the website www.windcraft.com and any of the many available books on the subject, including *Windsurfing* by Simon Bornhoft and *The Illustrated Dictionary of Boating Terms: 2000 Essential Terms for Sailors & Powerboaters* by John Rousmaniere.

## Wind words

**Upwind**  To windward. Sailing upwind is sailing into the wind, in other words, your boat or board is sailing toward the direction from which the wind is coming. You are sailing "against the wind."

**Downwind**  The opposite of upwind; you and your board are sailing away from the direction from which the wind is coming. You are sailing "with the wind."

**Windward**  Toward the direction from which the wind is coming.

**Leeward**  The direction away from the wind (opposite of windward).

**On the wind**  A position of sailing where the wind is blowing over the bow of the boat. You have your sail pulled in tight to the board to catch the wind.

**Off the wind**  You are sailing with the wind at your stern and your sail let loose in a "reach" or a "run."

She's more than halfway back to riding the wind after a spill. All she needs to do now is pull the sail up out of the water.

## Launching the board

The two most basic windsurfing questions are How do I stand up? How do I stay up?

First, practice standing on your board without the sail attached. Test your equilibrium by walking backward and forward on the board. Once you feel ready to try it with a sail, go for it. Put on your lifejacket and bring your mast with the sail on it into to the water. Next, carry your board into knee-deep water with the daggerboard not yet turned down. There you can insert (if they aren't already attached) or push down the skeg and daggerboard and then put the mast into the mast base. (If your rig is light and easy to carry, you can connect the sail and board on land and carry them together into the lake.) Attach the safety line to keep the parts together should the mast and board separate.

Always handle your rig with the mast on the windward side. If you haven't done this already, figure out where the wind is coming from. Keep the sail on the leeward (downwind) side of the board, with the mast at 90 degrees to the board. Climb on, first onto your knees and then rising to stand on the board.

Once you can balance, and standing on the board on the windward (upwind) side, pull the rig up by the up haul line. Keep your knees bent and your back vertical; your shoulders should never pass ahead of the line of your waist. With the back edge of the sail facing downwind, grab the boom with one hand,

release the uphaul line, then hold the boom with both hands. Put your back foot behind the base of the mast and then your other foot in front of the mast at a distance that makes you feel comfortable and stable. To compensate for the force of the wind, try emulating sitting on a chair. Slowly straighten your legs as the rig catches the wind.

It may sound easy, but it isn't—not right away. But practice makes perfect, so keep trying until you get up and going.

## Safety tips

- Never sail without a lifejacket.
- Before sailing, check the condition of your board, sail, ropes and accessories.
- Tie the mast foot to the board, so that if it breaks the rig will stay tied to the board. If the rig does break, hold on to the board—it floats but the rig sinks.
- Practice the buddy system when possible and sail with a friend.
- If sailing solo, report to somebody that you are going out.
- Consider the weather conditions.
- Recognize the limitations of your fitness, technique or equipment.
- Dress appropriately. Use a neoprene wet suit in the cold. Wear sun protection.
- Never abandon your board—it might be your lifesaver.
- Keep your energy level up: snack on dried fruit or energy bars. Keep well hydrated.

## Four traffic rules

1. Boats sailing leeward have passing priority over boats sailing windward.
2. Sailboats with wind coming from the starboard (right) have priority over sailboats with wind coming from the port (left).
3. When passing a vessel, do not obstruct its motion.
4. Windsurfers and sailors have right of way over powerboats.

# Steering your windsurfer

The wind is in your sail, you are skimming the waves, and life is grand. But your cottage is fast becoming a speck on the shore far behind you. If you can't get yourself turned around, the wind may carry you clear across the lake. So how do you turn? Remember, you are at the mercy of the wind. When the sail is in a position where it doesn't catch any wind, it will not sail. You can "catch the wind" by changing the position of the sail. You have to turn the board by leaning on the mast to bend it forward (a jibe turn) or bringing the mast back (for a tack turn) and by moving your feet around the mast to shift your weight on the board. But you also have to know where to point your board to set yourself on the right course home.

An excellent website, www.windcraft.com, has given us permission to use their helpful description of the "wind clock" and words of wisdom on using targets to help keep you pointed in the right direction.

## The wind clock

Windsurfers, and sailors too, use an imaginary wind clock to help make sure they have completed a turn, to catch the best amount of wind, and to get to specific destinations.

The wind clock is an imaginary analog (not digital) clock. You stand at the center of your wind clock. If you turn to face the wind you are looking directly at 12 o'clock. If you turn around, you are facing 6 o'clock. If you hold your hands out to your sides when you are facing either 12 or 6 o'clock, you will be pointing to 3 and 9 o'clock. 12 o'clock is also called "upwind" — the direction the wind is coming from. 6 o'clock is also called "downwind" — the direction the wind is going to. 3 and 9 are going "across the wind."

If you walk around or imagine yourself standing on your board in the middle of a lake, you should also notice that the positions of your clock don't change because you are always at the center of your clock and your clock moves with you.

When you are sailing, you are generally sailing across the wind, toward 3 o'clock or 9 o'clock. When you make your board turn toward 2 o'clock or 10 o'clock you are still sailing across the wind but you are now heading slightly upwind. If you make your board turn toward 4 o'clock or 8 o'clock you are also still sailing across the wind but now you are heading slightly downwind.

Last, remember you cannot sail directly toward 12 o'clock. You will probably be able to stand on the board in a good sailing position but you will not go anywhere. You will more likely drift backward toward 6 o'clock. You must correct this by turning your board to head across the wind again and then return to a sailing position.

Top view of a windsurfing board.

## Targets

Targets are essential to windsurfing. Before going out on the water, look at where you are launching from and find a landmark. Look across the body of water (assuming it's not the ocean on your first time out!). When you go out, you will start out moving across the wind, toward the 3 or 9 o'clock position) and find a target to aim for, preferably something a bit upwind from where you are starting (like 2:00 or 2:30 or 10:00, or 10:30, depending on which side of the clock you are on when you are starting). If you can consistently reach your targets, you are doing great. If you think about aiming for targets you will automatically learn how to steer the board to go where you want it to go. And you've got to remember your wind clock the whole time you are on the water until you have perfected getting where you want to go. Then you can forget it because it will be part of your subconscious!

## Five things to remember

Once you're out in the water, remember these general rules:

1. Your back is always facing 12 o'clock.
2. Your sail is always on the 6 o'clock side of the board.
3. When you turn, the board turns under your feet, the sail stays in the 6 o'clock position.
4. Pick land-based targets and landmarks to sail toward and from.
5. Use common sense.

Text courtesy of www.windcraft.com.

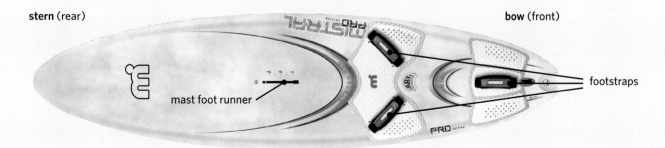

**stern** (rear)    **bow** (front)

mast foot runner

footstraps

Zipping around the lake in a motorboat is definitely exhilarating.

# Motorboats

I f you want to get there fast, bring lots of friends and stuff, and don't want to or can't depend on wind or muscle power, a motorboat is your best bet. Zipping around can be exhilarating, no question, and is a great way to see a large lake. However, always be respectful of the human and animal life you share the lake with. When the stillness of the morning is cut by the whine of an outboard, the world does change.

## Boating activities and their impact

Boating activities can have an enormous impact on life at the lake. Of primary concern are noise pollution, fuel and oil emissions, wash and bank erosion, disturbance to waterfowl and wildlife, and effects on aquatic life.

The maximum tolerable level of noise for boats traveling about 50 feet (15 m) from shore and going 36 miles per hour (58 km/h) is 75 decibels, according to the Environmental Protection Agency. Water ski and boat race competitions can create up to 105 decibels.

Fuel and oil emissions have the greatest potential for environmental harm, with hydrocarbons known to damage the ozone layer and affect animal health and human health. A gasoline additive called MTBE (methyl tert-butyl ether) is a possible carcinogen. Nearly 90 percent of the MTBE in lake water is due to recreational boating. Two-stroke engines are dirtier than four-stroke engines because of an inefficient "scavenging" process. According to the American Water Pollution Control Federation, an average of 10 to 20 percent (and a maximum of 55 percent) of unused fuel goes into lakes from two-stroke engines. *Cottage Life* magazine reported that a modern 50-horsepower, two-stroke outboard emits as many hydrocarbons in one hour as a typical car does in about 40 hours! New two-stroke motors now have direct injections and provide precise control of fuel and oil consumption, reducing emissions by up to 80 percent over conventional two-strokes.

# How the outboard motor works

The outboard motor has a spark ignition engine. Fuel enters the carburetor where it mixes with air, in a given proportion, to produce a gas-air mixture. The gas-air mixture enters the cylinder where a spark from a spark plug ignites the mixture, creating an explosion that drives the piston. The piston turns a crankshaft (or drive shaft) by a connecting rod. Numerous explosions in rapid succession in the cylinder turn the crankshaft and the gear assembly that rotates the propeller.

The internal temperature of an outboard is over 4,000° F (3200° C) and must be cooled. Lake water is drawn in through the water intake at the base of the motor to cool the engine, flowing around the cylinders before being pumped out into the lake through two water outlets. Water also exits as a jet through the water pump indicator located below the cylinder head to show that the water pump is working.

Outboard motors need to be taken care of or you'll spend hours of grief in the middle of the lake. The important components are shown here.

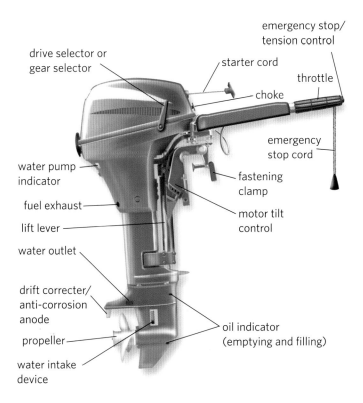

drive selector or gear selector
emergency stop/ tension control
starter cord
throttle
choke
emergency stop cord
water pump indicator
fastening clamp
fuel exhaust
motor tilt control
lift lever
water outlet
drift correcter/ anti-corrosion anode
propeller
oil indicator (emptying and filling)
water intake device

## Two-stroke versus four-stroke

Most outboards are two-stroke (cylinder) engines but four-stroke (cylinder) engines are becoming very common.

In two-stroke engines, oil is added to fuel in the tank itself (usually in a 50:1 gas-to-oil ratio). Some two-stroke outboards have two tanks, one for gas and another for oil. Although the oil and gas mix automatically before reaching the cylinders, it is a good idea to shake the gas container after adding the oil. In four-stroke outboards, the oil is added by the engine, as in an automobile engine.

The chart below compares the advantages and disadvantages of both types of engines.

| QUALITIES | TWO-STROKE | FOUR-STROKE |
|---|---|---|
| weight | lighter | heavier |
| cost | less expensive | more expensive |
| environmental issues | noisy; more pollution (oil); smoke emissions | quiet; more environmentally friendly |
| repair | simple design, easy to repair, but spark plugs more prone to fouling | complex design, costly to repair, spark plugs have longer lifespan |
| availability of used engines | good historical record (80 years) | new technology; few on used market |
| availability of parts | excellent | professional servicing needed for electronics |
| resale value | high resale value, demand | excellent |
| acceleration | very quick | slower |
| idling ability | rougher | smoother |
| starting ability | often harder to start | usually easy to start |
| fuel economy | high, gas-guzzlers | low, gas sippers |
| trolling ability | good to poor | excellent |

Don't be intimidated by your outboard. With a little knowledge and patience you can master all its idiosyncracies.

# Outboard operating basics

## Starting the motor

Every outboard has its idiosyncrasies—when to pull the choke, the ideal idle mixture, and other tricks—so it is wise to read the operating procedures manual for your model of outboard. Here is the basic routine:

1. Connect the fuel tank to the motor. If the tank cap has an air intake, open it. Squeeze the primer bulb until it is firm in pressure.
2. Examine propeller and cooling water intake and remove any debris.
3. Move the motor tilt lever to the Run position and the lift lever in the Lock position.
4. Turn the drive selector (gear selector) to Neutral.
5. Set the throttle to Start and use the choke as required.
6. While sitting or crouched, pull the starter cord until you feel resistance, then pull firmly in a single stroke. Remain seated or crouched to start the motor.
7. Check that the water control jet from the cooling system is flowing properly. If it is not flowing, service the engine, otherwise the engine will overheat and stop.
8. Once the motor is running well, adjust the choke if it was used.

*Right* The operator of the outboard on this beautifully maintained red motorboat also gets the best seat in the boat.

## Heading out

1. Cast off the moorings.
2. Shove off in the desired direction.
3. Set the throttle to the Shift position.
4. Set the drive selector to Forward, and increase the throttle setting.

## Stopping

1. With the drive selector set at Forward, move the throttle back to the Shift position.
2. Set the drive selector to Neutral.
3. Push the Stop button.
4. On reaching the shore, tilt the motor out of the water to avoid damaging the propeller and move the tilt lever to Tilt or Lock position.

## Outboard motor repair kit

The repair kit should be air-tight and contain these items:
- One funnel with filter
- One knife
- Pliers (long-nose and standard)
- Flat and star (Phillips) screwdrivers
- One feeler gauge for spark plugs
- One spark-plug key
- One container of penetrating oil
- Cotter pins and one shear pin
- Spare fuses
- Three disposable cloths
- Crescent wrench (for motor bolts)
- A roll of electrical adhesive tape
- Spare spark plugs
- One starter rope

# Mandatory equipment

The minimum equipment required on boats differs slightly in the United States and Canada but both conform to international regulations. The size of the boat determines the equipment required, but since most cottagers have powered boats not over 20 feet, the following are mandatory in both countries:

◆ One manual propelling device (paddle or oars) or an anchor with not less than 50 feet (15 m) of cable, rope or chain in any combination

◆ One Class 5BC fire extinguisher (if the craft is equipped with an inboard engine, a fixed fuel tank of any size, or a fuel-burning cooking, heating or refrigerating appliance)

◆ One bailer or one manual water pump fitted with sufficient hose to enable one person using the pump to pump water from the bilge of the vessel over the side of the vessel

◆ A watertight flashlight or 3 flares of type A,B or C

◆ One buoyant throw line of not less than 50 feet (15 m) in length

Seadoos, jet skis and the like — lots of people think these snowmobiles-on-water are great fun. Many more consider them the greatest nuisance ever to appear on the cottage scene. Not only are they loud (there are concerns about hearing loss in operators), these macho machines are dangerous if not operated responsibly.

◆ A sound signaling device, such as a pealess whistle, or a sound signaling appliance audible at distances of one-half a marine mile (0.93 km)

◆ One government-approved personal flotation device (PFD) or a lifejacket of appropriate size for each person on board

◆ Navigation lights that meet the applicable standards set out in the Collision Regulations if the pleasure craft is operated after sunset and before sunrise or in periods of restricted visibility (Collision regulations set by federal agencies in the United States and Canada conform to international standards.)

You should have lifejackets that fit each body, big and small, aboard your motorboat.

# Winterizing your boat and motor

After a long summer on the water, you owe it to your trusty boat to carefully store it for the winter. It may seem a tedious job, but it sure beats the hassle of repairs in the spring.

With proper maintenance and storage, you can extend the life of your motorboat, as have the owners of this 1963 Henry outboard with Evenrude motor.

## Remove water from the fuel tank

If there is a portable steel fuel tank, remove the fuel supply hose from the engine, remove the cap and use a flashlight to inspect the inside for water, which will appear in round globs on the bottom. If water is present, dump the tank and flush it thoroughly. If rust is present, replace the tank with a new, plastic-style tank.

## Prevent condensation in the fuel tank

To prevent condensation in the fuel tank over the winter and to prevent breakdown of the fuel during storage, add fuel stabilizer (follow label directions) to the fuel, which extends the shelf life of fuel from three months to six. After six months, the fuel degrades and will gum up fuel system components, including the carburetor. Shake the fuel tank to mix the stabilizer into the fuel. Connect the fuel hose to the engine. Run the engine for 10 to 15 minutes or until it is warm and enough fuel with stabilizer has passed through the carburetor. Stop the engine.

## Prevent moisture from forming in the carburetor

You will need a can of fogging oil to prevent moisture from forming inside the carburetor. It comes in an aerosol spray can. Remove the cover on the engine and look for a maintenance valve—it looks like a tire air valve (check your manual). Older outboards will not have a maintenance valve. The approach you take will depend on whether or not you have a maintenance valve, but must be done with the motor in the water.

**For carbureted engines with a maintenance valve** Attach the engine fogger to the maintenance valve fitting. Start the engine and bring it to about 1500 RPM. Push and hold the release button on the fogger until a steady, thick white smoke appears from the exhaust. Depending on the size of the engine, you'll use one quarter to half a can of fogging oil. Turn the engine off immediately to ensure as much fogger as possible remains in the engine.

**For carbureted engines without a maintenance valve** Carburetors without a maintenance valve are more difficult to access with a fogger. If there are removable plugs, remove them and squirt fogger through all of them. If there are small holes in the breather, squirt fogger through each hole making sure you fog all carburetor throats. If there are no plugs or pre-drilled holes, remove the breather cover to gain access. In all cases use the straw adapter that comes with the can of fogging oil and bring the engine up to 1500 RPM. Push and hold the release button on the fogger until a steady thick, white smoke appears out the exhaust. Make sure you spray fogging oil into each carburetor throat for three to five seconds, then move on to the next throat. Go from carburetor to carburetor until a steady thick white smoke appears. You will probably use half to three quarters of a can of fogging oil. Turn the engine off immediately to ensure as much fogger as possible remains in the engine.

## Drain water from the motor

No matter what model engine you have, pull the boat out of the water. If you have small motor, take off the boat. Keep the motor in a vertical position for at least ten minutes to drain all the water from the block and passages.

## Change the gear case oil

Change the oil in the gear case, ideally every 50 to 100 hours of operation, or at least once annually. If you change the oil only once a year, you should do so in the fall to remove any water in the oil. If water is present, it will freeze, expand and crack components containing water.

Your motor should have a slotted drain and vent screws on the shaft. The drain/fill screw is just beneath the bullet-shaped gear housing and the vent/overflow screw is just above the anti-ventilation plate. Remove both screws

and inspect the quality of the gear oil while it drains. Black oil indicates everything is fine. White or creamy oil indicates that water is getting into the gear case (through a leaky seal). Gray oil may indicate prolonged use of the same oil, or—horrors!—a bearing failure or chipped gears (very expensive).

If you find white or gray oil, or gray oil with a strong odor, have a dealer examine and repair any problems. If water is present, it will freeze and could expand and crack the block. Some gear cases use a magnetic drain screw, which pulls any fine metals filings out of the oil. If you find metal filings, have the unit looked at by a professional.

Refill the gear case with oil immediately. Do not leave it empty over winter. First, install new gaskets or O-rings around the screws (a few pennies for sealers now will save you big bucks and headaches later). Most gear oil comes in squeezable bottles. Insert the nozzle in the bottom hole and squeeze the bottle until oil comes out the top hole. Insert and tighten the top screw. Remove the nozzle and insert and tighten the bottom screw. Wipe off any excess oil.

You may be able do a lot of your own maintenance and, if you have the space, store your own boat for the winter, but that's not always possible. Either way, it's a good idea to get to know your local marina and boat repair shop. Chances are, you will need their services someday.

# More water fun

Water skiing was invented in Lake City Minnesota on the Mississippi River in 1922 by an 18-year-old Ralph Samuelson. His first attempt was on barrel staves but he fell off, so he tried snow skis but he fell off again. Finally he bought two boards and used leather straps as bindings and the rest is history.

You know spring has sprung when the annual boat show, cottage show and fishing derby are in full swing. It is at these venues you can best learn of the exciting variety of recreational things you can do on lakes. It's an opportunity to ogle the beautiful boats and snap up the latest coveted recreational equipment, sometimes at reduced prices. Most exhibits are manned by experienced people who can provide valuable tips on having fun on the water surface.

## Waterskiing

While many people prefer the quiet leisure of a canoe, kayak or paddleboat, others enjoy the thrill of pounding through the waves at speed in a powerboat, wind whistling past their ears, whipping their hair, and spray stinging their skin. The same thrills can be had in waterskiing, only closer to the water. If outboard motors are allowed on the lake, you are almost certain to see water skiers at some point during the summer. All you need is an expanse of fairly calm water and a boat that can pull you at speeds of at least 16 miles per hour (25 km/h) for the novice and 25 to 35 miles

per hour (40–55 km/h) for the experts. There should be two people in the boat, one to drive the boat and the other a "spotter" to watch the skier and inform the driver of spills.

Water skiers are pulled by a rope that is fitted with a handle on one end and attached to a powerboat at the other. Water skis are made from a variety of materials but fiberglass and carbon graphite are the lightest, strongest and most flexible, ranging in length from 62 to 70 inches (1.6–1.8 m). The length of water ski depends on your height, weight, skill and boat speed. The faster the boat, the shorter your ski can be; the more you weigh, the more length you should subtract as boat speed increases. If you are a novice, choose longer skis that offer plenty of balance and control. The wider a ski, the better your balance will be. Novices and intermediates usually use two skis but experts may use only one ski or go barefoot. Bare foot skiing is done at speeds between 37 and 62 miles per hour (60 and 100 km/h). Skiers control their direction by balancing their weight on different sides of their skis.

### Variations

There are many variations in waterskiing, each a unique thrill requiring different skills and different boards or watercraft.

**Water tubing or inner tubing** is probably the most common water sport on lakes. Tubes can be purchased but many people use inner tubes from large trucks and tape or tie the valve to the side of the tube so it doesn't scratch the person riding the tube. The tube is tied to a powerboat and then towed through the water by the boat. Children are generally given a slow, tame ride while thrill-seekers opt for high speeds, often challenging the wake of the boat.

Water tubing (*left*) and wakeboarding (*right*).

**Kneeboarding** is one of the easier skills to master. The rider sits on his heels on the board while securing himself to the deck with an adjustable strap over his thighs and then is towed in much the same way as a water skier.

**Wakeboarding** is riding the wake of a speedboat. The rider stands sideways on a wakeboard with stationary non-release bindings for each foot and rides the waves that follow the powerboat. The rope is normally mounted on a tower or a pole about 7 feet (2 m) above the water line. The boat is also unique, built to provide a large wake.

**Wakeskating** is an adaptation of wakeboarding where the rider is not bound to the board. Instead, the top surface of the board is covered with a soft, high-traction foam. The rider usually wears shoes to afford herself extra grip on the board.

**Hydrofoiling** requires a sit-down water ski or hydrofoil. The rider is strapped into the hydrofoil and secured by safety straps on the seat and the bindings. The skier is towed behind a powerboat with a driver and a spotter in deep water. The skier first leans back to keep the tip of the board out of the water and when the board begins to plane, he leans forward to keep the hydrofoil from leaving the water. He steers the hydrofoil by moving his knees in the direction in which he wants to go. To jump out of the water, the rider leans back.

**Ski jumping** is as thrilling to watch as it is to do. Many lakes have ski jumping competitions. The ramp is 5 to 6 feet (1.5–1.8 m) long, the shorter length being for woman. The boat is required to maintain a speed of 33.6 miles per hour (54 km/h) for women and 35.4 miles per hour (57 km/h) for men. The winner is the contestant with the furthest jump. The length of the jump is measured by taking the lake-surface distance between a point below the top edge of the ramp to the heels of the water skier after landing on the water. The best out of three passes counts.

A beautiful mahoghany runabout from a more elegant era gleams with the polish of glamour and luxury. There are antique boat clubs and societies spread across North America and most have an annual boat show. The antique boat museum in Clayton, New York, displays wooden launches like this one, but there is nothing like the sights and sounds of these beauties in action, racing and purring in regattas. If you ever get an opportunity to ride in one, take it!

# Essential knots

Here are four of the most useful knots for around your cottage and on your lake. For more on knots, see Hervey Garrett Smith's *The Arts of the Sailor: Knotting, Splicing and Ropework* and *The Marlinspike Sailor*.

## Clove hitch

This a good temporary knot for mooring boats around a log, post, spar or stake. There are two ways to make the knot.

**A** Tie the knot around the log.

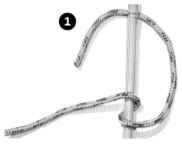 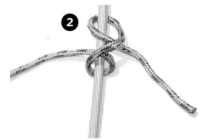 

Wrap the rope once around the log, bringing the bitter (or free) end over the standing end.

Make a second turn with the rope around the log, pulling the bitter end up under the second turn. It should sit between the rope and the log.

Regardless of the method you use to tie a clove hitch, it should look like the close-up above, a neat X.

**B** Make the knot first and then slip it around the end of the log.

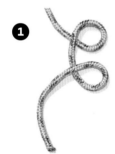 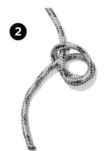 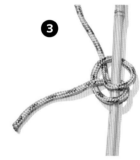

Make two loops in opposite directions.

Slide the back loop (the one closest to the standing end) overtop of the front loop.

Slide the two loops over the end of the log. Then tighten.

## Reef knot or square knot

The reef knot is often used to tie two ropes together but it is not a long-term or secure knot and often slips. Use it especially to finish tying bindings such as tow ropes or tarps and boxes. In other cases, use a more secure method of binding two ropes together. The basic rule for tying the reef knot is left over right, right over left. Draw the knot up tight.

## Bowline knot

The bowline is the king of knots when you want a loop that will never slip or jam. It's excellent for tying around a person in a rescue. This saying will help you remember how to make a bowline: "The rabbit comes out of the hole, around the tree and then back down his hole."

**1** Begin by making the hole by forming an overhand loop ("hole").

**2** Then take the bitter end ("rabbit") up through the hole.

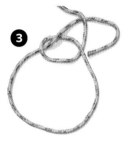

**3** Take the bitter end behind the standing part ("tree").

**4** Put the bitter end back into the hole.

For the final knot, tighten by pulling the standing end away from the loop and the bitter end.

## Rolling hitch

The rolling hitch is one of the few knots that can be tied and untied with a load on. It does not bind and does not slip when tied and used correctly. It is the best hitch for pulling lengthwise on logs or poles, such as towing a log behind a boat or for tying two ropes together. Never use it to pull parallel to your log, as it may slip. After tying it can be adjusted by keeping the standing part tight with one hand while sliding the knot along with the other.

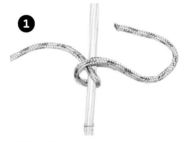

**1** Take a turn around a post or rope crossing over the standing part.

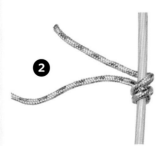

**2** Take another turn, again crossing over the standing part.

**3** Take a third turn around, wrapping above the standing part. Feed the bitter end under the last turn.

The final knot. Tighten the rope and pull firmly before loading.

If you are heading out on a large lake, know your local marine weather station, and bring a radio to keep abreast of the shifting situation.

# Weather

## Weather cones and sticks

Pine cones are amazingly accurate weather indicators. In dry weather, the scales open out stiffly. When rain is coming, the scales lie flat.

You can use a thin piece of willow or other wood, mounted perpendicular to a plaque, as a weather indicator. Hang it outside and watch as the stick rises in fair weather, and falls in wet weather.

For all our sophisticated technology, when it comes to life at the lake we are still at the mercy of the weather. While we all hope for sunny and warm days, cold and wet weather don't have to make your time miserable. Always come prepared with lots of games, books, and the best attitude you can muster. Although weather predicting is about as reliable as the stock market, learning to read the skies can alert you to dangerous conditions on water and on land.

Weather is what's happening outside in a specific area at a given time: rain, snow, thunder, lightning and sunshine. Climate is the average weather in a larger location over a longer period of time. Places that get a lot of rain over many years have wet climates. Places that stay cold for most of the year have cold climates. Knowing the climate helps determine when the best time would be for your family to plan a vacation at the cottage; knowing the weather forecast will help you decide when to go fishing.

Weather and climate affect the intensity and direction of winds over land and water, particularly on large lakes. In turn, the intensity and direction of winds greatly influence the intensity and direction of currents and waves in lakes. Conditions on big lakes in particular can change in an instant. When deciding whether or not to take your boat out, be aware of current conditions and weather forecasts as well.

## Natural weather predictors

Some of these sayings do seem to be true!
- Red sky at night, sailors' delight; red sky in the morning, sailors take warning.
- Flowers close before a storm.
- Crickets chirrup louder and louder as the temperature rises.
- Fish bite best before a rain.
- Flies bite before a rain.

# Predicting weather from cloud patterns

Clouds are our nearly ever-present weather indicators. They can be thought of as occurring in three layers, high altitude, mid altitude and low altitude. High altitude clouds at 20,000 feet (greater than 6,100 m) consist of extremely small ice crystals, whereas mid altitude clouds at 6,500 to 20,000 feet (2,000–6,100 m) and low altitude clouds at 6,500 feet (less than 2,000 m) are composed of moisture droplets.

## Peaceful, fairweather clouds

Wispy, white clouds indicate fair weather. Most of these clouds occur at high altitudes and include cirrus, cirrostratus and cirrocumulus clouds. Cumulus clouds belong to the vertical cloud family but are also a welcome sight. These high altitude clouds are typically associated with weather about six hours away.

**Cirrus** clouds are the thin wispy or feathery-looking clouds situated high in the sky at any time of day. Cirrus clouds can be the remnants of a thunderstorm.

**Cirrostratus** clouds appear as a thin layer. They are thickened but mostly transparent cirrus clouds still comprised primarily of ice crystals and at high altitudes. Cirrostratus clouds are often seen as a halo or "reverse rainbow" around the moon (or sun), created by light from the moon refracting through the cloud layer.

**Cirrocumulus** clouds are thin and patchy clouds that form a scaly pattern resembling the skin of mackerel fish, hence the term, "mackerel sky." They are most common during dry periods under high atmospheric pressures but are also seen when the weather is in transition. They can occur at any time of the day and can be very dramatic at night against a clear moonlit sky, or at sunrise when the almost transparent clouds refract sunlight. Although similar to altocumulus clouds in appearance, the cirrocumulus clouds are smaller, finer and hang much higher in the atmosphere.

**Cumulus** clouds look like suspended cotton balls or popcorn. They are common during dry periods with high pressure. Cumulus clouds form when the sun heats the air in lower levels of the atmosphere. As the air temperature in the lower atmosphere heats up, the air rises and the accompanying water molecules condense in the cool upper levels, producing the cotton-ball clouds. The clouds are loaded with moisture, but any precipitation that falls from them tends to evaporate in the dry lower atmosphere. This evaporation cools the surrounding air often creating a slight wind that is uniquely characteristic of cumulus clouds.

Weather tip: Stand with your back to the wind and look up. If high-altitude clouds move from left to right, the weather will worsen; right to left, it will improve. If clouds move toward or away from you, expect little change. (This rule applies only in the northern hemisphere: south of the equator, the opposite is true.)

Cumulus clouds are indicators of pleasant weather for several hours to follow.

*Below, from top to bottom* Cirrus clouds, sun halo effect with cirrostratus clouds and cirrocumulus clouds.

The distinctive scaly pattern of altocumulus clouds.

## Warning clouds

Many of these clouds are in the middle-cloud family and include altocumulus and altostratus clouds. Although humidity levels may be slight, these clouds consist of fair amounts of moisture and are good indicators of blustery weather, approaching fronts, or weather in transition. A third cloud type, the stratus cloud, is a low-altitude cloud but is usually seen after a weather system with steady precipitation has passed.

**Altocumulus** clouds often cover the sky, appearing as a broken layer of small, semi-transparent balls of cotton. "Mackerel sky" is used to refer to both altocumulus and cirrocumulus formations.

**Altostratus** clouds are best described as a consistent semi-transparent layer with a light to dark gradient covering the horizon. They often appear several hours in advance of a warm front that brings precipitation.

**Stratus** clouds often form a solid sheet covering the entire sky. They are the typical

Stratocumulus clouds produce intermittent rain showers.

dreary-day clouds that carry moisture and often release it as drizzle, especially after a main cloud burst has passed.

## Run-for-cover indicators

There are two low-altitude clouds and one high-altitude cloud that have obvious threatening appearances, especially when they are dark and angry-looking. The least-worrisome of the three types is the stratocumulus cloud. Run for cover when you see nimbostratus clouds, which are often accompanied by lightning and thunder.

> Really obvious weather tip: Low clouds are from close-by weather systems. Dense and dark clouds indicate ominous change.

**Stratocumulus** clouds are long rolling clouds that cover nearly the entire sky. Weather forecasters use the expression "partly to mostly cloudy skies," to refer to the presence of stratocumulus clouds. They can be seen at any time of day, but are particularly dramatic at sunrise and sunset when there are extreme contrasts in color. Stratocumulus clouds carry lots of moisture and can give enormous cloud bursts that often don't last long.

Stratus clouds produce drizzle or light showers.

**Nimbostratus** clouds are dark, raggedy-looking clouds that usually bring precipitation, such as rain or snow, which falls from them for extended periods of time. From a distance, you can usually see the streaks of rain falling from them.

**Cumulonimbus** clouds are tall and dark, cauliflower-like clouds that tend to form on hot, humid afternoons. When these clouds are present you can almost be certain that a thunderstorm is brewing. Sometimes called storm towers or thunderheads, they are full of moisture and contain strong up and down air currents. Thunderheads can form any time of day when the temperature falls rapidly higher up in the atmosphere. Occurring at more than 50,000 feet (15,250 m), some as high as 75,000 feet (23,000 m), they can cover from a few square miles up to 200 square miles (500 km²).

Cumulonimbus clouds form when a swift-moving cold front approaches and warm, moist air rises rapidly and condenses as it meets the sharply colder air mass. They accompany dramatic weather: heavy rain, hail, snow and thunderstorms.

Many cumulonimbus clouds form a disc-shaped feature, called an anvil, around the top of the cloud. The anvil occurs as a result of the rising air reaching a ceiling in the atmosphere. The cloud spreads out because there is not enough oxygen at this altitude to support the further rise of condensation. At such high altitudes, moisture exists exclusively as ice crystals, giving a cirrus appearance.

Weather tip: Avoid a storm's center by tracking its movement in relation to yours; put your back to the wind and point to the left — that's where the storm center lies.

Both nimbostratus clouds (*left*) and cumulonimbus clouds (*right*) clouds indicate it's a good day to stay in the cottage reading and playing board games.

### The danger zone

In our temperate climate zone, if storm clouds are to the west or north of your position, you are in the danger zone and may be in their path.

The anvil dome of a supercell peeks through some lower storm clouds.

## Beware the supercell

Supercells are very dramatic thunderstorms to watch form. The largest and most severe class of thunderstorm, they develop their unique features from the convergence of rising warm moist air in front and descending cold dry air to the back. When these two air masses come together in harmony, the storms develop a deep updraft that is in persistent rotation. An impressive sight to behold, supercells are responsible for heavy rain, strong downdrafts, high winds, hail, flash flooding, cloud-to-ground lightning. Most common on the Great Plains, supercells also occur in the eastern U.S., and in southern Ontario and Quebec.

# Lightning and thunder

It's untrue that lightning never strikes twice in the same place. For example, the Empire State Building, which was designed to serve as a lightning rod for the surrounding area, is struck by lightning on average 100 times each year.

At the same time, positive electrical charges build upon the ground below. When the difference in the charges becomes large enough, electricity moves from the cloud down to the ground (called cloud-to-ground lightning) or from one part of the cloud to another (in-cloud lightning), or from one cloud to another cloud (rare, but called cloud-to-cloud lightning).

In cloud-to-ground lightning, negative charges flow downward and positive charges on the ground leap upward to meet them. When the two meet, the jagged downward path of the negative charges suddenly lights up with a brilliant flash of light, appearing as though the lightning originated in the cloud. In fact, lightning (positive charges) travels up from the ground. The entire process takes less than a millionth of a second, so our eyes trick us into thinking that the lightning bolt shoots down from the cloud.

## Other kinds of lightning

In addition to seeing the three types of lightning mentioned above, you may also see:

- Sheet lightning is lightning within a cloud that lights up the cloud like a sheet of light.
- Chain lightning occurs when the lightning bolt appears to be broken into fragments because of varying brightness or because parts of the bolt are covered by clouds.
- Ribbon lightning occurs when a cloud-to-ground flash is blown sideways by the wind, making it appear as two identical bolts side by side.
- Ball lightning is rarely seen, and is lightning in the form of a ball the size of a softball and lasts only a few seconds.

**Bolt from the blue**

The expression, "bolt from the blue" originated from the form of lightning that seems to come out of the clear blue sky, when in fact it is a lightning bolt from a thunderstorm a few miles away.

From a safe vantage point, lightning is one of nature's most magnificent free shows. Lightning is electricity that forms inside cumulonimbus clouds as water droplets, hail, and ice crystals collide with one another. The more collisions there are, the greater the buildup of electricity. As with all electricity, there are positive and negative electrical charges, but in the cloud they separate from one another, the negative charges dropping to the lower part of the cloud and the positive charges staying in the middle and upper parts.

# Lightning rules

**The 30-30 rule** If the time between seeing lightning and hearing thunder is less than thirty seconds, you are in danger of being struck. Go inside. After the storm and the last flash of lightning or clap of thunder, wait thirty minutes before going back outside, but be cautious!

The 30-30 rule does not guarantee another lightning strike. Make a habit of listening to weather forecasts, and watch the sky for possible developing thunderstorms and be prepared to invoke the 30-30 rule several times.

**The 5 to 1 rule** When you see lightning, count the seconds until you hear thunder. At the speed of sound, it takes about five seconds to travel one mile (1 km for every 3 seconds), so it takes the sound of thunder longer to get to you than the lightning. Therefore, if you count to five just before you hear the thunder, the storm is about one mile away. For lightning that is far away, the thunder will sound like a low rumble as the sound waves reflect and echo off hillsides, buildings and trees. If the lightning is more than 15 miles away you may not hear thunder it at all.

# Avoiding death by lightning

Get off the water immediately. Go inside and stay away from windows. If you must stay outside during the thunderstorm, find shelter in a dense woods or thick grove of small trees. Stay away from tall trees. If you are trapped in an open space, get as low as you can in a valley or ravine and crouch down. Stay away from metals, like metal fences, flagpoles and lamp posts. Lightning that is about to strike near you usually gives a brief warning: your hair may stand on end, your skin may tingle, you might hear a crackling sound, and keys or other metal objects may vibrate. If there is a group of you when this happens, spread out 20 feet (5–6 m) or more apart and squat down with your head and feet together, your head tucked and your ears covered (the clap is going to be loud!). After the lightning flashes, keep moving to a safer place.

If you are indoors, avoid contact with corded phones, contact with plumbing (wait for storm to pass before washing your hands, showering, doing the dishes or laundry), stay away from windows and doors and electrical equipment, including TVs and computers.

Avoid pitching tents under large trees with exposed roots. The trees could act as lightning rods, and the charge can travel through the roots and fry you where you lie.

# Weather emergency plans

- Decide where to go when a flood, severe thunderstorm, or tornado warning is issued.
- Update these plans every year.
- Include in your disaster plan what to do with your pets.
- Make a weather disaster kit containing water, nonperishable food, a flashlight and radio with extra batteries, a first aid kit, important documents, medical needs, tools, and sanitation supplies. Be sure everyone in the family knows where your family disaster supply kit is located.
- Make a communication plan. Designate a friend or relative either living at your lake or outside your lake as your contact in the event you are separated from family members during a severe thunderstorm, flood, or tornado. Agree upon a place where the family members can meet if separated.

## Thunder and lightning

Lightning bolts are extremely hot, with temperatures ranging between 30,000 and 50,000° F (16,650–28,000° C). A lightning bolt suddenly heats the air around it to such an extreme that the air instantly expands, sending out a vibration or shock wave that we hear as thunder. If you are near the stroke of lightning you'll hear thunder as one sharp crack.

# Wind and waves

If you are in a boat, you will always care about the wind and waves. The wind sailors and windsurfers crave can make canoeists cantankerous. Too much wind isn't good for anyone out on the water—where there's wind, there are waves. Always make sure that your boat and everyone on board is capable of handling the conditions before you head out.

## Wind

Wind is the mass movement of air. Its patterns are dictated by variations in solar heating with latitude and season, as well as by the rotation of the Earth. Doubling of wind speed quadruples its strength (force); it is the strength of the wind that causes waves. On smaller lakes, the wind often rises in late afternoon because, as the sun begins to set, the change in air temperature creates the winds. For offshore winds, the water on your shoreline is quite calm but much rougher at the opposite end of the lake. Conversely, for onshore winds, the water on your shoreline is quite rough but much calmer at the other end of the lake.

If the wind changes in a clockwise direction, fair weather is on its way; if it changes in a counterclockwise direction, fair weather is leaving.

## Wave terminology

Wind will generate two kinds of currents or motions, periodic and aperiodic. Each type of wave has a characteristic length, height, period and frequency.

The wave length is measured between two adjacent crests or troughs. Wave height is the vertical distance between a crest and a trough. Wave amplitude is half the wave height.

Wave period is the time required for the passage of two crests or two troughs past a point. The inverse of wave period is known as the wave frequency.

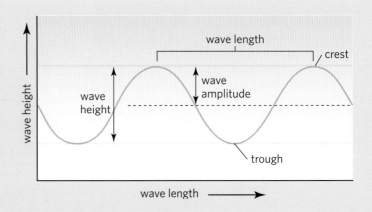

# Fetch and wave height

The distance that wind can blow across a lake without interruption by land, such as islands, is called the fetch. The greater the fetch, the higher the waves. If you are paddling into the wind, it's best to hug the shore, even if it makes a longer route; any land that juts out will protect you from the wind and from the highest waves.

You will want to estimate the wave height on your lake for a number of reasons:

- The taller the waves, the mightier they are. Consequently, shoreline erosion is dependent, in part, on wave height.
- Your ability to participate in certain watersports depends on wave height. You need waves for certain activities, such as body and board surfing. Waves that are too high will make other activities, such as waterskiing, canoeing and distance swimming, more difficult and even dangerous.
- Marinas are usually located in bays with low wave heights.
- Waves grow as they go. Big waves can damage your property and endanger lives, so you'll want to know how big your waves can get, and where along the shoreline they tend to be their largest.

# Langmuir circulation and streaks

Have you ever noticed streaks of floating foam or bubbles on the water surface? The Langmuir streaks, sometimes called windrows, can be spaced anywhere from 33 to 197 feet (10–60 m) apart, depending on the wind speed and the size of the lake. The length of the streaks can be anywhere from a few to several miles in large lakes. The streaks are typically aligned along the wind direction, but may vary by as much as 20 degrees, because as wind direction changes, the streaks will gradually shift to align with the new direction, lagging behind by 15 to 20 minutes.

Langmuir streaks. Irvin Langmuir noticed patterns of floating seaweed when crossing the Atlantic in 1938. He deduced that water movements can be organized into horizontal, helical currents in the upper layers of water. The Langmuir streaks coincide with lines of surface convergence and downward movements of water particles. Suspended particles accumulate in the streaks making them denser than the water on either side. Water swells up at the zones where the water particles move apart. The trip across the Atlantic is long; clearly, Langmuir was bored.

Once you have determined the fetch of your lake, use this chart to determine the maximum wave height possible on your lake. For example, if your cottage is at the end of a lake and located 2½ miles (4 km) from the farthest shore with no islands in between, you could expect a maximum wave height of 26 inches (66 cm) on your stretch of shoreline.

| | | | | | | | | | | | |
|---|---|---|---|---|---|---|---|---|---|---|---|
| **IMPERIAL** | fetch (miles) | ⅝ | 1¼ | 1⅞ | 2½ | 3⅛ | 3¾ | 4⅜ | 5 | 5⅝ | 6¼ |
| | wave height (inches) | 13 | 18 | 23 | 26 | 29 | 32 | 36 | 37 | 39 | 41 |
| **METRIC** | fetch (km) | 1 | 2 | 3 | 4 | 5 | 6 | 7 | 8 | 9 | 10 |
| | wave height (cm) | 33 | 47 | 58 | 66 | 74 | 81 | 88 | 94 | 100 | 102 |

If you'd like to calculate the exact wave height for your lake, use this equation:

$$\text{wave height} = 0.105 \sqrt{(\text{fetch in cm})}$$

# Seiches

## A mighty wind

The most common cause of seiches is the wind. It blows across the surface of the lake, piling up the warm, upper layers of water at the windward end. While this warm water piles up, the cold water from lower in the lake is forced up to replace it. When the wind stops blowing, gravity takes over and the lake begins to rock back and forth. The water rises and falls, usually less than 3 feet (1 m), at the ends of the lake. Most lakes have a seiche with a single node at the center where the water rocks back and forth without changing height. Some large lakes may have more than one node.

Cottagers on large lakes such as the Great Lakes, Lake Champlain in New York, Lake Wanapitei and Lake Nipissing in Ontario will undoubtedly have noticed periodic rising and falling of the water level, or surface seiche, on their shoreline. A surface seiche has a wavelength the same length as the lake basin. The water surface at opposite ends of the lake oscillates up and down, like a teeter totter, about a point, or node, somewhere near the middle of the lake. The to-and-fro horizontal motion is maximum at this point and minimum at the ends of the lake.

The most extreme wind-induced seiche on Lake Erie is reported to be 16 feet (5 m) between the ends of the lake, similar to a storm surge that is caused by torrential winds along ocean coasts. However, once a storm surge passes, it's gone; the seiche oscillates back and forth across the lake for some time. Lake seiches can occur very quickly, within 15 minutes on Lake Superior, causing the water level to fall and then rise again by 3 feet (1 m). Such high amplitudes can have destructive effects on the shoreline and many cottagers need to construct gabions to prevent erosion.

Once a surface seiche is set into motion, friction and gravity will dampen the oscillation and eventually the water settles down. While seiches occur in most lakes, their amplitudes are so small that they are almost undetectable.

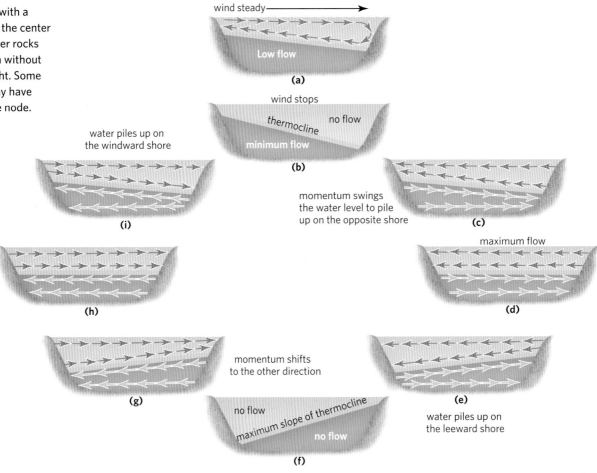

wind steady ⟶

Low flow

(a)

wind stops

thermocline    no flow

minimum flow

(b)

water piles up on the windward shore

(i)

momentum swings the water level to pile up on the opposite shore

(c)

maximum flow

(d)

(h)

(e)

water piles up on the leeward shore

(g)

momentum shifts to the other direction

no flow    maximum slope of thermocline    no flow

(f)

Watch your wake.

# Wake

Life at the edge of the water can be precarious. The plants and animals that inhabit the shoreline have adapted to natural waves and fluctuations in water levels. But wake, the moving waves a boat leaves behind it, can pose a threat to the delicate balance of shoreline ecology. Wake waves can cloud the water with sediment, destroying fish spawning habitat, smothering aquatic vegetation and accelerating shoreline erosion. When powerboats operate too quickly too close to shore, the wake they produce can be a safety hazard to humans as well, rocking or swamping other boats, endangering swimmers or wading anglers, and smashing docked boats against their moorings.

## Controlling wake: it's all about speed

By understanding how to control the wake your boat creates, you can limit its negative impact, and make waterways safer and healthier. Controlling your wake is easy: the slower the boat, the lower the wake. The lower the wake, the less damage it causes.

The shoreline is not significantly damaged by a wake up to 5 inches (13 cm) high. A 10-inch (25 cm) wake is five times more destructive, and a 25-inch (64 cm) wake is 30 times more destructive than a 5-inch wake. Your typical motorboat or larger fishing boat can create a 10-inch wake. Crafts such as houseboats or cruisers can create wakes of 25 inches or higher.

---

Local marinas generally have posted speed limits for boats passing by. Check with your local state or province to learn about wake restrictions. In some states, there are laws requiring boaters to limit wake in sensitive areas. Remember, you can be legally responsible for your wake and the damage or personal injury it causes.

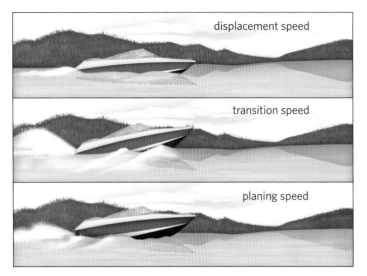

displacement speed

transition speed

planing speed

Boat speeds and the wake produced.

### Boat speeds

Understanding the speeds under which your boat operates is key to minimizing wake:

- Displacement speed creates the least wake. It is the slowest speed, with the bow down in the water.
- Transition speed creates the largest wake. As you increase speed to get on plane, the bow rises, causing the stern to plow through the water.
- Planing speed creates less wake than transition speed, but more than displacement. The bow drops back down, the boat levels out, and only a little of the hull contacts the water.

### More wake-reducing strategies:

- Slow down well in advance of sensitive areas to give yourself time to drop all the way down to displacement speed.
- When possible, boat in deeper waters (shallow water can increase wake), and avoid getting too close to other boats or the shore.
- A heavy stern will increase wake size, so distribute passengers throughout the boat. Bilges gather water after a heavy rain: remove the water by bailing or with a bilge pump if there is one.

*Right* To protect the loons on lakes, some shoreline areas should be left undisturbed to accommodate their nests (*right*), and boaters passing these areas should minimize wake. Keep boats well away from swimming birds, particularly when they are with chicks too young to dive or fly.

- Boats with trim tabs—extensions of the hull just above the waterline—keep your wake down, your boat level (planing) and limit your time in transition speed.

## How to ride wake and natural, wind-generated waves

- Warn your passengers so they can brace themselves.
- Particularly if you are in a canoe or other small boat, turn into the wake and come back on course when the swell is passed.
- Cross the wake at a slight angle, instead of crossing a wake perpendicularly, so your bow can grip the wave longer, and keep it from being thrown high in the air.
- You need some speed to be able to maneuver through the wake, so slow down to lessen its impact, but don't stop.

# Shoreline erosion

Not only do concrete, steel and stone breakwalls completely choke the flow of life along the shoreline, creating a lifeless wasteland, they ultimately will cost you more money and grief than you can imagine.

The erosion of your lake's shoreline is the natural consequence of water and wave action over time, a process you will not conquer, no matter how much concrete you pour or what kind of barriers you create. Fortunately, your shoreline has its own built-in erosion control: the plants, shrubs and trees that live at the water's edge. The roots of the natural vegetation hold the soil of the shoreline together, as well as contributing to the rich community of aquatic and land organisms that inhabit this zone. When you clear out this vegetation, you are not only destroying the ecological balance, you are putting your valuable property at risk of becoming lake-fill.

## Breakwalls

When a cottager removes natural vegetation, the only apparent solution to stop the inevitable erosion of soil is to construct an ugly, costly and often ineffective breakwall. When waves slam against the vertical wall, the energy bursts upward, and downward, where the ground is gradually washed away. Eventually, the wall has nothing to stand on, and topples.

## Restoring shorelines with breakwalls

If you own a breakwall, you can both reduce the pounding it takes from the waves, and improve shoreline habitat.

1. Plant a buffer zone, including lots of deep-rooted native shrubs to hold the soil behind the wall.
2. With the approval of local authorities, pile stones at a 45-degree angle in front of the wall. These stones will provide places for fish to hide, places for sediments to settle and plant life to establish, and will also absorb much of the wave action. "Shore ladders," made by piling up enough stones to reach from the lake bed to the top of the wall, allow frogs, snakes, and mink to travel back and forth from land to water.

## Going natural

If your breakwater is on its last legs, consider it the perfect opportunity to remove it and restore your shoreline to its natural state.

1. With the approval of local authorities, dig out the bank behind the wall to restore a slope of 25 degrees or less.
2. Line it with geotextile filter cloth to keep the soil in place.
3. Remove the wall if possible. If not, pull it back onto the new slope, reducing it to brick-sized pieces of rubble.
4. Add a veneer of additional stones known as "riprap" to cover the filter cloth.
5. Plant woody vines and shrubs, such as willow, dogwood, sweet gale, Virginia creeper, riverbank grape, which will eventually grow into the spaces between the stones.

If you have a serious erosion problem—on the Great Lakes, for example—you'll need professional advice from a coastal engineer, who can help you balance shoreline protection with habitat maintenance so everyone wins.

## Shoreline damage: ice jams

Variations in temperature over the winter cause forceful alternating contraction and expansion of the ice layer of your lake. The resulting stress results in tension cracks, which fill up with water, then freeze, then crack, and so on... Each cycle of contraction and expansion forces the thick ridges of ice up the edges of the shore, shoving anything movable or malleable in their path. Think of the scouring power of glaciers, only on a smaller scale.

# Building a dock

you a long-lasting, practical and safe structure. Before you begin, take stock of what you will use the dock for. Do you have a boat? Big or small? Do you want to swim, fish or sunbathe? With the right dock, you can do it all.

The best dock not only facilitates your favorite waterfront activities but exists in harmony with the delicate ecology of the shoreline. Your goal in building a dock is to maximize your waterfront enjoyment while minimizing environmental impact.

## Getting started

### Make a map

Begin your dock project by drawing a detailed map of your shoreline. Knowing the prominent features, such as rocks — on land and submerged — sandbars, water intake and power lines, will help you choose the best location for your dock and the type of dock that will suit your needs. A successful dock project is one that works with the natural environment; don't forget to include known fish spawning areas and nesting sites on your map. And be careful to note the property line, so you don't build your neighbors a dock. Use graph paper for your map to keep the proportions accurate.

### Clear the red tape

The powers that be will want to see the plans for your dock before they approve the shoreline alteration and construction. The better your plan — include your map, photos of the site, and construction details — the easier it will be to gain approval. Make your map and design in the summer, and present your plan in late fall or winter so you are clear to build come spring.

The dock can be either a sight for sore eyes or a sorrowful sight. Most cherish it is as a welcome mat to the cottage and a platform for a host of summer activities. At the end of the season it is either lifted in salute to another great summer or left as is to once more withstand the crushing groans of winter ice. Build it yourself or buy it, constructing a stable dock that serves your needs is not a difficult task. Whether you are replacing a wobbly old disaster-waiting-to-happen or are starting fresh, carefully considering the size, shape, material and type of dock before you start will guarantee

# Dock materials

Nothing lasts forever, particularly where water is involved. Even the best dock will not withstand the stresses of bashing boats, jumping children, wild waves and weather forever. Choose materials that are strong, and will resist rot and decay as long as possible.

## Untreated wood

Preferred woods include eastern red cedar, eastern white cedar redwood, and cypress, which make long-lasting, beautiful but expensive decks. For dock cribs and permanent piles, stronger woods, such as Douglas fir, hemlock, tamarack, pine, and spruce will do. However, they are not as rot resistant as the first group.

### Advantages
◆ easy to work with
◆ reasonably priced
◆ strong under short-term loads (rammed head on by a watercraft)
◆ easily rebuilt should nature win

### Disadvantages
◆ swells and shrinks with waterfront moisture, making joining pieces challenging
◆ wood eventually rots

**Extending wood life**

Standard wood preservation doesn't work for docks. Any coating you put on a dock will fade, blister, and peel, creating water pockets where fungi thrive. Naturally graying wood looks better anyway.

Consider a shape other than the standard rectangle for your dock to increase its stability and useable space.

Spring ice can destroy anything, so be aware of your usual ice conditions before you build.

## Size matters

Dock size is dictated by need. A small dock may not be practical for mooring a large boat, but could be perfect for a one-canoe family. The minimum width for a dock is 3 feet (1 m), with bigger docks being generally more stable than smaller docks. However, as dock size increases, so do expense and environmental damage. Docks shade the land beneath them, potentially disrupting your aquatic neighbors.

## Shape matters

If your pocketbook allows, consider building a T-, U-, or L-shaped dock instead of the basic rectangle. Adding sections allows you to allocate different activities to different parts of the dock (swimming off one section, boats moored to another). For the increased stability and useable space you gain, the extra cost is worth it.

A boy spaces the planks of a plastic lumber dock.

## Advantages

- waterproof
- decay-resistant
- stain resistant, never need paint or sealant
- don't crack, split, shrink or expand
- slip resistant (and no splinters!)
- lifetime warranty
- post-consumer plastic (preserves forests)
- preferred material for dock floats
- can be used as decking material
- costs between cedar and pressure-treated wood

## Disadvantages

- more fragile than wood and therefore not recommended for structural duties, such as for beams, joists, and posts. Railing post sleeves slide over top of 4-by-4-inch lumber posts, and decking is mounted over top of a standard lumber deck substructure

## Pressure-treated wood

Although pressure-treated pine or spruce is 20- to 30-percent less expensive than the preferred wood species, it is full of chemicals that can leach into the environment. Even the sawdust of this bright green wood is considered toxic. Some waterfront areas ban its use completely. If you have to use it for a dock, use it only for structural parts to minimize contact with skin. Any project should be done well back from the shoreline, and allowed to dry thoroughly. Choose pressure-treated wood labeled s-DRY, which is typically of better quality and longer lasting than s-GRN, which has had the preserving chemicals applied while the wood was still wet with sap and not as absorbent.

## Hardware

Don't scrimp on the metal brackets (usually steel), or the nails, screws, nuts and bolts that hold all the parts of your dock together, and add strength to any dock connection under load. Joints nailed or screwed together without proper dock hardware will inevitably pull apart. If using plastic decking, buy your hardware from a distributor. Otherwise, go to a hardware store that sells a wide variety of dock hardware.

## Plastic

When installed properly, plastic lumber decking can look great. It is available in several colors and wood grains and some manufacturers offer lifetime warranties. It comes in traditional "planks" of solid polystyrene or polyethylene (PE), extrusions made from polyvinylchloride (PVC), and composites of recycled PE and wood byproducts. Composites allow for some seepage into the pores of the product, while 100-percent plastic is nonporous.

*Right* No matter how good your hardware, if you take the lazy way to tie up your boat, you may find yourself searching the shore downwind for it. Better to pull the looped rope end through the hole in the centre of the cleat then pull it around each arm of the cleat.

# Types of docks

## Removable docks

### Floating docks

Floating docks are good economic and environmental choices. They work best when they are long, wide, low and heavy. The minimum size for a stable floater is 6 by 20 feet (1.8 × 6 m), weighing in at 1,000 pounds (454 kg). Anchor solidly for maximum stability. Install the floats closer to the perimeter of the dock, rather than set near the dock's center line to enhance stability. Use Styrofoam billets for flotation. They come in three sizes; 7" × 20" × 108" will support 480 pounds, 10" × 20" × 108" will support 690 pounds and 10" × 24" × 96" will support 730 pounds. Check out **Cottage Operations** for instructions on how to build a floating raft.

#### Advantages

- relatively easy and economical to build
- adaptable to most shorelines
- no maximum water depth to prevent its use
- cause minimal direct disruption to submerged lands
- where ice is a problem, floaters can be removed in the fall and replaced in spring

#### Disadvantages

- can block sunlight to aquatic plants and may cause shore erosion
- must have at least 3 feet (1 m) beneath it (measured at low water), so it won't bump submerged lands (less if water level stable and wave action moderate)
- often lack stability

## Pipe docks

Picture a ramp on long, skinny legs. The simple pipe dock is the most economical and least environmentally disruptive of dock types. As a general rule, the width of the dock should be at least 3 feet (1 m) and never less than the depth of the water. About 6 to 7 feet (1.8–2 m) is the maximum water depth practical for pipe docks.

#### Advantages

- least costly to build
- least disruptive to the environment
- light weight, easily installed and moved
- height of deck adjustable to water levels
- good for busy river channels, waves

#### Disadvantages

- must be removed in winter because ice action will crumple it
- severe wave action can damage lighter aluminum pipe docks
- not good for mooring larger vessels
- maximum water depth of 6 to 7 feet (1.8–2 m)

*Left* When ducklings are learning to swim, they cling to the shore and avoid areas where docks meet the land. To aid the swimming lessons, push the floating dock a bit further out and use a gangplank to bridge the short gap between dock and shore, giving mama duck and her brood a marine underpass.

A pipe dock.

Crib docks are susceptible to ice damage.

## Crib docks

A "crib" is a container that holds a few tons of rock and stone. A proper crib is made from new, square-cut lumber (occasionally steel or concrete castings). The timbers are assembled in opposing pairs, one pair laid out on top of the next, creating a slatted, box-like structure. Threaded rods run the full height in each corner to secure the timbers in place. The box is then filled with rock for stability.

### Advantages
◆ stable
◆ best above the high-water mark, and used as anchors for structures like floating docks

### Disadvantages
◆ maximum water depth 8 feet (2.4 m)
◆ for optimum stability, crib's total height should at least equal its total width (a lot of rocks)
◆ smothers a large area of submerged ground; second only to concrete piers in environmental destruction
◆ can destroy fish habitat, kill bottom organisms or introduce toxicants (from pressure-treated lumber)

## Fixed docks

Fixed docks are often misconceived as "permanent" docks, but no matter how well constructed your fixed dock is, it will eventually succumb to the elements. Fixed docks are probably the least preferred by environmentalists. If you absolutely must build a permanent dock, make sure you obtain the the appropriate permits, keeping in mind that it may be difficult to get one.

## A crib is not a gabion

The relatively inexpensive wire or plastic mesh baskets designed to hold stones, rock or concrete often seen in ugly retaining walls may seem ideal for dock construction but, if not properly constructed, won't stand the test of currents, waves, and ice, all of which cause the basket to sag and flatten. If properly constructed they do provide cost effective environmentally sensitive solutions for mechanically stabilized earth walls, vegetated slope reinforcement, slope stabilization, slope reinforcement and rockfall confinement for many Great Lakes cottages.

Poorly constructed, gabions will sag and collapse over time, the shoreline beneath them eroding away.

## Concrete piers

Picture a big block of cement, usually with an integral boat ramp. These monuments to human hubris (if you think it will last forever, think again) can be merged with shoreline to provide an anchor for other types of docks. You will most often see concrete piers in commercial, industrial and municipal settings. Because of the environmental damage they case over time, they are a poor choice for cottage use.

### Disadvantages

- expensive
- environmentally destructive; completely removes any aquatic environment
- erosion of land beneath pier eventually destroys it
- maximum water depth 8 feet (2.4 m)

Boats securely moored to a concrete pier.

## Permanent pile docks

Imagine a heavy-duty, immovable pipe dock, with long poles of wood or tubes of steel or plastic (all called piles) sunk into the earth by heavy equipment (not a home workshop project). They are only practical in areas where ice damage is not a factor.

Permanent pile docks share the environmental benefits of pipe docks for submerged land, as they have little contact with it.

A lift pipe dock is drawn up for the winter.

# Specialty docks

### Lift docks

Lift docks look like drawbridges. They come in lift pipe, lift float and lift suspension versions, all based on and having the same environmental impact as their non-lifting counterparts. Each version can be winched up in the air to prevent damage from winter ice.

### Finger docks

These narrow, wobbly structures jut out from much larger docks to increase spots to moor boats. This is their only practical application.

## Cantilever and suspension docks

A cantilever dock works like an overhanging balcony: the dock's frame stretches from the shore over the fulcrum point and then out over the water. For every foot that hangs beyond the fulcrum, you need 2 feet (0.6 m) of well-anchored onshore dock. If you have a large onshore dock (to smooth a rocky shoreline), and want only a couple of feet extension, a cantilever dock is a good option.

For a suspension dock, picture half of the Golden Gate Bridge; a rectangular tower holds up a pair of cables anchored well back on shore to keep the deck suspended over the water like a diving board. The practical limits to overhang length are 8 (2.4 m) feet for cantilevered and 50 feet (15 m) for suspension.

### Advantages
- docks sit completely out of water, not disturbing the environment
- look cool

### Disadvantages
- not great for lakes with extreme water level fluctuations
- potentially disruptive to shore land
- expensive

Finger docks branch off from a central floating dock.

# Dock damage

The increasing popularity of removable docks generally means you'll see less dock carnage in the spring than in years gone by. However, fixed docks can be shifted by the formidable power of ice. Docks that are supported by square, rock-filled structures called "cribs" are particularly vulnerable to the damaging effects of ice.

## Ice action on fixed docks

Fixed docks are not permanent and there's nothing that proves this quicker than damaging ice conditions. Even cribs filled with rocks can be moved by ice. Concrete cribs may not be lifted but they can be shifted by expansion and contraction of jacking ice. Pile docks are also vulnerable to the power of shifting ice, as the poles that support them must be sunk deep into the bottom of your lake.

Where your dock is situated along the shore can influence the amount of damage your dock may experience.

Docks most prone to damage and relocation are those near inflows or outflows. Docks in protected bays are less subject to ice damage but certainly not immune to the forces of ice.

If you have a new cottage and want a dock, carefully consider the winter conditions on your lake. If you are new to the property and haven't seen the winter conditions, ask your neighbors before you build. Consider environmental impact, shoreline aesthetics, overall function and municipal regulations as well.

## Better docks for icy conditions

Floating docks or pipe docks that can be easily removed every fall are now commonly found in areas where ice damage is a concern. Some docks are hinged to structures well up on shore and out of the water to which the docks are easily raised in fall by a winch with cables. These are also envonmentally sound choices: in addition to leaving the lake bottom undisturbed, they can provide shelter and shade for fish.

## An ounce of prevention

The best insurance against ice damage to your dock is to be aware of the likelihood and severity of its occurrence—before you even build your dock.

## The mechanics of ice damage

(**a**) In the fall, water levels are near their lowest levels, with only the base of the crib under water. (**b**) When winter arrives, ice forms and gradually engulfs the crib. If jacking does not occur throughout the winter, all will be fine, at least until spring. (**c**) When the snow melts, the melt water flows under the ice and raises it along with anything within it. (**d**) If the crib is not firmly anchored, the ice can lift the crib off its base. Any currents in the under-flowing water will move and relocate the dock and crib.

(**a**) November, low water level before ice-up

(**b**) December through March, ice forms and engulfs crib

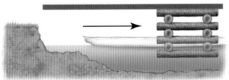

(**c**) March through April, spring runoff lifts ice and objects within it (e.g. crib)

(**d**) May through June, ice has melted and dock and crib are relocated during high water period

# CHAPTER 3

# Swimming

There's nothing like the sensation of swimming in a beautiful freshwater lake.

FLOATING ON THE MIRROR-STILL water of a lake at sunset, the air cool on your face and the water warm on your body... Cottage lovers conjure up this sensation to keep them going during the long, cold winter. Some people wait only until the ice has cleared to make their first breath-robbing leap. Others won't put a toe in until the summer sun has warmed at least the surface of the lake to bathtub temperatures. Some lakes are havens for the beach-loving sunbathers; others cater to adventure-hungry cliff jumpers, surfers or scuba divers. In the first half of this chapter we'll immerse ourselves in the physical characteristics of a good swimming lake.

Read on to discover the many creatures — innocuous and malevolent — that share the water with us. Whether you are a splasher, a floater, or a long-distance racer, when you swim in a lake you are never alone. It's wise to be aware of the potential dangers, animal, bacterial and otherwise, you might meet in your lake. But don't be afraid. Chances are good you've swallowed a number of tiny aquatic creatures by now, and they obviously haven't killed you.

And finally, we offer advice on swimming safety, as well as a review of some basic strokes.

One last swim before the sun goes down — a perfect way to end the day as the season draws to a close.

It's too cold!

# Water temperature

It's too cold, it's too cold! We shriek as the water inches up our bodies for the first swim of the year. Some people swear it's easier to just jump in. There are several factors at play in regulating the temperature of your lake, including sediment color, summer sun, rivers and underground springs.

## Near-shore and off-shore water

Why is near-shore water warmer than off-shore water? In nearly all cases, red light is being absorbed by the sediments and transfers its heat to the water. Since red light waves are most intense in the top few feet of water, the shallow water will nearly always be warmer. If it's a large lake, the Coriolis force tends to force the warm water shoreward and then downward as it is deflected offshore.

In the spring, as the water is warming up, the edges warm up so much more quickly than the center that there is a distinct vertical division between the two areas, called a thermal bar. As you wade into the water you'll feel the sudden, cold shock of the unheated open water when you hit the thermal bar. By the end of June, the lake will be warmed enough from the sun that the water is well mixed and the thermal bars are absent.

## The sultry summer sun

As spring advances, the sun gradually comes to lie directly overhead, rapidly heating the surface layers of the lake. These layers become much warmer and lighter than the water below. Because water is heated from the surface down, only the upper few feet or so can be heated by the intense red and infrared heating waves from the sun. The clearer the water, the deeper the red and infrared light can penetrate, and the deeper the heating process can occur. Nearly all the red light is absorbed within the first few feet of water. Only winds can mix the warm water of the surface layers with the

warm surface layer = epilimnion

colder with increasing depth = metalimnion

constantly dark and cold
at 40° F (4° C) = hypolimnion

cooler water below. The stronger and more frequent the winds, the deeper the warm water can be mixed in.

The heating and mixing processes eventually result in the formation of three thermal layers in the lake; an upper warm layer called the *epilimnion,* a lower cold layer known as the *hypolimnion,* and an intermediate layer known as the *metalimnion.* (The *thermocline* is within the metalimnion.) The metalimnion is the zone of rapid changes in temperature, usually more than $1.8°$ F ($1°$ C) per meter drop in the water column. In some lakes, the metalimnion may be extremely thin, as thin as an inch (8–10 mm). The thinner the metalimnion, the greater the resistance to mixing between the cold hypolimnion and the warm epilimnion. If you swim down through the metalimnion, you will feel the rapid drop in temperature as you pass into the cold hypolimnion below.

## Hot and cold spots

If you've spent much time at all swimming in your lake, you have undoubtedly experienced breath-arresting cold spots and heavenly hot spots. Hot spots tend to be in surface layers and cold spots tend to occur as eddies or as bottom layers. Both are especially common below mouths of rivers. Hot spots are warm slugs of water that have heated up over dark-colored bottoms. Dark-colored substrates absorb heat faster than light-colored substrates and the water heats up faster than the main body of water. This readily occurs in shallow lakes, and in the water of streams and rivers. When river water is heated it becomes lighter (less dense) and enters the lake as an *overflow.* Conversely, if the river water is cooler than the lake water, it is more dense and sinks and enters the lake as an *underflow.* If the river and lake water are at the same temperature, *interflow* occurs.

Groundwater springs can also create cold spots. For example, if the temperature of the groundwater is near $50°$ F ($10°$ C) and the bottom of a deep lake is at the characteristic $39°$ F ($4°$ C), the groundwater rises and creates a cold water eddy that is moved around the lake by currents until it mixes and dissipates with the lake water. In a shallow, warm lake, the colder, denser groundwater will stay at the bottom unless wind mixes it with the warm water.

A dry towel for a chilly swimmer.

Sandy beaches like this one on Lake Edith in Alberta's Jasper National Park do exist on many North American lakes (*top*), but if you live on a rocky or weedy lake, a removable dock can provide a comfortable — even joyous — way to enter the water.

# Sandy beaches

There is nothing more gratifying for sunbathers and swimmers than a beach with fine, white sand. The structure and mineral composition of sand grains on a beach depends on the geology of the ancient rock that has been eroded by wind and water into the current landscape. Most beaches and dunes are composed of quartz and feldspar grains. Brilliant snow-white beaches are mostly composed of gypsum, unless you are on the gleaming white sands of tropical coral beaches. Black sand beaches are made of fine volcanic particles.

If you are lucky enough to be on a lake with natural sandy beaches, there may also be sand dunes along the shore. These often occur around ancient lake beds or river deltas. Wind moves the sand grains into mounds or hills, but any objects, such as shrubs, rocks or fence posts obstruct the wind force and cause the sand to pile up in drifts and ultimately large dunes. Even ant hills can form the nucleus upon which sand dunes can be built. Some dunes tower above lake level.

Unfortunately for beach lovers, the shoreline of many lakes is composed of gravel, boulders, vegetation — anything but sand. However tempting it may be to cart in truckloads of sand to create a beach, don't do it. The sand almost inevitably erodes, harming aquatic life in its path. It buries insects such as mayflies and caddisflies, disrupts spawning areas for fish such as smallmouth bass, and covers the vegetation where snails, frogs and toads lay their eggs. Without the balance these creatures bring to the ecosystem, more oxygen-depleting algae fill the lake and more annoying bugs swarm the would-be sunbathers. Not only is adding sand to create a beach against the law in Canada, it could increase the risk of creating habitat for mosquitoes that carry the West Nile virus.

Instead, build a removable dock that reaches beyond the rocks, boulders and weeds, or at least to a depth that you can dive or swim without touching bottom. Even more welcoming to swimmers fearing the presence of sinister life on the bottom is a set of steps added to the end of the dock. Hinge the steps to the dock so the steps float and don't gather algae and other life that attach to surfaces, such as sponges, leeches and snails.

# The toe-tanglers: aquatic plants

Many a swimmer with an overactive imagination has felt the slimy limbs of a giant octopus reaching up from the murky depths to wrap its tentacles around their legs. But unless you're in the ocean, that's no octopus—it's very likely a plant. It's time to get to know the innocuous culprits lurking in your lake.

## Eel grass

Eel grass, or water celery, is an aquatic plant with ribbon-like, grassy leaves that can grow up to 3 or 4 feet (1 m) long. You can see the ends of the leaves floating on the surface, along with the small, white, eel grass flower. Watch closely and you might see those flowers disappear, spiraling suddenly downward to the base of the plant. The flowers are attached to a long, coiling stem that recoils when the flower is fertilized. The developing fruit takes root in the mud and germinates. The plants provide cover for fish and food for muskrats, fish and waterfowl.

## Maiden's hair

If you know a stream that feeds your lake, chances are you've seen the long strands of green algae known as maiden's hair. Sometimes the strands cover the entire stream bottom. The presence of maiden's hair indicates the water is hard (see the **Getting to Know Your Lake** chapter). If the siren song of these dead maidens pulls you under, relax—they live only in shallow water.

## Scouring rush

Also known as horsetails, these ancient, spore-producing plants have a jointed, bamboo-like look to them, with small leaves close to a sturdy stem. You will find meadows of scouring rush in bays and lagoons, where muskrats munch on them. The plant is rough to the touch because the stalks and leaves contain silica. This makes them perfect scouring pads for your pots and pans.

## Freshwater sponges

Sponges are not plants, but primitive creatures that lack organ systems and a body form. They usually wrap themselves around logs or rocks, filtering bacteria, particles and other microscopic organisms from the water, and can be recognized immediately by their garlic odor and gritty feel. The deep green hue of the sponge comes from the algae that live within and on the sponge. Most sponges are very sensitive to enrichment and pollution and their presence in large colonies usually indicates good water quality.

**Sponges and spongillaflies**

The spongillafly, a type of lacewing insect, has aquatic larvae that feed on sponges, sucking up the cell contents with a needle-like appendage. The adults, with their lacy wings, are active at night, attracted to lights, and short lived. At rest the adults hold their wings roof-like over their bodies.

Freshwater sponge

# Your swimming companions

## Leeches and bloodsuckers

Ever get the feeling that you are being followed as you float through the water? Swimming toward you is a flat, black ribbon, training its three or four or five pairs of eyes on you, thirsting for your blood.

Leeches and bloodsuckers are creatures that swimmers love to hate. Both leeches and bloodsuckers have a sucker at both ends of their long, segmented bodies. One bloodsucker species that preys on humans has a jaw with three sharp teeth ready to slice into your skin. After making a Y-shaped incision, they secrete a salivary anticoagulant to prevent the blood from clotting. Some species are able to take blood up to twenty times their body weight by storing it in numerous stomach-like sacs. Some bloodsuckers have been starved for two years after a blood meal and survive. Small consolation can be taken from the fact that many leeches lack jaws and teeth to bite with, so when they do attach to humans they go for a cut or abrasion, often between the toes.

Some species live to terrorize our body parts for ten to fifteen years. Not all species of leeches and bloodsuckers have an appetite for your blood. Some attack only fish; some feed on dead animal material, insects, or

Controlling leeches is futile, so use them as fish bait instead.

mollusks; others go after horses and cattle. Many species are elaborately colored in red, orange and green.

> Leeches have three or four pairs of eyes arranged in an arch close to their mouth. Bloodsuckers have five pairs of eyes — all the better to see you with.

### Getting rid of leeches and bloodsuckers

Leeches and bloodsuckers lurk in shallow waters with rocky, solid bottoms and avoid silty water and muddy bottoms to which they cannot attach. However, if your lake has leeches, you'd best resign yourself to the occasional blood sacrifice, because your little vampires are there to stay. They are able to tolerate harsh conditions and almost every deterrent humans can throw at them; trying to get rid of them is as difficult as killing their Transylvanian cousins. Most leeches and bloodsuckers can live in water with temperatures ranging from near 32° to 77° F (0°–25° C) and can handle low oxygen conditions and pH levels from 4.0 to 9.0. They happily survive in polluted waters and are tolerant of many chemicals.

If you do emerge from a swim adorned with feasting leeches, reach for the salt. Sprinkling it liberally onto an attached leech will make it release its grip and shrivel up. But adding salt to the water is not effective at killing leeches and bloodsuckers. Besides, adding salt to the water kills other invertebrates. Similarly, adding lime may discourage the leeches from approaching, but lime has to be added almost daily to keep them away. Some people "bait"

The Northern water snake preys on fish and amphibians. However, they avoid confrontation with humans and are not poisonous.

an area with fresh meat, wait for bloodsuckers to attach, then collect the bait and kill the bloodsuckers by burning or burying them in a box of salt. This is only a temporary measure. Releasing the bloodsuckers a little ways from shore is not effective either, because many can tolerate long periods (months) away from water and will crawl back to the lake.

Bottom line? Controlling leeches and bloodsuckers is futile. Collect them instead and use them for fish bait!

# Northern water snake

On a sunny summer morning you may come across one of these thick-bodied, gray-brown serpents basking on rocks or logs at the edge of your favorite lake. You can identify them by the reddish-brown or black crossbands near the head, and back and side blotches along their bodies. Although it can be unnerving to have a fanged, 4-foot-long reptile sharing your swimming space, have no fear. True to their name, water snakes are excel-

lent swimmers — far better than you are — and will slip silently into the depths rather than seek out confrontation. They will bite if cornered or if you try to handle them, but they are not poisonous.

Adult water snakes can live at least seven years. Courtship and mating occurs in May or June. If you are extremely lucky you may spot the frolicking couple slowly entering the water and emerging, intertwined all the while. Sometimes other males will continue to court the female, or attempt to dislodge the successful suitor. The females give birth to up to sixty live young in August or September. Over the winter, they hibernate in underground dens.

Water snakes prey on fish, frogs, salamanders and tadpoles. They are preyed upon by herons, hawks, raccoons, skunks and foxes. Through habitat destruction and the age-old prejudice against serpents, we are the water snake's biggest enemy.

# Snapping turtles

Yes, snappers do snap. With their serpentine necks, muscular legs and prehistoric-looking tails, these myopic turtles are the subject of many myths. As they live in ponds, rivers, lakes and streams all over cottage country, chances are good that you have swum with snapping turtles without ever encountering one. Contrary to popular belief, they will not attack you in the water. They prudently avoid human contact whenever possible, slipping away to the bottom to feed on carrion, fish, frogs and aquatic plants.

**A word on turtle soup**

Over their long lives, snappers accumulate high levels of toxins in their fat. The more polluted their environment, the higher the toxin levels. If you eat a turtle, you eat the toxins.

Snapping turtle (*left*).

Turtles you'll see basking on logs include the olive-colored midland painted turtle, with its beautiful yellow striped head (*top right*), and the map turtle (*below*), which has a brown shell with many yellowish lines resembling contour lines on a map.

Unlike other turtles, snappers cannot retract their heads and limbs into their relatively small shells so, particularly on land, they are vulnerable to attack. They will face the danger and hiss threats at you. But since a charging turtle is still a turtle, you have ample time to get out of the way. You are most likely to meet a female snapping turtle on land in the spring as she searches for a nesting site. If you see a snapper crossing a dangerous road and want to help her along, always move her in the direction she was headed. Otherwise, she will simply attempt the journey again.

Snappers choose the banks of marshes, sandy beaches, gravel pits, roadsides and railroad beds as nesting sites. If you follow at a respectable distance, you can watch as the turtle digs a hole, deposits up to forty perfectly round, Ping-Pong-ball-sized eggs, covers them over with sand, and returns to the water. The laying process is such an ancient reflex that, once she begins to lay, she cannot stop, even if danger is present. Skunks, raccoons, and foxes often feast on the eggs. The inch-long baby turtles emerge after three to four months and head for the water, sometimes a quarter mile away. The survivors of this first ordeal take five to seven years to sexually mature. The adults live more than fifty years, can attain a shell length of 18 inches (45 cm) and weigh in at over 33 pounds (15 kg).

# Swimming bugs

**Giant water bugs** *Belostoma* and *Lethocerus* feed on prey as large as tadpoles, small ducklings and small fish, and can be a nuisance in fish hatcheries. *Lethocerus* can grow to nearly 2 inches (40–50 mm) in length and can give you a mean and painful bite. But the tables are turned in Asia; giant water bugs are a delicacy there! The giants are good swimmers but hide among debris and vegetation in slow-moving streams or among plants in ponds and lakes. When disturbed they will feign death and go belly-up. But beware, they will go for toes if you kick at them.

**Backswimmers** also bite. However, they redeem themselves by feeding heavily on mosquito larvae and so they are being studied as potential biological control agents. Backswimmers are elegant bugs that swim on their keel-like backs. Their bellies are very hairy and trap air bubbles that are used for respiration. When the oxygen is used up they swim to the surface for more.

**Water boatmen** are extremely agile swimming bugs. They swim on their bellies using their rear pair of long, powerful oar-like legs simultaneously. Their beak is fixed to the underside of their head and, since they cannot sting or bite, they are vegetarians, feeding on algae, plants and detritus at the bottom. Water boatmen have long been a cherished food called "Ahuautle" in Mexico; they are also used as food for pet turtles and fish. If your lake water is teeming with them, rejoice, for they are indicators of good lake water quality.

**Pond skaters and broad-shouldered water striders** are truly adapted for life at the surface. To prevent rupturing the surface tension, the last leg segments have a plume of unwettable hairs that offer low resistance to the surface "skin" of water. The claws are used to dig into the surface skin to provide traction for gliding over the surface. The middle pair of legs propels the bug forward and the rear pair act as rudders. Pond skaters are among the few insects that can tolerate pH values of less than 4.5 and are among the last to disappear when lakes and streams acidify.

**Water scorpions** look like scorpions and are just as fierce, with powerful, grasping forelegs that close about their prey like a jackknife. They are terrible swimmers, preferring to crawl around on banks of streams, lakes and ponds. To breathe air, they have a pair of long breathing tubes that are fused along their length and look like a tail. Water scorpions drown easily if they don't have access to air, so they sit near the surface on plants with the tip of their breathing tubes pointed up in the air.

**Water sticks** are closely related to water scorpions, but are bigger, ½ inch (14 mm) long. Indeed, they are sometimes called long-bodied water scorpions because they share many of the same features.

**Water measurers** look more like a stick than water sticks. They are almost prehistoric in appearance, their stalk-like head one and a half times longer than their thorax, with eyes halfway along. Commonly called marsh treaders, they tread on the surface film in ponds and slow-moving streams. The term "measurer" comes from their stalking behavior in seeking prey (mosquito larvae, pupae and crustaceans).

**Whirligig beetles** are tiny beetles (less than ⅛–½ inch or 3–15 mm long) that swim rapidly in circles on the surface of the water with their flattened, oar-like legs. Their eyes are divided into two parts on each side of the head; the upper half is for viewing above the water line, watching out for predators. The lower eye is for viewing below the water line, searching for prey. The adults usually appear in large numbers and take flight in the evening in search of new ponds and lakes. Whirligig larvae are larger than adults and swim like leeches.

A *Lethocerus* nymph with fishy prey.

Water boatman.

Water stick.

Whirligig beetle.

# Swimmer's itch: liver flukes

If you emerge from a pleasant swim only to find yourself itchy all over, the culprit may be a tiny worm-like creature called a liver fluke.

A parasite of wild ducks, the adult liver fluke lays her eggs in the intestine of the infected duck. The larvae are passed by the duck with the feces into the water. The larvae find a snail and enter its liver. There the larvae transform into sporocysts, which produce the cercariae, the offending stage of the liver fluke lifecycle. These cercariae swim in search of a duck, which they enter through the feet or legs.

If you happen to swim by, the cercariae might mistake you for a duck, and try unsuccessfully to penetrate your skin, thus giving you "swimmers itch." Incidence and severity of the itch may vary from year to year and day to day, depending on conditions. Children often develop more severe cases than adults because their skin may be more sensitive, they usually swim more often, and they have a tendency to stay near the shore in the shallow water where snails live.

This annoying but usually not dangerous itching can be quelled or prevented by showering right after a swim and drying off vigorously and quickly.

Lifecycle of swimmer's itch.

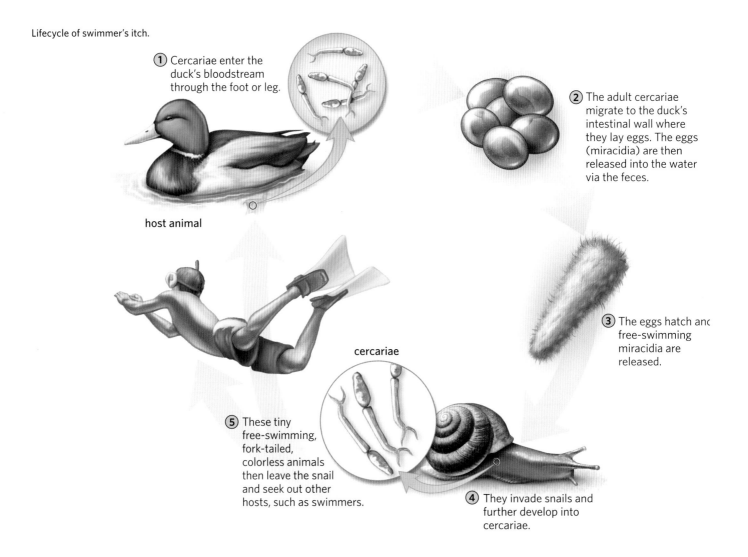

① Cercariae enter the duck's bloodstream through the foot or leg.

host animal

② The adult cercariae migrate to the duck's intestinal wall where they lay eggs. The eggs (miracidia) are then released into the water via the feces.

③ The eggs hatch and free-swimming miracidia are released.

cercariae

⑤ These tiny free-swimming, fork-tailed, colorless animals then leave the snail and seek out other hosts, such as swimmers.

④ They invade snails and further develop into cercariae.

# What's in an average glass of lake water?

"There was an old lady who swallowed a fly..." Anyone who drinks lake water is consuming pretty much what fish and ducks consume. So before you go drinking with the fish, you should know how potent a brew you may be imbibing.

Compared to the dangers of the ocean, lakes are human-friendly environments. But the average glass of lake water will probably contain some of these choice ingredients: living, dead and decomposed plankton that consist mostly of rotifers, crustaceans, protists, algae, bacteria and fungi. All of these organisms are essential parts of the lake ecosystem, but for those who want to swim in, drink, cook or wash with the water, they can be divided up into the friendly, the nasty and the hostile.

## The friendly

### Plankton

Plankton are tiny plants, called *phytoplankton,* and animals, called *zooplankton.* Both types are a key link in the food chain between the algae, the creatures that live on the bottom and fish. The numbers of zooplankton (includes protists, rotifers and crustaceans) in a glass of water varies according to trophic status of the lake (see **Getting to Know Your Lake**); in eutrophic lakes, 300 to 500 zooplankton are present; in oligotrophic lakes, anywhere from 1 to 10 zooplankton are present. The more enriched the water is with nutrients and algae, the more fungi, bacteria and plankton will be present, and the more likely it is that you will ingest something that will make you sick.

### Rotifers

Rotifers are minute animals that move by means of cilia located on a disc. The cilia beat synchronously, like spokes on a revolving wheel, lending the common name "wheel animals" to the group. Rotifers perform a vital function in the plankton: they filter algae and bacteria (good and bad) from the water column. Don't worry about rotifers. They are not dangerous to humans.

### Crustaceans

Crustaceans are related to insects and spiders. They have numerous segmented legs and two pairs of antennae and many have a protective "coat" called a carapace. The most common planktonic crustaceans are water fleas, copepods and opossum shrimps. Yes, we have shrimp in our lakes!

Crustaceans are known to control the growth of blue-green algae on lakes.

These blue-green mats with their characteristic orange surface layer indicate that this lake may be acidifying.

# The nasty

## Algae

Just when the water gets warm enough to swim in, you might wake up one morning to find that a massive smelly carpet of green has been spread over your lake. Look closer and you'll see that the floating carpet is made of microscopic algae.

Algae are helpful for at least three reasons: they are *the* major source of dissolved oxygen in water; they are an integral part of many nutrient cycles; and many species such as mayflies and carp depend on algae as a source of food.

Algae can be a nuisance when massive blooms become unsightly or downright foul-smelling. You won't feel them as you swim, but you won't be able to see your limbs below the water either. Massive die-offs of the algal blooms also cause oxygen depletion, especially during the winter under the ice, causing some sensitive aquatic species to "suffocate" under the mats of dead algae.

What causes algal blooms? Nutrient (for example, phosphorous, nitrogen) enrichment is at least one cause. But each species of algae has its own optimal requirements for light, temperature, and nutrients. Since light and temperature change with the seasons, we see a succession of species dominating throughout the year. Most blooms make the water look green, but some species give other hues, like red.

## Acidifying lakes

In some cases, water quality is such that only those algal species that can tolerate or adapt to it prevail. This is probably one reason that large algal blooms of specific species occur in acidifying lakes. If your lake is acidifying, you may see one of three types of bloom: *blue-green mats,* felt-like, dark blue-green to blackish mats, sometimes with an orange-colored surface layer, usually in water 7 to 10 feet (2–3 m) deep; *green mats,* coarser in appearance and less densely packed, varying from green to reddish purple and extending to a depth of at least 12 to 13 feet (4 m); and *green clouds,* loosely attached clouds of green algae in the littoral zone of acidic or acidifying lakes, often associated with aquatic plants, sometimes overwintering and appearing as whitish or grayish clouds in the spring.

**Getting rid of algal blooms** Getting rid of algal blooms is not easy. First you have to know the reason for the bloom. If it is nutrient enrichment, you as a cottager have some control of the nutrients you contribute to your lake:

- Cut back on, or eliminate, the use of fertilizers on lawns
- Ensure that outhouses and septic systems don't add to the nutrient buildup
- Don't treat your lake like a bathtub
- Limit the numbers of new cottages on the lake if it is beyond capacity

## Elephant snot

Basketball-sized blobs of jelly-like, whitish-gray elephant snot can be enough to clear the bravest swimmers out of the water. If your lake is acidic, the blobs may be the "green clouds" of algae discussed above. However, they could also be large colonies of bryozoans, or "moss animals." Many bryozoans appear greenish because the zooids (individuals that make up the colony) filter feed on algae and other organic material suspended in the water. The color depends on what the zooids' latest meal was, so yellowish and brownish hues are also common.

The blob of jelly is exactly that, a gelatinous material that holds the zooids in place in the colony. Some colonies can be nearly 3 feet (1 m) long and 1 foot (0.30) in diameter. Large colonies generally indicate good water quality.

One sure way to determine if the "blob" is an algal cloud or a bryozoan colony is to try and lift it out of the water. The algal cloud will collapse in your hands. The bryozoan is firm and will not collapse; if you *are* able to lift it out of the water, it will probably break into large pieces.

## Taste and odor problems

The smell of some algae will make you wonder whether the outhouse tipped over. Other algae will have you looking out for a skunk. Most of the algae that give a grassy odor are green algae (*chlorophytes*); those that give a septic smell are mostly blue-green algae, which belong to a phylum called Cyanobacteria. These days they are considered bacteria, not algae. If your lake smells like geraniums, the algae present are diatoms (*bacillariophytes*). All three types, with some yellow-green and yellow-brown algae (*chrysophytes*), contribute to a fishy smell. Most algae taste sweet; a few taste bitter.

Algal blooms often form in stagnant water, such as in this tidal pool.

## Sewage fungus

Sewage fungus is not a fungus at all, but a sheathed bacterium that attaches to logs and rocks in waters carrying domestic or organic wastes. The "sewer" odor produced is unmistakable and, along with its formations of long, white, slimy strands, is certain to discourage anyone from drinking or swimming in the water.

# The hostile

## Beaver Fever (*Giardiasis*)

Contracting beaver fever is a back country camper's worst nightmare. If *Giardia lamblia* sets up camp in your intestines, you can become dangerously, even fatally, dehydrated from the diarrhea.

*Giardia* is a microscopic animal called a protist. Protists propel themselves through the water by beating tiny hairs. Most mind their own business, but some, like *Giardia,* are parasitic.

The infective stage of the *Giardia* lifecycle is in the form of a microscopic, thick-walled cyst. When you drink contaminated water, the cyst makes its way to your intestine. The active form of *Giardia,* called a trophozoite, emerges from the cyst and begins reproducing by splitting in two about every twelve hours. This means that more than a million parasites are produced in ten days and one billion in fifteen days. The trophozoites attach to the cells of the intestinal lining and feed on fats. This is not, however, a recommended way to lose weight. Symptoms of beaver fever besides weight loss include one or more of the following over a period of one week or more: diarrhea, flatulence, bloating, abdominal cramps, and fatigue.

The parasite infects other mammals, such as beavers, as well. Beavers are often blamed for contaminating water with cysts of *Giardia*. It is highly unlikely that they are responsible for introducing the parasite into new areas, however, they can play an important role in

Lifecycle of *Giardia Lamblia.*

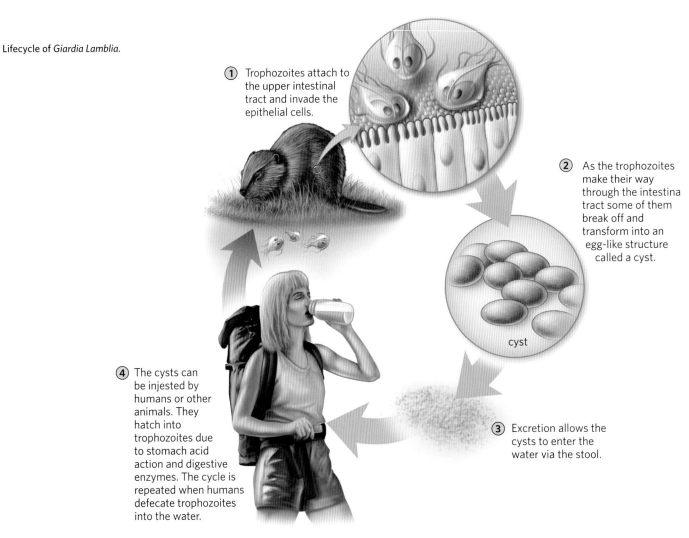

1 Trophozoites attach to the upper intestinal tract and invade the epithelial cells.

2 As the trophozoites make their way through the intestinal tract some of them break off and transform into an egg-like structure called a cyst.

cyst

3 Excretion allows the cysts to enter the water via the stool.

4 The cysts can be injested by humans or other animals. They hatch into trophozoites due to stomach acid action and digestive enzymes. The cycle is repeated when humans defecate trophozoites into the water.

amplifying the numbers, because beavers are easy to infect and can return millions of cysts to the water.

You can treat beaver fever using powerful drugs, but prevention is your best medicine. Protect yourself by boiling your drinking water. Cysts can be killed instantly by boiling the water (212° F, 100° C) but water heated to 176° F (80° C) or more for at least 5 to 10 minutes will kill all cysts. See the chapter on **Cottage Operations** for other water filter options.

## Cryptosporidiosis

*Cryptosporidium* is a common parasite found in warm and cold climates in untreated and treated drinking water supplies, swimming pools, rivers, streams, lakes and impoundments. The fact that this protist can be found almost anywhere is attributed to its broad range of host species, including mammals, birds and fish. Also, unlike most parasites, it completes its lifecycle in a single host.

*Cryptosporidiosis* is extremely infectious. A drop of water with as few as ten oocysts (the infectious stage) is enough to make you good and sick. Symptoms are profuse, watery, greenish, ill-smelling diarrhea, as well as vomiting, nausea, headache, abdominal pain, low-grade fever and potentially significant weight loss.

Because it can be found anywhere, isn't picky about who it infects, is highly infectious, and is resistant to most disinfectants, it is among the most difficult parasites to control. You can kill the oocysts with bleach, hydrogen peroxide, ammonia or formaldehyde. If you don't happen to have formaldehyde on hand, boiling the water for ten minutes is just as effective.

## Bacteria

It's a sad summer day when the beach is closed because the water is unsafe for swimming. But to ignore these warnings is decidedly unwise,
if you value your health. The less-than-friendly bacteria in contaminated water will show you no mercy.

*Escherichia Coli* is the most familiar bacteria we use to detect fecal contamination. We use it because it is present in the intestinal colon of all mammals. Everyone has "friendly" E. coli in their colon, however, it's the nasty strain of *E. coli,* the one that causes potentially fatal internal hemorrhaging, that gets all the attention. If any *E. coli* is present in water, beware: it is unsafe to drink or swim in. Its presence is also an indication that other harmful coliform bacteria might be in the water.

Here are some of the most dangerous other bacteria that can contaminate lake water:

- *Salmonella* is present mostly in spoiled foods, such as chicken, and can be contracted by handling infected turtles, or by drinking contaminated water. The bacterium causes diarrhea, fever and vomiting. One form, *S. typhi,* causes typhoid fever.

- *Shigella* belongs to a group of bacteria found in the intestines of humans. It is common in polluted water and can cause acute diarrhea in humans. Some species are fatal.

- *Leptospira* is a motile bacterium that causes a disease known as leptospirosis, an acute infection of the kidneys, liver and central nervous system. The primary hosts are rodents but humans contract the disease through cuts in the skin while wading through polluted water.

- *Vibrio cholerae* lives in the gut wall and produces toxins. The species causes cholera, an acute intestinal disease that may result in death within hours.

Take these notices very seriously.

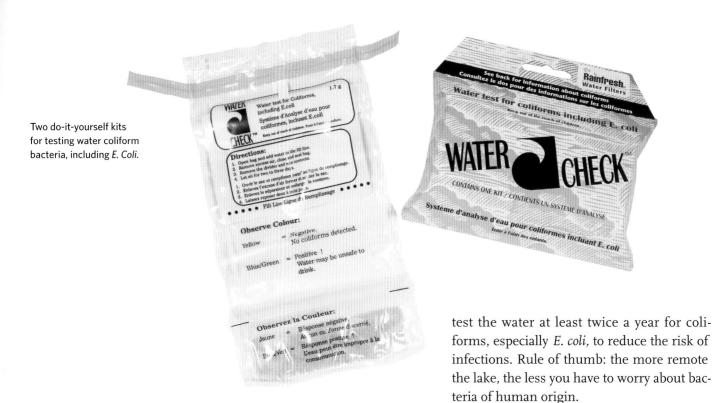

Two do-it-yourself kits for testing water coliform bacteria, including *E. Coli.*

### Other annoying bacteria

If you develop an ear infection after swimming, or an eye, throat, respiratory tract, or urinary tract infection, the culprits are most likely *Staphylococcus aureus* and *Pseudomonas aeruginosa.* These bacteria come from infected humans.

### Forewarned is forearmed

Don't panic! Your chance of being infected by these bacteria is remote in most lakes. However, the chances increase the more human activity is happening at your lake. Older cottages may still have outhouses too close to shore, where the potential exists for some coliform bacteria to "leak" into the lake. The further away from the lake the outhouse is placed and the finer the soil, the greater the probability that bacteria will be filtered by the soil before underground runoff reaches the lake.

The bad news: since cottage use and swimming and boating activities are greatest in the summer when, coincidentally, water temperatures are higher, the probability of pathogens occurring in lake water is greatest during the summer months. It is always a good idea to test the water at least twice a year for coliforms, especially *E. coli,* to reduce the risk of infections. Rule of thumb: the more remote the lake, the less you have to worry about bacteria of human origin.

## Testing your water

Many hardware stores now carry a do-it-yourself coliform testing kit as well as a do-it-yourself *E. coli* testing kit. The kit contains a chemical that you add to a sample of lake water. The chemical changes color if the offending bacteria are present. Do at least one test in midsummer, when bathing and swimming activities are intense and can provide the greatest potential for infections. Make sure to measure the total coliform count in water as well as the *E. coli* count. In general, water is considered unsafe for swimming if the total coliform count exceeds 200/100 ml.

Most municipalities have a local health unit that will make bacterial determinations for a nominal fee or even gratis. All have a specific protocol that needs to be followed if they are to analyze the samples. For example, you must submit five water samples weekly during the summer period. The health unit provides a mean number of total coliforms and fecal coliforms. If the mean exceeds standards for two consecutive weeks, beaches are closed. See **Getting to Know Your Lake** for more information on testing and filtering methods.

Aiming for a 10 out of 10.

# Swimming fun and safety

Swimming is considered the best form of exercise because it uses almost all the muscles in the body, especially the arms and upper body. Because the body is supported by the water and less stress is therefore placed on joints and bones, swimming is often recommended as an exercise for those with disabilities and in physiotherapy of many injuries.

Swimming is primarily an aerobic exercise requiring a constant oxygen supply to the muscles working over a relatively long exercise time. Prolonged exercise at lower intensity is better for fat-burning. However, for short sprints the muscles work anaerobically. Fast swimming requires a high level of effort, meaning glycogen rather than fat is burned. Although aerobic exercises burn fat and help with losing weight, the effect is in fact limited in swimming. Even though being in cold water burns more food energy to maintain body temperature, swimming does not significantly reduce weight. Take heart, though; as with most aerobic exercises, swimming is believed to reduce the harmful effects of stress. Some say that swimming may also be good for asthma sufferers.

Children should be provided with certified swimming lessons and close adult supervision while in the water.

**Wait an hour after eating before swimming?**

This adage has been almost universally accepted for generations. The fear is the possibility of developing severe muscle cramps and drowning from swimming on a full stomach. Neither the American nor the Canadian Red Cross makes any specific recommendation about waiting any amount of time after eating before taking a swim. However, it is recommended that you wait until digestion has begun, especially if you've had a big fatty meal and you plan to swim strenuously. It is unwise to chew gum or eat while in the water because both could cause choking.

## Take care!

While swimming can be beneficial in many ways, it can also be dangerous. The statistics tell the scary story. A recent North American survey revealed that non-swimmers and weak swimmers account for the majority of drownings; drowning is the second leading cause of unintentional injury death for people under 24; alcohol is associated with at least a third of all drownings; the majority of those 14 and under were alone or with another child when they drowned; for every child four and under who dies from drowning, there are an estimated 6 to 10 additional near-drownings; a small child can drown in only a few inches of water; and boys are the most frequent victims of drownings. Most drownings can be prevented — they are not "accidents."

Children love to splash and play in groups but the younger they are the more supervision they need. Young children should be kept within arms' reach, even if they are wearing a personal flotation device (PFD). Never rely on devices such as inflatable armbands, mattresses or tubes to provide floatation to weak or non-swimmers. Never use "noodles" or inflatable toys as floatation devices. Put toys away after use because children may try to get them from the water and risk falling in. On windy days, put light beach balls, inflatable toys, mattresses and "noodles" away. Don't let children chase after toys that are being blown off shore.

## Swim to survive

It is highly recommended that children be enrolled in a certified swimming program to learn different and proper techniques of swimming. All certified swimming programs have proper supervision and emergency treatments when needs arise. Supervise children at all times and communicate rules to them. Know your abilities and limitations and never go beyond them. When swimming in large lakes, be aware of currents and keep an eye on the shifting weather patterns. Swim parallel and close to shore when swimming in a lake or river. Keep emergency equipment and first aid kits close at hand. Never swim alone.

# Swimming strokes

Confident swimmers have more fun in the water. There are some basic swimming strokes that almost all good swimmers know. The easiest and simplest is the *dog paddle*; simply reach forward with the arms underwater, stroking from front to rear with left and right arms and kicking forward with your feet and legs. There are seven strokes that use four different body positions. There is one *sidestroke*; use a forward underwater stroke with the body turned on one side and propel yourself with a scissors kick. There are four strokes in the prone position: the *trudgen* is similar to the sidestroke but uses alternate overarm strokes in a prone position, with a scissors kick keeping the head on one side; the *breast stroke* alternates frog kicking with a simultaneous movement of the arms from a point in front of the head to shoulder level in the prone position; the *butterfly* is the most difficult and exhausting and uses a dolphin kick with a windmill-like movement of both arms in unison with body in prone position; the *crawl* uses alternating overarm strokes and a flutter kick with body in either supine (back crawl) or prone (front crawl) position. The back crawl is also known as the *backstroke*.

The front crawl.

## Cold water blues

North American lakes and rivers can be very cold, even during summer months. You may be one of those cottagers who takes particular pride in being first into the lake and last out each season. But cold water is dangerous even for good swimmers, because it reduces endurance, impairs judgment and causes muscle cramps.

Cold water robs heat twenty-five times faster than air at the same temperature and can induce hypothermia very quickly. The degree of hypothermia depends on water temperature, the length of time in water, the amount of body fat, the amount of body submerged, the type and amount of clothing/PFD worn and your age.

If you fall in, the Life Saving Society recommends getting as much of your body out of the water as quickly as you can. If unable to, hold your knees tightly together and to your chest; squeeze your arms against the sides of your trunk.

If there is a group (two to four people), face each other with arms interlocked to form a ring of people. Press your own legs together. Children can be placed in the center of the ring.

Try to relax; do not try to swim to "warm up" because it leads to faster heat loss.

Watch for these signs of hypothermia:

### Signs of mild hypothermia

- bouts of shivering and grogginess
- muddled thinking
- cold, red skin
- normal breathing and pulse

### Signs of moderate hypothermia

- violent, uncontrollable shivering or shivering stops
- inability to think and pay attention
- loss of judgment and reasoning
- memory loss
- slurred speech
- slow, shallow breathing
- slow, weak pulse

### Signs of severe hypothermia

- dilated pupils
- shivering has stopped
- loss of control of hands, feet, and limbs
- unconsciousness
- little or no breathing
- weak, irregular or non-existent pulse

# CHAPTER 4

# *Fishing*

A good helping of
patience and luck are
key to fishing success.

WHETHER IT IS THE PROMISE of fresh fish fillets, the thrill of the catch, or simply the quiet camaraderie that motivates a dawn trek to the water, fishing is a ritual many cottagers prize. The success of any fishing venture depends on a few key factors: the gear, the bait, some knowledge of the fish you are after and, as any seasoned angler will know, a generous helping of patience and luck.

We'll cover the essentials of fishing in this chapter, starting with the best times and places to fish. The different kinds of tackles, lines, and lures are covered, as well as various types of bait. There are several pages on flyfishing, plus recipes throughout for when you want you cook up your prize.

There is a page on unwelcome invaders and the effects a new species can have on the ecological balance of a lake. You can also learn about how to release a fish back into the water with minimal damage.

Teach your children that fishing is not a free-for-all and there will still be fish aplenty for their children when they're ready to join the fun.

Testing the shallows with a closed-faced reel on a spin casting rod.

# Where, when and how to fish

Although intuition can help, it doesn't take a psychic to figure out where the fish in your lake probably live. Inflows and outflows are favorite fish hangouts. The rivers and streams that enter the lake provide a constant supply of food, and their turbulent flows usually infuse a fresh supply of oxygen to the lake water. Where water flows out of your lake usually makes a great fishing spot because the water is compressed into a narrow channel; any food in the lake water is concentrated into a small area, making it easier to find the feeding fish.

The kind and quantity of fish that live in your lake depend on the lake's characteristics; temperature, oxygen levels and food supply are important features of a fishy home. Oligotrophic (pristine) lakes tend to be deep, cold, and have a high oxygen level and not much algal growth. Eutrophic (nutrient rich) lakes tend to be shallow with lots of algal growth and aquatic plants. In the summer, when the algae grow, die and sink to the bottom, the bacteria that eat them use up all the oxygen at the bottom of the lake. Fish such as walleye, perch, pike and bass don't mind the lower oxygen content of warm, reedy eutrophic lakes, but others, such as lake trout and whitefish, need the high oxygen content and cold water of oligotrophic lakes. See **Getting to Know Your Lake** for more information on lake types to figure out what type you've got.

Since fish tend to feed at dusk and dawn, these can be good times of the day to try to catch them.

## The best time to fish

Fish take bait when they are hungry. Sounds simple? Tell that to a fisherman who has spent the entire day without a bite. In general, fish tend to feed at dusk and dawn. To figure out the eating habits of particular fish is futile—not that that has stopped generations of fisher folk from attempting it. Charts that show the best fishing times under ideal conditions are available from many sport-fishing organizations, government agencies and fishing magazines. But traditional lore looks to moon cycles, wind, weather and water temperatures to divine the best conditions for a big catch.

## Cheating with fish finders

Fish finders operate on a Sound Navigation Ranging system (SONAR) that measures the time it takes for a burst of energy to travel to the bottom and return to surface. An electronic power pack (such as two six-volt batteries) generates very short bursts of electrical energy that are sent to a transducer attached to the bottom of the boat, which converts it into very short bursts of high-frequency sound energy. The transducer also acts as a microphone: after sending out a single burst of high-frequency sound, it picks up the sounds of the returning echoes created when a pulse of sound rebounds off the bottom of the lake and possibly other objects (fish, logs, stumps) that lie between the transducer and the bottom. The returning echoes of sound are received by the transducer, which converts sound energy back into electrical energy that you see on the monitor. The deeper the object, the weaker the return signal. The brightness of the display on the monitor indicates the range, or distance, from the transducer to the bottom, or to objects—even fish.

## Moon phases

The day before, day of, and the day after the moon phase changes usually give the best yields. Look on your calendar to see when the moon is full, new, at first and last quarter phases. The fish are said to be particularly hungry at these times. The full moon is apparently best. The quarter moons at sunrise and sunset are good too. Why? We know that the gravitational effect of the moon affects the tides as well as other aspects of life on Earth. Generations of fisher folk have noted the apparent connection between fish appetites and the moon. They have even tracked the moons of different seasons and named them. April's full moon is known as Fish Moon and August's full moon is known as the Sturgeon Moon, or Red Moon, because of the heat and haze of the month.

## Wind and weather

Old-timers rely on cloud patterns, avoiding hot, clear days when fish such as lake trout are apt to stay lower in the water column where it is cooler. They consider it futile to fish on the day of a change in weather or after heavy rains. Winds are good for stirring up the water, blowing food offshore and into the water. The food is followed by little fish, which in turn are followed by big fish, which in turn are followed by anglers. The wind makes ripples so the fish can't see you as well. Beware of high winds; no catch is worth drowning for.

## Fishing methods

There are three basic methods for fishing in lakes: jigging, casting and trolling. In streams, casting and flyfishing are most popular. Patient people tend to choose jigging. People who can't sit still gravitate toward casting or trolling.

**Jigging** is the most relaxing method; you sit on a dock or in an anchored boat with your rod over the side and jerk the line every 30 seconds or so. Live bait, such as minnows, worms or leeches, are best for jigging. You might need a weight or sinker to get the bait to the bottom. Let the bait sit about a foot (30 cm) off the bottom. If you are using a weight on the line, set it about a foot (30 cm) from the hook; the weight will sit on the bottom so the bait can float or swim up from it.

**Casting** means tossing the line out into the water and then reeling the bait in. When you are casting live bait, try to get the bait to the fish in near-perfect condition. Cast the line underhand or sidearm to prevent smacking the bait hard on the water surface. This will help to keep the scales intact and the bait stronger. Let the bait sink and do its job. Then reel it in slowly, about one revolution of the handle every two seconds.

**Spinning** is similar to casting but less accurate. Use a spinning reel for 4- to 10-pound test lines. Spinning reels tend to cause twisting, or "bird nesting," of the line.

**Trolling** is dangling the line behind a slowly moving boat. When trolling with live bait, hook the bait through both lips so you won't lose it. Make sure you put a swivel on the line or it will get twisted and you'll spend most of your time taking out twists and knots.

For more on each of these methods, read on. Would-be flyfishers, see **Flyfishing Basics** at page 127. Once you have an idea of where and how you want to fish, you'll need to get yourself some equipment.

### Astrology and fish appetites

The full moons in Pisces (February 19–March 29) and Cancer (June 21–July 22) are considered good for both fishing and hunting.

### Wind direction as guide?

Fishing is best
When wind is
from the west.

Fishing is least
When wind is
from the east.

The bait is in the mouth
When wind is
from the south.

The skilful fisher goes
not forth
When the wind is
from the north.

# The basic tackle

A tackle consists of a rod, reel, line, lures and accessories. Some tackle boxes contain a huge variety of lures, tools for removing hooks, three or four spools of nylon lines each of a different weight, and reels for different kinds of fishing, the total of which would make a good down payment on a car; others are more rudimentary and less designed to impress. How much you want to spend on building up your tackle box is up to you.

Every tackle box should contain at least these items:

- one spool of five-pound test monofilament line
- a variety of weights or sinkers: choose according to your fishing habitats
- hooks
- leaders
- swivels
- bobbers: smaller, camouflaged bobbers are better than larger, colorful bobbers
- lures: choose according to your fishing habitats
- long-nose pliers for removing hooks swallowed deeply in the throat by a fish ("gut hook")

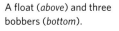

A float (*above*) and three bobbers (*bottom*).

A well-prepared fisher will have a well-stocked tackle box, a rod and reel and a net.

## Bobbers or Floats

Floats can be used for either jigging or casting. They are used to keep the line off the bottom by securing the line to the bobber when the hook is about 12 inches (30 cm) above bottom. They bob when the fish bites. Free-lining is using a bobber while jigging, casting, spinning or trolling to control the depth at which the bait stays. Free-lining works well in running water, as well as in deep water or on bright-sky days when fish stay low in the water column.

Single hooks (*left*) and a treble hook (*right*).

# Hooks

Two basic types are available, single and treble hooks. Single hooks come in different sizes and strengths and can have a short shank or a long shank. Single hooks are used with bait but treble hooks are generally used on lures. Every hook has an eye for the line and usually a sharp barb on the hooked end. Some hooks also have barbs along the shank to really snag the fish. Remember, they are twice as difficult to remove. Be careful not to puncture yourself with the barb. Some hooks lack barbs and are used by "catch-and-release" anglers.

# Leaders

A leader is a short nylon or stainless steel line with a swivel and snap at one end and a swivel and eye at the other end. Leaders provide strength to the line and help prevent it from twisting.

# Getting hooked: removing fish hooks from your body

The first thing a novice angler might hook is his or her own self. Here's what to do if more than your ego is injured. Fishhook injuries vary depending on the part of the body you've hooked, the depth at which the hook penetrates the skin, and the style of the fishhook. Never try to remove a fishhook that has penetrated an eye; see your doctor immediately. Fishhook puncture wounds cause pain, swelling, redness, potential loss of motion and, if not treated, infection. Most fishhook injuries involve only the skin tissue below. If possible, have a physician remove the hook. If you are in an isolated area, you can try one of two techniques:

**First technique:** You will need rubber gloves, antiseptic solution, tweezers, wire cutters, and adhesive bandage. If you don't have rubber gloves, wash your hands with hot water (as hot as you can tolerate) and soap.
- Clean the patient's skin with antiseptic solution.
- Grasp the shank of the hook with tweezers held by the thumb and forefinger.
- Rotate the hook to force the barb out through the skin.
- Cut the barbed end of the hook with a wire cutter. Back the rest of the hook out of the skin.
- Apply a sterile adhesive bandage.

**Second technique:** You will need rubber gloves, suturing line or fine, clean, nylon fishing line, antiseptic solution.
- Clean the patient's skin with antiseptic solution.
- Loop a fine-gauge nylon or silk suturing line around the belly of the hook at the point where it penetrates the skin.
- Grasp the shank of the hook with your thumb and middle finger and press against the skin. At the same time, apply gentle pressure to the belly of the hook with the index finger of the free hand to disengage the barb from surrounding tissue. The idea is to free any tissue behind the barb, then yank it out with a firm, quick tug. This should be done only with hooks that are shallowly set.
- Use your strongest hand to grasp the suture 10 to 12 inches (25–30 cm) from the hook and pull sharply. Caution: the hook may fly out; onlookers should get out of the way, unless they in turn want to be impaled. Dress the wound with a sterile adhesive bandage.

In most cases, fishhook injuries heal within three to four days. Inspect the wound carefully, liberally apply disinfectant, and notify your doctor if you experience any redness, swelling, puss or fever. Apply ice and/or heat to the injury to help relieve throbbing or pain.

# Lines

Fishing lines come in different strengths or "pound tests," such as eight-pound test, ten-pound test, twelve-pound test lines. The stronger the line, the thicker and more visible it is. The average size of most fish is less than three pounds, so a five-pound test line is appropriate most of the time.

You can catch fish heavier than the test of the line by adjusting the tension on the reel and "playing" the fish until it is tired and then reeling it back in.

There are three types of lines: nylon, fluorocarbon, and polyethylene.

◆ Nylon monofilament lines are the most popular since they are highly elastic and low in sensitivity (you don't feel the bait swimming around and mistake it for a bite), making them ideal for lighter baits on spinning rods. Monofilament fishing line is also a tough, abrasion-resistant line that works well on casting reels, and is excellent for casting into reedy areas. The line holds knots well and does not slip. It has limited stretch due to its thick diameter but is not as invisible as thinner lines.

◆ Fluorocarbon lines are tougher than nylon, but lack flexibility, making them better suited for jigs (see below) and live baits.

◆ Polyethylene (PE) lines are low in elasticity and high in sensitivity, making them better suited for floating lures.

Never, ever toss tangled line into the water. Birds such as loons get tangled up in it, are unable to fly, dive or eat, and die terrible deaths. Loons also die of lead poisoning after eating fish that have swallowed lead sinkers. The lead is partially dissolved in the loon's digestive tract and then absorbed into the blood and body tissues, causing nerve, kidney and other tissue damage.

Lures: (*top to bottom*) a spinner, a spoon, a floater, a bucktail and a jig.

# Lures

As the name suggests, lures attract the fish to the hook. They come in a variety of types:

- **Spinners** generally have a row of beads between the hook and spinner. There may be more than one blade (spinner). Good for yellow perch, walleye, bass.
- **Spoons** are shaped like a spoon, some elongated, others more oval. Good for lake trout, pike and walleye.
- **Floaters** are made of low-density material such as foam. They are used for floating live bait over weedy and rocky bottom areas. Good for walleye, bass, trout and panfish.
- **Bucktails** incorporate feathers and spinners. Good for northern pike and monster muskies.
- **Jigs and plugs** are designed to look like bait (worms, insects, leeches, minnows, frogs, crayfish) and have different actions to simulate movements of the bait. They have either a single hook or one or more treble hooks. Live bait is usually used on the single-hook jigs. Treble-hook plugs are used for trolling and casting and rarely are used with bait. Good for bass, walleye and pike.

# Reels

There are four basic types of reels: spinning, casting, trolling and flyfishing. Anglers who prefer to cast rather than jig or still-fish use either a spinning reel or casting reel. Fishing nuts will have both. You can achieve more accuracy with a casting reel, because your thumb is in control. Modern trolling reels are designed to give digital readouts of the length of line in the water. Trolling reels have stronger gears than spinning and casting reels because larger fish usually have to be reeled in. Flyfishing reels are designed for fast retrieval of lighter lines.

# Rods

There is a rod for each type of reel. Spinning and casting rods are designed for length and accuracy of the cast. In general, the longer the rod, the more accurate the cast and the farther you can toss the bait. Spinning rods are designed for lighter lures and they have larger guides (through which you thread the line) than casting rods, which are better suited for heavier lures.

Spinning reel and rod. The reel has a removeable spool and a mechanical pickup or bail. Most have a rear drag for small and moderate sized fish and a front drag for big fish.

# Sinkers

Sinkers are used as weights for sinking baits and lures. Most are still made with lead even though it causes lead poisoning in aquatic organisms, especially waterfowl. Some provinces and states have banned lead weights. Tin is replacing lead and is increasingly common in tackle boxes. Sinkers come in different weights and types. A good rule of thumb is to use the minimum amount of extra weight you require.

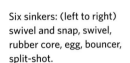
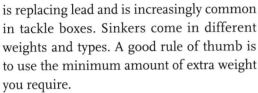

Six sinkers: (left to right) swivel and snap, swivel, rubber core, egg, bouncer, split-shot.

- **Worm or bullet sinker** has a stream-lined, tapered shape and a concave base, designed to sneak through weeds and brush, minimizing tangles and hang-ups. Works well with live bait when going after bass and walleye in the weeds.
- **Swivel and snap** takes the place of leaders that have a swivel incorporated into them. They help prevent the line from twisting, especially when reeling in the line.
- **Swivel sinker** is also egg-shaped but has a wire loop in one end. The line is placed inside the wire loop but not tied, so it slides easily along the line. It is used for trolling or bottom-fishing with live bait.
- **Rubber core sinker** is popular because there is no tying or line damage. Place the line in the slot and twist the rubber ears in opposite directions to lock the line in place.
- **Egg sinker** is shaped like an egg and has a large, smooth hole in the center to allow for uninterrupted movement on the line so the fish is unable to detect the weight of the sinker. The sinker can slip through weeds and rocks.
- **Bouncer** is designed to slide on the line, and "walk" live bait rigs slowly along the bottom. Some are made of wire with a feeler that glides over jagged rocks, logs, stumps, moss and weed cover without snagging. It is used with spinners, live bait rigs and floating plugs.
- **Split-shot** has a split down the middle with "ears" on the hinged end for opening them. Split-shot should be added at least 8 inches (20 cm) away from the lure. Heavier sinkers should be at least 20 inches (50 cm) up the line.

## Foreign invaders: the spiny water flea

Native to northern Europe, the spiny water flea entered the Great Lakes in the 1980s via the ballast water of a European ship. It is now common in many inland lakes in surrounding states and provinces. Spiny water fleas can be a terrible nuisance when they foul fishing lines and gear. They also cause rapid and substantial long-term declines in native zooplankton species, reducing the availability of food for young fish to eat.

Spiny water fleas can be spread by water currents, but humans are responsible for lake dispersal. The fleas don't live long out of the water, but even if you keep a boat out of the water for five days, drying out and killing any hitchhikers, their resting eggs could survive. On the next immersion in another lake, these dormant fleas wake up. It is impossible to eliminate spiny water fleas from a lake once they have been introduced. The best you can do is try to prevent their spread:

- Never dump bait from another lake in the water.
- Remove suspicious material from your boat. Clean fishing equipment, especially lines and downriggers where the line meets the swivel, lure, and downrigger ball.
- Drain water from live well, bilge, motor, et cetera.
- Inspect and remove aquatic plants, animals, and mud from boat and equipment.
- Wash boat and equipment with high-pressure water, 10-percent bleach, boiling water (212° F / 100° C), or dry boat and equipment thoroughly for at least five days before launching into another waterbody.

# Live bait for lake fishing

Anglers tend to prefer bloodsuckers, worms, minnows and crayfish for lake fishing. If nothing is working and you are getting desperate, try insects as bait (see **Flyfishing Basics** at page 127) or try the shell game — clams, mussels or snails.

There's much for fishers to like about the misunderstood bloodsucker, especially for luring smallmouth bass, yellow perch, bluegill and northern pike to bite.

## Bloodsuckers

Bloodsuckers are among the least understood and most underused baits. They are gaining in popularity but many people are wary of touching their slimy, squirming bodies. The terms leech and bloodsucker are usually used interchangeably but here they are distinct entities; bloodsuckers suck mammalian blood and can be used as fish bait; leeches suck body fluids from other aquatic animals but are too small to be used as bait. The bigger the bloodsucker, the better.

The most common bloodsucker used as bait is the ribbon leech (yes, its common name is leech, but it is a bloodsucker). Ribbon leeches are used for catching smallmouth bass, yellow perch, bluegill, crappie, northern pike and panfish. The pun "walleyes are suckers for ribbon leeches" may be true; rarely do you catch 8-pounders with minnows, but a good active ribbon leech will often land 8-, 9- or 10-pounders.

Ribbon leeches are easy to keep alive; they are not as sensitive to temperature changes as minnows, and they require relatively little oxygen. Ribbon leeches feel firm to the touch, while other bloodsuckers are soft and make poorer fish bait. Buy bloodsuckers by the pound; one pound will usually contain 10 to 12 dozen average-sized bloodsuckers. If you are lucky, you might get some that will stretch 4 to 6 inches (10–15 cm).

Bloodsuckers have jaws that make a Y-shaped incision in your skin. Learn more about bloodsuckers in the **Swimming** chapter.

### Leech hunting

You can make a leech trap by cutting both ends off a coffee can, flattening it and wedging or wiring a piece of meat (fish skeletons also work) into the middle of the can. Place it in shallow water overnight in a pond or swamp that has no game fish. The next morning check the trap and pick any leeches off the bait. If you catch your own bait, make sure you don't exceed your local leech possession limit. Yes, there can be a limit, as in Ontario, where resident anglers may have no more than 120 leeches in their possession at any time.

# Worms

Earthworms and night crawlers are a delicacy to many fish species, especially panfish and trout such as steelhead. Smallmouth bass, largemouth bass, pike, yellow perch and walleye will take the wrigglers too.

There are three species you can use as bait. Red wrigglers are the garden variety of earthworm and are used for vermicomposting. Night crawlers are larger than red wrigglers and can be as long as 10 inches (25 cm) and about half an inch (1 cm) in diameter—a mouthful for any fish! The European night crawler, recently introduced to the United States, is becoming a popular bait-shop worm. They are fat and approximately 4 inches (10 cm) long, widely used as bait for bass and other larger fish. Most anglers purchase the worms but rearing your own is becoming very popular. Like night crawlers, they can be kept at room temperature or refrigerated, and will hold in cups for several weeks.

The worm's body is divided into 100 or more body segments. Each segment has four pairs of bristles called "setae." When a bird or human tries to pull an earthworm out of the ground, the worm uses these bristles to cling to the wall of its burrow. Sometimes the worm holds on so tightly that it will tear apart. The puller keeps the front end but the hind end wriggles back into its burrow and regenerates the missing segments, as long as at least half of them remain. The earthworm has no head, but there is a concentration of sensory cells at the mouth end. Instead of eyes, worms have light-sensitive cells that can sense light. Worms have no ears, but feel the vibrations of animals moving nearby. They breathe through their moist skins.

Thread the hook through the worm in three places, all about one-third apart, the last (or first as the young lad at right is doing) through the "clitellum" or body thickening.

Earthworms were brought to North America by European settlers in the 17th and 18th centuries.

## Baiting the hook with a worm

When fishing with whole worms, hook them in thirds so that the ends hang free and the worm doesn't ball up on the hook. Worm pieces should be threaded onto the hook, starting at the broken end. Use as small a hook as is practical, from size eight for large nightcrawlers down to size twelve for smaller garden worms and worm pieces. Worms have near-neutral buoyancy and the line may need to be weighted; small and easily removed BB split-shot, with ears, are a good all-around choice (see **Sinkers**). Expert worm anglers constantly adjust the amount of weight on their line to match the depth and current of the water being fished. Use two- or four-pound monofilament line to help achieve a natural drift by offering less resistance to moving water. Large, whole 4-to-6-inch (10–15 cm) nightcrawlers are effective in spring on large rivers for trout. They are also effective after a heavy rainfall and higher water levels. A half of a crawler or 2-to-4-inch (5–10 cm) garden worm or a piece of it is a better choice for trout in smaller streams, or as water levels drop.

# Gathering and farming worms

Earthworms are barometers of soil health. They till the soil, keeping it porous, while their castings add nutrients to provide an ideal medium for plant growth and health. The materials needed to raise your own worms are simple and inexpensive.

## Good worm hunting

Some anglers still devote many evenings to catching night crawlers. You will need a flashlight and a container (16 ounces, or 500 mL) with a perforated lid. Fill the container with damp (around 60 percent moisture), organic soil or dirt that has an equal amount of peat moss mixed in. An evening with heavy dew on the grass is best for nabbing the worms. Wait until dark. Search closely with a flashlight, with your head about 2 feet (60 cm) above the grass, knees bent, ready to pounce on the worm. Move stealthily because they can feel the earth move as you approach them. When you spot one that is about 2 inches (5 cm) out of its burrow, quickly place your thumb on the worm at the hole opening so it cannot back into its burrow. With your thumb and forefinger, grasp the exposed portion firmly and slowly pull the worm out of its burrow. If it refuses to come out, stop pulling for a few seconds and hold it at its position; try pulling again a few seconds later and continue until you win the tug-of-war.

## Raise your own worms

Some bait shops and nurseries sell starter kits but you can make your own quite easily. You will have to purchase some worms to get started, but wait until you have constructed the hatchery. The materials needed are simple and inexpensive: a worm bin, bedding, water, worms and food. The worm bin can be a clean, plastic container or bucket. Select an opaque one because worms prefer darkness. The rule of thumb for selecting a bin size is approximately one square foot (0.1 m²) of surface area for 2,000 red wrigglers or 1,000 European night crawlers. This will allow sufficient oxygen to diffuse from the surface into the worm mixture. Drill small holes (approximately 1/16" or 1.6 mm) around the sides, just below the top edge for aeration. Use peat moss for bedding. Shredded newspaper, fallen leaves or old hay or grass clippings will also work. Thoroughly soak the moss by placing it in a large container and adding water while mixing it. Let it soak overnight. Take handfuls of soaked moss and wring the water out to reach the ideal moisture content. Crumble the bedding into the bin to a depth of 6 inches (15 cm). Keep the bin away from direct sunlight (in a basement, closet, under a sink). Place the worms on the bedding; they will burrow to evade the light. Feed the worms ground chicken mash, or rabbit, horse, or cow manure, but never pet waste, greasy foods, fish, or meat. Lightly sprinkle the food on the top of the bedding (too little food is better than too much — overfeeding kills the worms). Do not add additional food until the amount added is gone. Add water periodically to keep the bedding and food around 60 percent moisture.

Harvest worms before you feed them and never when food is present. Never mix food into the bedding because putrefaction of the food may cause a buildup of acids. If the worms die, immediately remove them from the bedding and start with new worms. Worms absorb oxygen through their bodies, so oxygen needs to be introduced by lightly toss the bedding every week or so, allowing the bedding at the bottom of the bin to reach the top. Earthworms and nightcrawlers are easy to keep and can provide an endless supply of highly nutritional food (worms are 70 percent protein) for toads, turtles and pond and aquarium fish.

## Worms in your kitchen

Vermicomposting is composting with earthworms; feed your food scraps to the worms in your kitchen. The red wigglers can consume organic material equivalent to their own body weight every day. Daily, they defecate or cast off a complete, natural fertilizer equal to 75 percent of their own weight. The earthworm castings provide your houseplants with fertilizer rich in nitrogen. The cast-vermiculite mixture can also be spread on flower and vegetable gardens and around trees and shrubs.

Use this method to grow your own bait or to provide live food for birds and small pond fish. And don't worry about the worms in your kitchen; besides a faint, earthy odor, you won't know they are there.

# Crayfish

Crayfish, crawfish and crawdads are different names for the same freshwater cousin of the lobster. This succulent creature can be found in most clean, flowing waters, ponds and shallows of lakes. Some live on land, but close to water. Crayfish are fussy about water quality and prefer clean, well-oxygenated waters that have a pH of at least 7.0. They are reclusive and hide under boulders and logs, or in burrows. They eat decomposing plant material but will also eat slow-movers such as snails, tadpoles, some fish and insects. If you are crawdad-hunting in the summer, look for the chimneys of soil or small rocks up to 5 inches (10 cm) high at the opening of the burrows females make. The burrows, as deep as 24 to 36 inches (0.6–1 m), provide protection from predators, and the water flowing through the tunnels aids in egg development.

Watch out for the first of the five pairs of legs, the one with the large claws or pincers. To avoid getting pinched, grab crawfish halfway along their hard shell. To use crayfish as bait, hook them through the abdomen and cast gently into a weed bed where many crayfish live and are prey for trout, catfish, bullheads, smallmouth bass, largemouth bass, pike, yellow perch and walleye. Herons, otters, mink and raccoons are also eager diners of crayfish.

Hook a crayfish through the abdomen, which has few vital organs. The thorax (swollen part) has the heart, liver and vital organs.

Crawfish have a hard skin called an exoskeleton that can have red, blue, green and yellow pigments in it. When cooked (see **Crayfish étoufée**, below), they turn red because all the other pigments are destroyed by heat.

# Spawn

The number one bait for rainbow trout is the spawn (eggs) from trout or salmon. It can be fished as a chunk or tied into "spawn sacs" with a thin netting material. Most anglers use the spawn from fish they catch, but it is available from bait shops bottled, frozen or fresh. Large salmon eggs can be fished singly on small hooks. Use real spawn in slow water; artificial spawn and flies are best in fast water.

## Crayfish étoufée

Crayfish are a popular delicacy for Europeans and Americans but many Canadians snub them. Europeans import millions of pounds of North American crayfish every year. Here is a good crayfish étoufée that serves four to five people:

6 tbsp butter
2 cups chopped onions
2 cloves minced garlic
½ cup chopped celery
2 tbsp finely chopped green onions
⅛ cup of water

1 pound / 2½ cups of crayfish tails or
   2 pounds / 5 cups of whole crayfish
1 ½ tsp of salt
½ tsp black pepper
⅛ tsp red pepper

Melt the butter in a skillet. Sauté onions, garlic and celery until onions are clear. Add water, cover and simmer until veggies are tender. Add crayfish tails or whole crayfish, salt, black pepper and red pepper and cook 15 minutes. Add green onions and 2 tbsp of minced garlic and cook 5 more minutes. Serve over hot steamed rice.

# Minnows and bait fish

Use minnows and bait fish to catch walleye, perch, and pike. The term minnow refers only to fish of the carp family, which includes Eurasian carp, dace, shiners, chubs and true minnows. Use the term bait fish for any small fish, including carp and young-of-the-year of fish in other families. Read all about carp near the end of this chapter.

Bait fish can be purchased at most bait shops or can be trapped. Check with local authorities on the regulations for capturing your own.

## How to hook a minnow

There are four basic methods for hooking bait fish. Slip the hook

- through the bottom lip, the nostrils or both lips;
- through the anal fin close to the backbone but not through the spine;
- through the middle of both sides; or
- through the back, down to the belly, then up through the back, avoiding the spine.

Bait fish live longer if hooked through the lips or anal fin. Hooking through the lips makes the bait swim up and away. Anal fin hooking will make the bait swim down and away. Hooking in the sides will make the bait swim up and away from the line but the bait tends to tire much more quickly and die sooner.

All four methods are good for jigging.

The third and fourth methods are recommended for casting because the bait fish usually breaks free after casting with the bait fish hooked through the lips or anal fin. However, even with these two methods, the bait fish will eventually tear free of the hook so plugs and lures are usually better for casting. Or consider using another kind of bait such as crayfish, which have a hard shell and don't tear free as easily as minnows.

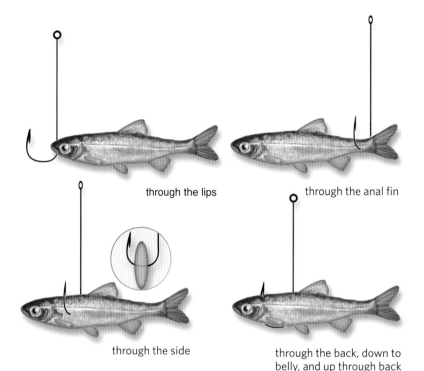

through the lips

through the anal fin

through the side

through the back, down to belly, and up through back

Four ways to hook a minnow

# Insects

Stream and river fish such as trout, bass and walleye like insects that land on the surface, as well as those that live on the bottom. Carp, suckers and other bottom feeders will go for the nymphs or larval insect forms from the bottom. Use fresh, active nymphs or larvae from your lake or stream. Keep them in a plastic dish with a perforated lid. Hook the insect through the middle segment, from either the top or the bottom.

Hook an insect through the middle section, from the top to the bottom.

# Clams, mussels and snails

When nothing else is working, try a snail or a clam. Remove the shell of snails with a nut cracker. Clams have a strong muscle at each end that attaches to each valve. Slip a sharp knife between the valves and slice the two muscles. For snails and small clams, thread the soft parts of the body onto the hook. For large clams and mussels, cut pieces off the large, hatchet-shaped foot and thread them on to the hook.

# How to fish

**The Econo-anchor**

You can make your own anchor by sinking an eye bolt in a large margarine tub filled with cement. Any weighty slab of steel is also ideal but you need to drill a hole into it for the rope.

The fisher who is casting will likely end up bringing in the fish for the one who is jigging.

## Preparing the rod

Try to prepare your rod before you head out to avoid having to spending half the day untangling your line or returning for something you forgot:

1. Tie a loop in the end of the line or use a fisherman's knot or fisherman's eye. The loop is easier to undo. Put a loop about 1 inch (2.5 cm) long in the end of the line. Hold the two lines at the base of the loop between thumb and forefinger. Wrap the loop around the forefinger, slide the forefinger out and push the loop into the hole created by the forefinger. Hold the knot and pull the loop until the knot is tight. Now make a lark's head knot on the eye of the leader by sliding the loop through the eye and then slide the entire leader through the loop. Pull on the loop and the leader until the lark's head knot is tight on the ring of the eye. A fishermen's eye (also called middleman's knot) can also be used. Tie a loose knot near the end of the line. Slide the line through the eye of the leader and then through the knot. Tie another knot and pull and slide the two knots together. The knot is also useful for carrying loads.

2. If the leader does not have an eye, use a fisherman's knot. The fisherman's knot is used for joining two fine lines such as nylon fishing leaders. It is two overhand knots, one holding the fishing line and the other the leader line. Pull each of the knots tight, separately. Then pull each line to bring the knots together, making the whole knot tight.

For photographs of knots, see the **Boating** chapter.

## Anchoring the boat

If you think you know where the fish are, set the boat up properly the first time or you may spook the fish each time you reset. Have adequate rope and heavy enough anchors to hold fast. Some people anchor the boat in front and rear to prevent shifting, but some motion is good, especially for jigging, because it moves the bait up and down and sideways. Anchors weighing 10 pounds (4.5 kg) will keep boats from shifting in most winds.

Anchors are available in three styles: dinghy, mushroom and hook. Dinghy and mushroom anchors are available in several weight classes, usually 5, 10 and 15 pounds (2.3, 4.5, 6.8 kg) and are recommended for all kinds of bottoms. Hook anchors are also available in different sizes but are lighter and rely more on wedging or hooking among rocks or logs and are not very reliable on mud or sandy bottoms. Use a fisherman's bend to attach a rope to the anchor. Make sure you secure the free end or the knot may slip.

## More on jigging

Jigging, also known as "still fishing", is the laziest of all fishing methods. The hook is baited and then line is let out until the bait is about a foot (30 cm) off the bottom. Then you wait, periodically moving the bait up and down (jigging) to attract fish. When you feel a nibble, set the bait quickly by firmly jerking the line upward. If the hook is firmly set, reel the fish in. When the fish is near the surface, use a net to bring it into the boat.

Open-faced fixed spinning reel and rod.

## More on casting and spinning

The kind of cast will depend on the type of reel you have. Spinning reels are of two common types, a closed-face and an open-face reel. The closed-face spinning reel has the mechanisms hidden and the line is released by holding a lever down and retrieved when the handle is rotated for reeling in the line. In the

Closed-faced spinning reel.

open-face reel there is a wire loop that must be flipped "open" for the line to be released when casting; when the loop is open, the line is held with the forefinger and released when a cast is made. The wire loop is flipped "closed" when the line is reeled in. The wire loop rewinds the line evenly on the spool. The spool is removable and usually two or three spools each with a different pound test line are kept in the tackle box for quick and easy replacement.

The casting reel has a gear system that moves a line guide along the spool to evenly rewind the line but the distance the line goes is controlled by your thumb. Fishermen who prefer to cast rather than jig or still-fish use either a spinning reel or casting reel. Some enthusiasts will have both. You can achieve more accuracy with a casting outfit, because your thumb is in control.

For any of the reels, you can use either an overhead cast or sidearm cast. For overhead, bring the rod back over your shoulder to the two-o'clock position, holding the line with your forefinger for open-face reels and your thumb for casting reels; the thumb is used to press a lever to release the line in closed-face reels. When at two-o'clock, flip with your wrist and forearm the tip of the rod forward to about the ten-o'clock position, releasing the line at about eleven-o'clock. For sidearm casts, use the same clock positions and technique but on a near-horizontal plane, starting with the rod low and swinging it upward.

Casting reel showing a geared line guide.

The spinning rod has a light tip for casting small lures, but thickens rapidly into the butt. The guides on the rod are large, especially nearest the reel. Casting rods are slightly heavier in the tip, have a slower taper and smaller guides and less whip than spinning rods.

## More on trolling

There is no need to cast when trolling but it is important to know how much line is let out. Trolling reels are designed now to give digital (usually) readouts of the length of line in the water. They have stronger gears than spinning and casting reels because larger fish usually have to be reeled in. Downriggers are used to keep the lure deep, where lake trout hang out. Read the instructions before purchasing because some models are easier to use and set up than others.

Trolling reel.

A fisher trolling from her canoe.

## Setting the hook

When a fish bites, set the hook by yanking the rod and line upward quickly and firmly to surprise the fish. But remember, nylon stretches, so retrieve all the slack smoothly by reeling the line in until you have made contact with the fish. Maintaining pressure with a bent rod while playing the fish will keep the hook firmly in place. If you are using a bobber, try to keep the time the bobber goes down to the time to hook is set at less than 30 seconds, so the fish doesn't swallow the hook (gut hook).

## Panfried fillets

How you prefer your steaks is a personal thing. It seems a sacrilege to marinate, broil, braise or sauté walleye, trout or bass fillets. The best way to eat these fish is pan fried. Here's a recipe:

1⅓ cups all-purpose flour
1½ tsp salt
½ tsp freshly ground black pepper
2 large eggs

6 large or 10–12 medium to small
   skinless fish fillets
Oil, for frying
Lemon wedges, for garnish

In a shallow bowl, mix together the flour, salt, and pepper. In another shallow bowl, beat the eggs until they are bubbly. Preheat the oil (use about a ½-inch deep layer) in a fry pan until a pinch of flour sizzles (usually about 375° F or 190° C). Dip the fish fillets first into the flour mixture, coating them lightly on all sides. Then dip the fillets into the eggs, shaking off any excess and place in the fry pan. Some people dip the fillets from the egg batter into 1 cup of cornmeal before placing them in the fry pan. Be careful: any excess water will splatter when the fillet hits the hot oil. Add as many fish fillets as will comfortably fit in the pan. Cook the fish for two to three minutes per side (less for small fillets), or until it is golden. Perfectly cooked bass and walleye are moist and nearly opaque; lake trout and salmon will be a dull pink. Some people eat these fish with quite rare meat in the center, only if very fresh. Fish that easily flakes and is slightly dry is overcooked. Transfer the fillets to a baking tray in the oven and continue frying the rest of the fillets as above. Serve the fish immediately and garnish with lemon wedges.

Releasing a rainbow trout.

# How to release a fish

There are anglers who prefer not to kill fish, and follow catch-and-release rules instead. They use barbless hooks and "play" the fish less than fishermen who catch fish to eat. However, there are times when anglers catch a fish for eating but must release it because the species caught is out of season, is beyond the legal catch size, or is a species that he or she does not like to eat.

## Tips for successful releases

- Keep the fish in the water as much as is possible.
- Make sure your hands are wet before touching the fish.
- Handle the fish gently so as not to remove the slimy protective coating. Do not squeeze or touch the gills.
- For pan-fish and bass, grasp the fish by the lower lip.

- If the fish is not deeply hooked, use long-nosed pliers to remove the hook quickly and to reduce the risk of tearing or injuring the fish.
- Never put a fish that you may release on a stringer; use a functional live-well or release the fish immediately.
- Revive any stressed fish before letting go. Hold the fish upright in a swimming position in the water, moving the fish slowly forward and backward so water runs through the gills. Let the fish swim away of its own accord.
- If a fish is hooked deeply, cut the line and leave the hook in when the fish is released. The hook eventually either dissolves, or the tissue around it will toughen.
- If you want to photograph a fish, be ready ahead of time! Take pictures quickly to minimize the time the fish is out of the water. Hold the fish in a horizontal position to support its weight.

# Preparing your catch

There is nothing tastier than pan-fried fillets from freshly caught fish. You will need some basic tools: a cutting board, a fillet knife (razor sharp with a highly flexible blade; 9 inches / 23 cm will do for most fish), strong but fine forceps such as jeweler's forceps or needlenose pliers, wax paper or plastic wrap, and a small garbage bag for the entrails.

## Skinning a fillet (walleye, perch, bass)

1. Start from the tail (narrowest part) of the fillet. Place it skin-side down on the cutting board. Hold the tail with your thumb fingernail of the free hand approximately ¼ inch (6 mm) from the tail end.

2. Beginning just in front of your thumbnail, hold the blade at a slight angle and cut down to the skin but not through it. Start from the heel of the blade and slice forward and away from yourself, keeping the blade as close to flat as possible. Slice the flesh from the skin using as few strokes as possible. Avoid sawing the fillet off the skin. If the knife is sharp and your hold firm, the skin should cut fairly easily from the meat.

## Skinning a whole fish (catfish)

1. Make a shallow incision all the way around the base of the tail, without cutting through any flesh. Make an incision along the length of the fish on both the dorsal and ventral sides.

2. Free enough skin at the tail to allow you to grasp it firmly with your fingers by scraping with the tip of the blade.

3. Using your free hand, hold the fish's tail down, and with the other, pull the skin toward and over the head, as if you were undressing it. If necessary, use pliers to pull the skin.

## Filleting a fish

1. Rinse the fish under cold, running water.

2. Lay the fish on its side on a cutting board.

3. Using your free hand, press down on the fish to pin it to the board.

4. Lift the gill and place the blade of the knife under it, with sharp edge facing the tail. Cut down to the spine and along the spine all the way to the tail, keeping the blade parallel to the spine. Make long, even strokes. If you have to saw back and forth, the blade is dull. Remove it and sharpen it. The sharper the blade, the flatter the blade is kept, and the more sweeping you keep your strokes, the neater the result, and the better the fillet will keep its shape during cooking. Remove the fillet and put aside.

5. Flip the fish over on its other side and repeat. Toss the fish remains in the garbage bag.

6. Place one of the fillets, flesh side up. Cut away any combs of tiny bones from the fins that may edge the fillet.

7. Cut out the rib bones that run across the bottom of each fillet by slicing under them, keeping the blade tight against them to avoid sacrificing any tasty flesh. As you cut, pull up gently on the rib cage. The bones get thinner near the edge of the fillet and you may be slicing through some of them. Make a shallow V-cut at the base of the ribs and than slice upward to the cut already made. The entire rib cage should lift out in one piece.

8. Feel for any small bones by rubbing from head to tail with your fingertips. Pull them out with your fingers, jeweler's forceps or needle-nose pliers. Pull firmly but gently to avoid tearing the flesh.

## Making fish steaks (salmon, burbot)

Steaks are a popular cut for meaty fish that you might want to broil or grill, such as lake trout and salmon. You will need a large, sharp, chef's knife to cut through the bones. Remove the gut contents first by slicing through the belly and pulling out the entrails. To steak a fish:

1. Lay the whole fish on its side on a cutting board.

2. Starting behind the head, make approximately one-inch-thick (2.5 cm) slices, moving down to the tail end. If the fish is a whopper, you may need to bang your blade with a rubber or wooden mallet, or use a cleaver.

3. Continue cutting fillets until you approach the tail where neat steaks are no longer possible.

Flyfishing at dawn.

# Flyfishing basics

## Fly selection

Perhaps the most challenging part of flyfishing is the selection of flies. The basic rule of thumb is "match the hatch"—use insect imitations that are similar to those emerging, crawling on the bottom, or floating on the surface, in both pools

An artificial fly.

and riffles. Caddisflies, mayflies and stoneflies are commonly imitated in artificial flies (see **Getting to Know Your Lake** for details on these species). Find out what is in the stream; lift rocks and look for insects and their life stage on the bottom and surface of the rock; use a dip net to scoop insects from plants, insects floating on the surface, and those living in and on the mud. You can either use the insects as bait or make or purchase flies that emulate the insects.

### For more on flyfishing

Flyfishing is too much of an art to give it proper attention here. Consult one of the many good books available on the subject for more information. A favorite is Jeannot Ruel's *Fly Fishing Equipment and Techniques.*

# Common bait insects

## Dragonflies and damselflies

Voracious predators of mosquitoes, dragonflies and damselflies are sometimes referred to as "mosquito hawks." They provide an important food for many fish, and are often patterned by fly fishermen.

Dragonflies and damselflies have chewing mouth parts; the nymphs have large teeth and a hinged jaw that extends to capture prey. Their eyes contain over 30,000 simple units, giving them the ability to see in front, above, behind and below. When at rest, adult damselflies hold their equally sized wings upright and together, or occasionally along the side of their abdomen. In dragonflies the wings are of unequal size, the hind wings being slightly larger. When at rest, dragonfly adults hold their wings horizontally. Dragonfly adults are among the best fliers; they can zip along at 22 to 25 miles per hour (35–40 km/h), fly vertically, forward and backward, and dodge from side to side. Although their bodies are large, they weigh very little.

![Mature dragonfly.]

Mature dragonfly.

*Right* Dragonfly nymph.

Damselfly nymphs have tapered bodies, two widely set compound eyes and three leaf-like tails. The tails are actually gills, but are also used for swimming. Many fly fishermen swear by the American ruby spot pattern broad-winged damselfly nymph for catching bass and trout. The nymph patterns of the speckled olive damselfly and the dark olive damselfly are also used.

Dragonfly nymphs have two large compound lateral eyes, sometimes joined at their bases; three wedge-shaped spines at the tail end; and the abdomen is often the widest part of the insect. All dragonfly nymphs can thrust water out of their rectums to propel them through the water. Fly tyers pattern the giant dragonfly nymph and the green darner nymph. The flies are used for catching trout, by letting the weighted fly settle to the bottom briefly, then jerking the line every few seconds.

## Dobsonflies, fishflies and alderflies

The larvae of dobsonflies and fishflies are huge (up to 3.5 inches or 9 cm long), very active and ferocious, and make excellent bait for stream fish such as trout. Both live on the underside of rocks in slow to fast waters, preying on other insects with their large, sickle-like jaws. The adults are also quite large (up to 1.5 inches or 35 mm long) and possess two pair of nearly identical, membranous wings that are held roof-like over the back when at rest. The larvae are aquatic, but adults are terrestrial, short lived and seldom seen.

Alderflies are much smaller, usually ½ to 1 inch (10–25 mm) long, and they have a long unsegmented tail. They inhabit both standing and flowing waters, on the bottom or sides of rocks or slightly buried in the sediments. The adults have two pair of dark, often brownish, wings, large eyes, and a pair of long, thin antennae. They are awkward fliers but good runners.

# The casting clock

It is absolutely essential to know how to cast a fly rod overhead. Think of a cast as an arc that passes through time on a clock. The 9:00 position is always the starting point, with the rod horizontal (or anywhere lower) in the direction of the cast; 12:00 is always vertical; and the other hours fall into other positions described below.

Try a dry run to simulate an overhand cast. Grip the rod with your right (or left) hand around the handle and your thumb on top. Begin with your arm hanging straight down by your side and the tip of your rod just above the water with no slack in the line. Bring your forearm to horizontal, the starting position for the cast. With your hand, wrist and lower arm held in a straight line, move your hand upward, bending your arm at the elbow and lifting your rod hand toward the top of your head, stopping when your index finger nears your ear and allowing your wrist to flex only a little as you do so. This is the top position at completion of the back cast. You should be able to see the palm of your hand out of the corner of your eye. This movement is called the backcast. Pause momentarily, then, using your arm and wrist, simulate a forward cast letting your elbow and hand fall forward to 10:00. You have just gone through the three stopping positions for a basic overhead cast. Remember the saying: tip (9:00), top (12:00), ten (10:00).

Now, for the real thing! To learn, it's easiest to start by facing downstream. Let about 20 to 30 feet (6–9 m) of line out into the water. Grip the fly line between thumb and forefinger of your non-casting hand. During the basic cast the line will be held at all times. Initiate the cast, accelerating through the motion, and adding speed and drive by snapping your wrist back crisply to 12:30. Overall, the rod arc should be slightly more than 90 degrees from start to finish. It is important that movement starts slowly but the speed of the rod tip increases rapidly

A flyfisher's spinner.

toward the end of the stroke. Just as the last of the line leaves the water's surface and speed is maximum, stop (at 12:00 to 12:30). The stop must be a dead stop, because any further movement will cause shock waves and produce a sloppy result. If done correctly, the line will fly upward and behind you and will become absolutely straight (horizontal) in the air. You'll feel the line as it pulls on the rod tip by your right hand holding the rod or by your left hand holding the line. Repeat the process if the line is not absolutely straight in midair. With practice, you can release more line with your non-casting hand to cast further away. When satisfied that you have a good cast, stop and drop at 10:00 with the falling line to keep the line straight as it falls to the water.

The direction that the line takes will be determined by movement of the rod tip. If you want your line to go in a straight line, make the rod tip move in a straight line. If you want the line to rise, stop the rod when the tip is rising. The same thing goes for circles or parts of circles, eclipses or any other shape.

A fisher pauses momentarily at the backcast before letting elbow and hand fall forward to the 10:00 position.

Just make sure that you perform a continuous motion for the duration of both the backcast and forward casting strokes.

When flyfishing, strikes to subsurface flies can be very subtle and are often detected more through sight than feel. Attaching a strike indicator to the leader will help to detect subtle twitches. Many strike indicators are pieces of bright, buoyant material, such as foam, placed just high enough on the line to rest out of the water and float on the surface. When fishing floating ("dry flies") imitations, the fish can be seen taking the fly at the surface of the water.

A trout about to strike a fly.

## After the cast

Once the cast is complete, there are several more steps to take before you actually catch and land a fish. If a fly line is placed across a stream, the current often places an unnatural drag on the fly, preventing the fly from drifting freely, as if it were a live insect. "Mending" the fly line is a method to reduce or prevent the current from dragging the nymph or dry fly. For a cast made upstream, a mend should be made the moment the fly and line are on the water by lifting the rod quickly and flipping the belly and forward part of the line upstream. If a long cast was used, the forward part of the line may need to be mended several times. Alternatively, throw a mend downstream and place the fly in swifter water. This will allow the fly to float naturally and quickly as it meets up with the line that is dragging downstream.

"Stripping" is a technique used to retrieve fly line, impart lively action to minnow-imitation flies, and to land a hooked fish. Fly line is not reeled in between casts so the angler must retrieve it by hand. First, using the index finger of the casting hand, grip the line between the finger and the rod. With the index finger, loosely hold the line while stripping in line and tighten the grip between strips. The line is pulled in or stripped using the non-casting hand. Any line that is stripped in is allowed to fall into the water if you are wading (or into the boat or on land, depending on where you are standing).

"Nymphing" is a technique used only when using weighted imitation nymphs for bait. Use short casts and hold the rod tip high to keep most of the fly line off the water and minimize drag. After the cast, let the weighted nymph drift along in the current, close to bottom.

Now for the exciting part: hooking and landing a fish. The non-casting hand is used to release or pull line according to the size of the fish and the strength of the battle. Large fish are often played "from the reel" instead of stripping and releasing line by hand. Control the fish using the pressure with the index finger on the line (as in stripping), using less finger pressure once a fish takes the fly and allowing extra line to fall into the water. Once a strike occurs, raise the rod straight up quickly to set the hook. Hold the rod high at all times, from the time the hook is set until the fish is in the net. (One exception—if a fish jumps and clears water, lower the rod tip to stop a fish from landing on the tight line and breaking free.) Allow the fish to run and tire instead of trying to manhandle it. When a fish is hooked, tension is released to allow the fish more line if necessary. Once the fish is under control, pull the fish in to within rod length and get the net ready for capture. Raise the rod high with the line taut in one hand while reaching for the fish with the net in the other hand. Bon appetit!

# Unwelcome invaders

The introduction of a new species can seriously affect the ecological balance of any lake or river system. Its feeding, spawning and habitat requirements may compete directly with the existing fish population. The resulting competition may even lead to the elimination of a native species — never a good thing.

The sea lamprey can scale walls of dams by using its mouth to attach itself and then releasing itself and leaping forward. It has been known to attach to boats for a free ride.

## The sea lamprey

The introduction of the sea lamprey to North America was a biological disaster on the scale of the introduction of the rabbit to Australia. Its arrival in 1930 coincided with the opening of the St. Lawrence Waterway, which provides a 1,864-mile (3,000 km) connection between the Great Lakes and the North Atlantic Ocean. It wreaked havoc with the Great Lakes freshwater fisheries, especially lake trout, salmon and whitefish species. Before the lamprey, the combined annual U.S. and Canadian catches of lake trout in the Great Lakes was 15 million pounds. By the 1960s, the catch had fallen to 300 thousand pounds. Since then the lamprey has come under control by chemical treatment of the larvae in spawning streams, a costly, ongoing necessity.

## The round goby

The round goby, which arrived in the St. Clair River via ballast water in 1990, possesses all the characteristics of an invasive species: tolerance of a wide range of environmental conditions, a broad diet, aggressive behavior, high fecundity (up to 10,000 eggs per nest per year), nest guarding by males and a small body size relative to other fish but large to competitor fish.

Round gobies larger than 3 inches (10 cm) long feed almost exclusively on zebra mussels, using their molar-like teeth to crush mollusk shells. At smaller sizes they feed on the same foods as mottled sculpins, darters, log perch and some minnows, changing the balance of the ecosystem.

Gobies have large heads and soft bodies, somewhat resembling large tadpoles. The gobies' unique feature is the suctorial disk on their bellies that anchors the fish to the bottom in flowing waters. Young round gobies are slate gray. Larger individuals tend to have blotches of black and brown over their bodies and their dorsal fin is often tinged with green. Round gobies look similar to some sculpins.

The round goby lives mostly in waters from 2 feet (20 cm to 60 cm) deep, on gravel, shell or sand bottoms. Spawning occurs in late spring and summer, with eggs laid under stones and mollusk shells and the male looking after the eggs of several females. Gobies live three to four years, occasionally longer, and are preyed on by bass, walleye and trout.

**To prevent the spread of exotics:**

- inspect live bait to ensure that no round gobies are accidentally released into fishing areas;
- discard live bait on land, and not into the water, to ensure that no exotic aquatic life is introduced into native water bodies;
- inspect boat, motor, trailer and boating equipment, such as anchors and fishing gear, centerboards, rollers and axles, and remove all visible animals and plants before leaving any body of water; and
- drain water from the motor, live well, bilge and transom wells on land immediately before leaving the shore of the lake or river.

The round goby.

## More on invaders

For more information on the spiny water flea and how to prevent its spread in lakes and rivers, read Foreign invaders: the spiny water flea earlier in this chapter.

The deliberate introduction of new species to your lake should not be undertaken lightly. Read Smart fishing later in this chapter. Never introduce a new species without permission from your local government agency of natural resources.

# CHAPTER 5

# Living with Wildlife

Respect the natural life around you at the cottage. The rewards will be many.

I F YOU GO OUT IN THE WOODS TODAY you could be in for a big surprise. Although your chances of running into a bear are slim, you'll discover a natural world around your cottage that is crawling, flying and buzzing with life. Most of the time, the animals that live around us go quietly about their business without us knowing they are there. Spotting a moose or elusive fox is a thrill, and hearing the call of loons and wolves sends pleasant shivers down our spines. But when mice breakfast on your bran flakes, skunks or wasps move in under the porch, and slugs, rabbits or deer decimate the garden, you may be less than awed by the wildlife around you. On the other hand, the spider in the corner is your ally in pest control, as are the insect-eating birds and bats, and the hawks and owls who hunt for rodents. And for every plant that will make you itch, there are many more that will heal and feed you. There are strategies you can use to avoid and thwart the pests and poisons and still keep the natural balance of things.

As cottagers, we can help support the web of forest and lake life of which we have become a part, respecting the natural world while marking out our own termite-, ant-, wasp-, bear-free territory. Keep in mind, though, that the wild creatures were there before us, and have first dibs on anything you let them get at!

Loon chicks can swim right away, but spend some time on their parents' backs to rest, conserve heat, and avoid predators.

# American black bear

The black bear's smooth, shiny fur is usually black but can be chocolate-brown, cinnamon and silver-gray to off-white.

**With bells on**

Going for a walk in the woods? Attach a bell to your belt or backpack, sing songs and make noise and you'll likely scare bears—and most other wildlife—away. Bears are capable of killing you if they have to, but generally they are passive and most preoccupied with berry hunting.

American black bears are the smallest and least aggressive of North American bears. Adult females weigh 100 to 200 pounds and adult males weigh 150 to 400 pounds. They have powerful limbs and large claws, are agile climbers, and have keen noses and sharp hearing. They love berries, mushrooms, acorns, grubs, ants, fish and small mammals.

Black bears are mostly solitary, preferring dense woodlands, and spend most of their time looking for food. The territories of males often overlap, but females don't share. Mating occurs from June to mid-July. At the end of hibernation, females usually have two to three cubs. The cubs are playful and often wander off, but mom is usually nearby.

Here are suggestions for how to avoid bears (see page 192 for more details) and what to do if you come across one.

## Black bear encounters

### Proactive Suggestions

To keep bears away from your cottage, don't invite them in the first place. Bears will come by to sample the goods if you've stored garbage and compost poorly, tossed food containers, have berry patches, birdfeeders or outdoor barbecues.

"Nuisance" bears rely on human food and generally end up being shot by scared residents. Killing a bear without a hunting license or out of season is illegal, but most jurisdictions give cottage owners the right to defend themselves if a bear attacks. If possible, call the local conservation authority to report the problem bear and get instructions on what to do. If the cottage is in a remote area with no telephone or Internet access, a last resort may be to kill the nuisance bear yourself.

In order to own a gun you will require a proper license, such as a PAL (Possession and Acquisition License), which is an authorization to possess and register a firearm and to obtain ammunition. You should also own a hunting license (laws differ among jurisdictions, so first find out what is required). A 12-gauge shotgun with 2¾-inch slugs is good to use to kill black bears if closer than 100 yards (90 metres). Try to shoot the bear broadside in the lungs, just behind the shoulder and middle area of the chest—never in the head. Report the kill to the authorities immediately. In most jurisdictions it is incumbent upon you to bury the bear, as far away from the cottage as possible. This last act should be enough to encourage more proactive preventions in the first place.

### Reactive Suggestions

Should you encounter a black bear, never approach it to try to drive it off. If the bear is not close—10 to 20 feet (3-6 m) away—freeze and don't threaten it. Grizzly bears are more ferocious than black bears, but if a black bear does attack, follow these guidelines:

- Curl into a ball on your side or lie flat on your stomach; clasp your hands behind your head to protect your neck (a backpack works as well).
- Pull your knees toward your chin to help protect vital organs.
- Try to remain calm and quiet until the attack ends; try not to scream; do not resist or fight back.
- Get up slowly, checking to see if the bear can be seen or heard.
- If the bear comes back, return to your position on the ground and stay motionless.
- Get out of the area or get help.

Moose have an inability to sweat so are limited to cool regions, and will seek shade and water to cool down in summer.

# The ungulates

Ungulate is a term used to describe plant-eating mammals with hooves. The hoof consists of hornlike tissue that is comparable to the human fingernail. Ungulates form an important part of the diet of large carnivores like wolves and bears.

## Moose

Moose is an Indian word meaning "eater of twigs." Moose are the largest members of the deer family and one of the largest land mammals in North America. Males are just slightly longer than females but weigh much more than females, with males ranging from 794 to 1,323 pounds (360–600 kg) and females from 595 to 882 pounds (270–400 kg).

Males carry wide, elaborate antlers, the largest of any mammal in the world, measuring up to 10 feet (3 m) from tip to tip. They are shed and regrown annually. The moose's long brown-black individual coat hairs are hollow, providing excellent insulation. Moose have a waddle of skin on the throat, a long, flexible nose and very long legs.

Moose breed once yearly, in September and October. Females attract males with long, moaning calls that can be heard up to 2 miles (3.2 km) away, as well as by emitting a powerful scent. Rival males compete for females during the breeding season. Two potential suitors may simply assess who is larger, the smaller bull retreating, or they may engage in violent battles.

## Deer parts

White-tailed deer have scent glands on the hooves of all four feet, as well as on the inside of their rear legs. The scent produced is used during mating season and for identification.

Deer are ruminants like cows, and have four-chambered stomachs for digesting plants that other animals can't, such as twigs and bark.

Eight months after mating, the cow produces one to two calves in late May to early June. The young reach sexual maturity at two years, but aren't finished growing until they are four or five. Adult moose are in their prime from 5 to 12 years, but begin to suffer from arthritis, dental diseases and other factors after about 8 years. The oldest moose recorded was 22.

Most of a moose's time is spent eating, about 90 pounds (40 kg) of food per day. Their stomachs, when full, can weigh up to 280 pounds (125 kg). Moose eat twigs, bark, roots and the shoots of woody plants, especially willows and aspens. In the warm months, moose feed on water plants—water lilies, pondweed, horsetails, bladderworts and bur reed. In winter, they browse on conifers such as balsam fir, eating their needle-like leaves. Moose prefer forested areas, where there is snow cover in the winter, and moist habitats, including lakes, ponds and wetlands, especially swamps, bogs and marshes. Although they are active throughout the day, you are most likely to spot them at dawn and dusk. They are powerful swimmers, able to sustain a speed of 6 mph (10 km/h) in water, and swift runners, running as fast as 35 mph (56 km/h).

Moose generally stay in one area 13 to 26 square miles (35 to 65 km²). They tend to be solitary animals, although two may sometimes be found feeding along the same shoreline. Mothers are very protective of their calves and have a strong social bond, frequently charging people if they get too close. Moose gather in larger groups during the mating season in alpine and tundra habitats.

Moose have poor sight, and are barely able to tell the difference between a fence post and a human standing still at 50 feet (15 m) away. But if you rustle, make a noise, or the wind is blowing in the moose's direction, watch out: their senses of hearing and smell are excellent. Their large ears can be rotated 180 degrees and their keen noses can whiff food under deep snow.

Moose usually avoid people and will not investigate or charge unless provoked. They generally are not a nuisance to humans and rarely damage gardens and shrubs. If you do find damage, in all probability it was caused by a white-tailed deer: compare footprints and scats; the hooves and scat of moose are much larger.

The moose's main predators are wolves, black bears and humans. Up to half of all calves fall to predators during their first year. Moose are able to aggressively defend themselves and their young with their stout antlers and sharp hooves. Car collisions also take their share, as do several diseases and parasites.

## Once upon a time...

... elk were once common over much of the temperate part of eastern North America but now exist only in small, reintroduced populations.

...caribou ranged from Greenland south to the northern border of the United States.

...bison (buffalo) was once very widely distributed throughout much of North America, but shooting them was a favorite frontier sport in the 19th century; hunters practically eliminated the bison by 1890. The bison is now protected and is restricted to small herds in parks and game reserves, like this member of a herd in Yellowstone National Park.

# White-tailed deer

The white-tailed deer is quite large, 4 to 6 feet (1.5–2.0 m) long, about 3 feet (1 m) high at the shoulders and weighs 100 to 300 pounds (22–67 kg).

The underside of the tail is white, but on top it is the same color as the deer's back — tawny in the summer, blue-gray in the winter. Male deer have antlers with unbranched tines, which they shed from January to March. The antlers grow back in April or May with a soft covering called "velvet" on them, which is lost in August or September.

Deer mate in November in the northern parts of their range and in January or February in the south. The doe has one to four fawns after about six months' gestation. Fawns are reddish-brown at birth with white spots that help camouflage them, the spots disappearing after about three months. The fawns are weaned at about six weeks. The mother leaves her fawns well-hidden for hours at a time while she forages, hiding them in different places if there is more than one fawn. The fawns lie on the ground with their heads and necks stretched out flat, and are scentless so predators almost have to walk over them to find them.

The white-tailed deer "lives on the edge," thriving on the borders of farmlands, woodlots and wetlands. They feed mostly on grass, leaves and twigs in the early morning hours and in the late afternoon. To avoid deep snow and chilly winds in winter, deer move from higher to lower elevations, congregating at feeding grounds such as cornfields. If food is plentiful, deer eat green plants in the summer, corn, acorns and other nuts in the fall, and the buds and twigs of woody plants in the winter. But if food is scarce, deer will often damage ornamental shrubs, young orchards, and blueberry vines in the spring and home gardens and commercial vegetable crops in the summer.

The white-tailed deer's main wild predators are wolves and mountain lions, and sometimes bobcats and coyotes. Humans outweigh all natural predators. Deer living in close proximity to humans are often involved in car accidents that sometimes result in injury to both deer and human occupants of the vehicles.

White-tailed deer are very timid and secretive, and constantly on the alert. When threatened, a deer will warn others by stomping its hooves, snorting and raising its tail to show the white "flag."

Wolves hunt singly and in packs.

# Dog kin: wolves, coyotes and foxes

## Wolf

Some day, if you are lucky, you may see a gray wolf, or at least hear its haunting howls. Until it became a protected species and recovery programs began, this beautiful creature was at risk of becoming extinct in many states and some provinces. While the species is slowly increasing its population sizes, cottagers should be aware of how desperate this animal is for its place on the planet.

The gray wolf is often confused with a large German shepherd. It has a thick, shaggy coat, usually gray, mixed with black and brown but may be nearly black, erect ears and a bushy tail. Hunting at night, gray wolves primarily prey on large mammals such as deer, moose, caribou and bison, pursuing smaller mammals such as rabbits and beaver only when larger prey are scarce or an easy kill presents itself. Humans

have been the gray wolf's most significant predator, ruthlessly hunting and exterminating them because of cattle and deer predation.

The wolf pack is a family group, including an adult pair, who mate for life, and their offspring. The leader is usually a male (the "alpha"), who initiates and guides activities and movements such as hunts. The males and the females have separate social hierarchies maintained by different degrees of aggression, greeting and submission. The alpha male retains his position for years, but is challenged by subordinate males or outsiders when he appears vulnerable through injury or old age. Young wolves generally do not remain with the parental pack past breeding age (24 months). As the young cub grows, it increasingly explores the edges of the parental territory (marked by urine and feces), eventually joining a lone wolf from another pack, or establishing itself in a small area, waiting for a member of the opposite sex to come by. Territories vary greatly in size, typically from 10 to 20 square miles (up to 52 km²), depending on the abundance and availability of prey. Gray wolves live 8 to 16 years in the wild.

Gray wolves hunt singly and in packs, which typically include five individuals. Under stressful conditions, especially in winter, or when food is scarce, several families may join together, forming a pack of up to 30 individuals. After the kill the wolves consume large amounts of meat, most often in a noisy, snarling scramble led by the alpha male and female.

Gray wolves are the among fastest and most agile of the wild canines, running as fast as 35 mph (56 km/h) and clearing 12 feet (3.6 m) in a single bound. While hunting they can maintain a lope of about 20 miles per hour (32 km/h) for many hours, eventually wearing down even the swiftest prey.

## Wolf talk

Gray wolves communicate through howling, body language and scent.

They howl to assemble the pack for a hunt, to talk to other packs, to assert territorial claims or just for the fun of it. People can hear howls in the open 10 miles (16 km) away. Other wolves respond to the howls of distant wolves up to 7½ miles (12 km) distant.

Scent markings are olfactory messages that announce a wolf pack's ownership of a territory, and indicate who is ready to breed. Wolves urinate at the same places and in the same patterns on a regular basis to mark territory. The particular smell of the urine declares who is "in the mood," which can help bring new pairs together.

Just like dogs, wolves use their faces and tails to articulate their emotions and status in the pack.

The coyote, *lupus latrans*.

## Coyote

The coyote can be recognized by its thick bushy tail, long pointed nose and ears. About the size of a German shepherd dog but slimmer and half the weight, coyotes are distinguished from wolves and dogs because they carry their tail low when running, creating a slinky outline. These much-maligned creatures are intelligent, adaptable predators.

Coyotes thrive in habitat disturbances such as clear cuts and survive well in urban areas, as long as there is food (garbage, cats, dogs) and shelter available. They use natural corridors such as ravines to travel between developed areas. Most of their natural diet is made up of rodents, birds and rabbits, as well as carrion, insects and fruit. Their most common enemies are disease and humans, but predators such as bears, wolves and cougars eat both young and adults.

Coyotes hunt alone or in pairs, one distracting and chasing prey into the waiting jaws of the other, alternating positions when one is tired. They have both speed and endurance, running as fast as 30 mph (50 km/h) for short bursts but sustaining a lope of 20 mph (30 km/h) for long periods.

### Coyote calling

Coyotes usually call at night, from an open area, where the sound can travel up to 3 miles (4.8 km) or more. The coyote's call is a series of short high-pitched barks and yodels (usually two short barks and a long wavering yodel). The young learn to call as soon as they are old enough to hunt, and their calls can be quite amusing as they try to mimic their parents. Occasionally, if you call back on a dark evening, you can get them to answer, but if your call isn't good enough, they will stop answering.

Coyotes cohabit in a den under a tree, stump or rock in February. After 60 days, four to six furry, blind pups are born. Both parents share in raising the young. By May, the pups begin to learn to hunt. They leave their parents in the autumn. The average lifespan for coyotes is eight years.

In the wild, coyotes are timid animals with a natural fear of humans, but they are curious and may watch you from a distance. Coyotes in cities and urban areas or around cottages may become accustomed to humans and stick around, usually because garbage has been left out, or people are feeding them. Often, coyotes are killed because humans attract them, they become a nuisance, and remind us again that "a fed animal is a dead animal."

If a coyote is bold or overly curious and does approach you, make yourself as large as possible (stand up, spread your arms and coat out), pick small children up in your arms, gather children in a group, make lots of noise and wave your arms. Usually, they will leave at a run.

## Red fox

The red fox resembles a small, slender dog, with rusty red or reddish-brown fur, black triangular ears and feet, a white-tipped bushy tail and furred foot pads. These shy, nervous animals are very wary of humans. Smart and alert, they have keen senses of smell, hearing, and sight, enabling them to live close to cottages without being noticed. They are agile, swift runners capable of reaching a speed of 30 mph (48 km/h) on their short legs.

Red foxes live in temperate forests and occupy territories of 1 to 3 square miles (3 to 8 km²). They build nesting dens for raising cubs and resting dens for safety. The dens are as long as 30 feet (9 m) in sandy or gravely soil and each have two or three entrances. Breeding usually takes place between mid-December and mid-February. Just over seven

weeks later, five to six cubs are born, blind and vulnerable. After five weeks of close care, they are weaned and venture outside to learn how to hunt. After the summer, cubs may choose to leave. However, only the females are allowed to stay within the family; the males must go start their own.

A fox on the prowl for food.

Foxes hunt mostly at night, traveling as much as 5 miles (8 km) in one night. They are not picky and will eat whatever they find or catch, dead or alive—small mammals, birds, fruit, insects, crayfish, vegetable matter —but mice are their favorite meal. Their winter diet consists mostly of small mammals, which they pounce on like cats. Foxes will come to cottages looking for anything to eat, like leftover bread, bird seed, fish trimmings, tomatoes, cooked peas, banana orange, and apple peels, and any other food that is left over, including pet vomit. Red foxes themselves are preyed on mainly by coyotes and bobcats.

> A red fox can hear the squeak of a mouse as far as 150 yards (137 m) away.

# Cat kin: lynx and bobcat

## Lynx

The lynx is found throughout the northern United States and Canada. The males are about five times heavier than the average domestic cat, although size can vary considerably. A lynx is a sturdy-looking animal with a small head, solid body and legs, large paws and a very short tail. The ear tips have tufts and the cheeks grow a ruff or "sideboard" in winter. The long fur on the paws aids in movement over soft snow.

Lynx are good climbers and swimmers. They have acute vision and will either stalk their prey, over long distances if necessary, or wait and ambush, pouncing in typical feline fashion. The most important prey is the snow-shoe hare, but lynx will also take fish, small rodents, ducks and ground-dwelling birds. A lynx will also take larger prey such as young deer and cattle that are at a disadvantage in the snow or when they have sustained injury. Two lynxes may cooperate in hunting to kill and share prey. Like a coyote, one lynx will drive a rabbit toward a waiting ambush by another, or a pair of lynxes will stalk from both sides.

Both males and females hunt beyond their territories in the mating season, normally in late February or early March. They occupy dens typically in hollow trees, under stumps, in thick brush. After two to two and a half months a litter of two to three kittens is born in early summer. The kittens are weaned by five months but even by winter do not have their adult teeth or claws and must accompany their mother on hunting expeditions. They stay with their mother until the next mating season, when they are usually chased away by suitors.

## Bobcat

The bobcat owes its name to its characteristic stumpy, dark-tipped tail. Bobcats have short ear tufts, cheek ruffs and sometimes spots or tabby stripes. These heavily built cats are found from the United States/Canada border down to Mexico.

Where territories overlap, the bobcat is more aggressive and tends to displace the lynx. However, lynx predominate in areas with deep snow because they have longer legs. Like the lynx, bobcats prefer forested areas and hunt cottontails, hares, rodents, bats and birds. They also will hunt larger animals such as deer when food is scarce. The lynx and bobcat hybridize quite readily.

Both the bobcat (*above*) and the lynx (*left*) prefer coniferous forests with dense undergrowth. However, the lynx has adapted to other kinds of terrain, including treeless slopes, open woodland, delta swamps, and rocky outcrops.

### Lost cats

The mountain lion, formerly found throughout the United States and most adjacent provinces of Canada, exists only in remote areas of its former range and is now rarely seen.

Adult raccoons may grow to 3 feet (about 1 m) long and weigh 30 to 40 pounds (14–18 kg).

# Raccoons

The name "raccoon" is derived from the Algonquin word *arakum,* which means "he who scratches with hands." Raccoons are adapted to forest nightlife. They have sharp claws for climbing but are slow runners. Their front feet are sensitive hands that can catch prey in and around water, and can pry open clam shells. Raccoons eat crayfish, clams, frogs, worms, fish, grubs, crickets, grasshoppers, large insects, turtles, bird eggs and nestlings, and small mammals such as squirrels, rats or mice. Around cottages they will also feed on dog or cat food, fruit on trees, garden vegetables, or garbage.

Raccoons don't hibernate. They mate from January to March; litters of three to five "kits" are born in April or May. If the young ones haven't left by about four months, mom will drive them away before her next litter is born.

Of all the wild animals that have adapted to urban life, raccoons are the most destructive. If you feed them, they will literally move in, building dens in attics, chimneys, wall spaces, woodpiles, under cottages and in soffits. Beware if you meet a mother and her young in an attic or other enclosed space—they will attack if cornered. Not only do these bold omnivores raid garbage cans, they damage gardens and fruit trees, and are carriers of fleas, ticks, lice, distemper, mange and rabies. Their feces may also contain roundworm eggs. Anyone—especially children—who contacts infected raccoon feces can become infected. The larvae may migrate to the eyes or brain, causing blindness or death.

Controlling them is usually difficult and time consuming. If you suspect unwanted masked tenants have moved in, listen for whines and growls. Watch for prints in mud or snow. The hind footprint looks like a human's footprint and the front looks like a human's hand, with claws on all feet. For control details, see **Living with wildlife** later in this chapter at pages 192 to 195.

A snowshoe hare in winter (*left*), and an eastern cottontail (*right*).

# Hares and cottontails

If you see a big rabbit with long ears and hind legs, soft fur and a short tail, you've met the snowshoe hare. In winter, the hare's fur changes from brown to almost white, or to a grayish-brown. Large (6 inches, or 15 cm), long-furred feet allow it to travel on heavy snow.

If you see a little rabbit with short ears, big eyes and a puffy tail that is white on the underside, you've met the eastern cottontail, the most common rabbit. Eastern cottontails have small rear feet (4 inches, or 10 cm), speckled brown-gray fur that's reddish-brown around the neck and shoulders and lighter around the nose and undersides.

Hares and cottontails have some other differences. The young of hares are born with eyes open, furred and mobile while baby cottontails are born blind, naked and helpless; hares seek safety in flight, cottontails by hiding; hares prefer open country, cottontails prefer shrubby cover. But in com-mon, hares and cottontails are timid, inoffensive animals. Their diets are vegetarian (garden greens, buds, bark, twigs, leaves); neither hibernates; they read the wind with their noses, and "thump" on the ground with their hind feet to warn others of approaching danger. Wolf, bobcat and lynx are their main predators.

If predators approach, the snowshoe and cottontail often "freeze" in place, relying on their camouflaged fur to blend into the background. Otherwise they use their strong hind legs to escape, the snowshoe running more than 25 miles per hour (40 km/h) and making 10-foot (3 m) leaps, the cottontail running more than 18 miles per hour (29 km/h) and making 8-foot (3 m) leaps. Both tend to avoid water but are excellent swimmers, and will jump into water when being chased. Population booms (5,000 to 10,000 per square mile) and crashes (3 to 4 per square mile) are common.

# Weasels, skunks and musky allies

This bunch of stinky critters is characterized by the presence of large, paired scent glands. The scent glands, used for identification, defense, marking territory and trail marking, are particularly powerful in skunk and mink. Weasels make up most of the group and include the ermine, ferret and mink. Martens, fishers and wolverines also belong. Weasels tend to have long bodies, short legs, rounded ears and fur that is brown during the summer, but white or whitish during the winter; martens and fishers are more wolverine-like and show little color change in winter.

The marten.

## Marten

The marten, also called the pine marten or American sable, was once widely distributed but is now rare. Aside from the lynx, eagles, owls and the fisher, humans are the marten's chief enemy. This beautiful animal has intense curiosity, which makes it one of the easiest fur-bearing animals to trap. Its pelt is exceptionally thick and soft and very valuable. Excessive trapping and destruction of habitat has dangerously decreased the marten's range.

The marten is a little smaller than a house cat. It lives in trees, where it hunts for squirrels and birds. When it does come down to the ground, it preys on marmots, chipmunks, hares, voles, mice, grouse and reptiles. When prey is sparse, it eats honey, nuts and berries.

*Right* The weasel.

## Fisher

The fisher is about the size of a fox. It is much fiercer than the marten, and spends more time on the ground, preferring swampy lowland forests but has the same diet. Although fishers are good swimmers, fish are only an incidental food; the name "fisher" was apparently invented to distinguish it from the marten. The long silky fur is valuable, but the animal is more difficult to trap than the marten.

## Weasel

The least weasel and the long-tailed weasel are both common in meadows, riverbanks, parklands, mixed forests, open woods, brush piles or grassy areas. Both have similar summer furs, but the long-tailed weasel, the largest North American weasel, has a black-tipped tail. Both species prey on small mammals such as voles, deer mice and ground squirrels and take over their nests, usually lining them with the fur of their prey. Weasels also prey on eggs of grouse and waterfowl and eat plants and berries. Weasels are hunted by owls, foxes and other larger carnivorous mammals.

Otters communicate with their diamond-shaped noses, mainly by smelling marked territories. When they do talk, it is with chirps, chuckles, grunts, whistles and screams.

## River otter

The river otter is at home on land and in the water, spending its life along the shores of deep, clear water lakes, rivers and large marshes. These graceful swimmers and divers can swim at an average speed of 7 miles an hour (11 km/h) and stay submerged for up to two minutes. Their ears and nose have a valve-like skin that closes and keeps the openings watertight. Mostly nocturnal and active all year, otters capture prey under water along lake or river bottoms. Their main prey is fish, but otters also feed on clams, snails, other invertebrates, frogs and small mammals including muskrats, voles and shrews. Bears, eagles and coyotes prey on otters.

River otters often raid muskrat burrows or beaver lodges, as they do not construct their own burrows. They make lairs of dry leaves, bark or wood chips in burrows, or use large open nests of grasses in thickets along marsh or river banks. Most otters travel daily along a 3-to-9-mile (5–15 km) stretch of shoreline; some may travel up to 60 miles (100 km) in a year.

Although mating occurs in the spring, the new young will not begin to develop until late in the fall. This process, known as "delayed implantation," enables the fertilized eggs to mark time, receiving only enough rations to stay alive for those months. Then an unknown signal awakens the tiny embryos, which resume their growth.

## Wolverine

The wolverine is an animal of boreal forests and tundra. In Alaska and Canada, they prefer the lowland spruce forests that support extensive wetlands. Wolverines will attack anything, even animals much larger than themselves, including moose and caribou, but they depend more regularly on small rodents, rabbits, porcupines, ground squirrels, marmots, birds and eggs, fish, carrion and plant material, especially roots and berries. Wolverines don't hibernate. They are notorious for raiding trap lines, cabins and food caches.

The wolverine is bear-like in appearance, but smaller, with a broad, white-masked head and short heavy neck, a long, bushy tail and short rounded ears. The feet are huge for the animal's size, 5 inches (13 cm) from heel to claw with semi-retractile claws.

Wolverines are found throughout northern North America but have become uncommon or even endangered in many areas in the south and east because of their characteristically low density, the threat of habitat change, and also as a result of hunting.

A wolverine.

# Skunk attack!

Skunks rarely attack unless they are cornered or are defending their young. If a skunk feels threatened, it will fluff its fur, shake its tail, stamp (dance) on the ground with its front feet, growl or snort, stand on its hind legs, turn its head and spit to scare the potential attacker. This is the enemy's cue to scram because the skunk will shuffle backward, raise its tail, bend its body to a U-shaped position and spray. The musk sprays up to 15 feet (4.6 m), from two small openings near the animal's anus. The glands that secrete the chemical hold enough for five or six full sprays.

If you or your pet is sprayed, act quickly.

- Skunk spray in your eyes is extremely irritating and can cause temporary blindness, but no permanent damage. Flush your eyes liberally with cold water.

- Wash your skin with carbolic soap and water, tomato juice, vinegar or douche. Several household products, including orange juice and toothpaste have also been used with reputed success.

- Don't dilute any of the products; thoroughly scrub the product into fur or onto skin. Let it soak in (at least five minutes) and then rinse thoroughly.

- If some odor still remains, repeat.

- When using any of the remedies, keep away from eyes, nose and mouth.

- You may be able to save clothing by washing repeatedly in vinegar water and hanging it outside for a month or so before dry-cleaning. For the worst sprays, however, it may be best to burn the clothing.

## Skunk odor remedies

Some people swear by a skunk odor-removing remedy made by mixing together 1 quart (1.14 L) of 3 percent peroxide (made by adding 1 fluid ounce (34 mL) drugstore-grade peroxide to 31 ounces (1,106 mL) of water), 2 ounces (57 g) of baking soda, and 1 tablespoon (15 mL) of liquid hand soap.

Commercial products, such as "Skunk Off" and similar products containing neutroleum alpha, work as well. Keep some on hand if skunks are known to be around. A 2-percent solution of vinegar (2 parts vinegar: 98 parts water) may also help to eliminate odor from pets, clothing, and furniture.

If any musk lands on lawn chairs or furniture, rinse with water immediately or the stains will be permanent. Burning a citronella candle or spraying ammonia water in a room will help reduce skunk odor.

Skunk spray contains musk — a sulfur compound called N-bulymercaptan — that is used as a base for perfumes!

# Skunk

If for some reason you don't recognize a skunk by the white stripe running down its black back and tail, you will know it if you smell it. The musk is a fetid, oily, yellowish fluid that is corrosive and will leave permanent marks on plastic and painted surfaces.

An individual skunk's territory may span 30 to 40 acres (12 to 16 hectares); to put it another way, several cottagers are probably dealing with the same skunk. In the wild, skunks tend to den in shallow burrows with well-hidden entrances or in hollow logs. Near camps and cottages, they like warm, dry, dark and defensible areas, such as below buildings, decks and woodpiles. They are rarely found more than 2 miles (3.2 km) from a water source.

Skunks feed mostly at night and begin foraging at sunset, looking for field mice and other small rodents, doing their part to help keep the rodent population in check. They also feed on lizards, frogs, birds, eggs, garbage, acorns and fallen fruit, and will dig for insects, especially beetles, larvae and earthworms. The skunk's chief predators are great horned owls, but automobiles and hunters also kill large numbers. Some skunks are trapped for their fur and pelt; more are killed accidentally every year by trappers.

> Skunks kill an estimated 70 percent of insects considered harmful to humans. They are also carrion eaters and help keep roadways and neighborhoods clean.

A beaver gnawing the bark of a poplar log for food.

# Beavers

The beaver is North America's largest rodent, growing to 4 feet (1.2 m) long (including tail) and weighing over 60 pounds (27 kg). Its webbed hind feet and powerful rear legs help the animal propel through water while barely making a ripple. The dark brown fur is waterproof, like the muskrat's, and provides protection and buoyancy for the animal's aquatic existence. Their short forefeet and heavy claws have amazing dexterity for feeding, grooming, digging and lodge construction. When a beaver is frightened, it slaps its large flat tail with a smack against the water and dives. Beavers don't see well, but have well-developed senses of smell and hearing. Like otters, their noses and ears have valves that close tightly under water. They also have a valve in their mouth behind the incisor teeth, which allows them to gnaw while underwater.

Beavers prefer fast-growing trees such as poplar, willow, cottonwood and alder. While tree felling seems destructive, it usually allows for bushier and additional growth of other saplings. The beaver's diet is mostly woody tissues (and some aquatic plants), so their digestive system is specialized to digest cellulose. Their respiratory system is also specialized, with strong lungs and low heart rates so they can stay under water for nearly 20 minutes at a time. The beaver has two chisel-like incisors in its upper and lower jaws that are very effective for tree cutting. These teeth are both self-sharpening and ever-growing, which means the beaver must use them continually.

Beaver chew.

### One smart rodent

Beavers know how to control the direction a tree will fall. First the beaver gnaws a notch at a comfortable height on one side of the tree, then goes to the opposite side and gnaws another notch a few inches below the first. The beaver continues chewing the wood away from between the two notches until the tree falls. The position of the notches dictates the direction the tree will fall. Beavers fell most trees toward the lake so they don't have to carry branches too far overland; the lower and deeper notch is usually lakeside.

Beavers live near rivers, streams, small lakes and marshes, and typically pile tree limbs and other debris together to make a large, bulky, dome-shaped lodge with one or more exits in deep water. Within the lodge is a bark-lined, above-water chamber that serves as the colony's main center of activities, including feeding and daycare. Sometimes beavers burrow from 6 to 20 feet (1.8–6 m) into the bank to make a den instead. Bank dens are often extended to the water's edge to form conical lodges called "half houses." Both lodges and bank dens are regularly reinforced with sticks and mud.

Beavers reproduce once a year, with mating beginning in January when rivers and wetlands are covered with ice. After three to three and a half months, three to four young are born with their eyes open, fully furred, able to swim, with their incisor teeth visible. The young usually remain with the family unit or colony for up to two years before leaving to establish a territory and colony of their own. The average lifespan of a beaver is three to four years. The main predators of adult beavers are wolves, bears, coyotes, lynxes and wolverines; owls, mink and hawks are known to prey on young beaver. Humans take their share of beaver for its valuable fur as well, selling for up to $150 for a good quality pelt.

Beavers play a major role in the management of river and wetland habitats. Their dams, and the subsequent formation of pools, create wetland habitat for a large number of highly beneficial wildlife species. Almost half of endangered and threatened species in North America rely upon wetlands.

Beavers use only the branches of large trees, conveniently leaving the main stem for us to cut up for firewood. Felled trees are important to the forest, adding to the soil profile over time. Beavers also make an important contribution to the balance of the ecosystem, for example, by raising downstream groundwater levels to help provide moisture to plants.

> Beaver fever: the reddish-brown water of beaver ponds often portends *Giardia,* or "beaver fever." See the **Swimming** chapter for the sickening details.

## Controlling beaver activities

Sometimes our aesthetic values clash with the single-minded rodent engineers, and we want to save our trees. Most cutting occurs within 20 to 30 feet (6–9 m) of shore. Also, while beavers prefer certain tree species, they do not necessarily take them in order of preference. Leave the trees that are already down, or use them for firewood, and protect the "precious" ones. If you are replacing trees along shorelines, use less palatable species, like conifers. For more specific methods of protecting your trees, see **Living with wildlife** at pages 192 to 195.

Relocating beavers is often not effective, at least over the long term. New litters of beavers in the area eventually must find habitat and build dens away from their parents, and sooner or later, another family of beavers ends up on your doorstep. Before moving any beavers, contact your local natural resources government agency for permission. They may help remove the beavers or recommend the most humane traps to use.

# The busy beaver

While beavers are best known for the dams they build, their activity also results in other feats of engineering, such as canals and ponds.

Beaver dams are generally about 5 feet (1.5 m) high, but some rise as high as 10 feet (3 m). They are usually more than 10 feet (3 m) wide at the base, and narrower at the top. A beaver dam more than 1,000 feet (300 m) long was found in Rocky Mountain National Park, Colorado.

## Beaver ponds

Beavers are masters at making dams large enough to create large ponds and small, shallow lakes. Beaver ponds attract fish, ducks and other aquatic animals. They are favorite breeding areas for several species of baitfish such as minnows. However, in most small beaver ponds, wood and leaf debris, much of it left by the beavers, turns the water brown and oxygen levels slowly drop over time. Only fish that can tolerate higher temperatures remain, and they often congregate at the dam near areas of higher flow. Although the dams cause local flooding, they also help control runoff and reduce flooding downstream. The ponds eventually fill with sediment, the animals move to a new location, and the abandoned area becomes meadowland.

## Beaver dams

Beavers build dams to widen the area and increase the depth of water around their homes. Some scientists believe that the construction is the beaver's response to the sound of running water. These rodents use sticks, poles, mud, brushwood and stones to construct what humans build using cement, a gaggle of engineers and millions of dollars.

As time goes by, the beaver repairs and adds to the dam. Floating material lodges there, and vegetation growing on the top adds its roots to strengthen the dam. For insurance, the beaver may build a smaller dam downstream in order to back up some water against the original dam, decreasing the pressure of water on it from the other side.

## Beaver canals

Although the beaver is a powerful swimmer, it has difficulty dragging logs and branches over the ground. Ever clever, colonies of beavers will dig canals from the pond to a grove of trees. Such canals are up to 3 feet (1 m) wide and deep and often a few hundred yards long, perfect for floating timber toward the pond.

## Beaver meadows

When the beavers have moved on, the neglected dam eventually breaks, leaving a stream flowing through the meadow. The soil is moist and rich. Reeds and then meadow grasses quickly grow, creating homes for birds such as red-winged blackbirds.

This shallow beaver pond is fringed by beaver meadows.

# Porcupines

A porcupine is covered by over 30,000 long sharp quills.

A robust rodent, the porcupine is about the size of a small dog, but the porcupine's rump and tail are covered with over 30,000 long sharp thick quills, 2½ inches (6.4 cm) in length, each with tiny, scale-like barbs that project backward. The front half of the body is covered with long, coarse guard hairs as well. Slow on land, porcupines climb trees with their powerful legs and long, curved claws. The tracks of the porcupine are distinctive: the tail leaves a corn-broom pattern between the pidgin-toed, clawed prints. Porcupines feed on twigs, leaves, buds and green plants in the summer, and on the inner bark of trees (especially spruce and hemlock) in the winter. Its main predators are the fisher, bobcat and coyote.

How do porcupines make love? Very carefully! The mating rituals of these prickly creatures are bizarre. In November to December, the male tours the area, rubbing objects with his nose. Males often sing during this period and become more aggressive with other males.

The male requires a period of close association with the female before he mates so he approaches the female, smells her all over and they rub noses. Then he rears up on his hind legs, penis erect. If the female is not ready, she runs away. If she is, she also rears up, faces the male, belly-to-belly, and then the male sprays the female with a strong stream of urine, dousing her from head to foot. Occasionally the female may either object vocally by barking, snorting or groaning, bash him repeatedly with her front paws, threaten to bite, shake off the urine and run away. If she is "in the mood," the courtship routine can occur several times in the days or weeks before they finally get down to it.

After a gestation period of 210 days in a rocky den, burrow or hollow log, one pup is born, eyes open, mobile and covered in hair and quills.

> Porcupines have a ravenous appetite for salt and glue and will chew on any salt-stained tools and lumber with glue, such as plywood.

## Porcupine quill first aid

Porcupine quills are very sharp and appear to have scales or shingles that point backward, like a rasp. There are no "barbs" on the shaft or end of the stiff, hollow quill, which will migrate through tissues if the entire quill is not removed.

Some dogs seem to be more prone than others to porcupine encounters; German shepherds and their crosses accounted for 18 percent of quill removal in one study of 296 dogs (57 breeds).

The mouth is a common spot for dogs to get quills as they try to bite the porcupine. If your pet has quills in the mouth, eyes or throat, take the animal to a veterinarian as soon as possible where it will receive the benefits of sedation and anesthesia. The risk of complications increases with increased time between quill injury and visit to the vet. The more time a quill remains in a dog, the more time it has to migrate deeper into tissues. A quill can travel a long way, from the chest to the heart tissue, for instance. It may resurface days, weeks or months later.

If your pet has just a few quills in other areas, you should be able to remove them yourself. You will need a pair of pliers. Cover the dog's eyes, grab the quill firmly and as close to the skin as possible with the pliers. However, do it fairly gently. Don't give a quick, sharp powerful tug. Give a gentle pull with continuous force. Speak softly and do not panic or your pet will panic if it hasn't already.

If a small part of the tip of the quill remains behind after you remove the quill, it could cause a problem. Consult your vet. Mark the spot on the dog with white-out or a black marker so as to quickly locate the broken quill if it needs to be surgically removed.

Don't be surprised if your dog goes back for a second time, but it's not necessarily for revenge: the delayed pain reaction quills provoke can mean the dog does not associate the porcupine with the pain.

### The prickly truth

Porcupines can't shoot their quills—if your dog comes home with a nose full of them, he simply got way too close.

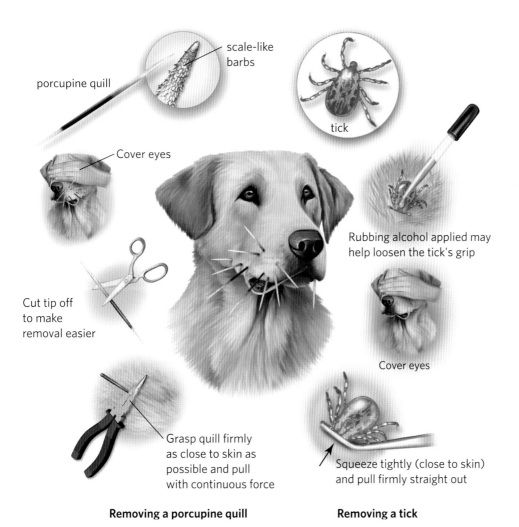

scale-like barbs

porcupine quill

tick

Cover eyes

Rubbing alcohol applied may help loosen the tick's grip

Cover eyes

Cut tip off to make removal easier

Grasp quill firmly as close to skin as possible and pull with continuous force

Squeeze tightly (close to skin) and pull firmly straight out

**Removing a porcupine quill**

**Removing a tick**

Removing quills and ticks from animals. Read more about ticks and Lyme disease at page 187.

# Chipmunks and other small rodents

A chipmunk.

## Eastern red squirrel

You may know the red squirrel from its cheeky chatter. Perched in a tree, it scolds you, then jumps from tree to tree in acrobatic leaps, descending to the ground only to search for or bury food.

Eastern red squirrels live in coniferous, mixed and deciduous forests. They breed during the spring and summer, nesting in tree cavities or woodpecker holes. Born blind and hairless, by eight weeks the young are completely weaned. Red squirrels are loners, active during the day all year long, only occasionally sharing quarters during the winter. They eat nuts, buds, seeds, mushrooms and fruits such as blueberries. Some red squirrels live as long as nine years. Their main predators are snakes, hawks, owls, foxes and other small mammals.

## Chipmunk

Chipmunks rarely climb trees: they generally scoot along the ground with tail erect. When you see these small, striped rodents popping out of dens between rocks or tree roots, or running across your deck, their cheeks are usually bursting with food. They have special internal cheek pouches designed for storing food as they gather it from the ground.

Chipmunks periodically emerge from their burrows to find food in the winter. They eat nuts—acorns, hickory nuts, beechnuts and walnuts—small seeds, berries, wild grapes, fungi, and invertebrates (snails, earthworms, insects). Litters of two to seven are born in May, a second litter often following. Chipmunks live from two to four years, if they elude snakes, hawks, foxes, bobcats and weasels.

The eastern gray squirrel is more urban and prefers the parks and backyards of town and city folk. There are two color phases, gray and black, the black phase being more common in Ontario and Quebec.

*Right* The eastern red squirrel.

# Groundhog

Also known as woodchuck, the groundhog has a bulky body, short limbs and sharp, sturdy claws. Groundhogs are common in woods adjacent to wide open spaces or rocky slopes. They like to live under cottages or decks, in garages and sheds or under woodpiles. They have an extensive burrow system, 15 to 25 feet (about 5-8 m) long, 2 to 4 feet (60–120 cm) underground. The main groundhog nesting chamber is usually at the end of the burrow, which has a main entrance and a side entrance marked by mounds of fresh earth around the openings.

Groundhogs move slowly, relying heavily on their keen eyesight and hearing to warn them of approaching would-be predators. They are most active by day. However, when the warmer spring and summer months arrive, they spend their days in the cool burrows, rising to feed during the very early morning and at dusk. They begin hibernation mid-October and emerge in February and March when breeding begins.

Groundhogs eat grass, seeds, leaves, flowers, fruit, eggs and some insects. Two groundhogs are capable of devouring a garden almost overnight. Their main predators are wolves, dogs, coyotes, bobcats, foxes and humans.

# Muskrat

The muskrat got its name from the musk glands located on the underside of its tail. Secretions from the glands warn other muskrats to leave the territory. Native Americans call it "musquash "or "ondatra"; others call it "mud cat" or "mud beaver." These medium-sized rodents have nostrils shaped like the number 7, which allow them to recover and inhale oxygen remaining from recently exhaled breath, and remain under water for at least 15 minutes.

Muskrats live in marshes and bogs, and near rivers and streams. They build their "lodges" in the riverbanks out of cattails, other aquatic plants and small branches held together with thick layers of mud that add insulation for winter hibernation. Tunnels with underwater entrances are hollowed out inside for quick escapes and for easy access in and out of the lodge. Muskrats also build a feeding hut near the main lodge, where they dine on a wide variety of plants and animals, including cattail roots, legumes, grasses, grains, garden crops, clams, crayfish, frogs, fish, and dead animals. Look for piles of clam shells. Muskrats are preyed on by foxes, mink, owls, herons and hawks.

Many thousands of muskrats (*above*) are trapped for pelts that range in price from $4.50 to $7.00 U.S., depending upon fur condition and color, black being the choice of fur buyers. The meat of the muskrat is also prized, at least in the southern United States.

If the groundhog sees its shadow on February 2, winter will be extended six weeks; if no shadow, spring will be early.

and munch on ripening tomatoes, beans, peas, cucumbers, and other fruit. In the winter, mice make runways below the snow cover to their food source.

## Hantavirus in mice

Hantavirus Pulmonary Syndrome (HPS) is a severe viral infection of the respiratory system spread by saliva, feces or urine of mice, especially deer mice. Human cases are rare, but you should always take precautions when coming in contact with rodents. The virus can be spread in the air as mist or dust, when droppings or nests are stirred up and inhaled. Humans can be infected by handling infected rodents but they are not known—nor are cats, dogs and farm animals—to transmit the disease.

There is no cure for the hantavirus. Symptoms are flu-like and include fever, shortness of breath, chills and muscle and body aches one to six weeks after infection. HPS is potentially fatal and immediate intensive care is essential once symptoms appear.

Prevention is the best approach. Take these steps to minimize contact with rodents:

- Clean up infested areas wearing latex rubber gloves.
- Thoroughly wet contaminated areas with a disinfectant to deactivate the virus; mixing 1½ cups (12 oz or 240 ml) of household bleach in 1 gallon (4 L) of water is effective.
- After everything has been wetted down, use a damp towel, mop or sponge to take up contaminated materials.
- If the area is dusty or if sweeping up or vacuuming up droppings, urine or nesting materials, wear an approved mask.
- Spray any dead mice with disinfectant.
- Disinfect latex gloves and double-bag them and all cleaning materials and dead mice and burn, bury or dispose in an appropriate waste disposal system. Wash your hands thoroughly with soap and warm water.

Mice can run up almost any vertical surface, smooth or rough, cross and balance on wires or ropes, jump straight up at least one foot (30 cm), squeeze through openings slightly larger than ¼ inch (7 mm), and swim. Don't try freezing them out; they'll be running around down to 14° F (-10° C) and looking for food. A pair of house mice can eat about 4 pounds (113 g) of food and present you with about 18,000 fecal droppings in six months.

*Far right* The Norway rat.

# Mouse

Most mice you'll meet inside are house mice, *Mus musculus,* but the white-footed mouse and the deer mouse also visit cottages. White-footed and deer mice have white feet and bellies, large ears and eyes, and tails as long as their bodies. They are dark gray to nearly black, weigh twice as much and lack the mousey odor of house mice.

White-footed and deer mice are more commonly found in open, grassy fields or brushy and wooded areas, spending the winter as a family group in a nest made of fur, feathers, shredded cloth, stems, leaves, branches and roots, built underground in old burrows, under boards, hollow logs or in buildings—occupied or vacant. They will explore in the winter for food, leaving footprints in a square pattern. Breeding occurs from spring to fall, with two to four litters of one to eight young per year.

The meadow jumping mouse and the woodland jumping mouse are also very common near cottages, but rarely enter the building. They eat the bark and roots of young trees, dig up potatoes, carrots, beets and parsnips,

# Vole

The eastern meadow vole and the pine vole look like big mice with tiny ears, short tails, and beady black eyes. Voles spend most of their time below ground in burrows. They use a maze of above-ground runways that lead to several burrow openings, each about 1½ inch to 2 inches (3.8 to 5 cm) in diameter. The runways are usually hidden beneath a protective layer of grass or ground cover, including wood piles, shingles, lumber and snow.

Voles are active day and night, all year around. They make underground nests of grass, stems, and leaves, and feed on grass and other plant roots and crowns. In preparation for winter, voles store seeds, tubers, bulbs and rhizomes in their tunnels in late summer and fall.

# Rat

The Norway rat, also called the brown rat, is the most common rat, ranging all the way from Hudson Bay south to Gulf of Mexico, coast to coast. It lives everywhere, in buildings, sewers, backyards, farms, fields, boat houses, attics, barbeques, basements, garbage dumps, you name it. The yearly cost to control rats runs in the millions.

These clever rodents can be quite large, up to 17 inches (44 cm) long, but average 7 to 10 inches (18–25 cm), the tail adding another 50 percent. They are omnivorous, feeding on a variety of plant and animal materials, are prolific breeders, producing litters of two to fourteen after three week's gestation, and live two to three years. Owls, housecats, dogs and other animals prey on rats, but can't control rat populations.

# Mousetraps

Mousetraps can be divided into two types: live traps and kill traps. Both need to be baited with food (cheese, peanut butter, or peanut butter with rolled oats), or nesting material (cotton batten or shredded toilet paper). Larger versions of these traps can be bought for catching rats.

## Live traps

The various types of live traps all work on the same principle. They are box-like (some look like houses), made of metal or plastic, and one or both ends have a door that is hinged and linked to a tripping mechanism. When the mouse steps on the baited paddle, the tripping mechanism releases the door(s), trapping the mouse inside. Closed doors do not mean a mouse has been trapped; some mice are fast and will escape before the door closes. See-through plastic traps make it easy to see when a mouse has been caught.

## Kill traps

The most common kind of killing trap is a snap-back trap. Bait them with cheese, peanut butter, or add oatmeal, sunflower seed, or rolled oats to the peanut butter. Put traps at each place where you see mouse droppings. Use two to three traps each time. You may have to "tweak" the trap if it isn't closing properly, but be careful—the trap hurts if you get your fingers caught. If there are no mice droppings, place the traps along the sides of runways and perpendicular to the runways.

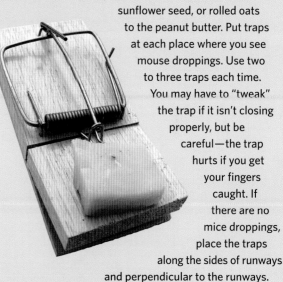

## Poisons

Beware of poisons such as warfarin, chlorophacione, brodifacoum, diphacinone, and bromadiolone, which can kill pets that eat the bait or the poisoned mice.

For helpful tips on mouse- and rat-proofing your cottage, see **Living with wildlife** later in this chapter, at pages 192 to 195.

# Shrews and moles

A hairy-tailed mole emerges from a tunnel.

Shrews and moles have small, sharp teeth, small eyes, long snouts and flat, five-toed claw-bearing feet used for digging in the leaf litter or deeply into the soil. Although they can cause considerable damage to lawns, their antics are often blamed on other creatures.

Shrews are 3½ to 6 inches (9–15 cm) long, and grayish or brownish with a pointed snout. They prefer moist habitats such as forest floors, marshes, swamps and bogs, as well as tundra and rocky areas. Voracious feeders, shrews eat their own weight daily in earthworms, insects, grubs, snails, other invertebrates and soft vegetation. They are active all year long, making small, round holes in leaf litter and using surface tunnels of mice and voles, so are hard to spot; watch for their corkscrew-shaped feces. The most common shrews you'll see are the water shrew, smoky shrew, arctic shrew and short-tailed shrew, which makes flattened runways through leaf mold and whose poisonous saliva paralyzes its prey; and North America's smallest living mammal at 2 inches (5 cm) without the tail, the pygmy shrew.

Moles are usually larger than shrews and have big front feet with powerful claws. They burrow close to the surface, often leaving visible ridges and hills with dirt removed from their burrows. They also make furrows with an opening into their burrow somewhere along its length. The mounds are most common during periods when the soil is damp, generally spring and autumn. Moles have very poor sight and feed mainly on earthworms and insect larvae that they find by touch and smell. The most common are the star-nosed mole, eastern mole and hairy-tailed mole.

The northern short-tailed shrew is active all year.

# Bats

Be happy to know that bats are the primary consumer of night-flying insects. A single little brown bat swallows hundreds of beetles, wasps and similar-sized insects each hour.

Bats are the only mammals that fly. Their wings are made of thin membranes that are actually double-layered extensions of body skin, connecting all limbs, digits and the tail. The arms have a thumb and fingers and are located halfway along the wing at the end of the arm. The middle finger is the longest; the thumb is free.

Bats roost by day, hanging upside down by their feet in attics, rock crevices, thick brush, the hollows of trees, caves, or behind shutters and clutter in sheds, garages and other buildings. Some species form colonies while others are solitary. In winter, bats either hibernate or migrate south. If they hibernate they seek shelters where temperatures remain somewhat stable, as in mines or caves. If the weather is warms enough, they may awaken to seek water, defecate and even breed.

Mating generally occurs from November through March. In the females of some hibernating species the sperm or embryo can lie dormant for several months before fertilization or development begins. After the breeding season, pregnant females seek areas with high daytime temperatures in which to raise their young. Females often assemble in "maternity roosts" away from the males before giving birth. The young bats, usually two to a litter, are born in late May to early June, or even July if the embryo had lain dormant. The baby bats are nursed in the roost, weaned at three or four weeks, then leave the roost for their first flights at four to six weeks. Some bats have lifespans as long as 18 years. Little brown bats have been known to live over 30 years.

A roosting bat.

Bats, in eastern North America at least, feed exclusively on insects, especially beetles and wasps, which they capture in flight, either in their mouths or in the "dragnet" of their tail membrane. Bats, like birds, provide a natural check on insects, with birds feeding on day-flying insects and bats on night-flying insects.

The dragnet is a membrane between the hind legs and helps the bat to maneuver in flight and to scoop up insects. The wings are used not only for flying but for crawling, catching prey and grooming.

> Encourage bats to move into your neighborhood. They won't hurt you, and they play a vital role in controlling many insect species. Unfortunately, bats feed very little on mosquitoes, so rearing bats as a means to control mosquito populations is futile.

## Bad rap on bats

Bats don't carry lice and bacteria; they are actually very clean animals. Contrary to popular belief,

- they don't try to nest in peoples' hair;
- they don't thirst for human blood;
- they don't eat through attics;
- they don't interfere with birds;
- nor do they attack pets and children.

In fact, bats play a major role in maintaining the balance of nature.

# Building a bat house

Install bat houses before the bats return in spring. Mount them on buildings or poles for protection from predators at least 12 to 15 feet (4 m) above ground, away from bright lights. Brick or stone buildings with proper solar exposure are excellent choices, especially under the eaves.

Bats find houses more quickly if located along forest or water edges where bats tend to fly; however, they should be placed at least 20 to 25 feet (7–8 m) from the nearest tree branches, wires or other potential perches for aerial predators. Wasps can also be a problem but the use of ¾-inch (2 cm) roosting spaces tends to reduce wasp tenants. If wasp nests do accumulate, remove them in early spring before either wasps or bats return.

This diagram is for a single roosting partition. Two roosting areas can be made by building them back to back. A roof is optional but recommended. Use a cedar board 1 by 3 by 28 inches (2.5 × 7.5 × 70 cm) for the roof. Do not use pressure-treated wood. Any hardware must be rust protected (galvanized, coated or stainless). Caulk all seams, especially around the roof.

For the exterior, apply three coats of exterior grade, water-based paint or stain. Use black paint where average high temperatures in July are less than 85° F (29° C); dark colors (such as dark brown or dark gray) where they are 85 to 95° F (29 to 35° C), medium colors where they are 95 to 100° F (35 to 38° C) and white or light colors where they exceed 100° F (38° C).

For the interior, use two coats dark, exterior-grade, water-based stain. Apply stain after creating scratches or grooves, since paint may fill the grooves, making them unusable.

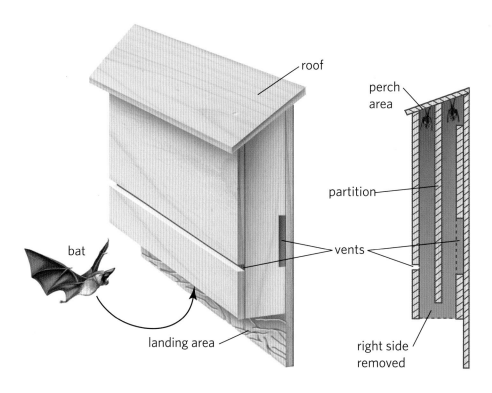

**Side view**

# Snakes

Snakes move by pushing against objects with specialized scales on their bellies called scutes. The scutes act much like tire treads, gripping the ground and giving the snake the traction needed to move forward. Scales cover the rest of the body and function to prevent excessive dehydration by retaining body moisture. The scales contain the pigments that form the color patterns of snakes. A single transparent scale covers the eye. Snakes lack ears, but "listen" by sensing vibrations through the bones in their heads. Snakes can also smell by "tasting" the air and ground with their forked tongue, which contains a specialized taste organ in the roof of the mouth called Jacobson's Organ.

Most snakes mate in the spring after they emerge from hibernation. Depending upon the species, snakes can reproduce by either laying their eggs or by hatching the eggs internally and bearing live young. Most snakes in the temperate zone, including water snakes, garter snakes, brown snakes, copperheads, cottonmouths and rattlesnakes, bear living young instead of laying eggs.

All snakes are carnivores, preying upon a variety of different animals including other snakes, fish, frogs, salamanders, rodents, insects, birds and slugs. Snakes eat their prey whole, dislocating their jaws to swallow any prey larger than their own head. Some snakes actively pursue their prey, while others remain motionless and well camouflaged, striking unsuspecting prey when they wander by.

Snakes are preyed upon by mammals, birds, and even other snakes, and have evolved varied defense strategies to avoid them. Some have cryptic coloration, camouflaging themselves against the background. Some snakes "freeze" when they sense danger, a behavior saving them from watchful hawks and owls. Some snakes "bluff" their would-be predators by vibrating their tails, making a rattling sound that would discourage almost any predator. The eastern hog-nosed snake makes itself appear larger and more threatening by flattening its neck, and hissing loudly. If this doesn't work, the snake will play dead by lying on its back and discharging a foul smell from specialized glands.

Like all snakes, the redbelly snake has specialized scales on its belly, which give it the traction needed to slither along the ground — and climb trees.

### Changeable reptiles

Reptiles are "cold blooded," having a body temperature that is the same as their surroundings. They regulate their body temperature by basking in the sun or seeking shade and reducing activity when they are too hot. This explains why snakes tend to be more active during the middle of the day in the spring and fall when evenings are cool, and more active in the morning and evening during the hot summer months. All reptiles have scales. Reptiles grow by shedding their skin two to four times annually.

# Common snakes

Eastern garter snake

Northern ribbon snake

Brown snake

Eastern milk snake

| SNAKE | LENGTH | DESCRIPTION | HABITAT |
|---|---|---|---|
| Eastern garter snake, *Thamnophis sirtalis sirtalis* | 19–28" (48–70 cm) | black with three yellow stripes, the lateral stripes on the second and third row of scales from the belly. Some individuals lack striping and are entirely black | marshes, along streams, fields, woodlands, urban parks and yards |
| Northern ribbon snake, *Thamnophis sauritus* | 18–26" (45–65 cm) | black with three bright yellow stripes, the lateral stripes on the third and fourth row of scales from the belly; whitish half moon-shaped spot in front of each eye | wet meadows, marshes, bogs, ponds, weedy shorelines and swamps |
| Northern water snake, *Nerodia sipedon sipedon* | 24–39" (60–100 cm) | gray-brown to dark gray with brown, saddle-shaped markings down the back and sides of the snake, especially distinctive on younger snakes and fades as the snake gets older (see the Swimming chapter for photo) | rivers, streams, swamps, marshes, bogs and lakes |
| Redbelly snake, *Storeria occipitomaculata* | 8–12" (20–30 cm) | brown, gray or black with a bright red-orange belly and three light spots on the nape of the neck (see previous page for photo) | woodlands, sometimes inhabiting urban areas, or hiding under logs and rocks and in woodpiles during the day |
| Brown snake, *Storeria dekayi* | 8–14" (20–35 cm) | brown with two rows of small, black spots bordering a paler stripe down the center of the back and has a black blotch behind each eye | moist, forested uplands and lowlands, old fields, meadows, and urban areas, hiding under logs, rocks and debris |
| Eastern milk snake, *Lampropeltis triangulum triangulum* | 20–35" (50–90 cm) | gray to brown with reddish-, brownish- or black-bordered markings on back and sides and has a light neck collar<br><br>* This species is often mistaken for the Massasauga rattlesnake because it vibrates its tail when threatened | woodlands, fields and farms, old buildings in urban areas, hidden under dry leaf litter, stones and boards |

Eastern Massasauga rattlesnake

# Snake bites

There are some simple guidelines to help you to identify venomous snakes. The guidelines will not work with exotic species. Poisonous snakes in the temperate zone tend to be

- very heavy-bodied, or appear "fat,"
- have broad, spade-shaped heads that are distinctly wider than their narrow necks (the heads of non-venomous snakes are typically about the same width as their bodies), and
- the pupils of the venomous snakes are usually vertical slits rather than round.

**Caution** These guidelines are not always completely reliable. For example, water snakes can be rather stout but are not venomous; some species of snakes will flatten their heads when bluffing, giving the head a spade-like shape as well; most snakes after having had a good meal will appear fat.

Don't try to handle or kill a snake that you believe may be venomous. Simply keep at a safe distance and move on your way. Snakes do not actively seek out people and bite them. Given the chance, snakes will almost always try to escape an encounter; if you leave them alone, they will leave you alone. Avoid the head when handling dead snakes; a snake's reflexes can remain functional hours after death.

If you know there are venomous snakes in your area, follow these guidelines:

- Wear high-topped, leather hiking boots.
- Do not reach under rocks or logs, and do not step over logs. Step on them, then over them.
- Be alert and survey the area ahead of you, not just the area below your feet.
- If you are bitten, stay calm, avoid excessive activity, and seek medical care as soon as possible. While it is helpful to identify the snake, do not waste time or risk being bitten again by capturing or killing the snake. Do not make any incisions at the bite.
- Non-venomous snakebites should be washed with soap and water to reduce the risk of infection.

**Relax** There is only one poisonous snake, the eastern Massasauga rattlesnake, in the northern part of the temperate zone and it lives mainly in wetlands where people rarely go. Cottonmouth and northern copperhead snakes are restricted to the southernmost part of the temperate zone and they too are rarely seen.

## Eastern Massasauga rattlesnake

The adult eastern Massasauga rattlesnake is 20 to 28 inches (50–70 cm) long, and gray with a row of brown-black markings down the back and alternating blotches down the sides. It has nine enlarged scales on the top of the head and a rattle on the tip of the tail. The species prefers wetland environments such as marshes, bogs, swamps, but is also found in dry upland areas in summer. It is quite rare now, and is the only rattler that cottagers are likely to see. The species has been officially designated as "threatened" in Canada.

# Cottage bird life

Common loon.

## Loon

With its ruby-red eye, black-and-white checkered back, glossy black head and white necklace, the common loon is among the most striking of birds. Loons swim low in the water, can stay under water for almost a minute and dive to depths over 260 feet (80 m). Many of their bones are solid, rather than hollow like most other birds, and aid in sinking. Their powerful legs are placed far back on their bodies, allowing for excellent movement in water but making them clumsy and shambling on land. Loons hold their heads directly in line with their necks during diving to help reduce drag.

In flight, loons have a humpbacked profile, with head and neck held low. The dense bones make lift-off challenging; loons usually have to run a great distance on the surface of the water before gaining enough speed to take flight. The wingspan is 4 to 5 feet (1.2–1.5 m) and loons can fly at average speeds of 75 miles per hour (120 km/h) during migration.

The loon spends long rest periods almost motionless on the water, occasionally rousing itself to stretch a leg or wing. Often it will peer underwater, moving its head from side to side to locate prey. When it spots a fish, the loon aims and dives, first compressing its feathers and forcing air out of air sacs to quietly and swiftly slide into the water. At night, loons sleep well off shore for protection from predators (fish, snapping turtles, gulls, eagles and crows).

Common loons generally build their nests close to the water, the optimal site being completely surrounded by water, such as an island, muskrat house, half-submerged log, or vacated beaver house. Loons reuse the same sites from one year to the next. Both the male and female loons build the nest using a variety of plant materials. Toward the end of June two chicks covered in brown-black down hatch. The chicks are fed exclusively by their parents until about eight weeks of age, diving for some of their own food by 11 or 12 weeks, when they are basically independent. By migration time, the young are strong and able to look after themselves, and leave soon after the adults. The life expectancy of the loon is 15 to 30 years.

Boaters beware: the survival of loons depends on chicks surviving for the flight south. However, parents will leave the nest if your watercraft comes within 150 feet (45 m) of it, leaving the eggs without warmth or protection. Young chicks are not waterproof and cannot dive. If washed or scared from their nest, they can drown or be run over by watercraft. To avoid their natural predators, loon parents move the chicks away from the nests, out into more open waters. Unfortunately this often puts the chicks into the direct path of boats going for joyrides or pulling tubers or water-skiers.

# American crow and common raven

The American crow, *Corvus brachyrynchosis,* is an intelligent, adaptable and opportunistic creature. Adults measure about 17 to 21 inches (43–53 cm) in length, are charcoal black and have a fan-shaped tail. Its relative, the common raven, *Corvus corvax,* tends to be larger (20–27 inches, or 51–69 cm) and has a wedge-shaped tail. Their flight patterns are also different: the crow has a steady flapping flight, seldom gliding for more than two to three seconds; the raven soars. Crows *caw-caw,* while the raven's call is a deep, guttural *wonk-wonk.*

The American crow.

Crows gather in small groups (two to eight birds) in the summer, but band together in huge roosts of up to thousands or even two million birds in the winter. During feeding, one or two crows perch at high places as sentinels, watching for signs of danger and warning the rest of the flock. They eat a variety of plant and animal food, including seeds, garbage, insects and mice, and the eggs and young of other birds. Crows are often criticized for their messy eating habits. However, the eggs and young they eat tend to be weak and feeble; the insects they feed on include injurious insects, such as grasshoppers and cutworms; they alert other animals in the neighborhood when danger approaches. They also clean up road kills. However, the American crow is not a specialized scavenger and must wait for other animals to open a carcass or for bacteria to decompose the carcass before eating it.

American crows do not breed until they are at least two years old, most not until they are four or more. The young generally stay with their parents for several years. Some families consist of 15 individuals and contain young from five different years.

The American crow appears to be the biggest victim of West Nile virus, a disease recently introduced to North America. Crows die within one week of infection, and few seem able to survive exposure. No other North American bird is dying at the same rate from the disease, and the loss of crows in some areas has been severe.

Although the common raven is the largest of the birds classified as songbirds, their raucous songs are hardly musical. The raven is similar to the American crow, with some differences, as described above. In addition, the common raven has elongated and pointed shaggy feathers on the throat. Common ravens will hide their stored food under rocks, in small holes in the ground or in cavities in trees and conceal their stash with leaves, twigs or other debris.

> How do tell the difference between a crow and a raven?
>
> A raven has one more pinion in its primary flight feathers than does a crow. It's simply a matter of a pinion!

## Loon language

Unforgettable loon calls are synonymous with life at the lake. Loons have four distinct calls—the tremolo, hoot, wail and yodel—which are used in combinations to communicate with other loons.

- The tremolo sounds like a crazy laugh and signals alarm or worry, annoyance or greeting.

- The hoot is a short *hoo,* used by family members to locate each other and check on their well-being.

- The wail is a social call. Mates use it to regain contact during night reprising and in answer to another loon's tremolo.

- The yodel, given only by the male, is a long (up to six seconds), rising call with repetitive notes in the middle and is used to defend territory from encroaching males. The yodel is different for each bird and can be used to identify individual loons.

The blue jay (*left*) and the cormorant (*right*).

## Moody blue jay

The shape of this mouthy jay's crest indicates the bird's mood. If the crest

- is fully erect, forming a prominent peak, the bird is highly excited and aggressive;
- points forward, the bird is greatly surprised or excited;
- bristles out like a bottle brush, the bird is frightened;
- is laid flat, the bird is feeding among other jays, ready to flee, or quietly resting.

# Blue jay

The blue jay is one of the more easily identified birds — the blue on its crest, back, wings and tail are real giveaways. Blue pigment is unknown in birds; the blue feather color results from the refraction of light through a microscopic substance or structure in the feather. If the feather is crushed, the blue color disappears. Adult jays go through a complete change of plumage between June and September. During this molting period, blue jays may be seen anting — picking up and applying ants (or other materials such as fruits, tobacco, mustard, vinegar) to the underside of its wings so that the bird can then preen and tidy its feathers in the process. Either this peculiar behavior relieves the skin irritation of new feather growth or the ant's excretions act as a needed irritant.

The blue jay prefers mixed wood and deciduous forest areas. It is non-migratory but may wander about in small bands after the breeding season, living from 10 to 15 years in the wild. Blue jays are well known for eating eggs and young of other birds but the bulk of the jay's diet consists of wild fruits, acorns, hazelnuts, beechnuts, corn and other grains, and insects.

The blue jay has adapted well in settled areas, as long as there are a few trees. In forested retreats they are usually more wary than the blue jays we see in towns and cities.

# Double-crested cormorant

Sometimes referred to as "crow-ducks," this large, greenish-black waterbird with a slender hooked-tip bill, orange facial skin, and two small tufts of feathers on either side of its head is frequently seen standing erect on rocks or posts, sometimes in a spread-eagle posture. It swims low in the water, often with only its head and neck exposed and can be distinguished from loons by the distinct upward angle of its head and bill. Flocks of double-crested cormorants often fly in V formations.

After colonizing the Great Lakes from 1913 to the 1950s, the cormorant population was devastated by the effects of chemicals, especially DDT. Human disturbance and nest destruction contributed to the decline.

With spectacular resurgence of the species on the Great Lakes, especially Georgian Bay, the birds now are appearing in large numbers in more inland lakes. Ample food supply, lowered concentrations of toxic contaminants, and protection by federal and state laws have helped their recovery.

Anglers and commercial harvesters are now concerned with the quantity of fish cormorants consume. To date, attempts to control exploding cormorant populations have met with little success.

# Hunted birds

These ground-dwelling birds are favorite game birds, and are also hunted by natural predators. Grouse have feathered legs and feed on buds, berries, seeds and some insects. Partridges and pheasants lack feathered legs and they feed on insects, grains and berries. The turkey is the largest upland game bird and is the species from which all domestic turkeys descended.

## Ruffed grouse

The *thump thump thump* noise that echoes through the woods like a deep heartbeat is the male ruffed grouse announcing his territory. He usually stands on a log, called a drumming log, and beats his wings against the air to create a vacuum, as lightning does when it makes thunder. The drummer only uses the drumming log as a stage for his display; he does not strike the log to make the noise. He drums more frequently in spring, advertising his address to hens. Males are aggressively territorial, defending woodland territories of 6 to 10 acres (2–4 ha) in extent, allowing one or two hens to occupy the area.

Ruffed grouse are slightly larger than pigeons and thrive best in young forests of aspens and evergreens, or forests with occasional clear-cutting or forest fires. Long, shiny, blackish neck feathers are most prominent on the male, especially when he is in full display defending his territory, or attracting a hen.

Ruffed grouse feed on a wide variety of green leaves and wild fruits, a few insects, and occasionally snakes, frogs and salamanders. In winter they feed almost exclusively on dormant flower buds or catkins of trees such as aspens, birches, and cherries. Ruffed grouse have a short lifespan, about half of a brood of 10 or 12 dying before next breeding season. Raptors, especially the goshawk and horned owl, probably kill more grouse annually than any other predator. Some die by accidentally hitting trees or branches while in a panic flight after being frightened.

## Spruce grouse

Also known as the fool hen, the spruce grouse is so tame, humans can approach within a few feet before it flies away. This little chicken-like bird is endangered in New York and threatened in Wisconsin.

The spruce grouse lives in spruce and pine forests, feeding on the needles and buds of evergreens, berries, seeds, mushrooms, leaves and some insects. During mating season, the male struts around ruffling his feathers, spreading his tail feathers, and beating and flapping his wings. The female lays four to eleven eggs in a hollow lined with moss, grass and leaves, usually under low-lying branches of a spruce tree.

The male ruffed grouse drums throughout the year by beating his wings against the air.

The colorful male spruce grouse has a red comb over its eyes; the female lacks a comb and is brown overall with black barring.

Also called Chinese pheasants, the ring-necked pheasant is native to Ukraine and was introduced into the United States in 1857 and southern Canada in the early to mid 1900s.

## Ring-necked pheasant

Ring-necked pheasants are large game birds with stout yellowish, chicken-like bills, short legs, short, rounded wings, and long tail feathers. The head and neck are strikingly iridescent green-blue or purple with a white collar that separates the head and neck region from the rest of the body. There are bright patches of red skin on the cheeks and around the eyes, red wattles below the eyes and iridescent greenish ear tufts on the sides of the head. The overall body color is an iridescent bronze, mottled with brown, black, white and green markings. The long reddish brown tail has dark barring across the feathers.

Commonly found in farmlands or areas with grasslands mixed with small woodlands, the bird also inhabits wetlands with suitable small dry sites. Pheasants feed shortly after sunrise, mostly on plant foods such as waste grains or seeds, weed seeds and wild berries. They will also eat large insects, including grasshoppers, crickets, caterpillars of gypsy and brown-tail moths, and mice or snails. Males defend territories from intruders and display during courtship, mating with several hens. Hens lay 5 to 23 eggs in nests of other birds such as mallards, blue-winged teal, turkey and grouse. A pheasant's lifespan in the wild is relatively short, males living about 10 months and females about 20 months. The maximum age in the wild is eight years.

## Wild turkey

Wild turkeys were widely used by American Indians as food but certain tribes considered the birds stupid and cowardly and did not eat them for fear of acquiring these characteristics. Although they were hunted almost to extinction in the 19th century, protection, restocking programs, and the return of its preferred mature forest habitat has helped the species make a comeback, from an estimated 450,000 in 1959 to 3.5 million in 1990.

Wild turkeys are dusky brown, barred with black, with iridescent bronze sheen; head and neck naked, with bluish and reddish wattles; tail fan-shaped, with chestnut, buff, or white tail tips.

Wild turkeys can fly at speeds up to 55 miles per hour (89 km/h) and run at speeds of 12 miles per hour (19 km/h). The male, called a tom, has spurs and a long (up to 16 inches, or 41 cm) beard on its breast. Females are smaller, lacking the spurs and beard. Toms gabble and strut to attract multiple hens in spring. Only about 35 percent of nests are successful in producing young because raccoons, skunks and opossums raid the nests. Adult turkeys feed on grapes, blackberries, beechnuts, acorns, grains, grasses, ferns, and insects.

*Right* A flock of wild turkeys in search of green grasses, acorns, buds, seeds, fruits of various kinds and, especially when they are young, insects.

Bald eagle (*left*) can lift about half of its own weight.

The broad-winged hawk (*right*) nest and perch near the forest edge.

# Hunting birds

## Bald eagle

This eagle is not bald; "balde" is Old English for "white." It is the only large brown bird with a white head and tail. The white head and tail plumage grows in when the bird is sexually mature, at four to five years old. An endangered species, its populations are recovering thanks to protection by the Endangered Species Acts in the United States and Canada.

Bald eagles live near water—lakes, rivers, marshes and seacoasts—roosting and nesting in old-growth trees that extend above the forest canopy, occasionally using cliffs or ground if no trees are available. Bald eagles lay one to three relatively small white eggs, incubated by both parents. While much of the bald eagle's diet consists of fish, they will also eat ducks, rabbits, herons, squirrels, opossums and carrion. An adult bald eagle can consume one pound of fish in less than four minutes.

## Broad-winged hawk

Broad-winged hawks will migrate 10,000 to 11,000 miles (16,000–17,700 km) round trip. A dark brown, crow-size bird with short, pointed wings and a tail with alternating broad bands of black and white, the broad-winged hawk glides and soars on flattened wings, occasionally flapping awkwardly. They nest and perch near edges of forest openings, usually near water, hunting for small mammals and birds, lizards, frogs and snakes. They either nest in a crotch in the lower third of a tree, or renovate old crow, other raptor, or squirrel nests, rarely reusing the nest in consecutive years. The female incubates two to four eggs while the male provides food.

## Northern goshawk

In North America, goshawks live in mature forests, largely in southern Canada and the northern United States. They are commonly seen darting in the open canopy beneath the trees in pursuit of songbirds, jays, flickers, rabbits and squirrels. Their long, rudder-like tails give them an acrobatic ability to spin around trees and quickly dive under shrubs and brush.

Each pair of goshawks builds and maintain between three and nine nests within their home range, but use and defend only one (or less) per year. Goshawks provide essential nesting opportunities for many species that cannot build their own nests, including spotted owls, great gray owls, Cooper's hawks, red-tailed hawks, great horned owls, and short-eared owls. Unfortunately, as mature and old growth forests become rarer and rarer, so do goshawks. They are an endangered species in all states west of the continental divide and threatened in British Columbia.

In medieval Europe, the northern goshawk (*below*) was the most prized of all falconry hawks.

# Hunting birds: natural mice control

Raptors will help alleviate your mice problems. These powerful birds of prey can be distinguished by their flight silhouettes:

**Accipiters**, for example, the Northern goshawk, are small, swift hawks.

**Buteos**, for instance, the red-tailed hawk, red-shouldered hawk, and broad-winged hawk and harriers, have longer wings.

**Falcons** have angulate wings that are pointed on the end. There are only two species in the temperate zone. Both the peregrine falcon and the gyrfalcon are rare and protected in Canada and the United States.

**Harriers** (for example, northern harriers) have angulate wings like falcons, but theirs have fringed flight feathers on the forward edges and ends.

**Eagles** are the largest of all the raptors and the feathers on an eagle's wingtips are curled upward.

The harrier's courtship flights include steep climbs and dives, with a series of loops, at the top of which the bird is upside down.

## Northern harrier

The northern harrier has an owl-like facial disc. The long wings and tail, a white rump patch and its hooded dark head are characteristic of the species. Males are gray with black wing-tips; females are brown with a streaked breast. Adult males have bright lemon yellow eyes; adult females have amber to pale yellow eyes. The harrier's courtship flights include steep climbs and dives, with a series of loops, at the top of which the bird is upside down. Males mate with up to five females, who lay two to eight eggs. They prefer wetlands, marshes, logged or burned wood lots, tundra or medium to tall prairie grass. Northern harriers will usually perch on the ground, but will use fence posts, or other low perches. They build nests on the ground within patches of dense, tall vegetation. Males eat mostly rodents, reptiles, and frogs while females eat mostly birds.

## Red-shouldered hawk

The red shoulders of the bird can be seen only when you are close to the bird. The adult's breast is reddish with fine, horizontal, brownish barring. The tail is blackish with three to four narrow white bands. Red-shouldered hawks prefer swampy lowlands or dense woods around streams and rivers, leaving if woods are cleared. Pesticides have probably reduced populations in some rural areas, but loss of habitat is the most likely the cause of long-term declines. Red-shouldered hawks usually construct a new nest halfway up a tree each year but may refurbish a nest from years before. Females lay two to four eggs that are incubated by both parents. They hunt rodents, birds, frogs and toads, snakes, crustaceans, fish and insects.

# Noises in the night

Great horned owls have prominent, widely spaced ears and large yellow eyes within a heart-shaped facial disc rimmed in black.

## Owls

Owls are nocturnal and are usually heard at dusk and in the early evening. These large-headed birds of prey have to rotate their heads to see things around them because their large eyes are fixed within their sockets. A good way to locate an owl roost is to search for a cluster of pellets on the ground. The pellets, regurgitated bundles of undigested fur and bones, also provide a good indication of the bird's food habits.

### Great horned owl

Great horned owls are the largest common owl in the temperate zone. They are best noted for their hoot, *whooo-whooo-whooooo-who-who.*

Great horned owls prefer densely forested regions consisting of conifers, hardwoods or a mix. Solitary and highly territorial, with only a mate sharing the territory, they have the most extensive range, widest prey selection, and most variable nesting sites of any North American owl.

Great horned owls perch and search for prey, diving down with wings folded to snatch the prey and kill it instantly with their large talons. They will wade into water to snatch a frog or fish. Seventy-five percent of the great horned owl's prey are mammals, including rodents, raccoons and bats. Owls pluck birds, which make up about six percent of the owl's diet, before eating them. The great horned owl generally uses an abandoned hawk nest but will nest in hollows in trees, on cliffs, artificial platforms, or even on the ground. The female lays two eggs in November or December.

### Eastern screech owl

The eastern screech owl is the smallest eared owl at only 8 inches (20 cm) long. It has as many as three color phases, red, brown or gray, depending on where it lives. In its red color phase, the eastern screech owl is North America's only reddish eared owl. Eastern screech owls avoid dense coniferous forests occupied by their predator, the great horned owl, preferring deciduous forests, parklands and orchards. The female lays three to seven eggs. Eastern screech owls feed on fish, insects, small mammals and birds. Their call is a whistle instead of a hoot.

### Northern saw-whet owl

The northern saw-whet owl.

Northern saw-whet owls are extraordinarily tame and may be approached closely or even handled. They are the only tiny earless owl likely to be seen in the central and eastern temperate zone.

Northern saw-whet owls are most common in coniferous forests, but can be found in deciduous trees along watercourses. They nest in woodpecker holes or natural cavities in woodlands. Females lay four to seven eggs in April. Almost entirely nocturnal, they prey on deer mice, voles, jumping mice, shrews, large insects, and occasionally small songbirds. The call is a monotone *toot, toot, toot, toot,* made rapidly and persistently throughout the night.

Screech owls roost mainly in natural cavities in large trees.

# Whip-poor-will

The nocturnal whip-poor-will is more often heard than seen. It sleeps by day on the forest floor, its coloration matching the dead leaves, but its call is a distinctive, three part WHIP-poor-WEEA with rising last note and first and last syllables accented.

Whip-poor-wills are mottled grayish-brown birds with long, rounded tails and rounded wings.

Whip-poor-wills use their large eyes to spot insects at twilight, dawn and on moonlit nights. At night, the eyes reflect ruby red in car headlights.

The whip-poor-will's breeding cycle is synchronized with the lunar cycle. They lay their eggs so that they hatch as the moonlight is increasing in intensity. Maximum moonlight aids in finding food for their growing young. One or two eggs are laid on the ground in a bed of leaves and both parents feed the young regurgitated food.

Whip-poor-wills live in open woodlands with well-spaced trees and low canopy. They hunt in sustained flight, wheeling and circling, sometimes gliding and even hovering. Sometimes seen perching on tracks or roads, they tend to sit lengthwise on branches and rails instead of across them like most other birds.

# Insect-eating birds

## Common nighthawk

The common nighthawk is neither strictly nocturnal, nor a hawk, but it does hunt insects on the wing. Its capacity to consume insects is extraordinary; it can capture more than 500 mosquitoes or 2,175 flying ants in a single day.

Not knowing that the birds fly around livestock to feed on insects, farmers once believed that the nighthawk sucked milk from goats' udders and caused them to dry up, and called them goatsuckers.

It is a jay-sized bird with mottled plumage, brownish-black above and below, perfectly matching and blending in with the ground. The wings are long and pointed with a broad, white wing bar and its flight is high and fluttery.

Nighthawks live in open woodlands, clearings, or fields, with roosting trees or fence posts. They are also common in towns and cities, where flat roofs provide excellent nest sites. The booming sound created by males during courtship is well-known: the male makes a power dive and then abruptly swerves upward, which produces the booming sound. The female lays two eggs on the ground or a on a roof.

## Chimney swift

Swifts spend all of their daylight hours flying and come to rest only at evening. They gather twigs for nests in flight and it is believed that they even sleep and copulate in flight.

The chimney swift is a uniform gray-brown, slightly darker above and on wings, light below, and palest on upper breast and throat.

Chimney swifts gather in communal roosts in air shafts or large chimneys, often whirling in a huge circle as they funnel down for the night. The nest is a shallow cup constructed of twigs cemented together with saliva. A clutch of four or five eggs is usually laid in late June or early July and both parents share in incubation duties. Swifts are like nighthawks, with huge mouths for catching insects on the fly, but are most active during the day.

## House wren

This is a tiny bird with a short tail usually held cocked over the back. It is dusky brown above, paler below, with few markings. The house wren is an aggressive bird during breeding season, often tossing the nest, eggs, and even the young of other hole-nesting birds, occasionally even killing its competitors. Their songs are loud and begin with a chatter of rapid notes, followed by cascades of doubled notes and groups of trills.

The house wren, *Troglodytes aedon,* is a ruthlessly aggressive bird during mating season.

The ruby-crowned kinglet (*left*) and the golden-crowned kinglet (*right*).

# Ruby-crowned kinglet

The ruby-crowned kinglet can be recognized by its constant wing-flicking and its small size (a bit larger than a hummingbird). Males have a red crown but it is usually hidden. This tiny bird lays a very large clutch of eggs for its size; although the eggs themselves weigh only 0.02 oz (0.65 g), an entire clutch can weigh as much as the female herself. The song starts with two or three high *tsees,* followed by five or six lower *tur* notes, and ending with repeated *tee-da-lett* phrases; the call is a rapid *di-dit.*

# Golden-crowned kinglet

Golden-crowned kinglets are social, lively and playful birds, commonly found traversing the tops of trees and bushes in the heart of forests or near swamps, and frequently gardens and yards. Mated pairs build a globular nest, attached to twigs of an evergreen, anywhere from 4 to 60 feet (1–18 m) above ground. They eat insects on the wing, seizing them among the leaves, bark or branches of pine trees.

The song of the golden-crowned kinglet is a series of high-pitched, ascending *see-see-see* and ends with similar but louder and harsher descending notes. In winter, they socialize and roam with flocks of chickadees, brown creepers and woodpeckers instead of migrating south.

*Right* An alder flycatcher.

# Flycatchers

These medium to small land birds have feet well adapted for perching, and catch insects on the wing. Most build nests of twigs, leaves or other plant material and lay two to six eggs, depending on the species, of which there are many.

### Acadian flycatcher

Common in moist woodlands, particularly deciduous forest floodplains, mostly below the canopy, its song is an explosive *peet-suh.*

### Alder flycatcher

Common near water, they hunt in the airspace below the canopy of tall alders in swamps or along creeks, sitting erect on a twig, then darting out after flying insects. Its song is a moderately rapid *fee-bee'o.*

### Olive-sided flycatcher

This bird is most common in northern coniferous forests, usually near openings, burns, ponds and bogs. Also occurs in mixed forests of aspens, birches, and maples. Its song is a loud and melodious whistle, *whip-three-beers,* and its call is *pip-pip-pip.*

# Swallows

Graceful swallows skim the water and woods, catching insects on the wing with their short, wide beaks. Swallows have long, pointed wings and most have a deeply notched tail. They tend to flock and perch on wires, nest in colonies and lay four to seven eggs to a clutch in nests generally made with mud, leaves, twigs, feathers and hair. There are many species of swallow, including the bank, barn, cliff, tree, northern rough-winged swallows and the purple martin.

## Purple martin

This is the only swallow that is dark all over, with purple iridescence on the head and top of wings. The wings are broad and built for soaring. Starlings are known to usurp purple martin nests, and along with sparrows are thought to have contributed to the decline in purple martin populations. There is a huge contingent of people who are actively "managing" martin populations by maintaining the martin colonies, periodically cleaning sparrow and starling nests during the nesting season, cleaning and closing martin houses when the martins are gone and placing feeders out. Where legal and feasible, some people eliminate sparrows and starlings by either trapping or shooting them. Martins are not exceptional consumers of mosquitoes; diets of purple martins consist of larger insects such as dragonflies, damselflies, mayflies, butterflies, moths, beetles, bees, wasps, grasshoppers, cicadas and midges.

Concerned for the well being of the purple martin (*below*), many cottagers now safeguard their resident populations. Here purple martin houses flank a boathouse on Lake Ontario.

# Making a birdhouse

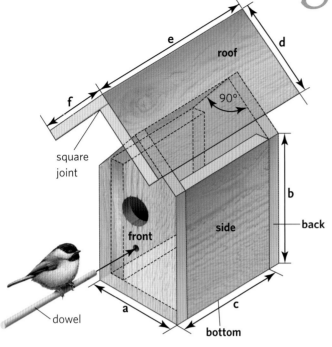

square joint

roof

90°

front

side

back

bottom

dowel

Encourage your favorite species to move into your neighborhood by building a birdhouse. Using the birdhouse schematic to the left and the chart below, you can build nest-boxes for a variety of bird species.

Don't be surprised if other birds of the same size decide to nest in a box you intended for someone else! In particular, if you've built a purple martin birdhouse, watch for signs that house sparrows and European starlings have moved in. These birds will displace purple martins instantly. Consider cleaning and closing the birdhouses for the winter.

| | | American robin* | Barn swallow** | Bluebirds | Chickadees |
|---|---|---|---|---|---|
| **IMPERIAL** | Front & back, a x b (inches) | 6½ × 8 | 5½ × 6 | 5½ × 6 | 5½ × 8 |
| | Sides, b x c (inches) | | 6 × 5½ | 6 × 4 | 8 × 4 |
| | Bottom, a x c (inches) | | 4 × 5½ | 4 × 4 | 4 × 4 |
| | Left roof panel, f x e (inches) | | | 4½ × 8½ | 4½ × 8½ |
| | Right roof panel, d x e (inches) | | | 4 × 8½ | 4 × 8½ |
| | Entrance above door (inches) | | | 6–8 | 6–8 |
| | Entrance hole diameter (inches) | | | 1½ | 1½ |
| | Height above ground (feet) | | 8–12 | 4–6 | 4–15 |
| **METRIC** | Front & back, a x b (cm) | 15.5 × 20.3 | 14 × 15 | 14 × 15 | 14 × 20.3 |
| | Sides, b x c (cm) | | 15 × 14 | 15 × 10 | 20.3 × 10 |
| | Bottom, a x c (cm) | | 10 × 14 | 10 × 10 | 10 × 10 |
| | Left roof panel, f x e (cm) | | | 12 × 21.6 | 12 × 21.6 |
| | Right roof panel, d x e (cm) | | | 10 × 21.6 | 10 × 21.6 |
| | Entrance above door (cm) | | | 15–20.3 | 15–20.3 |
| | Entrance hole diameter (cm) | | | 3.2 | 3.2 |
| | Height above ground (m) | | 2.7–3.7 | 1.2–1.8 | 1.2–4.6 |

\* prefers nesting shelf

\*\* prefers nesting shelf with sides

The dimensions (**a** through **f**) shown in the schematic correspond to those in the chart below if you use lumber ¾-inch thick. Use cedar, if possible, because it resists decay. Boxes less than 5½ inches on one side can be made with ¾ by 5½ inch cedar fence boards. Don't use pressure-treated lumber because the preservative may be toxic to the birds. For larger boxes, use wider cedar planking or plywood.

The front and back will have the same dimensions, but the front will also have a hole of the diameter specified in the chart below.

For all boxes, make the roof pitch on the front and back panels 90° so the roof boards will squarely butt up to one another during assembly; one roof panel will be ¾ inch narrower than the other. The two sides will have the same dimensions. The floor will be 1½ inches smaller (**a**) on width than the bases of the front-back (**a**) and the same length as the side (**c**).

Use 2-inch finishing nails to assemble the nest box. Adding outdoor glue to all joints before nailing will strengthen the box.

| Flycatchers | Great horned owl* | House finch | Nuthatches | Purple martin | Screech owl | Tree swallow | Wood ducks | Wrens |
|---|---|---|---|---|---|---|---|---|
| 7×6 | 24×24 | 7×6 | 5_×9 | 7½×6 | 9½×15 | 7×5½ | 11½×21 | 5½×7 |
| 6×5½ | | 6×6 | 9×4 | 6×6 | 15×8 | 5½×6 | 21×10 | 7×4 |
| 5×5½ | | 5½×6 | 4×4 | 6×6 | 8×8 | 6×6 | 10×10 | 4×4 |
| 5½×9 | | 5½×9 | 4½×8½ | 6×9½ | 6½×11½ | 5½×9½ | 7½×13½ | 4½×8½ |
| 4½×9 | | 4½×9 | 4×8½ | 5½×9½ | 6×11½ | 4½×9½ | 7×13½ | 4×8½ |
| 6-10 | | 4 | 6 | 1 | 9 | 4½ | 15½ | 5 |
| 1-1½ | | 2 | 1½ | 2½ | 3 | 1½ | 4 | 1½ |
| 5-15 | | 8-12 | 5-15 | 10-15 | 10-30 | 5-15 | 10-20 | 5-10 |
| 17.8×15 | 61×61 | 17.8×15 | 14×23 | 19×15 | 24×38.1 | 19×14 | 29.2×53.3 | 29.2×17.8 |
| 15×14 | | 15×15 | 23×10 | 15 x 15 | 38.1×20.3 | 14×15 | 29.2×25.4 | 17.8×10 |
| 14×14 | | 14×15 | 10×10 | 15×15 | 20.3×20.3 | 15×15 | 25.4×25.4 | 10×10 |
| 14×23 | | 14×23 | 12×21.6 | 15×24 | 17.1×29.2 | 14×24 | 19.7×34.3 | 12×21.6 |
| 12×23 | | 12×23 | 10×21.6 | 13.3×24 | 15×29.2 | 12×24 | 17.8×34.3 | 10×21.6 |
| 15×25.4 | | 10 | 15 | 2.5 | 23 | 12 | 39.4 | 12.7 |
| 3.8-4.8 | | 5 | 2.9 | 6.4 | 7.6 | 3.8 | 10 | 3.8 |
| 1.5-4.6 | | 2.7-3.7 | 1.5-4.6 | 3-4.6 | 3-9.2 | 1.5-4.6 | 3-6 | 1.5-3 |

You can catch fireflies with a glass jar lined with a bit of grass — just remember to punch air holes into the lid. You can also catch them with your hands. Be sure to let them go shortly after catching them because these fragile insects do not survive in captivity.

# Nocturnal bugs

## Fireflies

Also known as glow worms and lightning bugs, fireflies are actually beetles. The adults are ⅜ to ⅝ of an inch (9–15 mm) long, flattened, with large, widely spaced eyes and thread-like antennae. The head and front thorax are a dull yellow, the latter with a black spot surrounded by reddish ring. The forewings are brown or gray with yellow bands along their sides. Adults of both sexes, and in some species, all life stages, including eggs and larvae, are able to produce light. The light is produced by a reaction involving three chemicals produced by the beetle: a substrate called luciferin,

an enzyme called luciferase, and adenosine triphosphate (ATP). This mixture in the presence of oxygen produces a practically heatless, flashing green or yellow light. Depending on the species, the light organ is either on the side or bottom of the abdomen.

No one knows the reason for the light. One theory is that it is a sexual attractant, but this doesn't explain why eggs and larvae produce light. Another theory is that it warns nocturnal predators not to eat them, but being undetectable at night is better than "advertising." Fireflies eat soft-bodied insects, mites, slugs and even their own species.

# Moths

## Gypsy moth

The gypsy moth is one of North America's most devastating forest pests. The species was introduced to North America by artist and amateur entomologist E. Leopold Trouveot around 1868. He was interested in using the caterpillars from France for producing silk and brought some to his backyard near Boston. A few escaped and about ten years later gypsy moth outbreaks were occurring everywhere and state, municipal and federal governments began trying to eradicate the species.

Today, the gypsy moth is still one of the most serious threats to our deciduous trees, including oaks, maples, elms, apple, alder,

Most deciduous trees can survive a moderate degree of defoliation, or even one complete defoliation by the gypsy moth caterpillar. However, continuing attacks will fatally weaken a tree or leave it vulnerable to insects or disease.

birch and willow trees, or evergreens if these are not available. Depending on the degree of infestation, tree damage can range from light to complete defoliation.

The adults are seen in midsummer; males are smallish, grayish brown and can fly, females are larger, whitish with black marks and cannot fly. Mating occurs from July to September. The male dies and the female lays an egg mass with 50 to 1,500 eggs, covers it with body hairs to act as insulation and to help protect the eggs from predators. The egg masses are 1⅕ inches (4 cm) in diameter, tan or buff-colored and laid on tree trunks, outdoor furniture or the sides buildings. The eggs overwinter and hatch in early spring through mid-May. The larvae crawl up the trunks and braches to the leaves of trees and begin to eat, mostly at night. Feeding continues until mid-June or early July when the caterpillar enters the pupal stage emerging as a moth.

## Eastern tent caterpillar

This caterpillar is known for the tent-like nests it spins in trees. More a nuisance than a threat, tent caterpillars only kill already weak trees. Occasional heavy infestations can defoliate trees more severely. You'll mostly see the tents on black cherry trees, but other cherries and fruit trees are also infested. The adults are moths, emerging in July to mate, lay eggs and die.

Blue jays are an important predator of tent caterpillars. One pair of blue jays feeds hundreds of tent caterpillars to their nestlings in early summer, carrying several caterpillars inside their mouths at one time to the young.

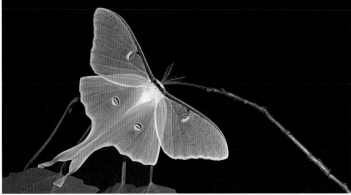

The cecropia moth (*left*) and the luna moth (*right*).

### Cecropia moth

This moth has stunning wing colors and patterns and is the largest moth in North America, with a wingspan of 5 to 6 inches (13–15 cm). You are most likely to see them at night around bright lights. The body is reddish-orange with a white collar and white bands on the abdomen. The forewings are red at the base, dark brown with a white frosted appearance and crescent spots.

Cecropia moths emerge from their cocoons in late May or early June. They live for only about two weeks because the adult has no mouth parts.

The male cecropia can sense the female's scent with its antennae from as much as a mile away. The eggs are laid in small groups on the underside of leaves and hatch in 7 to 14 days. The newly hatched caterpillars grow and molt several times until reaching about 4 inches (10 cm). They are bluish green, with a pair of yellow projections on each body segment. The caterpillars feed mostly on maple, birch, willow, cherry, plum, apple, and elderberry, but will also feed on lilac, elm and linden. Many species of birds and insects prey on the caterpillars.

Cicada adults have broad heads with bulging red eyes, red legs and veins through transparent wings. These fierce-looking bugs are harmful only to young saplings.

### Luna moth

With their yellow-green colors and long tails, luna moths are among the largest and most stunning North American moths. The smooth green larvae eat white birch and sumac leaves in the northern states and Canada, and munch on hickory, walnut and sweetgum leaves in New Jersey and states of that latitude. The caterpillar builds a brown, tent-like cocoon in which to pupate.

Adults fly from early June to early July. When females are ready to mate, they release pheromones into the air from a scent gland to attract the male, which is easily achieved. After mating, the pair remains connected until the following evening. Females will lay eggs in brown paper sandwich or grocery bags for those who want to try to raise luna moths. Adults live only about a week.

## Summer sound: cicadas

The cicada is a small bug with a big noise. Their unmistakable buzz echoing through the treetops is the loudest sound in the insect world, and can be heard as far as 440 yards (400 m) away. The male cicada produces the sound to attract a mate by vibrating ribbed plates in two amplifying cavities at the base of his abdomen. Cicadas hold another record in the bug world: nymphs feed on tree roots underground for 13 or 17 years. After the long wait, the nymphs mysteriously emerge at the same time, morph into adults, lay eggs, and die in a few short weeks.

# Biting bugs

Fun times can turn bloody when clouds of black flies, mosquitoes, deer flies and horse flies emerge from their aquatic stages to become terrestrial terrors. Many people avoid opening their cottages in spring when mass emergences of these two-winged vampires are looking for their first blood meal. Some, like mosquitoes, may be transmitting fatal diseases such as encephalitis and West Nile virus. Although most flies are non-venomous, some people are deathly allergic. Most of us have to just grin and bear the painful or itchy bites.

The best defenses are bug repellent (see page 180), bug hats and jackets, and avoiding cottage country during the worst spring swarms.

If you want to improve your hand-eye co-ordination, try the badminton zapper. The kill yields a loud zap and the smell of burnt protein! They are inexpensive, run on D-cell batteries and available at most hardware stores.

## Mosquitoes

Many a quiet evening has been marred by the crazy-making whine of female mosquitoes, thirsty for the blood meal that will help their eggs mature. The males (and sometimes the females) feed on nectar and other plant juices. Different species enjoy different host animals.

Mosquito larvae, also called "wrigglers" or "wiggletails," inhabit ponds, lakes, swamps, bogs and other standing water. They live at the surface, breathing through a tube-like siphon and feeding on floating or suspended micro-organisms. After a few days they pupate. The pupae ("tumblers") fall to the bottom, and after another few days the adults emerge and mate. The duration of the life cycle varies from ten days to several weeks.

## Black flies

The common name is not very imaginative but it does describe the color of the little adult pests that swarm and bite mercilessly in the spring. Unlike mosquitoes, female black flies bite in the daytime. Although black flies are non-venomous, their bites can cause blood loss or serious allergic reactions, even death in cattle and "black fly fever" in humans, characterized by headaches, fever, nausea, dermatitis, and allergic asthma. Black flies also transmit blood-borne parasites to waterfowl, geese and turkeys.

Black fly larvae are adapted for life in flowing waters, attaching themselves to rocks with a sucker-like disc, and with a silk thread. Thousands of larvae can be found on the same rock. The larvae molt six times before building a silken case for the pupae to develop within. There may be one to several generations per year but the largest emergences occur in springtime.

### Common mosquito genera

- *Anopheles* is the only carrier of malaria in tropical countries, and transmits encephalitis in North America. It bites with its proboscis, head and body held on a straight line to each other but at an angle to the surface.

- *Culex* is a carrier of viral encephalitis, West Nile virus. It bites with its body parallel to the resting surface and its proboscis bent downward relative to the surface. Humans are dead-end hosts of West Nile virus in that the virus cannot reproduce or be transmitted to other hosts; birds, especially crows and ravens, are primary hosts and can transmit the virus to other hosts.

- *Aedes* transmits yellow fever, dengue and encephalitis. It holds its body parallel to the surface with the proboscis bent down. It usually breeds in floodwater or rain pools, the eggs being capable of withstanding long periods of dryness.

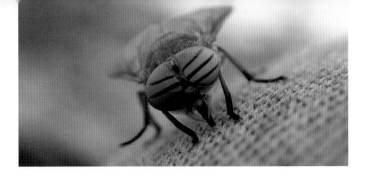

Adult horse flies have brightly colored eyes and broad, flat abdomens.

## DEET

DEET, short for N,N-diethyl-m-toluamide, is the most effective insect repellent ingredient around. It will protect you from mosquitoes, black flies, and a variety of other bugs that are out for your blood. DEET is a thoroughly tested chemical that shows no adverse effects as long as it used according to label instructions.

Mosquitoes especially likely to bite around dusk and dawn but they do bite in the daytime. They are attracted to skin odors (some species adore stinky feet) and carbon dioxide from breathing. DEET repels mosquitoes, making them unable to locate you. Repellents are effective only at short distances, so you may still see mosquitoes buzzing around, but they won't land and bite.

The more DEET a repellent contains, the longer the protection time (the protection is longer, not stronger). As a rule of thumb, calculate hours of protection as one hour for each 5 percent increase in DEET content, so 10 percent DEET would provide about two hours protection, and 25 percent DEET will provide about five hours of protection. Sweating or getting wet will limit DEET effectiveness; you'll know when you need to reapply it!

### Alternatives to DEET

Using repellents on skin is not the only way to avoid mosquito bites. Wear long pants and long sleeves while outdoors. Mosquito hats and jackets are quite effective. Mosquito netting can be used over infant carriers. Reduce the number of mosquitoes in the area by getting rid of containers with standing water (old tires, bird baths) that provide breeding places for the mosquitoes.

Some folks use incense coils (*see photo*), which do a slow burn, filling the air with smoke containing insecticides.

Citronella oil is one-sixth as effective as DEET, 10 percent citronella providing only about 20 minutes of protection. Some campers use a citronella candle, which is a fragrant smoke repellent that burns for nine hours, but you may have to play musical chairs to stay downwind of the smoke. Products with oil of lemon eucalyptus plus p-menthane 3,8-diol, commonly known as PMD, will provide two hours of protection.

## Horse flies, deer flies and breeze flies

These are nasty, painful biters that plague particularly on sweaty days. Horse flies are huge, black buzzing menaces, larger than the triangle-shaped deer flies and breeze flies (often called "clegs"). Horse fly larvae are mostly found in swamps and marshes preying on other insects, sucking them dry, while deer fly larvae are more common in the margins of streams and ponds, feeding on detritus.

In flight, horse flies are fast, 19 to 31 miles an hour (30–50 km/h) but at take-off they are slow and easy to kill. The females suck the blood of vertebrates, especially cattle, horses and humans, cutting a triangular hole in the skin with razor-sharp mouth parts. The bite is very painful and often causes large welts and allergic reactions, some of which may be fatal. The innocent males feed on nectar from flowers.

Horse flies like to bite when the body is wet or sweaty and will follow or chase you when swimming, waiting for some body part to emerge from the water. There are two theories for this; one is that the cool water desensitizes the skin enough for the insect to get a good bite and slug of blood before the person feels it; the second is that the water may aid in the flow of blood.

## Biting midges (no-see-ums)

Small enough to pass through most screens on doors, these almost invisible insects have a painful bite. The slender, needle-like larvae lack legs, and are bottom dwellers feeding on eggs of other insects, small detritus or algae in lakes, streams, ponds, marshes and bogs. Some live in moist beach sand, which gives rise to another common name, "sand flies." The gnat-like adults have piercing mouth parts, the females of most species feeding on blood of vertebrates. Some feed on other insects, even their own species.

A pollen-dusted honey bee feeds on nectar.

# Stinging bugs

Bees and wasps are most active during the summer. Since they are not detered by insect repellants, it is best to avoid them. For suggestions on controlling wasps and bees nearby your cottage, see **Living with wildlife** in this chapter at pages 192 to 195.

## Honey bees

There are three types of bees in a hive. The "queen" bee is the boss. She lays several hundred eggs each day. "Drones" mate with the queen. "Workers" are also female. They lay no eggs and do all the work, visiting thousands of flowers each day and collecting food needed to sustain the colony.

Each bee has a long, straw-like tongue to suck the nectar out of the flower and into her nectar sac. During this activity, pollen sticks to her body and is brought back to the hive for food or pollinates flowers and fruits of other plants. The worker uses her front and middle legs to comb the honey into pollen baskets on her back legs. Inside the hive, the workers help each other out by performing specific dances that tell other bees where to find the flowers.

Wax is secreted from openings in their abdomens and is shaped into thousands of small "cells" that make up the honey comb. The cells house both pupae and honey. The nectar changes into honey sugars when workers add enzymes from glands in their heads. The workers spread out honey droplets and fan them with their wings to help evaporate the water and leave thick, sticky sweet honey. The color and flavor depends on the age of the honey and the kind of flower that the nectar was extracted from. It is one of the easiest foods to digest and is the only food that does not spoil.

Wild colonies of honey bees nest in hollow trees or in wall voids. Honey bees may become a nuisance in the spring at bird feeders and swimming pools as they forage for water. They are rarely, if ever, a nuisance in summer or early fall. Control of honey bee nests can be challenging. Consider hiring an experienced pest control service.

## Power in numbers

The average honey bee will make only one-twelfth of a teaspoon of honey in its lifetime. To produce a pound (0.45 kg) of honey, worker bees must collect nectar from about 2 million flowers, traveling 50,000 miles (80,465 km) while doing so. Some bee colonies have been known to produce 300 pounds (135 kg) of honey in a single season.

A bumble bee.

*Right* A mining bee.

# Wild bees, aka bumble bees

Wild bees rarely sting unless stepped on or squeezed. These small- to medium-sized insects come in many colors, including yellow, black, red, blue, green or copper, or a mix of these. They feed on the nectar of many plants, gather pollen and are excellent pollinators of vegetable and fruit crops. The nests are mounds (½ to 2½ inches or 1.5 to 6.0 cm wide, and ⅛ to ½ inch or 0.25 to 1.5 cm high) formed from excavated dirt in well-drained soils that have relatively little plant growth and organic matter, sometimes in a deserted mouse or bird nest. Occasionally they nest in wall cavities or in clothes dryer vents.

After overwintering in their soil burrows, the adults emerge by early April to begin digging new burrows, abandoning the old nest. Like honey bees, each colony has a single queen producing larvae, but unlike some bees, there is no worker caste or nest guarding. Eggs hatch in early May and the larvae develop throughout the summer. Pupation occurs usually in August. Some species overwinter as adults, others as larvae.

When a bumble bee nest is in the way, treat it with the same insecticides and methods as described for ground-nesting or concealed wasp nests.

# Mining bees

Some ground-nesting bees don't form colonies. Common "Andrenid bees" or "mining bees" are solitary ground-nesting bees that are important pollinators of native plants. They usually nest in sun-exposed, dry areas of yards. There is just one bee per nest but many bees nest close to each other. You may find these bees flying around

their nests in the spring, but they are gentle and rarely sting people. They avoid dampness so sprinkle the area of their nests with water if you want them to move.

## First aid for bee and wasp stings

Wasps and bumble bees do not leave their stinger in your skin and can sting more than once, but honey bees have barbs on their stinger and will remain hooked in the skin. The stinger is connected to their digestive system, so when the stinger is torn out, so is the digestive tract, and the bee dies. If you are stung by a honey bee, remove the stinger with its attached venom gland with tweezers or scratch it with your fingernail as soon as possible. Trying to remove the stinger between two fingers is a bad idea because it may force more venom into your skin and cause even greater irritation.

Most people have only local reactions to wasp and bee stings, but some experience everything from burning, itching, redness, and tenderness to massive swelling and itching that may continue for a week. Try treating the itch with ice, vinegar, honey, meat tenderizer, or commercial topical ointment.

Some allergic reactions may include hives or rash, swelling away from the sting site, headache, minor respiratory symptoms, and stomach upset, but these are rarely life-threatening and can be treated with an antihistamine.

In the worst-case scenario, a person may experience anaphylactic shock (fainting, difficulty breathing, swelling and blockage in the throat) within minutes of being stung. Get immediate medical attention and purchase an auto injector with epinephrine (an EpiPen) to have handy for the next time. An EpiPen has a one-year shelf life and needs replacing annually.

# Killer bees

African honeybees were imported from South Africa by a researcher who wanted to produce a variety of honeybee that was better adapted to the tropics. While the bees produced better honey than European bees, they were also much more aggressive at defending the nest. Some bees escaped in the 1950s, and began expanding their range from Brazil across South America, then northward to California and Texas. Killer bees and honey bees look so much alike that specialized tests such as DNA analyses are needed to tell them apart.

The bees react quickly, attack in large numbers, and swarm for long periods of time. Many people have been killed by mass stinging. They may not expand their range beyond the southern United States because they are adapted for tropical conditions. However, they can tolerate up to three and a half months of freezing weather.

## Hornets and wasps

The names "hornet" and "yellow jacket" refer to kinds of wasps. They all build large paper nests but of different shapes and locations. The bald-faced hornet (black and white and about 1 inch or 20 mm long) tends to build pear-shaped, mottled gray nests in trees or shrubs and, occasionally, under decks, porches, roof overhangs, or in attics, crawlspaces and walls. The insects make the paper-like building material from chewed wood. They feed on flies and other insects.

Yellow jackets are the size of house flies, with distinctive yellow and black markings.

A yellow jacket.

They build similar nests but they are tan in color, smaller than a hornet's nest, and usually constructed in underground cavities. These scavengers frequent fireplace cookouts and trash cans, attracted by the smell of food. They often congregate around sugar solutions in hummingbird feeders.

Wasps and hornets live for only one year. Each colony dies in the fall with only the new queens surviving the winter. The queens leave their nests during late summer, mate with males, seek shelter in rotting logs, under loose bark, under siding, in wood piles or other small crevices, and become dormant. Emerging in spring, they search for sites and construct new nests.

Wasps don't reuse old nests, so you can remove them safely in autumn.

A hornet's nest.

An orb weaver spider.

# Spiders

Remember Charlotte? The vast majority of spiders are harmless to humans. Most spiders have venom but it is not very toxic to humans, usually resulting in no more than a slight swelling or itch, and the fangs of most spiders are too small and weak to puncture skin. In fact, spiders are beneficial predators that reduce pest flies, crickets and mites.

Spiders have four pairs of legs, find their way around with six or eight simple eyes and have a pair of jaws, each of which ends in a hollow fang through which venom can be injected. The venom paralyzes the prey and begins the digestion process. Spiders can only ingest liquids, so they must wait for the prey's internal organs to turn to a broth that they can suck in.

The tip of the spider's abdomen has a group of small finger-like spinnerets that produce silk for spinning webs. All spiders pro-duce silk, which is secreted as a liquid through the spinnerets and hardens on contact with air. The silk is used for making egg sacs, capturing prey, holding prey, making shelters or retreats, and transferring sperm during mating. Also, young "spiderlings" extrude silk threads so that they can be transported by air currents, a process called "ballooning."

Spiders that use the web for capturing prey in camps and cottages are cobweb spiders, orb weaver spiders, cellar spiders, and funnel web spiders; spiders that use the web as a resting place and actively hunt for their prey are wolf spiders, jumping spiders, and nursery web spiders.

> Ants are busy, gnats bite, crickets sing louder than usual, spiders come down from their webs, and flies gather in houses just before rain and possible severe storms.

# Orb weaver spiders

Orb weaver spiders construct the circular, elaborate webs that catch flying insects, usually outdoors. Each species constructs a web with a distinctive design. The spiders have poor vision and locate their prey by feeling the vibration and tension of the threads in their web. They use silk to wrap and store the victim. Orb weaver spiders can be tiny (less than ⅛ inch or 2.5 mm) to quite large (over 1 inch or 2.5 cm long), like the brightly colored yellow garden spider, with silver hairs and a large abdomen marked in black and bright yellow or orange. It lives in bushes and tall grasses in open sunny places.

# Funnel web spiders

Funnel web spiders make large funnel-shaped horizontal webs of non-sticky silk. The spider hides at the narrow end of the funnel and, when it feels the vibration of an insect strolling the web, dashes out, bites the insect and carries it back to digest the broth. Generally

A funnel web spider has moth for dinner tonight.

brown, about ½ inch (1 cm) long with banded legs, some species have spinnerets that extend out beneath the rear of the abdomen. The bites of most funnel web spiders are not known to be toxic to humans. The silk of funnel web spiders was once used to cover wounds to stop bleeding.

# Cobweb spiders

These are the spiders that are responsible for the face-full of web that we often walk into when we're looking down instead of up. The outer sticky threads of these irregular webs entangle insects. Some cobweb species hide during the day in a retreat built into the web, and hang upside down in the center of the web at night. The common house spider is gray to brown, lined with several dark stripes near the tip of its globular abdomen. It prefers damp basements, cellars, crawlspaces, and outbuildings.

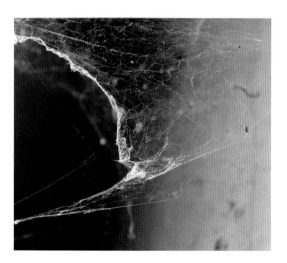

Cobweb spiders abandon webs that do not catch prey, constructing new ones until it finds a productive site.

A wolf spider.

# Wolf spiders

These hunting spiders will chase down their prey. Wolf spiders are hairy, dark brown and usually large, up to 1⅜ inch (1 cm) long with long spiny legs. They hunt day and night, usually outdoors. When they wander indoors they tend to stay at or near floor level. Females produce a large, globular egg sac attached to spinnerets under the abdomen. She carries the spiderlings on her back for several days. Wolf spiders are not aggressive, but may bite if you pick them up.

# Dock spiders

Also called nursery web spider, dock spiders usually live near lakes and streams, but can be found indoors too. They can run over the surface of water and dive and stay submerged for some time if threatened. They can be huge, some with a leg span of 3 inches (7.5 cm). They hunt day and night for aquatic insects and even small fish and are often referred to as "fishing spiders." The silk webbing is used solely for the egg sac which the female carries using her mouthparts. When the spiderlings are ready to emerge she fastens the egg sac to leaves and encloses it within a "nursery" web, within which the spiderlings remain until they are ready to leave. The female guards the nursery while the young are developing. A fishing spider will not bite unless threatened, or it may bite in defense of its egg sac. However, encounters with dock spiders are usually one of surprise for both parties and the hasty retreat is usually by the spider. The venom of a dock spider is effective in paralyzing or killing prey, but it is harmless to humans. Nevertheless, bear in mind that there in very rare instances, an individual may have a severe or medically significant reaction to a bite.

*Right* A daddy long-legs.

# Harvestmen or daddy long-legs

Close relatives of spiders, daddy long-legs do not bite humans, lack venom glands, and don't construct webs. They do have eight very long, slender legs, but lack the narrow waist of spiders. Their bodies are oval, compact and small (1/16–3/8 inch or 1–10 mm long). During the fall, large numbers of harvestmen often cluster together. The adults usually don't survive outdoors when temperatures drop. The female deposits each egg deep into the soil. They hatch the following spring. The adults usually are inactive and hidden during the day, but at sunset they wander about hunting for live insects, especially aphids, or dead insects and plant juices. Harvestmen commonly live among plants or on tree trunks. They are often found in crawlspaces, basements, and outbuildings of cottages that don't freeze in winter.

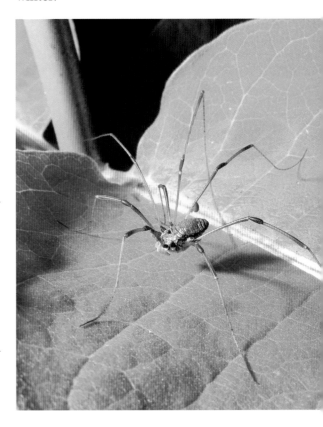

# Unwelcome cottage visitors

## Chiggers

Chiggers are biting mites. The adult, sometimes called a harvest mite, is bright red and can be seen crawling over the ground. It's the microscopic larval stage that attacks humans and other animals. Shores of lakes and streams, woodlands, berry patches and orchards are their preferred habitats, and they are most numerous in early summer when grass, weeds and other vegetation is lush and damp.

Chiggers move to a feeding site, such as human skin, rodent ears or around the eyes of birds, and firmly attach themselves. They don't burrow into the skin, but jamb their mouthparts into a skin pore or hair follicle, secrete digestive enzymes to liquefy the tissues, and suck up the broth. Their bites produce small, reddish welts on the skin accompanied by intense itching. There is one generation each year with chiggers most abundant during July, August, and early September.

## Ticks and Lyme disease

There are two closely related deer tick species that harbor and transmit the bacteria and the protist that cause Lyme diseases in people and animals. The bacteria cause a Lyme disease called "Ehrlichiosis." After incubating for one to three weeks it can cause fever, headache and muscle aches. A typical early symptom is a slowly expanding red rash at the site of the tick bite, often followed by fatigue, gastrointestinal complaints, nausea, vomiting, and/or diarrhea. The illness may vary from mild to severe and life-threatening. In some, the joints,

A tick.

the heart and the central nervous system can be involved. The Lyme disease "Babesiosis" is an infection caused by a protozoan. The disease begins with flu-like symptoms one to three weeks after a deer tick bite. Like malaria, the protozoan inhabits red blood cells and can cause anemia and fatigue. It can be severe and even life-threatening in people with blood disorders and without spleens. Antibiotics eradicate both Lyme disease infections.

The greatest risk is in spring, summer, and fall when the smaller nymphal form of tick is most active. Adult ticks are active in the fall, warm days of winter, and spring in a variety of habitats, principally woodlands and bushy areas, feeding on birds, mice and deer. Domestic animals, such as cats, dogs, horses, and cows, can also carry ticks. Children appear to be at higher risk for tick bites than adults.

Use DEET to keep ticks off you. If one does attach, use tweezers to pull the tick straight out from your skin. For tips on removing ticks from your family pet, see page 151.

Carpenter ants. The large one is an adult and the others are all workers preying on insect larvae.

# Ants

## Carpenter ants

Carpenter ants chew on wood but do not ingest it. They leave a sawdust behind while mining tunnels for nests. Termites eat and digest wood and do not leave sawdust behind.

Most carpenter ants fall into five size classes between ⅛ and ¾ inch (3–20 mm) and all sizes can be found in one nest, in living or dead trees, logs or wood piles. If you are building a cottage in a forested area, you can be certain that carpenter ants will be around to watch you provide their next hangout! The ants typically have a parent colony in an outside nesting area. A new queen can lay 70,000 fertilized eggs so it does not take long for the colony to outgrow its space expand to a satellite colony, which can quite readily develop in a nearby cottage.

If you are lucky enough to locate a nest, remove it with a vacuum cleaner, disposing the bag outdoors.

Unfortunately, locating nests is difficult. Carpenter ants chew wood and make a gnawing sound. To find a nest, start by listening for faint rustling sounds and then tear lumber apart to find the slit-like tunnels, usually carpeted in sawdust. Look for piles of sawdust-like borings in basements, under porches, or accumulations of sawdust at cracks or crevices between walls and partitions.

While chemicals may not be in your repertoire of control options, you can either watch your cottage slowly come down around you or apply an insecticide (available from most hardware stores). Form chemical barriers in tunnels that ants use as they forage for food. The ant's body becomes contaminated with the insecticide and carries it back to the nest, where other ants are poisoned. Use slow-acting, persistent insecticides. There are insecticidal dusts that can be applied between walls, in attics, and in other areas where liquid sprays might harm fabric, wallpaper, carpet or tile. Treat inside and outside along walls, entry ways and in crawl spaces.

## Fire ants

Fire ants are even a greater problem than carpenter ants and termites, particularly in the southern United States where they have infested more than 318 million acres of agricultural land. Introduced from South America, they are a significant health hazard and hundreds of millions of dollars are spent annually to control them.

A colony of fire ants.

Termites enter a tunnel (*left*). An example of termite damage (*right*). Imagine this happening to your cottage!

Very aggressive and competitive, they eliminate most other competing ants. Fire ants become very aggressive when anything disturbs their sandy mound. If they get on you, shake them off or brush them off quickly because within seconds the ant will grasp the skin with its jaws, arch its back, insert its rear-end stinger into the flesh, and inject venom from the poison sac. As if that isn't enough, it then pivots at the head and rapidly jabs seven to eight stings in a circular pattern. Fire ant venom is unique because of the high concentration of toxins, which are responsible for the burning pain characteristic of fire ant stings.

Each summer, fire ants produce hundreds of new queens that fly off to begin new colonies. There are insecticides that can be applied to kill the colony. Digging the mound can be dangerous and usually the ants will return quickly anyway.

## Termites

Termites are social insects that eat wood. There are two basic types, drywood termites that live entirely in wood, and subterranean termites that tunnel into the ground.

Drywood termite colonies excavate "galleries" inside dead branches, logs, lumber or furniture. Once the wood is consumed the colony dies.

Since single pieces of wood cannot support large numbers, the colonies are small, less than a few thousand termites. The tell-tale sign for drywood termites is the coarse, sand-like fecal pellets that the nymphs leave behind.

Most termites are subterranean, tunneling to find wood. They are not limited to one piece of wood so their colonies can be massive, usually hundreds of thousands to several million, and can be very serious structural pests. The queens are grossly huge. The workers can transform into soldiers and reproductives, but never alates, which fly from the colony to start new colonies. Subterranean termites don't produce fecal pellets like the drywood termites but are revealed by the presence of mud shelter tubes on walls. Many species have specialized diets and may eat plant litter, grass, dung or humus instead of wood. In spite of their pest role, most termite species are considered highly beneficial because they break down wood, turn, aerate and enrich the soil.

Ants differ from termites in three ways: Ants have elbowed antennae, termites have straight antennae; ants have a narrow waist, termites have a broad waist; the hind wings are smaller than the forewings in ants but the same size in termites.

You will encounter earwigs indoors and out. They average ⅜ to ½ inches (10–14 mm) in length.

Insecticides control earwigs outdoors but indoor control is not really required. Earwigs need moist soil to lay their eggs and will move outdoors eventually to find it. Just bear with them, then keep them out using the methods described for spiders. If you really want to hunt them down, try spraying them with soap and water. They usually die right away.

## Silverfish and firebrats

Silverfish and firebrats, sometimes called "bristletails," have flat, elongated, tapering bodies that are covered with tiny scales. They have two long, slender antennae and three long, tail-like appendages. Silverfish adults are about ⅜ to ⅝ inch (1–1.5 cm) long with a uniform silvery or gray color, depending on the species. The firebrat is about ⅜ inch (1 cm) long, grayish and mottled with spots and bands of dark scales.

Silverfish and firebrats eat a wide variety of foods, including glue in wallpaper paste and book bindings and paper; fabrics such as cotton, linen and rayon; grains such as wheat, rye, rolled oats, flour, and cereals; and dried meats, leather and dead insects.

Silverfish tend to live in damp, cool places such as basements and laundry rooms, often frequenting bathtubs and sinks but unable to escape the porcelain walls. Firebrats prefer hot, humid places such as attics in summer and near furnaces, fireplaces and heating ducts in winter. They enter buildings by hitch-hiking in food, furniture, old books, papers and clothing. Populations build up slowly so a large infestation usually indicates a long-time infestation. Adults lay eggs in cracks and crevices near food sources. Silverfish and firebrats are long-lived insects. Combined, the lifespans, including the nymph stage, can be up to six years for silverfish and three to four years for firebrats.

## Earwigs

There's an old superstition that earwigs crawl into the ears of people sleeping on straw beds, bore through the eardrum and attack the brain. Earwigs will pinch you if you disturb them, and some species have scent glands that squirt a foul-smelling liquid, but they aren't interested in your brains.

Most earwigs have a pair of short, leathery forewings, but are poor fliers. They have a pair of forceps-like appendages for defense and during courtship. Earwigs are good runners and can migrate short distances in this manner. Tough and good feigners, they'll lie still for a while and then crawl off.

Earwigs are primarily scavengers on live aphids, dead insects and rotted plant materials; a few species are predators. They are active at night, some species being attracted to lights in large numbers. During the day they seek shelter beneath baseboards, stones, lumber, sidewalks or debris. They lay eggs in small batches beneath the soil surface. The mother guards the eggs and the newly hatched young. Most species have one generation per year, overwintering as eggs or adults in the soil.

A firebrat.

# Snails and slugs

Ugh, slugs, those slimy little creepers that devour our garden vegetables. The gray garden slug in particular is infamous for its assaults, using a rasp-like tongue called a radula on lettuce, strawberries, seedlings, tomatoes and several flowering plants, including lilies, iris, narcissus, amaryllis, coleus and tulips.

Not all species are pests. Many are predators that only eat other plant-eating species. Slugs are a good source of food and when abundant will attract frogs and birds such

A garden snail.

as crows, ducks, jays and owls. Like earthworms, slugs contribute to the breakdown of plant debris and the recycling of nutrients, particularly dog and cat feces, back into the soil. Many eat mostly dead vegetation and fungi. Most live for only one to two years but some can live for many years.

Snails have an obvious shell but the shell in the slug is hidden underneath the mantle in an elevated region on the back. They breathe atmospheric oxygen using a lung, the air entering the lung cavity through a breathing pore. Slugs move by sliding along mucous secreted by their large foot. They sense with two pairs of tentacles, the first having eyes at the tip of each one.

Slugs use their tentacles to follow slime trails they left the night before. Other slugs pick up on different trails, creating a slug "map" to host plants. If you get slime on your hands, pour a little white vinegar on your hands and wash it off with lukewarm water.

## Edible land snails

The favorite edible land snails raised as escargot are the brown garden snail, *Helix aspersa,* and the Roman snail, *Helix pomatia,* both introduced into several eastern and gulf states in the mid 1800s.

The brown garden snail seems to be more popular than the Roman snail, which has a lifespan of two to five years and is adaptable to different climates and conditions. Their shells measure about 1 to 2 inches (30–45 mm) across and they can be found in woods, fields, sand dunes and gardens.

The wood snail, *Cepaea nemoralis,* which measures about 1 inch (25 mm) across the shell, is more common than the brown garden snail. It too was introduced and inhabits woods and dunes in many U.S. states, from Massachusetts to California and from Tennessee to Canada. It mainly eats dead plants and dead animals (worms and snails), but it likes nettles and buttercups.

The garden snail, *Cepaea hortensis,* measures about ¾ inch (20 mm) across the shell and has distinct dark stripes. It was introduced into Maine, Massachusetts, and New Hampshire in colonial times, but it never became established in these states. The garden snail is found in colder and wetter places than the wood snail. Both the garden and wood snails are used as escargot but their smaller size, and the adage that snails with striped shells do not taste as good, make them less popular than the brown garden snail.

### Caution!

Although some people eat garden snails as escargot, some other people use poison bait to kill slugs and snails; since snails move everywhere, those in your own backyard may be carrying poison. If you consumed enough of these snails, the poison could kill you! Be snail smart and buy your escargot from a reliable source or collect in known safe areas.

# Living with wildlife

When you are sharing space with nature, a little knowledge and respect goes a long way. You may be delighted to watch chipmunks chasing each other up trees and across the deck but appalled to have their mousey kin skittering across your kitchen floor. A fluffy cottontail is a delight to see, except when it is devouring your carefully tended vegetable garden. A wasp is just as fascinatingly elegant as a dragonfly but, alas, it has a sting. Yet it's unreasonable for us to expect animals to know that our gardens and kitchens and bodies are off-limits. If you know what to expect in the behavior of the animals that live in the vicinity of your cottage, you can prepare for it. If it's too late for that, there are some reactive measures you can take.

### Proactive measures

As in almost everything, prevention is easier than the cure. Don't tempt creatures into the spaces you don't want them to occupy. There are a number of things that will attract wild creatures to your cottage, inside and out. Be aware of what they are and take measures to prevent problems before they happen. The goal is to remove sources of food, water, and shelter.

- Don't leave food or garbage out.
- Always wash containers that had food in them, or throw them in the wood stove to burn the waste food.

- Clean your barbecue after each use, burn off the grease before closing it, and keep the grease trap empty.
- Remove pet food and water during the night; pick up bones, chew sticks, and other pet treats.
- Keep the yard clean and woodpiles stacked neatly.

### Bears

The number one way to keep bears away is not to leave out food to attract them. Also be considerate of your neighbors by not leaving garbage on anyone else's property — and encourage your children to do the same. Whatever you do, don't make a game of going to feed the bears at the local dump. Incredible as it may seem, some cottagers think that's a fun thing to do. If there are bears in your part of cottage country, and you do happen to have one visit, make a lot of noise and get safely inside. And then notify the authorities. Don't try to take action yourself.

squirrel · rat · bristletail · mouse · ant · termite · honey bee nest · barbeque · beaver · raccoon · skunk · garden · deer · bear · bird seed · kibble · garbage · gypsy moth · vole · snail · slug · coyote · fox

## Deer

Before implementing any control solutions, make sure it is deer that are destroying your garden. Decide from tracks and droppings. The height of the browsing can also be a clue: deer browse below 5 feet (1.5 m); large moose may browse as high as 12 feet (2.3 m). If the deer are an annual nuisance, plant trees and shrubs that deer tend not to eat such as box elders, pines, and spruces. They also aren't keen on hollies, tree peonies, rhododendrons and lilacs. Try scare tactics that relate to sight, hearing, taste, and smell — but do it early, before the deer get too used to seeing people around.

- Vary your tactics frequently. Scarecrows made from fertilizer bags inverted over stakes in gardens will bring relief for only a week or so.
- Try streamers, balloons, aluminum pie plates, and other spinning or fluttering objects.
- Set lights on a timer to turn on and off at half-hour intervals.
- Try placing a radio tuned to an all-night station under cover.

Deer are infamous for browsing on buds, twig-ends and leaves of woody plants in winter, destroying new growth and deforming shrubs and trees. To deer-proof your trees (if you don't want to fence them out) the only alternative is to fence individual plants:

- Place fence around trees or shrubs of 7 feet (3 m) high or less.
- Drive three or four tall wooden stakes into the ground around the tree, far enough away to keep the deer from reaching in to eat the lower branches. The stakes should be 10 feet (3 m) long, with at least 8 feet (2.4 m) above the ground; attach woven wire or plastic mesh to the stakes to form a fence around the tree.
- Young trees and shrubs should be fenced every fall until their primary branches are about 5 feet (1.5 m) high. You may need to make the fence taller after accumulated snowfalls.

Garbage, especially food waste, attracts wild animals. Be on the lookout for wildlife you might encounter when visiting rural dump sites. Remember that you invite trouble for your fellow cottagers whenever you dispose of your garbage anywhere but designated dumping grounds.

- Chemical deer repellants are available at garden centers. A homemade repellant made from six spoiled eggs, three gallons of water and three tablespoons of 75-percent Thriam, a mild fungicide, works reasonably well, but it must be painted on the trees after rain or snowstorms.

## Rabbits

Rabbits can do a number on young trees and saplings too. They gnaw a ring of bark entirely around the trunk and kill the tree. Fortunately, rabbits can stand only about 2 feet (60 cm) high, so fences can be short.

- Rabbits travel well on deep snow so it is best to protect at least 3 to 4 feet (1–1.5 m) of the tree and its branches.
- Drive four stakes into the ground so that the fencing is at least 6 inches (15 cm) from the longest branch.
- If you use chicken wire, increase the distance from the branch because rabbits can lean on and push the fence inward. Use fencing with holes no larger than one inch (2.5 cm).
- Dig a trench around the base of the mesh and bury 4 to 6 inches (10–15 cm) so the rabbits cannot burrow below the fence.

- If the young tree has only a few branches, use plastic coil wrapping with holes. It is available in 3- to 6-foot (1–2 m) lengths at most garden centers and is easy to work with.
- Chemical repellents are available at garden centers, but need to be reapplied frequently, especially after rain or wet snow.

## Raccoons

To get the raccoons out of their dens:

- Loud noise: during the early evening when they are probably on their way out for food, encourage them to leave by using horns, scarecrows, bright lights, or loud music. Some stubborn raccoons may think you are playing games and return soon after.
- Live-trapping: Use cage-type live traps that are at least 10 inches wide by 12 inches high by 32 inches long (25 x 30 x 81 cm) constructed with heavy-gage wire. However, finding a new home for the raccoon is not easy; no one wants a nuisance animal in their area, including the raccoons already established there.
- Modify habitat: Because adult males have large territories, a community-wide effort may be more successful.

## Beavers

To protect from beavers.

◆ Use cylindrical cages or fences made of chicken wire or sturdy 2-by-4-inch (5–10 cm) welded wire fencing, about 4 feet (1.2 m) high. Leave a 6-inch (15 cm) space between the tree and the fence. Join the ends of the chicken wire with nylon or wire ties, or cut every other horizontal wire and bend into hooks to connect with the other side. Anchor the cages to the ground with rebar stakes.

◆ Make a sand and paint mixture by using 8 fluid ounces (240 mL) of fine sand (mason sand) to one quart (1.1 L) of oil or latex paint. Stir often while painting trunks up to 4 feet (1.2 m) high. Do not paint young trees (less than about 6 feet / 2 m tall).

## Skunk control

If you are worried about the skunk next door, modify your own habitat to discourage it from hanging around. It's a bad idea to live trap, or even dead trap, skunks. Preventing the skunks or young from escaping a den is not only inhumane but can cause even worse odor problems.

◆ If a skunk strays into a shed, leave a door open and let the skunk exit on its own.

◆ Remove debris and brush piles or stack neatly to eliminate den sites.

◆ Putting a light, tape recorder with human noises, a portable radio, or moth balls in the den may encourage the skunk to move out.

## Mice and rats

How can an animal as tiny as a mouse be such a colossal nightmare? It's best to keep mice out of the cottage in the first place,

◆ Get a flashlight, a roll of aluminum foil, a flat-head screw driver, and a silicone gun. Crawl under the building. Find every opening between every floor joist, including those where electrical wires and plumbing enter the building. Seal every space larger than ¼ inch (5 cm) inch with silicone, or aluminum foil. The silicone will also keep out centipedes, ants and other pests.

◆ Find openings larger than ¼ inch (5 cm) in eaves, soffits, facia, gable ends, windows, doors, and anything else suspicious. Seal the openings with silicone, aluminum foil or both.

◆ See **Mousetraps** at page155.

You will see rats all year around. In winter their nests are easy to locate by following their tracks. If rats move in, remove or exterminate them.

◆ Rat-proof garbage cans and all buildings to keep them out.

◆ Use the same control methods as for mice, but larger traps and cages.

## Voles

Voles tear up lawns. The easiest solution is to give up your lawn — what are you doing with a lawn at the cottage?

◆ Live mousetraps or snap-back killing traps can be effective. Place the traps perpendicular to the runway with the trigger end in the middle of the runway.

◆ Place a third of a roofing shingle over the burrow opening and bait with an apple slice. Bend the shingle to form a V-shaped roof and place a trap under it. Leave the shingle in place for a few days before baiting to allow the animals to become accustomed to it.

◆ Cylindrical wire mesh (with ⁵⁄₁₆-inch or 8 mm openings or less) cages at least 12 inches (30 cm) high can be wrapped around the bases of small trees, blueberries and other shrubs to protect them. Keep the cages at least one inch (2.5 cm) from the trunk.

## Gypsy moths

The gypsy moth can be controlled at the egg, caterpillar and adult stages.

◆ Burn or soak egg masses in water or kerosene.

◆ Wrapping the tree trunk with sticky bands, or slippery bands (available at garden centers) will help keep the caterpillars from reaching the foliage from the ground.

A live trap for rodents. You can generally tell when an animal is a nuisance in an area because hardware stores will keep traps in stock. If you have to order them in, reconsider trapping. Every animal is important to the balance of the ecosystem.

Glass wasp traps are a functional and beautiful way to prevent stinging bugs from crashing your outdoor meals. Sugar water or any other sweetened liquid lures the hornet to fly onto the jar through a hole at the bottom. Trapped, the hornet drowns in the liquid.

◆ Spraying them with water under pressure to kill or knock them off.
◆ Garden centers carry various brands of "insecticidal soaps." These are soaps that do not contain synthetic insecticides but instead are soaps that have abilities to kill certain insects. Be sure to follow label directions.
◆ Small and large caterpillars can easily be drowned in a bucket of soapy water.

## Wasps

The best time of the year to control wasps is in June, while the new colony is still small.

◆ Dress with long-sleeved shirts and pants, rubber boots, gloves, and head and face protection. Tuck your pant legs into the boots and pull your sleeves over the gloves. At night, when they are less active, apply a "wasp and hornet spray" into the entrance of the nest according to label directions. Stand to the side to avoid pesticide raining down on yourself. Use steady ladders and plan an escape route. If wasps are still flying the next day, repeat the treatment.
◆ Alternatively, but a bit riskier, cover the nest with a large, heavy, plastic bag and seal it shut, cut the nest from its hold and freeze it.
◆ For ground nests, try pouring a soap (dish or laundry detergent will do) and water solution into the entrance.
◆ You can also apply an insecticide that is registered for use in lawns or soil into the nest opening.

## Spiders

If spiders become a nuisance, keeping them out is a better strategy than trying to kill them.

◆ Install tight-fitting screens on windows, soffit vents, foundations and roof gables, and weather stripping on door sweeps.
◆ Use yellow or sodium vapor light bulbs outdoors and turn lights off when not needed.
◆ Clean up clutter, store things off the floor, and vacuum.

## Bristletails

Making sure there are no bristletails in the materials you bring to the cottage is the first step.

◆ If they get past you, remove old stacks of papers, books and clutter.
◆ Repair any leaky plumbing.
◆ There are many insecticides available to treat infestations of silverfish and firebrats. Apply thoroughly to all potential hiding places such as floor moldings, seldom-moved furniture, crevices around steam and water pipes, closets and even attics.

## Termites

Once they move in, they aren't leaving. Termites get into places you can't treat. Use pressure-treated lumber on outside parts, such as floor joists and supporting structures, to deter them.

## Slugs

Some commercial products will discourage or kill pest slugs and snails, but there are several environmentally friendly techniques:

◆ Spread cedar or oak bark chips or gravel chips, which irritate and dehydrate slugs.
◆ Wood ashes dry the slugs up.
◆ Spread well-crushed eggshells or ground shells of filberts, pecans and walnuts around the plants.
◆ Use a mulch of strong-smelling herbs (for example, wormwood, mints, tansy, rosemary, lemon balm) mixed with conifer twigs or needles.
◆ Quack grass tea apparently damages the nerves of slugs: cut up quack grass, soak in 1 quart of warm water for 24 hours, then use as a barrier spray on soil (but not on plants).
◆ Epsom salts sprinkled on the soil apparently deters slugs and also helps prevent magnesium deficiency in plants.

# Poisonous, noxious, nuisance plants

## Jack-in-the-pulpit

Also called bog onion, brown dragon, Indian turnip, wake robin and wild turnip, this peculiar-looking perennial appears in the spring. The unusual flower is greenish-yellow with purple or brown stripes, and consist of a spathe, or "pulpit," and a spadix, or "jack". The spadix is covered by thousands of tiny flowers that fruit into a cluster of smooth, shiny red berries in late summer.

The plant contains asparagine, an amino acid that is required by the nervous system to maintain equilibrium.

The striped spathe of the jack-in-the-pulpit conceals a white spadix that is covered by small flowers (*left*).

However, it also contains oxalic acid, which is toxic to animals. The most toxic parts are the tuberous root and the stem. Fortunately, the roots are inaccessible to most animals. Symptoms of toxicity are burning in the mouth, swelling of tongue or mouth, slurred speech, burning pain in the throat, teary eyes, nausea and vomiting, diarrhea. In rare cases, the swelling may be severe enough to block the airway.

The best treatment is to wipe out the mouth with a cold, wet cloth and give milk to drink. Don't induce vomiting. Wash skin with water. If eyes are watery, wash with water.

Nightshade.

## Natural itch-relief: spotted touch-me-not

Touch-me-not, also known as spotted jewelweed, can be recognized by its trumpet-shaped orange flowers, which are speckled with red dots. The plants stand 3 to 5 feet (1–1.5 m) tall. When gently squeezed, a touch-me-not seed pod will burst and spread its seeds, hence this common name. The name jewelweed comes from the bright turquoise color of the inner parts of the seeds.

Touch-me-not is a natural remedy and preventative for poison ivy, oak and sumac. Conveniently, it often grows near these plants.

Crushed leaves or the juicy insides of stems quickly ease the irritation of plant-induced rashes. Boil the leaves to make a tea, strain it and then freeze it into ice cubes to use on irritated skin. You can also apply a healing poultice made from the leaves and stems to bruises, burns, cuts, eczema, insect bites, sores, sprains, warts, and ringworm.

No touch-me-not in sight? Use ointments or lotions that contain calamine or zinc oxide to stop the itch.

# Bittersweet nightshade

This pretty plant with deep purple flowers was introduced as a medicinal plant but in fact is very poisonous to humans and animals. The poisonous, bright red berries often attract children and unwary adults.

# Common tansy

This aromatic herb was introduced from Eurasia for its medicinal properties. People used it to kill intestinal parasites and to flavor liqueurs, salads, cakes and puddings until someone discovered it contains a toxic chemical called thujone that can be fatal!

Common tansy.

Some people apparently are immune to poison ivy but you have to find out the hard way!

# Poison ivy

Most of us know the effects of this poisonous plant but surprisingly few of us spot it until it's too late. To recognize poison ivy, remember the rhyme "leaves in three, let it be" — the glossy green leaves are divided into three pointed leaflets with smooth or slightly toothed edges. The plant can be sprawling and bushy, covering the ground, or a tall, woody vine. The leaves turn red in the fall and carry white, berry-like fruits. Unfortunately, it grows in a variety of places, including shady, moist areas and open, sandy areas. The leaves, stem and roots of poison ivy contain a resin called urushiol that causes an itchy rash if left for more than ten minutes. If you catch it quickly, you can wash off the resin with strong, soapy, lukewarm water. Urushiol does not evaporate and can linger for a year. Clothing, pets and shoes can carry it and cause rashes. Don't burn poison ivy because smoke can carry the resin. To get rid of poison ivy permanently you need to remove/kill the roots. Call a professional if you have a lot of plants. Otherwise, spray them with a herbicide, keeping in mind that it can also kill surrounding plants.

**You give me fever**

Itchy eyes and runny nose? Don't blame goldenrod for your hayfever. The pollen is so heavy that wind can't carry it very far. It's ragweed, which often occurs with goldenrod, that is the main cause of hayfever.

Poison sumac.

Spotted water hemlock (*above*) and young stinging nettle (*below*).

# Poison sumac

Poison sumac grows in some peat bogs and swamps of southern Ontario, southern Quebec and in the eastern United States. Because of the plant's habitat, few people are likely to experience the poison ivy-like itch.

Poison sumac is the only sumac species with whitish-green fruit growing between the leaf and the branch (nonpoisonous sumacs have reddish fruit growing from the ends of their branches). It is a tall shrub or small tree with 6 to 13 leaflets, 6 arranged in pairs with an additional single leaflet at the end of the midrib. The foliage turns to brilliant orange or scarlet in the fall. The male and female flowers of poison sumac are on separate plants, as in poison ivy and western poison oak, which thankfully does not occur in the temperate zone of North America.

# Spotted water-hemlock

A single rootstock of spotted water-hemlock is capable of killing a horse. All parts of the plant are toxic; the stem is thick and tough, but even touching it can cause stomach pains, vomiting and convulsions. To identify the plant, look for side veins that go to the notches of the leaf teeth, not to the tips; remember the saying, "vein to the cut, pain in the gut."

# Stinging nettle

Nettles have coarse teeth and sharp stinging hairs (the sting is from formic acid, not the bristle). The formic acid within the hairs causes skin irritation that can be cured by rubbing aloe vera on the affected area. If great mullein is around, crush the flower and rub it on the affected area.

You can eat this plant—use rubber gloves to pick it! The stem and leaves are loaded with vitamins A and C. The formic acid needs to be boiled (15–20 minutes will do) to kill the sting and convert it into a digestible protein. After cleaning in water and boiling, melted butter and lemon juice make stinging nettle a delicious vegetable.

# White death camas

This extremely toxic plant has chemicals more potent than strychnine. The bulb looks like wild onion and if eaten can be fatal. Symptoms are salivating, diarrhea, a low body temperature and a slow heart beat. Induce vomiting immediately if you suspect a person has eaten the bulbs and then rush to a hospital.

White death camas.

# Foreign invaders

## Purple loosestrife

Purple loosestrife is native to Eurasia and is now naturalized over large areas of North America. Because of its attractive purple flowers, it was planted as an ornamental garden species but escaped from cultivation, and now occupies at least 40 states and most of Canada.

This tall (7 feet or 2 m), much-branched perennial spreads so aggressively that it takes over from native vegetation, altering the structure and function of wetlands and reducing the value of wetlands for wildlife. It may also impede the flow of water in irrigation canals and degrade the quality of pastures and hay. It is estimated that nearly 5 million acres (200,000 ha) of wetlands in the United States are degraded annually through invasion of purple loosestrife.

Purple loosestrife grows anywhere with a source of water, such as in marshes, along margins of ponds, lakes and rivers, and in canals, wet meadows, prairies and ditches, creating seas of purple flowers. It spreads asexually, from a strong root stock, and sexually, with a single plant producing as many as 2.5 million seeds annually. Long-range dispersal occurs by seeds spread by the water currents, wind and animals, including humans.

### Control options

You can help control small patches of purple loosestrife:

1. Place a garbage bag over each plant to capture all the flowers and seeds.
2. Cut the stem at the ground and invert the bag so that the contents remain inside.
3. Dig up the roots and place them in the bag with the rest of the plant.
4. Tie the bag tightly and dispose of or burn.

Mowing, cutting, burning or drowning can also eliminate small and young stands, but these labor-intensive methods require continued long-term maintenance. Herbicides have also been used but they are non-selective and environmentally harmful.

### Biological control: beetles to the rescue

The leaf-eating beetle (*Galerucella pusilla*) is especially effective at killing purple loosestrife, reducing the plant biomass of purple loosestrife by at least 90 percent. The beetle eats only purple loosestrife leaves; it cannot complete its life cycle on any other plant. Over 100,000 adult beetles were released in Ontario between 1992 and 1995; another 200,000 adults were released in 1997. Huge hectares of purple loosestrife are now being controlled by the leaf-eating beetle.

Common reed in the autumn.

# Common reed

Common reed is a widely distributed grass species, found all over Europe, Asia, Africa, Australia and North America. There are two strains in North America, one introduced and the other native. The invasive version occurs throughout the United States, except Alaska and Hawaii, being most abundant along the Atlantic coast and in freshwater and brackish tidal wetlands of the northeastern United States and Canada. In North America the species is a threat to natural biodiversity. Dense stands decrease the quality of wetland habitat, particularly for migrating waterfowl species, impede water flow, recreational activities such as fishing, and restrict views from shoreline areas.

Common reed is a tall (up to 13 feet / 4.5 m), coarse perennial with stout rhizomes that are deeply set in ground. The stems are leafy throughout, the sheaths overlapping, teminating in a silvery, branched plume. Seeds germinate in spring on exposed, moist soils. Once established, *Phragmites* spreads by rhizomes, which supply the plant with water by creeping along the ground to a ditch or depression that contains water, growing up to 7 feet (2 m) per year. They can reach 66 feet (20 m).

Butterflies, moths, midges, aphids, wasps and mites — 26 species in all — eat the common reed. Of these, 21 were accidentally introduced by humans. Eradication programs using some of these bugs are currently being tested.

## Introduced or native?

You can tell the introduced and native strains of reeds apart by the stems, leaf colors and leaf sheaths. Stems on introduced plants are typically green with a bit of purple at the base, while the native variety has some purple color and are often shiny. Black spots often appear on native stems late in the growing season. Leaf collars are green on the introduced variety and purple on the native variety. One of the best indicators is on dead stems: the leaf sheaths on introduced variety remain attached but are lost or loosely attached on the native variety.

# Eurasian watermilfoil

Eurasian watermilfoil, native to Europe, Asia and Northern Africa, was introduced in the 1940s, and spread quickly through the eastern states and Canada by way of anglers, boaters, and waterfowl.

This aggressive species colonizes reservoirs, lakes, ponds, streams, small rivers and brackish waters of estuaries and bays. It is most abundant in the near-shore depths of nutrient-enriched lakes. Stems of Eurasian watermilfoil near the water surface branch profusely and usually form a dense canopy that reduces light available for other submersed species. It dies back during the winter, and spreads by releasing fragments of itself. The plant has a seven-year life cycle, which may explain the periodic

Eurasian watermilfoil, *Myriophyllum spicatum,* at flowering stage.

nuisance growths of the plant. Water currents, boat trailers and waterfowl transport fragments of watermilfoil over long distances.

Some notable nuisance aspects of watermilfoil include:

- shading out and out-competing desirable native species to form huge colonies;
- creating dense mats and colonies that restrict swimming, boating and bank fishing;
- detracting from the aesthetic appeal of the lake;
- clogging water intakes at power generation facilities and potable water intakes; and finally,
- providing habitat for, and increasing populations of mosquitoes.

## Control options

Eurasian watermilfoil is extremely difficult to control. Chemical and physical control options have limited success:

- Mechanical harvesters quickly remove large masses of milfoil, but the plant grows back quickly, harvesting is expensive, and must be repeated three or four times per year.

- Underwater rototilling and cultivating uproots the plants and allows them to float away, a more effective method than harvesting. However, it too is slow and costly, and releases plant fragments.
- Slow, costly diver-operated dredges are like underwater vacuum cleaners that remove plants (and other organisms) from the bottom.
- Water level manipulation is effective in reservoirs. Lowering water levels in winter exposes the plants to below-freezing temperatures but may be of limited usefulness because of the potential for fish kills, damage to docks and boathouses, and rapid reinfestation.

Biological control has good potential. Experiments are now underway to determine the effectiveness of an aquatic weevil, *Euhychiopsis lecontei,* native to the Kawartha Lakes area in Ontario, that eats the leaves and stems of watermilfoil.

Waterfowl eat the fruits and leaves of the watermilfoil, while muskrats eat the entire plant.

Spring bounty: fresh fiddleheads (*left*) and violets (*right*).

# Edible wild plants

**What's old is new again**

Some familiar domestic plants have wild relatives that can be prepared in the same way, such as leeks, wild garlic (spring bulbs are tasty), horseradish (eat the root), wild spinach and alfalfa.

The tap root of wild parsnip is more aromatic than domestic parsnip, and tastes best at the end of the first growing season. The seed-like fruits are oil rich and can be used as a spice.

Try the boiled young leaves of wild mustard, a prolific plant whose seeds can survive for 60 years.

The fleshy root of common goat's beard can also be roasted or boiled like parsnips.

From juicy snacks to the fixings for a complete meal, there's much wild food to be found within distance of your cottage or cabin. Many wild plants have medicinal uses; for information, see **Cottage Operations**.

## Spring and summer delicacies

### Fiddleheads

Good eating can be found in the young shoots of ferns such as the cinnamon fern, whose spring golden leaves turn cinnamon in fall; bracken fern, which grows in fields and burned areas and has wavy, dark green leaves; and ostrich fern, which grows about 5 feet tall by creeks and in marshes and has dark black-ish leaves that turn dark brown in fall.

French fiddleheads are excellent. Wash the heads thoroughly, blanch in boiling water for one minute, rinse in cold water, boil in fresh water until just tender, and serve with lemon butter.

## Edible flowers: violets, daylilies and common fireweed

Violet leaves and flowers are high in vitamins A (more than spinach) and C (as much as four oranges). Orange daylily blossoms last only a day. The flowers are edible raw, pickled, steamed or fried or added as a spice to soups. The young shoots, leaves and roots are also edible, the roots tasting like chestnuts. The flowers of common fireweed are edible and used as a salad garnish. The leaves and stem of young fireweed plants are tender and taste like asparagus.

## Wild spring salads

The young spring leaves of nasturtium, violets, land cress, chicory and dandelion (before they bloom) make great salads. The young tap root of Queen Anne's lace smells and tastes like carrot but is white and more fragrant. The leaves and root are edible raw or cooked. Do not eat greens from roadsides, where they may have been sprayed with pesticides, or from polluted ground.

# Autumn harvest

## Canadian or Jerusalem artichokes

A relative of the common sunflower: explorers took this plant to Europe where Italians noticed the flower turning and following the sun, so they called it "girasole" (meaning turn toward the sun), which eventually led to "Jerusalem artichoke." Later it was introduced to France where it was dubbed "artichaud de Canada."

Serve the tubers, dug in late fall, as a vegetable. They can be boiled for 10 minutes in salted water, drained, diced, mixed with chopped hard-boiled eggs, some chopped onions, relish and mayonnaise and served on lettuce leaves as a salad.

## Rose hips

The fruits of roses, called rose hips (or haws), are present on all varieties, including wild roses. They ripen in the fall and should be harvested after the first frost. Rose hips have about forty times more vitamin C than oranges. Their high pectin content makes an excellent rose hip jelly. Rose hip tea is blood red.

## Chicory coffee

In the fall, the roots can be dug up, cleaned, dried in an oven and ground up into coffee-size grounds. A tablespoon is added to coffee for added flavor, but it can be brewed and used as a caffeine-free hot drink.

## Mint julep

A handful of mint leaves steeped for 3 to 5 minutes makes a delicate tea. It can also be crushed and used as an herb in many soups and desserts.

**2 stems of mint, 8 inches (15 cm) long**    **crushed ice**
**2 tsp confectioner's sugar**    **bourbon whiskey**

Take 2 stems of mint about 8 inches (15 cm) long, wash, strip the leaves of one of the stalks into a cup, add 2 teaspoons of confectioner's sugar. With a wooden spatula, bruise the leaves with the sugar, grinding and mixing them together until the sugar is thoroughly stained with mint and the leaves are mashed. Fill a glass with crushed ice, add bourbon whiskey, stir, place the other mint stalk in the glass and serve.

## Blueberries

There are at least 40 different species of blueberries, *Vaccinium* spp, that grow from the arctic to Mexico and from the east coast to the west. Blueberries need acidic soil. They grow in dry or moist, sandy or rocky clearings, in sphagnum bogs and swamps, beaver meadows, and especially in burned-over areas.

Three common species are the low-bush blueberry, the high-bush blueberry and the velvet-leaf blueberry. All three species have elliptical to oval leaves 1 to 2 inches (2.5–5 cm) long. White, bell-shaped flowers in spring fruit to clusters of round, blue to black berries in summer. Not shiny, they are often dusted with a white powder. The lowbush and velvet-leaf blueberry bushes grow less than 3 feet (1 m) and the highbush to 6 feet (2 m). The leaves of the lowbush blueberry are naked while those of the velvet-leaf are fuzzy, with numerous short hairs on both surfaces. Otherwise, blueberry species are difficult to tell apart. But who cares—the berries of all three species are divine raw or cooked.

---

Virginia strawberry.

### Superfood: blueberries

Blueberries' health and anti-aging benefits put them among the top three "superfoods." Blueberries have ellagic acid, an antioxidant that may block the metabolic pathways that can promote cancer. People who consume fruits with the most ellagic acid—blueberries, raspberries, blackberries and boysenberries—are supposedly three times less likely to develop cancer than those who eat little or no ellagic acid. One serving of blueberries provides as many antioxidants as five servings of carrots, apples, broccoli or squash. Blueberries, like cranberries, help maintain urinary tract health.

# Wild fruit plants

Although some berries fruit in spring and others in fall, summer is the best season for seeking out these nutrient-packed treats. Avoid picking from areas with abundant dead vegetation: it has probably been sprayed recently with herbicide. Also, unless you are a well experienced forager, avoid vine fruit as most are poisonous or difficult to differentiate from look-alikes that are. Finally, make lots of noise in the berry patch to warn away bears, your biggest berry-picking competitors.

## Virginia strawberry

These tiny wild strawberries are much sweeter than domesticated varieties, and the leaves make great tea. The leaves, three per plant, roundly toothed on the end, are rich in vitamin C and minerals and are professed to cure all kinds of maladies, including insanity, tuberculosis, diarrhea and skin problems.

Use only fresh or fully dried leaves because wilted leaves contain toxins. The white flowers with five saucer-shaped petals bloom from April to early June. Virginia strawberry grows on dry to moist, sunny to shaded, disturbed or undisturbed grounds.

## Wild red raspberry, common blackberry, and smooth blackberry

All three of these *Rubus* plants produce delicious berries. Look for them in thickets, fencerows, roadsides, pastures, borders of woods and railway ballasts. Raspberry canes have numerous prickly, bristle-like hairs; common blackberry canes are similar but also have spines, while the smooth blackberry has a smooth stem with no hairs but a few spines.

Red raspberries.

The roots, leaves and berries of all *Rubus* plants have medicinal qualities and, as a tea with leaves or roots steeped in water, have been used as eyewash and for curing stomach aches, diarrhea, dysentery and colds. The berries are popular flavorings for candies, ice cream and medicines.

## American cranberry, small cranberry, and mountain cranberry

These trailing or creeping vines with narrowly triangular, leathery and tiny leaves less than ½ inch (15 mm) long produce red, tart berries. American cranberry and small cranberry grow best in peat bogs, on wet, acidic soils, on the shores of ponds, lakes and streams and in tundra. Mountain cranberry grows best in open rocky and sandy areas, on moss-covered boulders and stumps or in peat bogs.

Sweetened, these berries make an excellent sauce with white meats such as chicken and turkey. The American cranberry is the largest, with berries from ⅜ to ¾ inches (10–20 mm) in diameter.

Along with the blueberry and the concord grape, the cranberry is one of only three fruits that are native to North America.

The American elderberry: sprays of white blossoms that appear in the spring fruit to clusters dark red-purple berries.

## American elderberry

American elderberry is a shrub 5 to 10 feet (1.5–3 m) high that grows close to the ground in thick stands in wet woods, near streams and rivers. The pithy stems make great whistles, flutes or blowguns. The pea-sized fruit, purple to black when ripe, is high in vitamins A and C, potassium and iron and very delicious. However, they need to be cooked because raw berries can cause vomiting and diarrhea.

**Caution:** The fruit goes through color changes as it ripens, and is red before it is ripe. Do not pick ripened red berries—they belong to the red-berried elder, which produces clusters of inedible, poisonous berries. The stems, roots and leaves of all elderberries are poisonous.

Native Americans dried both pin cherry (left) and choke cherry (right) and used them in pemmican, trail mixes and other winter foods.

## Pin cherry

The stems and berries look like glass-headed pins stuck in a cushion. The plant can grow as a shrub or as a tree in areas recently cleared by cutting or burning. The shiny reddish-brown bark has conspicuous horizontal pores. The flowers are white, in tassel-like clusters of four to seven and appear in late May to June. The fruit is a small, bright red berry on a slender stalk and occur in small clusters of three to five. The berries ripen from July to September, are sour and need to be sweetened before making into pies, jellies and preserves.

**Caution:** The leaves, bark and pits (stones) of the berries are toxic.

## Choke cherry

Many animals and birds eat the leaves, branches and bitter berries of the choke cherry. The tree is mostly a shrub but can grow to about 30 feet (9 m). The leaves are widest near the middle and have a sharply (almost hair-like) toothed margin. The bark is a dark grayish-brown that turns blackish when mature, and rather smooth with vertical pores. The berries are yellow, red or black, and hang in clusters of six to twelve along a common stem and occur from August to early September.

## American mountain ash and showy mountain ash

These slow-growing shrubs or trees may reach 50 feet (10 m) under their ideal conditions in moist, shady sites near swamps and lakes, rocky hillsides and in coniferous forests. In both species, the trunk is pale gray with horizontal pores in a thin, smooth bark. White, clustered flowers appear in June to July. The wood is pale, soft and burns quickly.

The berry-like fruit— bright orange-red in mountain ash and shiny red in showy mountain ash—is present from August through winter. Gather it after first frost for the mildest and sweetest berries. These bitter berries need to be sweetened before making jam, jelly, marmalade or juice. Some people use them to make wine or to flavor liqueurs.

American mountain ash.

# Mushrooms

An astonishing 90 percent of the living forest floor (not including plant roots) is made up of fungal material, including mushrooms. The other ten percent is made up of bacteria, protozoa, nematodes, insects—larvae and adults—worms, algae, and so on.

The survival of forest trees depends on fungi associated with their roots. Hundreds of thousands of miles of fungal threads (hyphae) are associated with the roots of each tree. The hyphae supply the tree with the water and nutrients needed for growth, and the tree responds by giving the fungus sugars that are manufactured in its leaves.

A few wild mushrooms are deadly and several are mildly poisonous, but there are many edible mushrooms that are easy to recognize and hard to confuse with anything lethal. This information here is not meant to serve a definitive guide to mushrooms—we are presenting only a few of the more easily identified common and safe and/or dangerous fungi out there. For a more comprehensive education, consult a specialized mushroom guide or, better yet, read about them and go hunting with experienced 'shroomers.

> One tip we can't emphasize enough: If you aren't sure what it is, don't eat it!

## Collecting and storing mushrooms

Collect the entire mushroom, including the base. Take only fresh, young specimens that are free of insect damage. Wrap each type of mushroom separately in waxed paper (do not use plastic wrap—it hastens decay), along with any notes you might want to make about the habitat and appearance of the mushroom. Note where the mushroom is growing (on wood, soil, moss); whether it is single or in clusters; the color of the cap, gills and stem; and any other distinctive features. The more information you gather about the mushroom in the field, the easier it will be to identify later.

## Making a spore print

The color of spores is important for identifying many mushrooms, especially the gilled ones. Individual spores are too small to see with the naked eye. A spore print shows the color of the spores in mass. To make a spore print, cut the stalk off the mushroom. Place the cap gill-side or pore-side down on a piece of white and black paper taped together side by side—place the mushroom at the junction of the two papers so that half the print is on black and half on white. Cover with a bowl or jar. If the mushroom is at the right stage—not too young, not too old or deteriorated—the spores will slowly collect on the paper. A spore print will be visible in one to twelve hours.

The best time of year to collect mushrooms is in the spring and fall, when the weather is warm and damp and cottagers are usually opening or closing their havens.

## Nobody does it better

Fungi are the best wood decayers in the world, returning hundreds of billions of tons of carbon dioxide to the atmosphere annually. It takes 20 years or more to reduce a hardwood trunk to dust. Fungi and a few bacteria are the only microorganisms that can digest wood (see **Termites** at page 189).

# Friendly mushrooms

Puffballs.

## Puffballs

Puffballs are round or pear-shaped mushrooms, lacking stalks, 1 to 12 inches (2.5–30 cm) in diameter, sometimes larger. The interior of a puffball is solid white at first, gradually turning yellow, then brown as the mushroom ages. Finally, the interior changes to a mass of dark, powdery spores. Gently squeeze them and they'll release their spores in a cloud of black "smoke." Best collecting is late summer and fall, in lawns, open woods, pastures, barren areas, or on soil or decaying wood. Remove the outer skin if it is tough, then slice, dip in batter and fry.

**Caution:** Slice each puffball from top to bottom and examine the interior. It should be completely white, like a slice of white bread. Puffballs with traces of yellow or brown are less tasty. Most important: There should be *no* sign of a developing mushroom with the stalk, gills and cap. Amanitas, which are lethal, can resemble small puffballs when they are young, but cutting them open will quickly blow their cover.

## Inky caps

**Shaggy mane**, or lawyer's wig, is the largest of a group of edible mushrooms called inky caps, which have dark spore prints. They are delicate and should be picked young and eaten the same day as they do not store well. Shaggy mane is large and distinctive.

Shaggy mane.

The cap of a fresh specimen is long, 4 to 6 inches (10–15 cm) tall, white and cylindrical with shaggy, upturned, brownish scales and whitish gills. As shaggy mane matures, the cap and gills gradually digest themselves and dissolve into a black, inky fluid, leaving only the standing stalk. It is found in the spring, summer and fall, growing in grass on lawns and pastures, soil or wood chips.

**Caution:** Pick before the caps begin to turn black. Always check for the developing ink to be sure of your identification.

**Tippler's bane** is another member of the inky cap group.

**Caution:** It must never be consumed with alcohol because it contains a compound that has a toxin called coprine that acts like Antabuse, a compound that is given to alcoholics. With alcohol it has unpleasant symptoms including dilation of blood vessels. Do not drink alcohol for three days after eating tippler's bane.

Tippler's bane.

Dog stinkhorn.

## Dog stinkhorn

Also called Ravelen's stinkhorn, this mushroom stinks so strongly you usually smell it before you see it. It has a single, erect pinkish to reddish stalk, up to 4 inches (10 cm) tall, and a conical head that is up to 1 inch (2.5 cm) long, with a reddish tip. Most of the head is covered by a slimy green spore mass. The smell attracts flies which land on the spore mass and disperse the spores to new sites.

## Morels

Also known as sponge, pinecone and honeycomb mushrooms, morels, *Morchella* spp., are easy to recognize and delicious to eat. There are three common species of morels: the common morel, black morel and half-free morel. The surface of a morel is covered with pits and ridges, and the bottom edge of the cap is attached directly to the stem (with one exception, see below). All three species can be found from spring to early summer, on the ground in a variety of habitats, including moist woodlands.

The common or yellow morel goes through color stages as it ages. The young white morel has white ridges and dark brown pits. As it ages, both the ridges and the pits turn yellowish brown to become yellow morels. When conditions are appropriate the yellow morel can grow into a giant morel, which may be up to a foot (30 cm) tall.

In the black morel or smoky morel, the ridges are gray or tan when young, but darken with age until nearly black. Black morels are best when picked young. Discard any that are shriveled and shrunken or have completely black heads.

The half-free morel is the exception to the rule that morels have the bottom of the cap attached directly to the stem. The cap of the half-free morel is attached at about the middle. They have small caps and long bulbous stems.

Wash carefully. Morels can be breaded and fried, sautéed, stewed, baked, creamed or stuffed with dressing.

**Caution:** Cut morels in half to check for insects. Morels are quite distinctive, but there is a small chance they could be confused with false morels (see page 213).

## Oyster mushroom

The oyster mushroom, *Pleurotus ostreatus*, is a large, wide (2–8 inches / 5–20 cm), white, tan or ivory-colored mushroom named for its oyster shell-like shape. It has white gills running down a very short and slightly off-center stem. The spores are white to lilac and the flesh is very soft.

They grow in large clusters of overlapping caps, always on trees or fallen logs in spring, summer, fall and during warm spells in winter. They are a treat when dipped in beaten eggs, rolled in cracker crumbs and then fried. Small black beetles sometimes infest this mushroom. Soak in salted water to remove bugs.

**Caution:** There are a number of look-alikes, and although none are poisonous, they may be unpleasant-tasting, best confirmed by tasting a small piece and by making a spore print.

Common or yellow morel.

Oyster mushroom.

On the culinary scale, the king bolete is a mushroom of choice.

## Boletes

Boletes look like a hamburger bun on a thick stalk. They are up to 10 inches (25 cm) tall and wide, sturdy and fleshy, and easily mistaken at first glance for gilled mushrooms. However, on close inspection, the underside of the cap has a spongy layer of pores rather than bladelike gills. The pore layer can easily be pulled away from the cap. Bolete caps are brownish or reddish-brown, while the pores may be whitish, yellow, orange, red, olive or brownish. There are more than 200 species of boletes in North America:

- king bolete, *Boletus edulis,* 6 inches (15 cm) tall, is probably the best edible bolete;
- old man of the woods, *Strobilomyces strobilaceus,* has black scales on a grayish to gray-brown background and fruits on the ground or on dead wood where it produces a black spore print;
- slippery jack, *Suillus luteus,* has a persistent ring and a slimy coating on the brown cap, fruits under conifers and has an ocher spore print (note: may cause stomach upset in some people) and
- painted bolete is an attractive mushroom that commonly fruits under white pines. It has a shaggy look with cap and stalk covered by reddish scales on a yellow background.

Look for boletes summer and fall. Remove tough stems, and peel off the pore layer in all but the youngest specimens. Sauté in butter and add to any cheese dish. Dried boletes are tasty in soups.

**Caution:** A few boletes are poisonous. Do not eat any boletes that have orange or red pores. Some boletes, while not poisonous, are very distasteful. Confirm by tasting a pinch of the raw mushroom cap. If bitter or otherwise unpleasant, throw it away. To make them more digestible, boletes should be cooked before eating. If the cap is slimy, peel off the slime layer as it sometimes causes diarrhea. Many insects like boletes so check your specimens carefully. Boletes tend to rot quickly. Collect and eat only fresh specimens. Is it worth the trouble? On the culinary scale, the king bolete is a mushroom of choice.

## Wax caps

Another group of gill fungi are species of wax caps that belong to the genus *Hygrocybe.* The large group has many colorful species with a waxy appearance. They come in brilliant shades of red, yellow, orange, purple, green, scarlet, chocolate-brown and snowy white. The wax caps are extremely common and widespread. Stunning beauty and edible, but not tasty.

The vermillion waxy cap mushroom is particularly common — and lovely.

Chanterelles.

Tooth fungi.

bearded tooth may grow quite large, four to twelve inches (10 to 30 cm) across. Its size and whiteness make it easy to spot against the dark hardwood logs, trees or stumps on which it grows, mostly in summer and fall.

The bearded tooth is distinctive and has no poisonous look-alikes. There are several closely related species that are more open and branched, but all are edible. Edible toothed fungi are best when sliced, parboiled until tender and served with cheese sauce.

**Caution:** Only young, white specimens should be eaten; yellow, older ones are sour.

## Chanterelles and horn-of-plenty

The funnel-shaped chanterelles have wavy cap edges and are ½ to 6 inches (1–15 cm) wide, 1 to 6 inches (2.5–15 cm) tall. Chanterelles are bright orange or yellow, and have a pleasant, fruity fragrance. The black trumpet is brownish-black.

Check the underside of the cap to identify. A few species of chanterelle are nearly smooth underneath; others have a network of wrinkles or gill-like ridges running down the stem. Chanterelles always have blunt-edged, crisscrossing ridges and cross-veins. (Some poisonous look-alikes have knife-like gills.) They are usually found in scattered groups on the ground in hardwood forests in summer and fall.

Chanterelles are highly regarded as edibles but are tough and need long, slow cooking. They are best when sautéed slowly in butter until tender, seasoned with salt, pepper and parsley, and served on crackers.

## Tooth fungi

Tooth fungi contain only a few species but most are common and widespread. Although many are edible, it is best not to eat any fungi in this group. The spores are born on spines on the underside of the mushroom. The bearded or comb tooth looks like clumps of hanging white fur. It is pure white when fresh and young, but yellows with age. The

## Bracket fungi

These are shelf-like and grow from the sides of trees. The spores are produced inside tubes that line the underside of the shelf, giving it a perforated look. Most mushrooms die into a putrefying mass within a few days, but bracket fungi have a tough leathery texture and last for months, even overwinter, or last for 50 years.

Most bracket fungi are inedible, but Ling-Chi, or lacquered polypore, has herbal properties. The Chinese use it for its apparent anti-aging property and strengthening of the immune system. It is widespread and common on hardwoods.

Sulfur tuft is also called chicken of the woods because uncooked, it tastes like chicken. These mushrooms have brilliant orange-red caps and a pale sulfur-yellow underside that has minute pores. It has no stalk, ranges in size from 2 to 12 inches (5 to 30 cm) in width and always attaches directly on trees or dead wood, usually in large masses of overlapping caps, in summer and fall.

Cook only the tender outer edges of the caps; the rest is tough and woody. Slice and simmer in stock, then serve creamed on toast.

**Caution:** It may cause a mild allergic reaction (swollen lips) in some people.

Chicken of the woods.

Amanitas: deadly destroying angel (*left*) and yellow patch (*right*).

## Poisonous mushrooms

### True or false?

False morels differ from true morels in two obvious ways: the cap surface has lobes, folds, flaps or wrinkles, instead of pits and ridges, and the bottom edge of the cap of a false morel hangs free around the stem, like a skirt. On true morels, the bottom edge of the cap is attached to the stem.

There are three dangerous groups of fungi: the amanitas, the false morels and a catch-all group known as little brown mushrooms (LBMS). Mushrooms in these groups cause virtually all the fatal mushroom poisonings, the amanitas alone accounting for 90 percent of mushroom-related deaths.

There are hundreds of other mushrooms that will cause anything from a mild stomach upset to cramps, vomiting, diarrhea, and loss of coordination. Usually the symptoms pass in 24 hours or less. To be on the safe side, notify your doctor immediately if you suspect mushroom poisoning of any kind.

There is no quick-and-easy test that will separate poisonous from edible mushrooms. Peeling the cap, testing with a silver spoon, checking for insect damage or any other folk method will only go so far.

To avoid mushroom poisoning, follow these five rules:

1. Identify each and every mushroom you collect. When in doubt, throw it out.
2. Strictly avoid any mushroom that is parasol-shaped with white gills (amanitas), all LBMS and all false morels.
3. The first time you try a new wild mushroom, eat only a small amount and wait 24 hours before eating more.
4. As with other foods, rotting mushrooms can make you ill. Eat only firm, fresh, mushrooms.
5. Most wild mushrooms should not be eaten raw or in large quantities because they are difficult to digest. Keep in mind that some people are allergic to even the safest mushrooms.

### Amanitas

Several members of this group contain amanitin, one of the deadliest poisons found in nature, and phalloidin. One capful of a destroying angel can kill a person. Another lethal amanita is fly agaric which comes in yellow and red varieties. Yellow patches is one of the most common amanitas in cottage country and northern Ontario. It is recognized by its yellow to orange-yellow color and sulfur-like dustings on its stalk. If the edge of the mushroom is radially streaked, it is Frost's amanita. Perhaps the most common amanita is the tawny grisette, usually found on or close to forest trails. It has a smooth, brown, radially streaked cap and a white stalk.

Amanitas begin as egg-shaped buttons, which often resemble small, innocent puffballs. The button breaks open as the mushroom grows. When fully developed, amanitas are gilled with parasol-shaped caps that may be white, yellow, red or brown.

To avoid amanitas, watch for these four characteristics:

- a saclike cup surrounding the base of the stem (this may be buried beneath the soil surface and not obvious);
- a ring on the stem;
- white gills and
- a white spore print. Since both the ring and cup may be destroyed by rain or other disturbance, simply avoid all parasol-shaped mushrooms with white gills.

Amanitas are usually found on the ground in woodlands in summer and fall, but you should be on the lookout for them whenever you hunt for mushrooms.

## False morels

False morels are tricky, because some people consider them a favorite wild mushroom while others get very sick. Because these mushrooms have definitely caused deaths, we can't recommend that you eat them.

The basic problem seems to involve the amount of a toxic chemical, called monomethyl hydrazine (MMH), present in the mushroom. MMH causes diarrhea, vomiting and severe headaches, and occasionally it can be fatal. Because of different cooking techniques and differences in individual sensitivities to MMH, false morels poison some people but leave others unaffected. Also, false morels contain more MMH in some areas of the country than in other areas.

False morels have convoluted or wrinkled irregular caps that are brain-like or saddle-shaped. They may be black, gray, white, brown or reddish and range in size from 2 to 8 inches (5–20 cm) tall. The brain morel, *Gyromitra esculenta*, has a highly convoluted reddish-brown cap. False morels are found in spring, summer and fall, on the ground in woodlands.

## Little brown mushrooms (LBMs)

This catch-all category includes all small to medium-sized, hard-to-identify brownish mushroom with spores of hundreds of colors, brown being among the more common. Avoid all LBMs with brown spores because so many are poisonous. Many LBMs are harmless, some are mildly poisonous or hallucinogenic, and a few are deadly.

The innocent-looking mushrooms of the genus *Galerina* are probably the most dangerous of the LBMs, particularly the deadly galerina. They contain the same toxin as amanitas and have caused a number of deaths. Galerinas grow in clusters on wood and have brownish spores.

Do you take your dog camping? Don't let it eat this nasty little LBM, scaly fiber cap. It contains muscarine, a toxin dangerous to children and small dogs. It is known to cause serious symptoms and even death in puppies and small dogs that chew and swallow the mushrooms. It grows on the ground in mixed woods and is often found in campsites in Ontario.

False morel.

Two little brown mushrooms to watch for the deadly galerina (*above*) and the scaly fiber cap (*below*).

# CHAPTER 6

# Cottage Operations

If you are handy you will enjoy keeping up your cottage yourself. If you are not handy, you will either learn to be handy or enjoy cottage life with deep pockets and a good list of local tradespeople.

BEHIND EVERY WELL-MAINTAINED cottage is a diligent crew of cottagers keeping things warm, dry, clean and cozy. A few good tools and some patience will see you through most cottage repairs, from zebra mussel-clogged foot valves to toilet troubles. A satisfactory septic system is one that doesn't announce its presence, ever. The same principle applies to a well, although cottagers have to stay on top of all filtration and purification of drinking water, no matter the source. Maintaining woodstoves, safely felling trees and storing firewood are important cottage activities, as are keeping lamps and generators working well. For the cuts and scrapes that come with cottage repairs and antics of all sorts, we have suggested first aid kits for people and pets, along with natural plant options growing close by. For those who stray further afield, there are tips on finding your way in the woods, with and without a compass. And finally, we offer a few tips for those who haven't quite got the knack of the campfire yet.

For those who are buying a cottage for the first time, we begin with a checklist of things to watch out for in both the property and the built structures, so you can celebrate and not rue your decision for generations to come.

The same well may serve your cottage for a century, but test your well water at regular intervals.

# Buying your cottage

If you plan on using your cottage year round, you'll want to check that it has been properly winterized.

B uying your piece of paradise is much like buying a house. However, most of us are thinking more about what we will do out of doors, on the land and in the water, rather than indoors. Call it your cottage, cabin, camp, chalet, lodge, vacation home or whatever you like, but location is everything when it comes to your personal paradise. Do you want to hear nothing but the call of the loons, or are you a jet-ski fanatic? Do you crave a beach? Is fishing your favorite activity? Skinny-dipping? Before you fall in love with a cottage, make sure that the privacy, noise and activity levels on and around the lake or river suit your lifestyle.

## Cottage associations

Cottagers on many lakes have formed cottage associations with regulations to protect the lake against pollution and destruction, and to help pay for things such as road maintenance. Contact the directors before buying a cottage to find out the cost of the annual membership fee and what it covers.

### Setback

There is a minimum distance, called setback, that a cottage can be located from a lake or river. The setback is regulated by local authorities but cottagers should be concerned with flood levels. If there is little slope to the land, build the cottage beyond the 50-year flood level (see the **Getting to Know Your Lake** chapter for flood details).

## Inspection checklist

The best time to inspect a cottage is in the spring, after winter has taken its turn at freezing and heaving all the buildings, the trees around the cottage, the beach and shoreline on the lot. Even if you've owned your cottage property for years, it's a good idea to go through this checklist every spring to keep ahead of developing problems. When you do the internal and external inspection of the cottage, keep in mind that, unlike your house, your cottage may sit vacant over the winter. If you love snowshoeing or cross-country skiing, make sure that the property is accessible year round.

## The lot

### Accessibility

◆ How remote is the lake?
◆ If access is by water only, ask if a boat and a raft (for moving big items such as lumber) are included in the sale.
◆ If access is by road, who maintains it and what is your share of the cost?
◆ Is there winter access?

### Slope, Drainage and Size

◆ The best lots are those with a slope of less than 10 percent. Unless you are a mountain goat, the slope should not exceed 30 percent. No part of the lot should ever be submerged.
◆ Check that the drainage is good and away from the cottage or camp. The soil should be permeable and have good forest cover.
◆ The ideal lot size is greater than one acre but many older cottages have smaller lots.

### Ecology

◆ If the lot has a wetland, make sure it has been preserved.

◆ Check that natural vegetation along the shoreline is intact and has not been back-filled.

◆ If the lot is on an island, check that most of the island is still in its natural state.

◆ Make sure trees are not encroaching on the roof or foundation of any buildings. The cottage should be surrounded by natural vegetation but large trees, especially poplars, are a potential hazard and often break or can be wind-blown onto the cottage.

◆ Lawns are a bad idea, but if present, should not be fertilized.

◆ The cottage should be at least 75 feet (23 m) from the lake.

### Docks and boathouses

◆ Check the quality and operation of the docks and learn how they are stored for the winter if they have removable components.

◆ If there is a boathouse, check the structure and condition inside and out. Ask about variations in water level through the year to make sure the boathouse is usable all ice-free times of the year.

## Exterior

### Roof and chimney

◆ Ask when the shingles were last replaced and what the warranty lifespan of the shingles is. What is the overall condition of the roof? Are there loose or missing shingles, rotten eaves, or a wavy roof, indicating wet or rotting sheathing below the shingles?

◆ Look for evidence of leaks. Inside, look for water stains on ceilings around chimneys of stoves and fireplaces and areas around windows. If there is attic access, examine the interior of the roof structure.

◆ Outside, look under the soffit areas for water stains and cracked or peeling paint. Look at the condition of the eavestroughs — have they been cleaned and well maintained?

### Foundation and walls

◆ Are there obvious cracks or any apparent shifts in the foundation? If the exterior is brick, check for any cracks that indicate shift.

◆ Look for dampness in the basement and crawlspaces. Is there a musty odor? Is there a vapor barrier and adequate insulation in the walls?

◆ Is the cottage going to need paint soon?

Thoroughly inspect the roof, eavestroughs and chimney.

Remember to ask about seasonal fluctuations in lake levels, as they can affect your ability to use your boathouse. Be sure to check the condition of any docks.

*Right* Look for level floors. Unlevel ones can indicate that bigger problems lurk underneath.

## Interior

### Electrical

◆ Check the electrical panel to determine whether it has fuses or circuit breakers and count the number of spaces available for new circuits. Fuse panels are typical of older cottages but have been replaced by circuit breakers in the past 30 years. The number of available circuits will partly determine the number of upgrades (new rooms or buildings) possible in the future.

◆ Look for any malfunctions in switches. Bring an electric night light (or any small electric appliance) with you and check to make sure all outlets work.

### Doors and windows

◆ What is the quality of the windows—are they single pane, double pane or sealed window panes?

◆ Check for mold around the window edges, indicating leaking or sweating window panes. The doors and windows should be tightly sealed but easily opened and closed, with sills and jambs still plumb and level.

The windows that offer you stunning views of your lake can also let in drafts and moisture.

### Floors

◆ Check the levelness of the floors to make sure they are not tilted or heaved, indicating either a shifting foundation or warped floor joists.

◆ Check for musty odors, especially in carpets, that would suggest poor ventilation and/or dampness from leaky roofs.

Squeaky or bouncy floors can usually be repaired (by screwing rather than nailing the sub-floor to the joists) but they could indicate weak floor joists that are more difficult to repair.

### Stoves and fireplaces

Many camps and cottages have a wood stove and a gas (propane or natural) or electric range.

### *Wood stoves*

◆ Lift the stove plates and examine the walls of the stove box. Are the fire walls intact or cracked with chunks missing?

◆ Are the stove grates (usually three) still operational?

◆ Open the oven and check the condition of the walls and base to make sure they are solid and not corroded.

◆ Is the ash box still of good quality (not rusty or corroded)?

◆ Are the stove dampers (usually one on the side below the grates and one on the stove top or on the chimney) still operational?

◆ Is there a wood box or holder?

### Gas ranges

- Check for smells of propane or natural gas.
- Turn each burner on, including the oven, and make sure all burners work at low and high settings.
- Make sure there are instructions for locating and lighting the pilots.

### Propane stoves

- Check the sizes and conditions of the propane tanks. Heavy, awkward 100-pound (45 kg) tanks hold more propane but 60-pound (27 kg) tanks are lighter and more convenient.
- For any tanks not attached to the copper line that feeds the range, tilt them back far enough to check for rust on the bottom; propane suppliers will not fill tanks that have rusty or degraded bottoms.
- Check the ages of the tanks — all tank valves have a ten-year lifespan and have to be replaced. New propane tanks now have an overfill protection device (OPD) that will not allow propane to flow until it is attached to the proper regulator.

### Refrigerators and freezers

- If the cottage or camp has no electricity, the options are very limited, propane refrigerators and freezers being the most common. They are very expensive and hard to come by. The freezer space in the refrigerator is much smaller than in electric refrigerators.
- Lighting the pilot varies from model to model so ask for instructions or owner's manual.
- How much propane does it use per day?

### Plumbing

- Open all taps and let the water run for one or two minutes. Check for leaks around the taps and drainage in the sinks, tubs and showers. Check for any unusual noises or malfunctions.
- Flush all toilets to make sure they work properly.

### Septic system

- Most cottages have an indoor washroom, which means that a septic system and a gray water system are present. Because septic systems are buried installations and hidden from normal visual inspection, many problems may not reveal themselves right away. It can be difficult to determine the condition of the system.
- Find out when the septic tank was last pumped clean. If the system has been serviced recently, contact the septic pumping company to inquire about the type and condition of the waste disposal equipment.
- Find out what the septic tank is made of. See **Septic systems** at page 221.

A few camps have outhouses only; you need to know how old any outhouse is. A new outhouse may have to be built if the cottage is older than 30 years, but this depends on the number of people using it and the frequency of use.

# Basic tools and hardware

Here's a list of everything it would be nice to have in your cottage work shed. Make a copy of this list and distribute before your birthday.

There's nothing quite like a well-stocked and well-organized set of tools.

1 **safety glasses**

1 **hammer**

1 **tape measure** wide blade is recommended

1 **cross-cut saw** for cutting across the grain; blade has many small teeth

1 **rip saw** for cutting with the grain; blade has fewer large teeth

1 **hack saw** for cutting metals and plastics

1 **miter box with miter saw** for cutting angles in trim

1 **needlenose pliers** infinitely handy

1 **regular pliers**

1 **crowbar or wrecking bar**

1 **set of Robertson screw drivers** for screws with square holes

1 **set of Philips screw drivers** for screws with star holes

1 **set of slot screwdrivers** for screws with slots

1 **set of open and box-end wrenches**

1 **ratchet set with short and long sockets** for rapid removal of nuts and bolts

1 **set of crescent wrenches**

1 **pipe (monkey) wrench** a must for loosening or tightening pipe joints

1 **level/plumb** for leveling (horizontally) and plumbing (vertically)

1 **large vice** indispensable at any camp or cottage

1 **large square (with construction scales)** 24 × 16-inch (61 × 41 cm) for "squaring" corners of walls, frames, etc.; scales are used for building stairs, rafters, roof valleys, etc.

1 **set square** has a slide with a 45-degree-angle piece; very useful for squaring small projects, marking lines at uniform distance from edge of material and drawing 45-degree angles for cuts

Needlenose pliers are indispensable for cottage use. In addition to gripping, bending and cutting small-gauge wire, they can reach into tight places that are inaccessible to other kinds of pliers.

1 **⅜ inch (1 cm) electric drill** (at least 4 amp recommended); or **⅜ inch cordless drill**, 15–16 volts recommended

1 **set of drill bits** ¹⁄₁₆ to ½ inch (2–18 mm) recommended

1 **circular saw** at least 10 amp is recommended with a 7-inch blade for cutting 2-inch (5 cm) thick lumber; for cutting straight lines

1 **saber saw** at least 3 amp recommended; for cutting circles and odd shapes

1 **box of each of various sizes, 1- to 3- inch, #8 wood or deck screws**

1 **box of each of various sizes, 1- to 3-inch #8 sheet metal screws**

1 **pound of each of various sizes finishing nails/brads** use galvanized nails outside; non-galvanized nails tend to rust and show through paint

1 **pound of each of various sizes galvanized standard spiral nails/ brads** use galvanized especially outdoors

# Septic systems

There is usually a patch of ground close to the cottage that grows the best wild-flowers every year; the flowers growing in the nutrient-rich soil over the drainage bed are the only sweet aspect of your septic system. It's vital to understand, maintain and respect this essential system. Ignore this warning at your own risk.

## How it works

When you have a septic system, what goes into your toilet is not washed away down the drain into some municipal sewage system. It all travels into a septic tank on your own property. There the solids must be broken down into sludge and liquid before the waste can be released to the soils. The septic tank does this by first removing solids from the liquid. As sewage enters the tank, the heavy solids settle, eventually forming sludge. Grease and other light solids rise to the surface to form a scum. Bacteria break down the sludge and scum while the liquid, called clarified effluent, is discharged to the drainfield for soil absorption.

## Breakdown

The breakdown process is biological, with aner-obic bacteria reducing the solids in the sludge and scum to a small volume. Tanks in warm climates don't need to be pumped or cleaned out as often as those in cold climates, because the bacteria are more active. Regardless of climate, always leave some sludge—and its resident bacteria—in the tank, so that the biological breakdown can continue.

If the process is somehow altered (by using the toilet excessively), or stopped (by pouring in chlorine), the solids fill the tank, enter the drainfield piping and clog the openings in the pipe or the soil in the drainfield.

A typical septic system for gray and black water. See text for details.

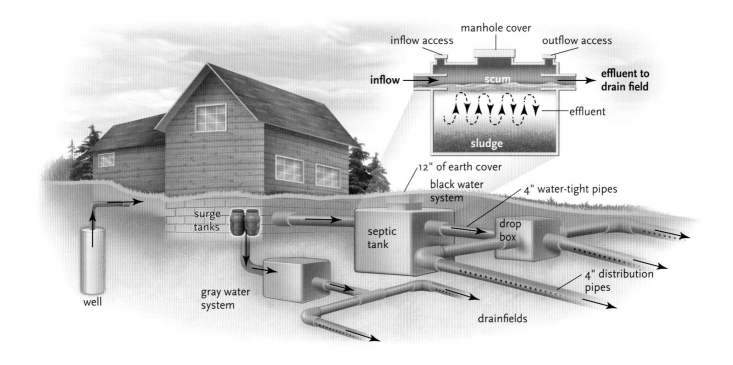

# Location

The first thing to do is decide where to place the septic system. If you can, place it some distance from your well, because effluent leaching from the drainfield could reach the groundwater that the well is drawing from. Next, select an area with good soil for the drainfield. Soils made of a mix of sand, silt and clay work best. If there is too much clay, the effluent may percolate poorly through the soil. If the soil contains too much sand and gravel, wastewater may pass through to the groundwater too quickly, without being treated by soil microbes.

Every district or municipality has guidelines on minimum setbacks and clearances for septic system absorption area, septic or holding tank, privies and wells. Check before digging, but in general, septic systems should be a minimum of 150 feet (45 m) from wells or water bodies and privies at least 100 feet (30 m) from a well or water body.

The permeability of your soil will determine the size of your drainfield. To determine the permeability of the soil, and hence the size of your drainfield, do a percolation test, which measures the rate at which the water infiltrates the soil. This is usually done by an expert. If you would rather undertake this yourself, see **The do-it yourself percolation test**.

# Septic tank specs

The size of the tank will depend on the number of people using the septic system and the frequency of use. A good rule of thumb is about 300 gallons (Canadian 250 gal or 1136 L) per bedroom for full-time use. If you use the cottage four months of the year, the tank capacity should be at least ⅓ or 100 gallons (380 L) per bedroom. To give you some idea of size, a tank 5 feet long by 3 feet high and 3 feet wide holds 336 gallons (1274 L / Can 280 gal).

**What is your septic tank made of?**

Steel tanks last 20 to 25 years, rust and collapse, and baffles may rust off. Concrete tanks are generally more durable, but still may have damaged baffles or cracks that permit the seepage of groundwater in or septic effluent out around the tank. Look for septic effluent seepage downhill from the septic tank (you'll smell it first). Seepage may be due to an overloaded tank, failed absorption system (both very expensive to repair) or blocked or broken piping (less costly).

## The do-it-yourself percolation test

If you'd rather not pay a professional to determine the permeability of your soil, you can do your own percolation test. The information you collect can then be used to figure out the size of the drainfield you need.

♦ Dig several holes (use a hole-digger or auger) at least 4 inches (10 cm) in diameter and 10 inches (25 cm) deep, down to the area to be used for the drainfield.

♦ Roughen or scratch any compacted clay or soil in the bottom or sides of the holes by scraping lightly with a nail or screw driver.

♦ Remove any loose soil, add 2 inches (5 cm) of fine gravel, and then add water to the holes to saturate the soil, allowing time for any clay to swell. Soak all soils, except sand, for at least four hours.

♦ Insert a ruler or tape measure into the hole. With your stopwatch ready, add 6 inches (15 cm) of water to the hole. Measure the distance from the surface of the ground to the surface of the water. Time how long it takes for the water to percolate (a few seconds to minutes, depending on soil composition). Repeat for all holes.

♦ Add more water if the depth of the water over the gravel falls below the two inches of gravel. Take measurements at approximately the same time intervals until you can determine a constant rate of percolation. The time in minutes required for the water to drop one inch is the percolation rate in minutes per inch.

♦ There are tables to help you compute the size of the drainfield from your results, but the data vary from one province and state to the other because the size of the drainfield depends on the numbers of people using the septic system and the frequency of use. Your local ministry or department of environment or natural resources can advise you on how to estimate the size of your drainfield using the percolation data you have collected.

Drainfields and septic systems at cottages can be difficult to create. Trees with extensive root systems will make your life miserable so hire a company with the proper equipment and knowledge to install your septic system.

The most durable tanks are made of concrete 6 to 8 inches (15–20 cm) thick, reinforced with rebar, but fiberglass and heavy plastic tanks are available commercially.

Septic tanks must have access openings over the inlet and outlet baffles, as well as a manhole cover. Cap the pipes over the inlet and outlet so odors do not escape. Mark the access location for easy inspection. Use 4-inch (10 cm) diameter ABS pipe for the inlet and outlet. Place a T at the end of each pipe.

## Drainfield construction

Drainfields should be at least 100 feet (30 m) from the closest well or spring, at least 10 feet (3 m) from water supply lines, and not closer than 50 feet (15 m) to a pond or stream. As a rule, drainfield trenches are 25 to 36 inches (64–91 cm) deep. There should be a minimum of two trenches of less than 100 feet (30 m) long. The tile drain, consisting of open-jointed, 4-inch diameter drain tile or perforated plastic pipe, must have at least 6 inches (15 cm) of crushed aggregate under it and 12 inches (30 cm) of soil over it. Ideally the drainfield should be nearly level.

The drainpipe must be laid with the holes down and must be level throughout its length. Place a distribution box or drop box every 10 to 15 feet (3–4.6 m) or so (length depends on the slope) and run a 4-foot (1.2 m) length of nonporous pipe laterally from each side of the box. Glue a 90-degree elbow at the end of each lateral piece and then run porous pipe down another 10 foot (3 m) stretch of trench in the drainfield. Add distribution boxes with their solid lateral pipes and trenches as needed.

### Garbage in...

Overloading the septic system is a bad idea. Waste systems are designed to treat and dispose of a specific volume and type of wastewater in the conditions found at the site. Dispose of hazardous chemicals and large amounts of grease in the garbage, not the septic tank. Better yet, install a gray water system to conserve water and extend the life of the system (see page 224).

# Maintenance

Maintain your septic system diligently. Have your septic system pumped/cleaned regularly, at least every two years. Mark the location of your septic tank and distribution box with stakes for ease of locating. Keep detailed records of inspections, permits issued, repairs, pumping, and other maintenance activities. It is wise to open and expose the distribution boxes to check for even distribution of effluent. If a distribution box has sunk or tipped, re-level it.

How do you know your septic system is failing? Check for

- patches of abnormally healthy grass over the drainfield;
- soggy areas with gray water on or near to the drainfield;
- constantly wet lawn above the drainfield;
- sewage back-ups in the toilet and drains;
- sinks, toilets and showers drain more slowly;
- a sewage odor over drainage field area.

# Gray water

While most cottagers and campers have one septic system that treats all the water they use, there is an increasing trend to separate gray water from black water. Gray water makes up 50 to 80 percent of residential "waste" water, which is a waste; plants can thrive on this used, nutrient-laden water. The reuse of gray water is part of the solution to the many abuses that we impose on the natural water cycle. Light gray water includes water from the shower, bathtub, bathroom sink and laundry, dark gray water includes kitchen sink water, and black water includes water from the toilet.

### How to make a gray water system

When you get permission to build a gray water system, ask what materials can be used (concrete blocks, plastic, fiberglass), what the minimum size requirements for the leaching tank are, and what the minimum setbacks are (distance from lake, wetland, wells, groundwater). In general, gray water leaching tanks are approved for seasonal cottages only with a non-flush toilet, but check with local authorities to make sure. The size will depend on the number of bedrooms, number of cottagers and days of use, as well as soil permeability.

### Method one

- Dig a hole to accommodate the volume of the tank. If you are lucky, you may be able to use a plastic or fiberglass barrel that is riddled with ⅛- to ¼-inch (3–6 mm) diameter holes in the bottom and sides for the gray water to seep through.
- Fill the barrel with 1- to 2-inch (2.5–5 cm) diameter gravel. The surface area of the gravel will get covered by bacteria and protists that will help digest organic materials in the gray water.
- Place the inflow that collects all the gray water near the top of the barrel. Put a lid on the barrel and mound at least 6 inches (15 cm) of soil on top, using the dirt that you originally removed to make the hole. Add enough so that rain water drains away from the system.

### Method two

- Build a crib with concrete blocks but do not use mortar between the blocks.
- Dig the pit at least 36 inches (91 cm) deep and lay 6 inches (15 cm) of 1- to 2-inch (2.5–5 cm) diameter gravel on the bottom. The walls of the crib should be a minimum of 2 feet (60 cm) high.
- Place the inflow that collects all the gray water near the top of the crib. Put a lid on the crib (patio slabs often work) and mound at least 6 inches (15 cm) of soil on top so that rain water drains away from the leaching pit.

**Benefits of gray water recycling:**

- Less strain on the septic system
- Greater longevity of the septic system
- Recharge of groundwater
- Lower fresh water use (for gardens)
- Plant growth
- Reclamation of otherwise wasted nutrients
- Less energy, chemicals and artificial fertilizers

# Basic plumbing: toilet problems

If you are stuck with the unenviable task of fixing the toilet, don't worry. It's not that hard, and you will be a domestic hero.

## How the toilet works

When you hold down the flush handle, the chain attached to the flush-handle extension bar lifts the drain plug and water exits the tank through the drain, flushing the toilet. When the tank is empty, the plug falls onto the drain opening and plugs it. Water enters the tank through the inflow tube via openings below the inflow cap. As the tank fills, the float rises and exerts pressure on a valve inside the inflow tube and closes the valve when the float is at its maximum height. You can adjust this height by the float adjustment set screw.

## Four foul problems

**Lack of flush or slow flush** is usually caused by a broken flush-handle extension arm or handle or a detached chain. Simply replace the broken part. The other more serious cause is a plugged toilet—water (and contents!) spills out of the bowl. You have two options:

- Place a toilet plunger squarely on the opening on the bottom of the bowl and plunge down and pull up (keeping plunger on the bottom) rapidly 10 to 15 times. Remove the plunger and hope the bowl drains. If not, try again.
- If the plunger fails, use a pipe cleaner called a "snake," available from any hardware store. The toilet has a P-trap (somewhat S-shaped) at its base, where the blockage is likely occurring. Twist the snake up and down the S-curve and pull back and forth on the snake until you remove the blockage (and the water drains). Flush the toilet to flush out any remaining material that made up the blockage.

**Continuously running water** occurs when the drain plug fails to sit properly either because the chain gets caught (shorten the chain) or the chain is kinked (remove the kink) or too short (replace the chain or add a link).

---

You can expect a toilet to "wear out" over time, but a screwdriver can fix most problems. To avoid serious problems, treat the toilet like a throne and flush one-ply (preferably) or two-ply tissue paper only.

**Slow filling** occurs when the inflow is plugged or water is draining out as the tank is filling (see page 225 for remedy). To increase the flow,

1. Turn the inflow valve — below and behind the toilet — toward but not completely off to reduce the pressure in the line.
2. Remove the inflow cap by removing the three or four screws attaching the cap to the inflow tube.
3. Take a length of clothes hanger wire and run it into the narrow inflow tube (a smaller diameter tube within the main tube).
4. Now, slowly open the shut-off valve until water exits and flushes the tube; this will remove any material inside the tube before replacing the cap.
5. Close the shut-off valve again, replace the cap and three or four screws, and open the shut-off valve completely. Water should flow freely and quickly. If not, repeat the process.

> For gravity-fed toilets, you need not close the shut-off valve, but be prepared for a good gush of water when the tube is cleaned!

**Leaking seal between the toilet base and the floor** is a tricky problem. Although wax seals can crack, they are better than rubber seals, which dry out. To fix the leak, you must begin by removing the toilet:

1. Close the shut-off valve.
2. Flush and empty the toilet tank and bowl *completely*.
3. Remove the inflow pipe from the shut-off valve. Remove the two bolts attaching the toilet base to the flange on the floor.
4. Lift the toilet off its base and place it to one side. Tip the toilet enough so that you can clean the groove that receives the seal.
5. Clean the groove in the flange on the floor. Put a new wax seal on the floor flange.
6. Replace the toilet carefully and squarely on the new seal (use the bolts to help align the base). Don't drag the toilet onto the seal or you will displace and/or damage it. Apply downward pressure to force the wax well into the grooves.
7. Replace the bolts and inflow pipe. Slowly open the shut-off valve; let the toilet fill and then flush the toilet.
8. No leaks? You have passed basic plumbing!

## Alternatives to flushing

Without question, the most popular "green" alternative to the flush is the composting toilet. Many of them are about the same size as a standard toilet.

Composting toilets digest human waste and tissue paper through a process involving atmospheric oxygen, moisture in the waste, organic material (such as peat moss, the kind we use in gardens) and microbes (from waste or enriched organic soils). Heat speeds up the process by stimulating microbial activity. Electric fans or a vent chimneys also help by evaporating excess fluids and exhausting air.

It is important to provide the digestion process with plenty of oxygen. Non-electric models use a rotating drum, which is hand-turned by an exterior handle, to speed up the composting and help prevent odors caused by putrefaction. Add about one cup of peat moss per person per day. The microbe population usually needs to be rejuvenated periodically through the addition of microbe-rich top soil.

If the toilet is to survive cold winters, install fiberglass or marine-grade stainless-steel units which can survive freezing temperatures without cracking.

When the bucket is full, it is removed and emptied onto a composting pile. Keep this composting pile well separated from other composting materials, such as kitchen or garden waste. The compost can eventually be used as fertilizer but the process of converting human excrement into safe and usable compost material can take between three months to a few years depending on climate, temperature, and the efficiency of the conversion of waste to compost. In most cases, the compost will become highly mineralized soil in four to six years.

# Mending pipes

Imagine you return to the cottage in the spring to discover that, although you did drain the copper line, some water remained in it, froze and burst the pipe. There is one sure way to find low spots in your water lines: the burst point(s). Mending the pipes becomes routine, especially if you have a lot of sags in the line. Smart people eliminate the sags. The rest of us get used to the smell of solder.

You will need
- a hacksaw or a tube cutter,
- a propane tank with torch attachment,
- a flint lighter,
- a fine emery cloth or steel wool,
- a pipe fitting brush,
- acid paste flux,
- lead solder, and
- ½ inch (1.3 cm) diameter copper union (one for each split).

## Mending the pipe

### If the split is shorter than ½ inch

- Cut the pipe in the middle of the split. The two ends must butt close together. Pull both ends of the cut pipe down to drain excess water. Note: make sure all water is drained. If there is any left inside you will not be able to solder the joints. To get rid of any excess water, heat the pipe with a propane torch until no more steam leaves the pipe. Let the pipe cool before continuing.

**Caution:** the pipe will be burning hot.

- Polish each end of the cut copper line with fine emery cloth or steel wool so that at least ½ inch (1.3 cm) gleams of new copper. Polish the inside of both ends of the copper union with emery cloth or a wire brush. Apply soldering flux to both ends of the copper pipe and to the inside of the union.
- Slip the union on to one pipe end and then on to the other. Push the pipes fully into the union.
- Uncoil a 3- to 4-inch (7.5–10 cm) length of solder and light the propane torch. Using a back and forth motion with the torch, heat the union and copper pipe evenly and all around. Starting at the top of the union on either end, apply solder to the joint. If the pipe and union are hot enough, the solder should flow around the entire joint. Repeat at the other end. Take a good look at the joints and make sure there is solder all the way around at both ends. If not, apply more heat and solder.

### If the split is longer than ½ inch

- Cut out the split portion with either a pipe cutter or a hacksaw. If you cannot pull the pipes close enough to butt, you will have to add a short length of copper pipe. In this case, cut off another 3 to 4 inches (7.5–10 cm) and then cut another length long enough for the two pipes to butt up to one another. You will need two unions, one for each end of the new length of pipe. Repeat the procedures above for each end of the new pipe.

Cutting a pipe.

### Multiple bursts

If you have more than one burst, install a drain valve at the lowest burst point and open the valve in the fall to avoid bursts in the same place next year. If there are sags in the line, apply shims so that all water will drain into a valve at the lowest point.

# Water sources

In most parts of the temperate zone of North America, we are lucky to have an abundance of freshwater. The typical sources of water for cottages and camps are the lake, the inflow or outflow streams or tributaries, shallow water wells, deep water wells and springs.

## Wells

A well is simply a hole that has been dug, bored, driven, drilled or excavated into the ground to extract water. The source of water is an *aquifer*. Aquifers are found both in the bedrock and in the soil overlying the bedrock (called overburdens). Rainfall percolates through the soil to replenish aquifers. Ground water travels downward and laterally through permeable soil (such as sand or gravel) on top of hard or impermeable layers.

Overburden aquifers are readily recharged by percolating water from the surface, and are the most commonly used aquifers for wells. Overburden aquifers composed of sand and gravel yield lots of water, whereas those with fine sand or silt yield water more slowly. In bedrock aquifers, water flows through joints, fractures and channels, but the quantities of water are generally variable and unpredictable.

### Water table wells

Water will percolate downward until it reaches a depth where water fills all the spaces in soil and cracks in rock. This is called the saturated zone. The top of the saturated zone is called the water table.

When the upper limit of an aquifer is the top of the saturated zone (water table), the aquifer is called an unconfined or water-table aquifer. An aquifer that is overlain by material through which water cannot easily pass is called a confined aquifer. Water in confined aquifers is under pressure caused by the weight of the materials in the confining layer, the difference in elevation in the aquifer, and any resistance to flow of water within the aquifer. When a well is drilled into a confined aquifer, water rises in the well to a point somewhere above the top of the aquifer. Sometimes the pressure is so high that water rises to ground surface.

### Shallow water wells

A shallow water well is usually less than 25 feet deep (7.6 m), although some set the maximum limit at 50 feet (15 m). Shallow water wells usually intercept only the uppermost (or most easily reached) water, such as in perched water tables. These layers of water are stranded or "perched" upon a relatively impermeable layer of soil. The soil within or below the impermeable layer is not saturated with water.

> The depth of the water table depends on the types of geological materials and the topography of the land surface. Water tables rise during rainy seasons and fall during dry seasons and periods of heavy water use.

## Well safety

Know exactly where your well is located.

Secure the top of the well with a well cap or sanitary seal. Periodically check the cap or seal for cracks and holes.

Inspect the inside of the well annually to check for seepage and remove any debris.

Plug and seal any well that is no longer in use.

Sources of well water.

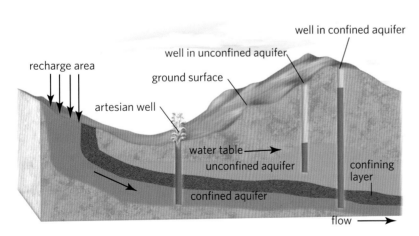

recharge area

well in confined aquifer

well in unconfined aquifer

ground surface

artesian well

water table
unconfined aquifer

confining layer

confined aquifer

flow

### Artesian wells

The best wells are artesian wells, which penetrate into confined aquifers. Rainfall percolates into and recharges the aquifer through permeable layers at high elevations, which causes the ground water to be under pressure at lower elevations. This pressure raises the water level in the well above that in the aquifer. A well that yields water by artesian pressure at the ground surface is a "flowing" artesian well or spring.

## Digging a well

As you withdraw water from the well, the aquifer must eventually be rejuvenated or recharged from local sources of precipitation. If you find that your well is no longer producing, it may be because you formed a "cone of depression" around the well intake. You will have to relocate your well to another point in the aquifer. Several wells on the same aquifer or an aggregate pit in the area may also be lowering the water table.

The worst case scenario is a contaminated aquifer. Since aquifers can extend over a large area, you may have to wait until the contamination source has been removed or depleted. Often confined aquifers receive recharge many miles from the well and will flush the system.

If you need a new well, your construction choices are drilled, jetted, driven, dug or bored. Only one of these is a viable option for the do-it-yourselfer: the driven well.

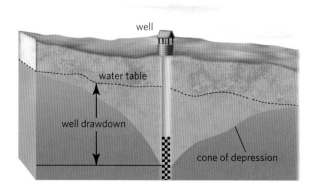

Cone of drepression.

## Driven wells

Driven wells are the simplest and least expensive wells, not requiring professional well diggers or drillers using heavy or specialized equipment. You basically drive a point into the ground. The point is made of hardened stainless steel and has a stainless steel screen to allow water to enter. It is screwed on to the end of a 6- to 8-foot (1.8-2.4 m) length of 2-inch (5 cm) diameter galvanized pipe. The other end of the pipe has a short malleable drive cap screwed on.

◆ Install the drive cap and drive the full length of pipe into the ground with a sledgehammer.

◆ Remove the drive cap, tightly screw on a well point drive coupler followed by a second length of galvanized pipe. Screw the drive cap back on to the end and pound the new pipe section into the ground.

◆ Continue this process until you reach water. The pipe sections act as a casing. Once you reach water, feed another galvanized or PVC pipe of smaller diameter, usually 1¼-inch (3.2 cm) diameter, down the middle of the casing into the water. Attach a foot valve to the pipe before lowering.

◆ Depending on the depth of the water, attach the 1¼-inch pipe to either a shallow-well suction pump (a "pitcher pump" for less than 24 feet/7.3 m) or deep-well suction pump.

◆ Build a box or housing and bolt the pump to the surface. The housing acts to stabilize the pump as well as provide a place to set water containers for filling.

◆ Before building the housing, have the water tested for E. coli and nitrates. Depending on provincial or state laws, water must be tested regularly, usually every 12 months for E. coli and every 36 months for nitrates. E. coli test kits (many including nitrate analysis) are available at many stores.

An artesian spring bubbles up from the ground.

## Artesian springs

Some lots have flowing artesian springs, a point where the aquifer meets the ground surface and water bubbles up. Most springs arise from a shallow groundwater source with a variable flow rate. The origin of a spring is often difficult to find, but the better springs are those that emerge from rock formations.

As groundwater moves through rocks and subsurface soil, minerals dissolve into it. Depending on the geology through which the water passes, these minerals may give a distinctive flavor or even carbon dioxide bubbles to the water. Naturally occurring contaminants such as aluminum, selenium and manganese can dissolve into the water. Have spring water tested to be sure it contains premissible quantities of any contaminants.

You'll also want to be sure that your family likes the taste of the water before considering making an artesian spring your main source of drinking water.

Many health departments don't consider springs appropriate sources for drinking water. To be used as drinking water, spring water must meet two criteria:

1. The spring must provide adequate, good-quality water to meet cottage needs throughout the year.
2. Since the spring's source is at a higher elevation than its outflow, you must protect the source. The most common protection is fencing to prevent animals from contaminating the spring source.

Those who do have such an oasis usually use a jet-pump to pump water from the spring to the cottage or camp. Yearly water testing for coliform bacteria and nitrates is still necessary to monitor the sanitary condition of the spring.

## Lake and river water

Obtaining lake and river water for non-potable uses is much easier than obtaining well water. All you need is a length of hose (usually 1–1¼-inch ABS) long enough to extend from the 2- to 3-foot (0.6–0.9 m) depth of water of the lake or river to the pump, usually a jet pump.

### Foot valves

Attach a foot valve at the lake end of the hose. The foot valve is a form of check valve, and is an inexpensive way to prime a centrifugal pump such as a jet pump. Most foot valves are designed with a 10-percent larger flow area than the pipe size to insure minimal loss of pressure at the outflow end. Since foot valves are continually submerged, it is important to select one with high-quality, long-wearing construction, like a brass valve with a stainless steel screen.

Foot valves are susceptible to fouling by zebra and quagga musselss. See **Foot valve menace** for more information.

### Priming the jet pump

- Prepare the jet pump by attaching nipples (usually 1-inch / 2.5 cm diameter) to the inlet and outlet openings.
- Prepare for priming by first gradually submerging the entire hose from the foot valve end up; do not submerge the open end or an air lock will occur. Gradually push the entire hose under water.
- When water appears at the open end, pull the hose to the pump and attach it to the inlet nipple. Attach another length of hose to the outlet nipple of the pump; this hose will go to the distribution system.
- Pour enough water into the primer opening until water flows out the opening. The water level should remain stable if there are no airlocks or leaks in the pipe.
- Wrap Teflon tape around the threads of the primer plug and screw it tightly into the primer opening.
- Plug the pump into a 110 V or 220 V outlet (depending on the manufacturer's electrical configuration) to start the pump. Water should be pumped immediately into the distribution system if the prime was maintained. If not, detach the hose from the pump and refill the hose by repeating the process, submerging the foot valve first and refilling the hose.

## Distribution system and storage tanks

The distribution system includes the network of pipes, valves, connections and other fixtures between the pump, storage tank and the buildings being served. A pressure of 30 to 50 pounds per square inch (psi) is usually maintained throughout the system. The two most common types of storage facilities are a pressurized storage tank on or close to the pump or an elevated holding tank remote from the pump but close to the cottage.

## Pressurized storage tank

Having a pressurized storage tank protects the pump from having to turn on every time someone flushes the toilet. Compressed air in the tank maintains water pressure throughout the distribution system. You can control the pressure by resetting electrical switches. Typically, only 10 to 40 percent of pressure-tank volume is usable for storage; pressure tanks are designed only for peak water demands.

## Elevated storage tank

An elevated storage tank uses gravity to maintain pressure in the distribution system. The higher and larger the tank, the greater the pressure provided to the distribution system. Tanks with 265 gallon (1000 L) capacity provide good pressure and last three to four days for three people. It takes about 30 minutes for a ½ HP jet pump to fill the tank, the pump being about 10 feet (3 m) above the water and the line from the pump to the tank being about 150 feet (46 m) and the tank elevated about 30 feet (9 m) above the pump.

Your lake or river can supply you with the water you need for washing clothes, flushing toilets, watering flowerbeds and other non-potable uses. With additional filtering and sterilization, it can be made safe for drinking too. See **Potable water at the cottage**, starting at page 234.

A submerged foot valve attached to a hose.

# Foot valve menace: zebra and quagga mussels

By 1992, a whopping $113 million had been spent to combat the zebra mussel since its arrival in North America in the mid 1980s in the ballast water of a ship from Eurasia. The costs included research, prevention, control and lost revenue due to shut-downs of industries and utilities whose valves were clogged by massive mussel colonies. These same bivalves can wreak havoc on foot valves and other intake structures at your cottage.

In the spring, massive accumulations of mussels scoured off rocks by the ice wash up on cottage shorelines. The piles of mussels rot and putrefy, producing terrible odors, attracting swarms of flies and squawking gulls. Not only are the accumulations ugly and smelly, the broken shells cut the feet of beach walkers and swimmers like razor blades. Hulls of boating and sailing vessels encrusted with zebra mussels are a common sight, as are navigation buoys so covered with mussels that they partially sink.

The impacts to lakes and organisms have been enormous. The filtering rates of zebra and quagga mussels are actually less than those of our native mussels. However, the prolific exotic mussels often number over 100,000 per square meter, compared to 1 to 1,000 per square meter for our native clams. Even a lazy zebra mussel colony of 100,000 or more per square meter can strip the water of its food pretty quickly! No wonder our native mussels disappear soon after zebra mussels arrive. In 1988, there were 16 species of native mussels in Lake St. Clair; by 1991 zebra mussels had smothered and killed all but two or three species.

While the increase in water clarity is a boon for scuba divers, it is not so great for fish and other organisms that feed on the plankton in the water. Their food is gone or depleted to the point that many species of fish, such as alewife, and bottom organisms such as clams and crustaceans, have been replaced by invasive bottom-feeding fish, like round gobies, and burrowers like worms and tube-building insects. The increase in water clarity created an increase in the quantity and diversity of plant life. However, many nuisance plants are part of this change.

## Appearance

Zebra mussels are bivalves with "zebra stripes" that come in a range of colors, from three colors of zigzag stripes in white, yellow and brown, to two stripes — yellow and black — to solid white, black, brown or yellow. Quagga mussels, on the other hand, are rather bland, usually without stripes or if striped, then only two colors.

Zebra and quagga mussels secrete strong threads used for attaching to hard surfaces, like rocks, submerged parts of docks, boat hulls, and inside and outside pipelines including foot valves. Some infestations are so massive that they break apart into clumps called "druses," which create new surfaces for the mussels to attach to. The druses can be found even on sandy bottoms, which otherwise are poor substrates for these mussels to settle on. Zebra and quagga mussels are the only bivalves that attach to hard surfaces. All native bivalves live either partially or entirely buried in the bottom sediments.

Like native bivalves, zebra and quagga mussels obtain their food by filter feeding. Small hairs on the gills sort the nutritious from the non-nutritious material in the water and send it to the digestive tract. The unusable material is spewed out and collects on the bottom as soft, fluffy ooze. The ooze is fed upon by a few bottom creatures but in general it covers the natural substrate and creates miserable conditions for invertebrates and fish.

Not only is a hard substrate needed by the exotic mussels, the water temperature and chemical composition are crucial for their life cycle. Zebra mussels need temperatures of at least 59 to 64° F (15–18° C) to complete their lifecycle. The quagga mussel can grow and reproduce at lower temperatures than the zebra mussel, so has a greater potential to infest more northern lakes. Quagga mussels seem to prefer the relatively constant temperatures characteristic of deep water over the highly variable temperatures found in shallow waters.

## Zebra mussels and pH

Lakes that have low pH (< 7.0) and calcium levels (< 10 mg/L) will have few to no mussels. Lakes with a pH near 7.5 and calcium levels near 15 mg/L will have some mussels which over time may accumulate to nuisance levels, but annual cleaning, or removal of intake structures (e.g. foot valves) for the winter, would prevent large infestations from forming.

If you don't know if your lake is susceptible to infestation by zebra mussels, call the district ministry or department of natural resources or environment and ask for data on pH and calcium content of the water in your lake, or collect the data yourself with standard pH and calcium hardness kits, available from most swimming pool stores.

## Lifecycle

Zebra and quagga mussels are the most prolific mollusk species in freshwater, producing more than one million eggs per female each year in their two- to three-year life span. They may spawn once or twice a year. If they spawn only once, spawning peaks mid to late August, with settlement occurring from July through October. If twice, the first lasts about three months (early May to early August) with settlement occurring from July to September; the second occurs in August or September, and settlement occurs as late as October or November. When the water temperature peaks and is maintained at an average of at least 59 to 64° F (15–18° C) over a two- to three-week period, only 10 to 15 days may be required for development from egg to settlement stage.

> A good rule-of-thumb for initiating zebra mussel control is to begin before the water temperature reaches 59 to 64° F (15-18° C).

## Dispersal prowess

Zebra and quagga mussels can traverse continents and oceans. To invade North America, zebra mussel larvae survived a seven or eight day trip across the Atlantic Ocean in filthy, grimy ballast water. Adult zebra mussels may have attached to the anchor chain as the ship was moored at a pier; when the ship departed, the anchor chain was stored in a hold moist enough for adult mussels to survive. The zebra mussel has a dispersal prowess that is unmatched by any other freshwater organism!

Both fishing and pleasure boats have nooks and crannies where water with larvae can hide. The boats also have hulls, motors and anchors to which adults can attach, especially if they are left in the water for a day or two. Mussel larvae can survive in bait buckets and wet wells for weeks if the water is aerated. If kept damp, they can survive even out of water for at least a week.

Even if every single cottager works to keep them out of the lake, natural vectors disperse the offending mussels. Waterfowl and some adult aquatic insects, such as giant water bugs and predaceous diving beetles, are capable of transporting small adult mussels overland to other bodies of water.

## Control options

There are two basic strategies used to control zebra and quagga mussels: proactively preventing the infestation before it begins, or reactively controlling the infestation just before it reaches nuisance levels. The proactive strategy generally employs low, sub-lethal doses of a control chemical such as chlorine when mussels are settling; the reactive strategy employs high, lethal doses to a specific life stage for part of the year.

For example, as a proactive strategy, chlorine may be applied at levels that do not kill the larvae but disturb them enough to prevent the settling stage from attaching to the inside walls of pipes or holding tanks of cottages, at least those that use gravity feed to supply water. The chlorine is applied from about June to November, while the larvae are in the water. As a reactive strategy, wait until October or November, after all the larvae have settled, and then kill all the attached adults by immersing the foot valve in boiling water.

While the reactive strategy is less expensive, there are disadvantages. First, large numbers of dead and often putrefying shells must be discarded. Second, the effluent water usually has to be detoxified because such high levels of chemicals are needed to kill the adults. If chlorine is used, sodium metabisulphite must be used at the end of the pipe to dechlorinate the water before it enters the receiving waters.

Biofouling occurs when living organisms such as zebra mussels coat objects, such as the stick above, or other organisms submerged in the water. Zebra mussels kill native clams by attaching to exposed shell and filtering food and oxygen from the water before the native clams.

## Pick your strategy

Three main areas require protection in most cottages: the intake structure (foot valve), delivery system (piping and pumps) and the cottage itself. You may be able to avoid the use of filters and other devices if you have only low to moderate infestations. Six devices have been evaluated by scientists for cost-effective control of zebra mussels. Several cottage associations in the Great Lakes area have made available material detailing the scientists' findings. The complete report on control options is published on the website www. georgianbay.ca/gbafoundation/zebra/.

Chlorine is the only chemical being used in low-volume intake devices. Chlorine cottage devices are available, but a reactive strategy is recommended by the manufacturer. Before selecting this option, contact the district ministry or department of natural resources or environment for permission to use the device.

# Potable water at the cottage

Dealing with drinking water at the lake isn't as simple as it is in the city, where we usually turn on the tap and trust that all is safe. The chapters **Getting to Know Your Lake** and **Swimming** should convince you that lake water must be treated if you want to drink it.

Boiling for five minutes will kill any pathogens in temperate latitudes. Most pathogens are dead by the time the water reaches 85° F (30° C) but a five-minute boil will ensure sterilization. However, since boiling all your drinking water is largely impractical, you will have to choose another method of ensuring your supply of clean, potable water. The options for most cottagers are filtration and sterilization.

If the water that comes from your cottage kitchen tap is drinking water, you won't hesitate to use it for washing fruits and vegetables.

Many cottagers opt for a combination of filtration and sterilization to purify their drinking water. Water *filtration* removes particles (including organisms) and impurities (pesticides, metals, contaminants), but often misses pathogens such as viruses. Water *sterilization* kills pathogens by chemical or physical means but doesn't remove particles, toxic chemicals and contaminants.

Normally, water is first prefiltered to remove large particles, then is purified using a process appropriate for the contaminants present in the water.

## Water filters

Filters are made of metal or plastic screens; of cloth bags or woven thread candles; or of hollow ceramic cylinders of sintered ceramic-oxide particles. Water molecules pass through the pores in the filter, while larger particles can't fit.

### Pore size

The smaller the pore size, the more expensive the filter. When choosing a filter, you'll come across two terms for pore size: absolute and nominal pore size. Absolute pore size describes pores that are of equal size throughout the screen. Only metal and ceramic screens have uniform pore size because they don't shrink or stretch the way cloth screens can. Flexible materials, including plastic screens and woven-thread candles, may stretch and distort. Their pore size is described as nominal—the size of the holes can vary considerably.

## Washing your filter

Most filters will clog over time and either must be backwashed, where water is forced through the filter in the wrong direction to unclog collected impurities, or replaced. Only metal and ceramic screens can be backwashed. The more particles in the water, and the smaller the pore size, the more often you have to backwash. Be sure to clean ceramic filters as often as the instructions recommend; forcing water through a clogged filter will eventually crack it.

Cloth filters can't be backwashed. Wound thread filters cannot be washed effectively. Once clogged, they have to be discarded.

## Reverse Osmosis

Reverse osmosis (RO) will remove all impurities and pathogens. These heavy, bulky and expensive systems are designed for large volumes of water, using semi-permeable membranes with tiny pores that allow water molecules to pass through but not chemicals.

# Sterilization

## Chemical treatment

Many jurisdictions prohibit the use of chemicals for purifying lake water for drinking water. Check with local authorities to determine if chemical treatment is a viable option.

## Chlorine: Sodium hypochlorite

Chlorination is the most commonly used method for water sterilization. While it is possible to use "chlorine pucks," like those used for swimming pools, to regulate the amount of chlorine sterilizing the water supply, chlorination at the cottage has a number of drawbacks. If you have a septic system, discharging chlorinated water to the system kills the bacteria needed to digest waste. You also need to be extremely careful that no chlorinated water leaks back into the lake. A major disadvan-

tage of chlorine is the production of cancer-inducing byproducts such as trihalomethanes (THMS).

The effectiveness of chlorine decreases with

- pH values above 7.5;
- decreasing water temperature (ineffective below 39° F or 4° C);
- increasing organic content of the water (the organic matter imposes; a "chlorine demand" that leaves little chlorine available for disinfecting the water);
- decreasing chlorine concentration.

## Liquid chlorine bleach

You can use liquid chlorine bleach to sterilize smaller quantities of water. The chlorine bleach sold in grocery stores has 1 percent, 4 to 6 percent, or 7 to 10 percent chlorine. Read the label to determine the amount of chlorine in the bleach. If the water is cold (less than 50° F / less than 10° C) or cloudy, double the number of drops.

A water filter with a wound thread filter.

| chlorine % | drops to add per US gallon (3.8L) of clear water |
|---|---|
| 1 | 10 (38) |
| 4–6 | 2 (8) |
| 7–10 | 1 (4) |

## Distillation

Distillation is akin to boiling water in a kettle. The evaporated liquid flows to a cooled surface where it is condensed and then collected. All the dissolved minerals, good and bad, as well as most of the toxic chemicals and tastes and odors are left behind in the boiler. A continuous feed distiller is more expensive but more convenient than the batch type.

## Ozonation

Ozone is a powerful sterilant with few drawbacks. Unfortunately, ozone generators are expensive and use up a lot of electric power.

## Ultraviolet Radiation

uv light is often used to destroy harmful volatile organic compounds, bacteria, viruses, and molds. When living microbes are exposed to uv rays, their nuclear material absorbs the uv energy and scrambles the DNA structure of the cells, rendering them dead or sterile and no longer able to reproduce.

uv light is effective at killing microbes only if the water is not turbid or cloudy. You should install a uv system that pre-filters the turbid water before treatment with uv rays. A common residential-use system with a pre-filter has a mesh with 10 micron absolute to filter sediment and a 0.5 micron absolute carbon block to filter out most impurities.

Water quality can change. To make sure your drinking water is safe, you should have it tested each spring, at the very minimum. Your testing laboratory will provide you with detailed instructions to follow.

## Iodine

You can use a 2-percent tincture of iodine from the medicine chest to sterilize small volumes of drinking water. To make a 2-percent solution, add five drops of iodine from the medicine bottle to 1 quart (1 L) of clear water or ten drops to 1 quart (1 L) of cold or cloudy water. The effectiveness of iodine decreases with the same factors described for chlorine.

# Water testing

In the U.S., many country health departments will help you test for nitrates and bacteria. You can also have your water tested by a state-certified laboratory. You can locate your nearest lab at www.epa.gov/safewater/labs. In Canada, contact your local health department or your provincial water/envionmental agency for water testing advice.

# Water treatment options

| TYPE/ PLACEMENT | ELIMINATES | | | | | COST* | PROS & CONS |
|---|---|---|---|---|---|---|---|
| | Bacteria, *Giardia, Cryptosporidium* | Viruses | Metals | Pesticides | Zebra mussels | | |
| **Boiling** for 5 minutes | ✓ | ✓ | | | ✓ | low | **Pros:** simple, kills all pathogens; cheap<br><br>**Cons:** treats only small amounts at one time; difficult to store large amounts of boiled water |
| **Distillation** by distiller which boils water then condenses it; placed on counter near tap | ✓ | ✓ | ✓ | | ✓ | med | **Pros:** Removes almost everything but volatile pesticides; also removes minerals like calcium, iron<br><br>**Cons:** very slow process, hydro costs can be very high; not energy efficient |
| **Chlorination**; device either in the lake for zebra mussel (ZM) control or attached to main water line for cottage use | ✓ | ✓ | | | ✓ | high | **Pros:** kills all pathogens and ZM larvae<br><br>**Cons:** expensive; risk of chlorine entering lake for ZM control device; risk of THMs produced; for main line device, carbon filter needed to convert residual chlorine into chloride before going to septic tank |
| **Iodinated resin with carbon filter**; column placed on/under counter or on main line | ✓ | ✓ | ✓ | ✓ | ✓ | med | **Pros:** kills all pathogens and removes some metals, pesticides; septic tank unaffected<br><br>**Cons:** excess iodine can lead to thyroid disorders |
| **Carbon-block filter**; column placed on tap or on/under the counter | | | ✓ | ✓ | | low | **Pros:** simple, reduces taste/odour problems; great for "polishing" water after treating it for microbes.<br><br>**Cons:** should be used with other devices so costs rise; ineffective on pathogens |
| **Ceramic filter**; cylinder placed on tap, on/under counter | ✓ | | | | ✓ | low | **Pros:** simple, inexpensive<br><br>**Cons:** ineffective for viruses, pollutants; filters are fragile, easily damaged (absolute pore size of 1 μm) |
| **Ultraviolet radiation**; cylinder with UV lamp placed on main water line on/under counter | ✓ | | | | ✓ | med to high | **Pros:** treats whole cottage; harmless byproducts<br><br>**Cons:** ineffective on cysts; greatly affected by water turbidity; sediment filter needed if water is cloudy; requires hydro, constant maintenance |
| **Reverse osmosis with carbon filter**; on/under counter | | | ✓ | ✓ | ✓ | med | **Pros:** whole cottage filter<br><br>**Cons:** not designed for removing pathogens; needs 35–45 psi water pressure that cottage pumps cannot provide; 90% of water is "rejected" to septic tank |

\* low < $100–$500   med $500–$1000   high > $1000          ✓ effectiveness depends on several factors; check your owner's manual

# Powering your cottage

Hard-core cottagers snub their noses at the necessity of electric power. The truth is, most people don't need too much power for a summer cottage season.

While some cottages have hydropower electricity, many others rely on alternate sources, such as generators, wind and solar power, or a combination of all three. In our energy-hungry world, looking to "free," renewable energy from the sun and wind is making more and more sense, particularly for life at remote lakes.

A portable generator.

### How much propane is left?

Propane is a liquid at very cold temperatures but turns to gas when released under pressure. Determine the propane level in the tank by pouring hot water down the side of the tank. Wait for two or three seconds and then slide your hand up and down the tank. The walls of the tank will be quite hot where there is no propane but remain cold where there is liquid propane. Where cold meets hot is the level of the liquid propane.

## Generators

Generators are great for "energy on demand" but not recommended if you run appliances or pumps 24 hours a day, 7 days a week all year because they can be gas-guzzlers and expensive to run. They should be stored in a sound-proofed shed with doors open or good ventilation while running the generator. Run a pipe from the exhaust of the generator to the outside to reduce the risk of carbon monoxide poisoning.

### Size matters

Generators vary in the wattage that they provide, from about 1,000 watts to over 10,000 watts. They can be gas-guzzlers and quite noisy, depending on the make and wattage, so it is wise to shop carefully. Some are incredibly quiet, rated at less than 60 decibels.

A 2,500-watt generator will run power tools under 10 amps and ⅓ horsepower water pumps quite nicely but if you want to run power tools with 10 amps or more, or run 220 volt machines such as welders, you will need a 5,000-watt generator.

The greater the wattage, the more fuel is required and the more costly it is to run the generator. The newer models have four-stroke engines, which are quieter and produce less fumes than two-stroke engines.

## Propane "power"

Most cottages and camps without hydroelectric power use propane stoves and propane refrigerators. They are much more costly but as or even more efficient than electric-powered equivalents. The downside is hauling propane tanks to the cottage or camp every few weeks. The tanks come in 100, 60 and 40 pounds (45, 27, 18 kg). You must transport propane cylinders in the upright position, which makes if difficult to transport the 60-pound tanks if you have a cap on your truck. (Someday they'll come up with short and wide tanks.)

Propane tanks must be kept outside but protected from rust-causing precipitation. Check the bottom of the tank for rust and corrosion. The valves have to be replaced every ten years. New propane tanks now have an overfill protection device (OPD) that will not allow propane to flow until connected to the proper regulator.

## Solar radiation

Solar panels are becoming as prevalent as satellite dishes on the roofs of cottages from coast to coast. The panels consist of photovoltaic cells, usually made of silicon, that convert solar rays into electricity. They tend to have a high initial cost but once installed are usually low maintenance, easy to operate, quiet and environmentally friendly.

Solar power systems consist of a solar panel, a power pack, an AC charging adapter, DC charging cables and jump start cables. A 300 watt system with an 18 amp power pack will run small appliances and electrical devices that draw less than 300 watts. It takes 10 to 12 hours of full sunshine to charge a 300 watt system, or longer if it is cloudy. Today's panels no longer require full sunshine all day.

## Wind power

Wind power is a great power alternative if you can place the windmill in an area that gets fairly constant wind. Wind is an indirect form of solar energy (heat from the sun drives the winds). As with solar power, the cost of wind-generated electricity is in the initial manufacturing of the wind turbines. After that, wind is free! The main environmental concerns for the use of wind turbines are impacts on land use, noise, effects on wildlife and the disruption of radio transmissions.

Wind is a clean and renewable energy source.

Wind turbines that produce 100 watts are sufficient to provide power for single cottages. At present, most wind turbines have three blades, 50 to 100 feet (15–30 m) in diameter. Wind passes over the blades, producing mechanical power (turns the wind mill), which is fed through a transmission line to an electrical generator. The transmission keeps the generator operating efficiently throughout a range of different wind speeds. The electricity generated can be used either directly, fed into a transmission grid or stored for later use.

### How much wind is enough?

Every location on the globe has wind, but the absolute amount of wind in any one area is highly variable. Wind speed depends on elevation above ground level. This is why most wind turbines are on the top of tall towers or on mountains. You can buy wind speed maps for most locations in North America from most state or provincial electrical generating companies.

Solar panels have become a common sight in cottage country.

### Wind math

The average wind speed of a site is an important factor in determining the cost of electricity generated from wind turbines. The amount of energy captured by a wind turbine increases as the cube of wind velocity. For example, the potential amount of energy that could be captured by a wind turbine in an area where wind speeds average 12 mph (20 km/h) is about 2.5 times that in areas where the average wind speed is 9 mph (15 km/h).

*Left to right* Naptha gas lantern, hurricane lantern, candle lantern, kerosene lamp.

# Let there be light

Life without electricity can be beautiful, particularly in the evening when the only light comes from candles, lanterns, fireflies and stars. Planning a summer evening of romance? Kill the generator and light the lamps.

## Naptha gas lanterns

The most common naptha gas lantern is the famous, allegedly indestructible Coleman lantern. Naptha gas lanterns produce a hot, bright white light. Be careful: even the handle will be too hot to touch if the lamp is suspended from the ceiling.

The gas is kept under pressure in order to feed it to the lamp device. The gas supply is in the center of the lamp and is housed by a mantle which you tie around the gas feed device. Frequently pump the air pump to supply compressed air to the lamp device. The mantle is very delicate once it is burned for the first time; if you touch it, it will collapse and turn to powder. If a black spot appears on the mantle while burning, turn the air supply down to prevent burning a hole in the mantle.

## Hurricane lanterns

Hurricane lanterns, sometimes called blizzard lanterns, are usually kerosene lamps whose flame is so well protected that even a hurricane will not blow it out. They are great in boats, will burn at least 24 hours on a full tank of kerosene and the flame will automatically go out if the lantern is tipped over.

## Kerosene lamps

Kerosene lamps use a wick soaked in kerosene along its entire length. Use the knurled knob to feed the wick through a slot at the base of the lamp. Trim the wick with scissors, absolutely flat to provide an even flame. Keep the flame low or the wick will smoke and blacken the glass globe. Clean the glass globe frequently with rolled-up newspaper.

## Candle lanterns

Candle lanterns are simply candles protected from the wind. Some cottagers and campers make their own. Some have a glass globe, others merely have a candle stuck into a hole in the base.

## Flashlights and head lamps

No cottage or camp can do without a flashlight. Purchase a waterproof flashlight that can be used in a boat or even under water. Head lamps are flashlights (often with white LEDs) attached to a strap that you wear around your head. They are fabulous for working in the dark, because they keep your hands free, and point wherever you are looking (watch you don't shine it in your friends' eyes).

# Woodstoves

Many camps and cottages rely on the venerable woodstove for heating, cooking or both.

## Starting the fire

- Check to make sure the ash box below the grates is empty or at least has enough room to accommodate more ashes, and empty if needed. Remove the front plate cover over the firebox. Using a poker, scrape the ashes back and forth to force the ashes past the grates and into the ash box. Using a grate shaker, rotate the grates (usually three of them) to clear the spaces between them. You should be able to see the ash box below.
- Open the dampers. Usually there are two knobs on the outside of the stove, one below the grates and one on the chimney or just before the chimney opening.
- Loosely crumble up three or four sheets of newspaper, placing one behind the other. Have five or six sticks of kindling at the ready. Ignite the crumbled sheets from the back to the front.
- Crisscross the kindling sticks and then place a small log on top. Replace the cover plates.
- Close or partially close the dampers as needed once the fire is ablaze. Place a larger log on the fire after about five minutes. Crisscross the logs at first but once the fire is going well, pile them side by side—they will burn longer.

If you have a woodstove, you probably have a wood box and a kindling box. The boxes should be large enough to store at least a spring or fall day's supply of wood, when the stove is usually kept going all day and night. Don't forget the supply of newspapers to start the fire.

## Maintaining woodstoves

- The firebox of the woodstove is lined with firebrick or mortar. The lining will crack over time, and bits of brick will break off. Purchase some cement made specifically for repairing the lining of woodstoves. Follow directions on the box. It works!
- Keep the ash box half empty. If it gets too full, it interferes with the flow of air through the grates from below.
- Let the stove cool and then rub stove black or olive oil on the top of the stove to keep it looking in top condition. This is especially important when closing the cottage as it will keep the surface from corroding.
- Keep the chimney clean of creosote, a chemical mixture created when wood is burned. A trip up to the rooftop once a year with chimney sweep equipment is a good idea and will help to prevent chimney fires.
- Burn hardwoods such as birch and maple when possible. Softwoods such as poplar have a lot of creosote and should be used only when cooking because they burn quickly and give excellent heat.
- Keep animals such as squirrels out of the chimney by putting a wire mesh around the chimney opening on the roof. Once the animals get in the chimney it is a messy job convincing them to leave.

Ashes are useful for keeping rabbits away from vegetable gardens.

### Creosote

Creosote is created by high-temperature treatment of beech and other woods, coal, or from the resin of the creosote bush. Wood creosote is a colorless to yellowish greasy liquid with a smoky odor and burned taste. It has been used as a disinfectant, a laxative, and a cough treatment, but is rarely used these ways today.

Felling a tree: first cut a notch on the side of the tree you want to fell. Second, make a diagonal cut on the oppsite side, leaving a "hinge" between the two cuts. Finally, shout, "Timber!"

# Firewood

## Felling trees

### Burn, baby, burn

The greater the BTU produced by a cord of wood, the better it is for heating your cottage.

| Species | BTUs* |
|---|---|
| Hickory | 27.7 |
| Apple | 26.5 |
| White Oak | 25.7 |
| Sugar Maple | 24.0 |
| Red Oak | 24.0 |
| Beech | 24.0 |
| Yellow Birch | 23.6 |
| White Ash | 23.6 |
| Tamarack | 20.8 |
| Paper Birch | 20.3 |
| Cherry | 20.0 |
| Elm | 19.5 |
| Black Ash | 19.1 |
| Red Maple | 18.7 |

* BTUs measured in millions per cord

There are a number of reasons why you might want to or have to cut down a tree on your cottage property. The possible firewood gained is often a secondary motivation that comes after safety considerations about, for example, partly fallen or overgrown trees.

Once you have decided that there is a good reason to remove a tree, consider first where you would like to fell it. Look at the lean of the tree in two directions. If there is a wind, determine its direction. Is the path clear? If the lean and wind will help place the tree in an open area, great.

Cut a notch about 1 foot (30 cm) above the ground and on the same side as you want the tree to fall. First make a horizontal cut about one-third way through the diameter of the tree. Then make the diagonal cut. On the opposite side, make another horizontal cut (the felling cut) about 2 inches (5 cm) above the horizontal cut of the notch. Do not cut all the way through; leave a "hinge" of 1 to 2 inches (3 to 5 cm) thick (rule of thumb is 10 percent of

tree's diameter). If the tree does not fall on its own, place a wedge in the felling cut and pound it into the cut until the tree falls.

Tree felling conditions are often challenging. The more trees you fell, the more expert you become at landing the tree exactly where you planned. You learn to deal with wind, sometimes waiting for a calm day, other times using it to help you fell the tree.

Felling trees for firewood is usually easier than clearing trees around the cottage because you have more options in selecting the tree and its direction of fall. Near the cottage, a tree will often lean toward a building or other trees sit in the direction of the lean. The felled tree can get hung up in them, becoming what lumberjacks term a "widow-maker" (see facing page). Always be prepared for the unexpected when a tree gets hung up and be ready to scramble.

It is better to risk hanging up a tree rather than having it fall in the direction of a building because there are ways to dislodge a tree. When buildings are at risk, an expert should be brought in.

# Chopping firewood

Once the tree is felled, cut it into sizes that will fit the stove firebox using an axe or log splitter. Most wood stoves have a firebox that is 14 to 16 inches (36–40 cm) long and 14 to 16 inches deep. It will have access from the top through openings that are 8 inches (20 cm) in diameter. However, this does not mean you can fit a piece 14 by 8 inches (35 × 20 cm) into the stove. Cut the logs into maximum widths of 3 to 5 inches (8–12.5 cm). The lengths should be about 1 inch (2.5 cm) shorter than the firebox.

If using an axe, start by selecting a small area of ground that is firm and level. Use the largest diameter block of wood as a chopping block; it is usually the second block cut from the base of the trunk, the first being the remains of the hinge. There are two basic approaches to splitting logs, depending on the log size. For logs 6 to 8 inches (15–20 cm) in diameter, split them into quarters, first by cutting them in half and then splitting each half in half again. Cut logs 8 to 10 inches (20–25 cm) in diameter into eighths by halving each quarter. For larger logs, make the first split at one edge; rotate the split block 90 degrees and make a split at right angles to the first chop. Rotate 90 degrees again and make the third split; rotate 90 degrees for the fourth split. This will result in a center that is more or less square and free of bark, as well as four pieces with bark. This squared block is useful for kindling by cutting slabs 1 inch thick and the slabs into 1-inch wide pieces.

Log splitters are becoming more popular, especially on properties that use large amounts of firewood. Log splitters vary in terms of tonnage, chopping pressures and how they are powered. In general, the higher the power is, the larger and the harder the wood that can be chopped. Most log splitters are convertible from horizontal to vertical splitters.

Your chopping block should have squared ends and should sit evenly on the ground. You don't want it rocking when you are splitting your logs.

The log splitter has grown in popularity in recent years and makes chopping wood much easier.

## The widow-makers

**The lodger** Lodgers are felled trees that get hung up in nearby trees. If the hinge is still intact, leave it; it will help prevent the trunk from rolling or sweeping. Don't cut the trees holding the lodger. Instead, first make a cut on the top side, about one-third of the way into the diameter of the tree. Next make the cut on the underside of the felled tree to prevent the bar of the chainsaw from getting pinched. Scramble when you hear cracking or see the lodger starting to move.

**The sweeper** Sweepers are trees that slide down between two trees. The trunk gets swept off its stump, swinging sideways and clearing anything in its path, including you.

Avoid a sweeper by standing well clear of the tree as it falls, preferably directly behind the fall. If the trunk remains attached, cut away from the direction of the swing.

**The barberchair** Common with hardwoods like birch, oak and maples, the barberchair happens when the trunk splits vertically upward as you make the horizontal cut on the felling side. The butt swings high up into the air and when the top hits the ground, the butt either bounces off its hinge and comes crashing down or it remains attached, until it eventually breaks or you bring it down yourself. Be ready to scoot. Don't cut the trunk; instead carefully tie a rope to the trunk and pull it down or winch it down with a come-along.

**The foolcatcher or time changer** When the tip of a small tree or sapling gets caught below a felled log, the sapling springs forward when the log is removed. It either knocks you back or you fall back just in time to avoid the wallop. Stand on the inside of the time changer's arc so it swings away from you.

**The chicot** Every forest has dead standing trees that are partly or totally rotted through. Birches are the most common chicot, with only the birch bark keeping the tree standing. Giving a judo kick to the trunk may seem like a fun idea until the top half of the tree lands with a clunk on your head.

## Axe safety

Never swing an axe if someone is directly in front of you or behind you; you never know when the axe head may fly off or the handle may break and become a lethal projectile. If more than one person is chopping wood, chop side-by-side but distance yourselves to stay clear of flying pieces of split wood.

## Tarps: all cons, no pros

Polyethylene tarpaulins degrade quickly from ultraviolet light. In addition, they are difficult to tie down so that they do not blow them into your neighbor's yard, or shred to pieces in a good wind. If you must use them, avoid wrapping them so tightly around the woodpile that no air can enter and circulate.

# Kindling

Use softwoods such as poplar, spruce or pine for kindling. Get rid of old lumber by chopping it into slats about ½ by 1 inch (1.3 × 2.5 cm) and of firebox length. Otherwise, chop softwoods or hardwoods into slats. Pile the kindling and let it dry for six to nine months.

# Drying firewood wood

While cutting trees and splitting wood is fun and great exercise, it gets tougher as you get older. But buying a cord of wood can be ridiculously expensive. If you do have to buy your wood, it is probably already dried.

Wood should dry two years before burning to reduce the amount of moisture in the logs. Green wood burns less efficiently than dried wood. It also gives off far more creosote than dried wood, reducing the efficiency of stoves and chimneys. More importantly, creosote produces chimney fire hazards, which have reduced many a cottage to ash.

Ordinarily, wood should be dried for a minimum of six to nine months, but it should be left for twelve months if it's cut in the fall. Wood cut in October will experience some water loss before ice-up, but none during the winter freeze. Wood cut in spring has all summer and most of the fall to lose its moisture. By cutting firewood a full year or more in advance, you could halve the amount of wood required to heat your cottage.

# Piling and storing firewood

Many cottagers store the wood under the cottage or camp. Others build wood sheds or shelters. The key is to protect the wood from the elements and keep it off the ground. Used wooden or plastic pallets make excellent platforms to keep every precious stick off the ground where it can dry. The closer the wood pile is to the cottage, the better; one mad dash for wood in a downpour will show you why!

If you have to pile the wood outdoors, orient it so that sunlight and prevailing winds work to your advantage. If possible, avoid overhanging eaves, trees, and structures that are conduits for funneling rain onto your fuel. If you must pile the wood against a wall, provide a roof or other shelter from the dripping eaves. Keep the rows of wood separated so that air can flow easily through them and the wood in the center will have enough circulation to dry properly.

There are several alternatives for keeping the wood pile from collapsing at the ends:

- Crisscross wood at the ends. Be sure to allow a slight incline towards the wood pile as it grows in height.
- Cut a point on the end of four logs, each about 7 feet (2 m) long, and pound them at least 1 to 1½ feet (30 to 45 cm) into the ground and brace them.
- Use walls or structures—pillars supporting the cottage, for example.
- Build a shed or shelter for the wood pile. A door or entry at each side allows you to use wood on one side of the shed for a year or so, while wood on the other side dries. When one side is empty, fill it with fresh wood and use the wood on the other side of the shed. Make separate rows for softwood and hardwood.

A wood shelter.

The female downy woodpecker (*above*) has a white head patch while the male has a red one.

# Woodpeckers

When woodpeckers peck, they can kill a tree. However, woodpecker activity often signals that a tree is already in trouble, infested with some sort of bug, and may need to come down. Woodpeckers have a strong, sharply pointed bill for digging and chipping into tree trunks and a stiff tail that is used as a prop while hunting for wood-boring insects. They find their food by feeling the vibrations made by insects moving and munching on wood. Most woodpeckers hammer on a dead limb as part of their courtship ceremony and to proclaim their territory.

## Downy woodpecker

The small downy woodpecker is the most common woodpecker in North America. They are often seen with mixed flocks of chickadees and nuthatches that gather in the woods during winter. In the winter, males feed on wood-boring insects in small branches in the tops of trees, whereas females feed in large branches on the lower half of the tree. Males aggressively maintain this separation by chasing away any bird that approaches his half of the tree. In the summer, a mating pair shares the food resources, the larger male chiseling deep into the wood with its longer, stronger bill, the female prying under the bark with her shorter bill. Downy woodpecker also feed on insects of weed stems, like gall fly larvae in goldenrod. Females lay three to six eggs in tree cavities.

The downy woodpecker's identifying features are a short, chisel-shaped bill, a black forehead and crown. A broad black band extends through the eye to the back of the head and down the neck, with broad white stripes above and below the black band.

The holes of the pileated woodpecker can be so broad and deep they break small trees in half.

## Pileated woodpecker

The pileated woodpecker is one of the largest woodpeckers in North America, at 15 to 19 inches (38 to 48 cm) in length. Nesting only in large old pine trees, the birds peck the bark around the nest entrance until sap (resin) flows around the hole, the sticky sap keeping predators such as snakes away from the nest cavity. The female lays two to four eggs, both parents incubating the eggs during the day and only the male at night. Pileated woodpeckers eat insects, fruits and nuts, and lots of carpenter ants and beetle larvae. It has a sharp, strong bill to pull bark off trees and expose ant colonies and a long tongue to reach into holes to pick the ants out.

The male pileated woodpecker has a black body, a flaming red crest and white stripes on its neck. The female has a blackish forehead, and lacks the red mustache below the eyes.

## Hairy woodpecker

Hairy woodpeckers look very similar to downy woodpeckers but are larger, shyer, robin-sized birds with longer bills and a black comma on their breasts. They have a barbed tongue for extracting insects, many of them harmful like the wood-boring beetles. Hairy woodpeckers prefer deciduous forests and are most common in winter and during their migration. The female lays four white eggs in a tree cavity.

## Yellow-shafted flicker

At 12 inches (30 cm) long, the yellow-shafted flicker is a strikingly large woodpecker. Lacking a strong hammering beak, they are the "anteaters" of the bird world, searching on the ground for ants and beetle larvae among leaf litter or in rotten logs.

Yellow-shafted flickers have a gray head with a large red patch on the nape of the neck, a long, narrow black bill and a black crescent on the breast. The face and upper breast are cinnamon. They have a prominent white rump and a dark blackish-brown tail.

*Left* The hairy woodpecker lives in close association with the pileated woodpecker, foraging for insects the larger woodpecker has missed.

*Right* Common in open country with trees, parks and large gardens, yellow-shafted flickers nest in tree cavities, utility poles or birdhouses.

The yellow-bellied sapsucker return to the same tree again and again, drilling sap wells in regularly spaced rows or columns.

### Yellow-bellied sapsucker

Yellow-bellied sapsuckers are medium-sized woodpeckers infamous for boring holes into the inner bark of living trees, letting the sap exude and then wiping up or sucking the oozing sap with their brush-like tongues. The extent of damage varies depending on the frequency of attacks. Lightly attacked trees usually recover. Trunks and branches girdled with several rows of holes are usually permanently damaged, and smaller trees or tops of trees may be killed by severe attack in several successive years. Harmful insects and disease organisms often enter the tree via these holes to cause secondary damage.

Each pair of birds establishes a territory that other sapsuckers do not trespass. If the territory is productive a pair may return year after year to the same location. The drumming pattern of a yellow-bellied sapsucker is distinctive and is used to establish territory limits and in courtship. Both males and females announce themselves with staccato drum rolls that sound like *tap, tap, trrrrrrrrrrt, tap, tap, tap, tap-tap*. They will even use human-made materials such as street signs and chimney flashing to tap their message. The metal amplifes their drumming.

Sapsuckers usually nest in cavities well above the ground in the heartwood of dead or partly dead trees. Three to seven white eggs are laid per nest. About 50 percent of the sapsucker's diet is composed of sap and sapwood, the remainder being wild berries, fruits, and flying insects attracted to the sap exuding from the holes drilled in the trees.

The forehead and throat of male yellow-bellied are red and bordered with black. Wings are mostly black spotted with white and have a large white patch. The rump is white, and the under-parts are pale yellow. Females have a white throat and lack red.

## Stopping woodpecker damage

To limit the damage, place noisemakers and frightening devices (flutters) in affected trees; wrap damaged areas with strips of burlap or other protective material and leave in place from April to late summer when the birds are most active; clean hardened sap and debris with a sharp knife and then spray the holes with pruning paint to reduce sap flow and prevent entry of insects and diseases. Varnishes, shellacs, and paints are not recommended as sealers because they are toxic to the tree.

# Cottage projects

## Saunas and sweat huts

Saunas are an integral part of a Finn's life. A sauna is not only a place to get clean, but also a place to relax and socialize. The relaxed atmosphere contributes to many positive outcomes in business and other meetings.

### Gerry's do-it-yourself sauna

Let's assume that you know how to erect a building, complete with walls, concrete floor and roof. Here are the considerations and details unique to saunas and steam-baths, using my own saunas as examples.

I have a wood stove in my sauna at the cottage and an electric heater in my sauna at home and it sucks up a lot of power. The wood stove heats up the sauna faster than the electric heater and really sizzles water and blasts off steam. Both saunas have concrete floors.

**Nails and knotholes burn**

If you use tongue-and-groove construction, the nail heads will be hidden. But if you use slat boards, use finishing nails; never use standard nails because the nail heads will get hot and burn you. This is especially true for the bench. You'll also want to spend the extra bucks on 2-by-4-inch knotless cedar for the bench. If you don't, you will be sorry as soon as one cheek touches a knot.

cold water tank

hot water tank

wood stove

concrete wall

chimney

rocks

**sauna**

bench of knotless, cedar lumber

concrete floor sloped to drain

door

windows

**change room**

tile floor (to resist water stain and wood rot)

wood box

door

Cutaway view of a sauna with a change room.

Don't use wood for the floor, especially pressure treated wood, because you'll slowly kill yourself with the toxic fumes.

Carefully consider sauna size: the smaller the better, but make it large enough to accommodate four or five people. The larger you make it, the larger the heater you will need and the longer it takes to heat it. Both saunas I have are 7 feet (2.1 m) high, 7 feet (2.1 m) wide and 6½ feet (2 m) deep, all inside dimensions.

The cottage sauna is a separate building; the home sauna is a room in the house. Each has a change room, as wide and as high as the sauna but one is 7 feet (2.1 m) deep and the other is 6 feet (2 m) deep. Make the change room of your sauna large enough for a person to dress and undress with a bit of dignity. The floor of the change room is plywood on 2-by-8-inch floor joists with 16-inch centers.

The cottage sauna has a 2-by-4-inch spruce frame, R-12 insulation in the walls and R30 in the ceiling. The door is homemade and is insulated with 1½ inches blue Styrofoam and has a slatted vent about 8 inches high by 12 inches long (20 × 30 cm) near the bottom and glazed glass window. On the back wall, there is a window that is hinged along the top, which we open slightly to help circulate air around the room. There is one light on the ceiling with a switch on the change-room side. The light fixture is waterproof and has a neoprene seal.

It takes about an hour and a half to get the water hot. By that time the rocks are almost red hot and water sizzles and dances on them. You can tell if the room has good ventilation because the steam will rise and flow around the room in waves, compel the skin pores to open and compel some visitors to step to the lower level or rush out of the room.

## Directions for the building:

1. Pour a 3-inch (7.5-cm) thick concrete floor that slopes toward a drain that drains to a gray water system. Lay chicken wire down before pouring cement to help prevent the concrete from cracking.

2. Build the frame, roof and exterior walls. Insulate walls with fireproof R-12 insulation.

3. Attach heavy-duty aluminum foil to the walls and ceiling. This isn't the aluminum foil sold at grocery stores; this foil has a a reflective surface and an R value of 2.6 or more. It comes in several widths and lengths. Start at one side of the door at the bottom of the wall and staple it to the studs, running it horizontally. Overlap the next row by 2 inches (5 cm). Continue up the wall and across the ceiling, making sure there is no overlap at the corner of the wall and ceiling. When finished, apply duct tape to the overlaps.

4. The walls and ceiling should be lined with tongue-and-groove cedar. It not only smells awesome but it will last much longer than spruce or fir. Knotty cedar is fine for the walls, but use knotless cedar where your body contacts the wood, such as the bench walls and bench.

5. You can either purchase stones or use quartz boulders from around your property. Don't use limestone rocks as they will explode when heated.

6. We have gravity feed for water and store water in two tanks. One sits on a concrete pad beside the wood stove and is used for hot water. The other sits near the bench and is used for cold water.

**Electric heaters** If you install an electric heater, the size you need will depend on the volume of the room, as shown in the chart on the right. A temperature control comes with the heater. Follow the owner's manual to install (distance from walls, protection, etc.). I highly recommend having the electric heater

installed by a licensed electrician. The stove requires a 240 volt supply and the connections must follow code for wet rooms.

**Woodstoves** If you use a wood stove, place it well away from the walls or pour a 4- to 6-inch (10–15-cm) thick concrete wall around the back and two sides. Buy the stove first then pour the wall. Put a damper on the chimney and make sure there is a damper on the stove for controlling flame height. An insulated chimney insert must be installed through the ceiling and roof. The chimney must extend beyond the highest point on the roof.

Sweating in a sauna is not only a physical act of cleansing, it is also a ritual that relaxes the body and calms the mind.

The size of electric heater (in watts) required for saunas of various total volume.

| ROOM VOLUME | | WATTS |
| --- | --- | --- |
| **Cubic feet** | **Cubic meters** | |
| 100-150 | 2.83-4.25 | 4000 |
| 150-250 | 4.25-7.08 | 5000 |
| 250-300 | 7.08-8.50 | 6000 |
| 300-350 | 8.50-9.91 | 7500 |
| 350-450 | 9.91-12.74 | 9000 |

## Willows for stick furniture

Furniture fashioned from sticks has been around for centuries. The oldest surviving examples date from the Egyptian Empire and include chests made from reeds and rushes, as well as chairs and hassocks made from sticks.

While stick furniture is durable, you should shield pieces kept outdoors from direct weather. Seal them with a clear exterior wood finish for extra protection. Indoor furniture requires no protection, although rubbing a coat of linseed or tung oil on every few years will keep it looking new.

With over 170 species of willow in North America, you should be able to find plenty of material for your stick furniture projects. Here are a couple of favorites:

**Shining willow** has shiny leaves and twigs. The branches are good for making twig and lawn furniture. The leaves are a favorite food for moose, deer, rabbits, squirrels and porcupines. Shining willow is more like a shrub than a tree but can grow to 30 feet (10 m) with an 8-inch (20 cm) diameter trunk. It is found on floodplains, shorelines, lake shores and in marshes and bogs.

**Black willow** is North America's largest willow. Mature trees have strikingly black bark, hence the common name. The wood is used for making furniture and wicker baskets. Black willows are small trees, up to 40 feet (12 m) high, 12 inches (30 cm) in diameter and grow for 70 years. They are most common on moist sites, on stream banks or in swamps.

### Prefab saunas

If you don't know how or don't want to erect a building yourself, prefab saunas are available commercially and can be assembled in three to four hours. Most are constructed from solid cedar and include walls and ceiling with insulation, a vapor barrier, preassembled benches, molding, a door and heater. Sauna kits are also available but they include the inside "skin" only; you build the frame walls, insulate and finish the exterior. They take three or four days to build, not including the framing and floor construction. The layout is entirely up to you; some have a two-level bench, others three levels. The bench can go against one wall, or form an L on two walls. The heater is always across from the bench.

# Camp furniture

The most common woods used to make camp furniture are birch, maple, willow and cedar. Use freshly cut branches when a lot of bending is required. Use rounds cut from tree trunks for table tops. Older logs are better to work with that green ones. All woods will shrink, and you will never eliminate checking and cracking when wood is air dried. Besides, it adds character to the furniture.

### Stick furniture

Making stick furniture has become a popular hobby, with specifically designed tools widely available. Those who want a jumpstart will find a plethora of how-to manuals. Sooner or later you will become an expert and design your own chairs, tables and garden furnishings.

To join pieces, you can either nail them together or use mortise and tenon joints. If you decide to nail your furniture together, use galvanized finishing nails. They won't rust and mark your furniture like non-galvanized ones will. To prevent splitting, pre-drill your nail holes with a bit that is smaller than the diameter of the nail. While mortises and tenons can be tailed to prevent slippage, good quality waterproof glue is usually used. Mortises are made with drill bits. Tenon cutters are available at most hardware stores. They come in different sizes, the most common being ⅜ inch (9.5 mm), ½ inch (12.7 mm), ⁹⁄₁₆ inch (14.3 mm), ¾ inch (19 mm) and 1 inch (25.4 mm) diameters. The tenon cutters fit any standard ⅜-inch drill.

*Left to right* The rounded leg end with the drill and tenon cutter; the legs and braces assembled together; the finished stool.

## Making a stool or small end table

Twigs and rounds or boards can make a solid, good-looking end table or stool.

1. If you have access to a large-diameter trunk, cut a 2-inch (5 cm) thick slice off the end for the table top and leave the bark on. Otherwise, use boards or cut 2-inch (5 cm) thick slabs from a tree trunk. Use a chainsaw or bucksaw to cut the tabletop. Use the smoothest side of the round or slab for the top of the table.

2. Use 1 to 2 inch (2.5 5 cm) diameter branches for the legs. The legs should be 18 inches (46 cm) long.

3. Use eight cross braces to square and firm up the legs. The braces should be about ½ inch (1.3 cm) in diameter and 20 inches (51 cm) long.

4. Nail the pieces together or use mortise-and-tenon joints. If you use mortise and tenon, drill four ¾-inch (1.9 cm) diameter holes into the underside of the table top and ¾-inch (1.9 cm) diameter tenon cutters to round off one end of each leg.

5. Nail the cross pieces onto the legs with 1½-inch (3.8 cm) long finishing nails.

Is there a cottage or camp without a comfortable wooden chair with a sloping back and armrests big enough to hold a drink? Call it Muskoka or Adirondack, depending on which side of the 49th Parallel you make camp, these traditionally hand-built chairs are so popular that chair kits are now available in most hardware stores. The cost is so attractive that it is difficult to make one for less money from your own lumber pile.

## One good hammock

A good hammock is made of 100 percent cotton or rot-proof, soft-spun polyester and will cost at least $100 — but it's worth it. Cotton hammocks should be brought indoors when it rains. If you hang the hammock between two trees, use tree straps; they are non-marring and make it easy to hang a hammock without damaging the trees. Don't drive spikes or screw hooks into the tree.

# Remote access

While owning a cottage without direct road access is not for everyone, it can be just the thing for some cottagers. Cottages on islands or on sites across the lake from a road entrance have some definite attractions.

Depending on the size of the island, privacy is usually one advantage. Other attractions include (usually) lower cost of real estate, proximity to good fishing right in your own "backyard," your own plant, bird and animal communities, and a sense of adventure.

Small islands generally have only small populations of large animals, many of which access and colonize it during the winter, then leave before the ice is out. Consequently, bears, raccoons, deer and other animals that can be nuisances to mainland cottagers are generally not a problem. Any animals that stay year-round are certainly easier to control. In fact, some island cottagers even have pet names for the "wild animals" that stay.

Last, but not least, islands are generally named after the people who own it—your name could end up being on a topographic map.

Although getting to your cottage can be a chore, after a year or two of trekking across the lake, you will generally find ways to make it increasingly more fun and memorable.

# Rafts

If you are an island or water-access cottager who finds the need to haul lumber every year to maintain or upgrade the cottage, you'll want either a raft or a pontoon boat. These sturdy craft are also useful for hauling propane cylinders back and forth.

The design for a raft can be as simple as a dock structure with Styrofoam billets below it or quite complex with billets supported by floor joists. The dock design can be somewhat unstable. Usually the deck is close to the water and will submerge if overloaded.

## Gerry's Wunderbarge

Because my cottage is across the lake and I haul lumber and gravel routinely with my all-terrain vehicle (ATV), I needed to build a raft (actually a barge) that can carry two tons. The barge has two parts: one long raft carries the ATV and most of the load; the other is a shorter raft that has the outboard motor and drives the entire barge. Because ATVs are difficult to back off the barge, especially if the trailer is fully loaded, the drive part of the barge is detachable and can be moved to either end of the long raft. The two rafts are joined by removable pins.

You too can build yourself a floating dock that can also be used as a motorized raft. The motorized raft consists of two parts, a *hauling raft* and a *pushing raft*. Make the hauling raft long enough to haul an ATV with a trailer attached—14 feet (4.3 m) will do. The pushing raft accommodates a 9.9 HP motor and can be shorter—8 feet (2.4 m) is a good size. For ultra buoyancy use 10-inch-deep by 20-inch-wide by 8-feet-long (25.4 cm × 50.8 cm × 2.4 m) blue plastic foam billets. One billet of this size will support 610 pounds (277 kg). The 14-foot hauling raft will accommodate up to seven billets and provide you with 4,270 pounds or over two tons (1,937 kg) of buoyancy.

The hauling raft is actually 16 feet (4.9 m) long. Each end has a 1-foot (30 cm) indentation with a 45-degree angle on the inner corners. The indent makes it easier to line up the pushing raft when engaging the two rafts. Why indents at each end? Having one at each end allows you to drive your ATV on and off without backing up. Use two ramps to drive the ATV straight on, put the emergency brakes on, turn off the motor, throw the ramps on the deck, and back the raft off shore. When you get to where you are going, but well off-shore, disengage the pushing raft, back out of the indent of the hauling raft, drive the pushing raft to the other end, carefully line up the 45-degree bevel on the front of the pushing raft with the indent of the hauling raft, engage the two rafts, and off you go to shore. Drive the ATV straight off the hauling raft.

The pushing raft will accommodate up to four billets, or 2,440 pounds, or over a ton (1,107 kg) of buoyancy. The diagrams that follow show three rows of billets but you can use four. The bottoms of the billets are protected by skids made from 2-by-6-inch lumber.

The ATV was driven directly onto the hauling raft part of the barge and then the barge was backed out from shore. The pushing raft has been detached and is now backing off to go around and reattach at the other end. That way, when the ATV arrives off the other shore, it can be driven straight off the barge.

## Tools

You will need

- a circular saw
- a drill
- hammer crescent wrench
- 3-inch (7.6 cm) galvanized spiral nails or 3-inch decking screws
- a square

Use only cedar or pressure treated lumber.

## Instructions

### Hauling raft

Start by making two frames for the hauling raft: one from two 2-by-10-inch-by-16-feet sides and two 2-by-10-inch-by-7-feet-9-inch ends for the top; one from two 2-by-6-inch-by-14-feet sides and two, 2-by-6-inch-by-7-feet-9-inch ends for the bottom.

Use nails or screws to join the corners; make sure the corners are square. I recommend 3-inch screws—they hold better than nails and don't come loose.

Having made the two frames:

- Attach a 4-by-4-inch-by-16½-inch post to each corner of the bottom frame.
- Attach four cross ties, evenly spaced, to the top of bottom frame.
- Lower the top frame down to sit on the cross ties. Leave one foot of the 16-foot board extending beyond each end of the bottom frame. The one-foot extension will form the 45-degree indent at each end. Attach the top frame to the four corner posts.
- Turn the entire unit upside down and place as many billets as you want for the buoyancy needed across the cross ties.
- Place a 2-by-6-inch-by-14-foot board along the middle of each row of billets.

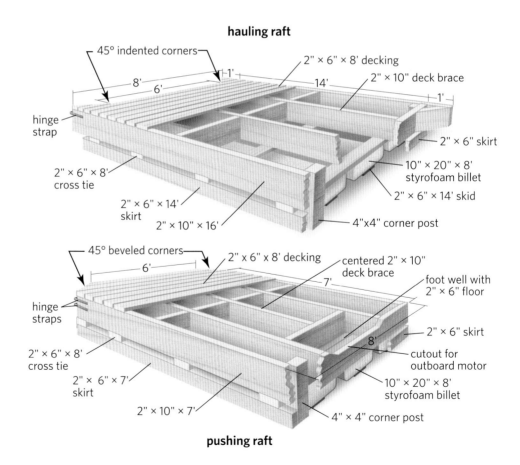

**hauling raft**

45° indented corners
8'
6'
1'
2" × 6" × 8' decking
14'
2" × 10" deck brace
1'
hinge strap
2" × 6" skirt
2" × 6" × 8' cross tie
10" × 20" × 8' styrofoam billet
2" × 6" × 14' skirt
2" × 6" × 14' skid
2" × 10" × 16'
4"x4" corner post

45° beveled corners
6'
2" x 6" × 8' decking
centered 2" × 10" deck brace
7'
foot well with 2" × 6" floor
hinge straps
2" × 6" skirt
2" × 6" × 8' cross tie
8'
cutout for outboard motor
2" × 6" × 7' skirt
10" × 20" × 8' styrofoam billet
2" × 10" × 7'
4" × 4" corner post

**pushing raft**

The pushing raft has driven to the other end, has reattached to the hauling raft and is now landing on shore, allowing the ATV to be driven directly off the hauling raft.

- Drill ½-inch-hole through the board at each end of the billet, through the billet and through the cross tie.
- Use ½-inch-by-14-inch (1.3 cm x 36 cm) long carriage bolts or threaded rods to attach the billets to the skids and cross ties.
- Flip the entire unit upright and install length-wise bracing first, then the cross bracing. The bracing sits on top of the cross ties.
- Cut four boards 2 by 10 by 17 inches with a 45-degree angle at each end. Screw them in place.
- Attach 2-by-6-inch-by-8-foot boards for decking, using a ½-inch plywood board for spacing the deck boards ½-inch apart.

### Pushing raft

The pushing raft is built in the same fashion, with the following exceptions:
- The back end is square
- The front end has a 45-degree bevel on each corner
- The backend also has a cutout to accommodate a 9.9 HP outboard motor. A foot well is built into the center rear of the raft for the raft driver. To center the well, an additional length-wise brace is installed on the front portion of the top frame. Use 2-inch-by-6-inch lumber for the floor of the well and attach them to the bottoms of the deck braces that form the two sides of the well. Leave enough room to accommodate the rear cross tie, which will form one of the foot well boards.

### Linking the two rafts

The two rafts are linked together using two foot-long (30 cm), ½-inch (1.3 cm) diameter eye bolts and eight 10-inch (25.4 cm) hinge straps.
- Pull the two rafts together, the bevel of the pushing raft fitting inside the indentation at either end of the hauling raft, leaving about ¼-inch to ½-inch gap between them.
- Attach two hinge straps, one about 6-inch above the other, near the front bevel on each side of the pushing raft and one hinge strap on each side of the hauling raft, situated about half way between the two straps on the pushing raft.
- Line the holes up in the three straps using the 12-inch-long eyebolt.
- Attach all straps using ⅜-inch-by-2-inch lag bolts.
- Turn the hauling raft end for end and attach a strap to each side of the opposite end of the raft.
- Attach a motor and celebrate with a scenic cruise! Invite 20 others—it'll hold 20 to 30 people.

A detail of the linkage between the pushing and hauling rafts.

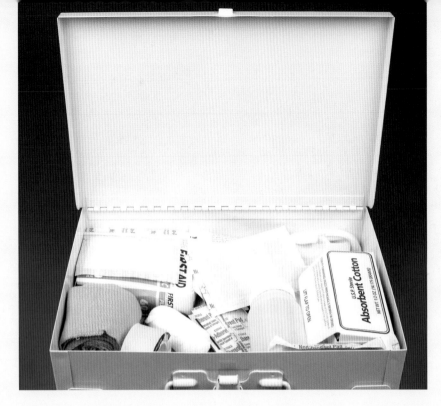

# Basic first aid

Here is a basic first aid kit to help you survive the mosquitoes, stubbed toes, cuts, snake bites, hangovers and other minor emergencies that happen at the lake. Common sense is, as usual, the best way to avoid calamity.

## Phone numbers

*Doctor*
*Fire*
*Police*
*Poison control*
*Veterinarian*

## Hardware/supplies

1   *flashlight* with batteries or without if you have a hand-crank-powered radio/flashlight
1   *tweezers*
1   *thermometer*
1   *bandage scissors* have a flat-tipped blade that glides safely under tape, bandages, coflex tape and gauze
1   *EMT shears* have serrated edge, used for cutting tough materials (clothing) and thick bandages

1   *emergency blanket* prevents shock by preserving body heat
6   *pairs of disposable* (usually rubber) *gloves* to protect hands and prevent contamination of open wounds, burns and abrasions
24  *sponges* for soaking with antiseptic solutions such as ethanol and rubbing alcohol and cleaning injuries
6-8 *safety pins* small to large for holding pads and large bandages together

## Bandages

25  *adhesive bandages* for cuts and scrapes
5   *adhesive spot bandages* the common bandage for protecting smaller injuries

5   *adhesive extra large spot bandages* for protecting larger injuries
5   *adhesive fingertip bandages* have V-notch on each side, for bandaging fingertip cuts
5   *adhesive knuckle bandages* have a U-shaped notch at each end, for bandaging knuckle abrasions
5   *medium butterfly bandages* shaped like a kayak paddle, wide at each end, narrow in the middle, for closing simple lacerations
5   *large butterfly bandages* same as above but for closing larger lacerations
*Note: there are some lacerations that should be stitched by a doctor; butterfly bandages are not recommended for deep lacerations*
1   *3-inch elastic bandage* designed to provide comfort for injured or weak joints and muscles. Use 2-inch (5 cm) for wrist or ankle, 3-inch (7.6 cm) for foot, elbow or knee, and 4-inch for knee, lower leg, upper leg or shoulder
1   *triangle bandage* ideal for use as a sling or cover for head dressing

## Pads/Dressings

3   *2 x 3-inch sterile pads* for placing on smaller wounds before bandaging
3   *3 x 4-inch sterile pads* for placing on larger wounds before bandaging
10  *iodine prep pads* for sterilizing wounds and burns
20  *alcohol prep pads* for cleaning areas around wounds
10  *gauze pads* for general-purpose use on wounds
4   *eye pads* for protecting eyes
2   *5 × 9-inch pads* for large scrapes and abrasions
2   *4 × 4-inch Burnfree dressings* are non-adherent and do not shed fibers; they provide immediate pain relief by cooling the burn, which in turn helps stop the burning process and minimizes depth of the wound

## Tape

1 **roll of cloth surgical tape** porous and breathable and stretches to accommodate swelling and movement; useful for securing wound dressings and repeated applications where preservation of "at risk" skin is critical

5 **rolls of micropore tape** for securing dressings, especially on damp skin, anchoring light to medium weight tubing, and when repeated taping is needed on fragile, at-risk skin

## Pain relievers and treatments

20 **acetylsalicylic acid** (Aspirin, Anacin) for general pain relief, headaches

20 **non-aspirin pain relievers** (e.g., acetaminophen, Tylenol) for people who react to acetylsalicylic acid

1 **oral analgesic**, such as ibuprofen (Advil, Motrin); used to relieve headaches, pain, inflammation, and muscle aches

1 **instant ice pack** to help reduce swelling and pain from sprains and bruises

1 **Burnfree gel** for applying to burn wounds; cools the burn and prevents sticking of bandages

1 **calamine lotion or hydrocortisone or prednisone** soothes the irritation of common skin rashes and insect bites and stings; dries the oozing and weeping of poison ivy and poison sumac; hydrocortisone is also used for the relief of itching and inflammation associated with a wide variety of skin conditions

20 **antihistamine tablets** basic treatment for hayfever and some other allergic illnesses; also a treatment for hives or "nettlerash"

1 **Epipen** for anaphylactic reactions to allergens such as bee stings; use for immediate treatment, but get the person to a hospital
*Note: Epipens have a shelf life, usually one year; check the label*

1 **antivenom** for each venomous snake species known to be around the camp or cottage
*Note: antivenoms have a shelf life; note the expiry date.*

## Cleansers and inhalants

1 **antiseptic soap bar** for washing hands before treating patients

1 **sterile eye wash** for flushing out materials in eyes

10 **antiseptic towlettes** for cleansing wounds

2 **ammonia inhalant** for reviving faint patients

5 **Polysporin or other antibiotic ointment** helps prevent infection in minor cuts, scrapes and burns

> Be sure to bring along medicine regularly needed by any member of your family. Stock up on essentials like asthma inhalers just in case.

## Basic first aid kit for pets

Pets get into all kinds of trouble at the lake. Here are some basic components of a pet first aid kit.

For the pet who pawed the porcupine, startled the skunk or met with a tick, see the **Living with Wildlife** chapter for remedies, and include the instructions in the first aid kit.

**scissors** to cut tape, gauze and to clip hair around wounds

**Biocaine lotion** for treatment of wounds, abrasions, minor burns and hot spots

**gauze pads** to clean, cover and cushion injuries

**alcohol prep pads** use to clean scissors, tweezers, and hands; do not use on wounds

**cold pack** use to reduce swelling or pain; do not leave animal alone with it; it might get eaten

**vet wrap** a flexible bandage used to wrap and stabilize injuries; adheres to itself, so no clips or tape needed
*Caution: do not wrap so tightly that circulation is cut off*

**povidone-iodine ointment** provides antiseptic action in the prevention of infection in burns, lacerations and abrasions

**gloves** to protect hands and prevent contamination of open wounds, burns and abrasions

**iodine prep solution** antiseptic solution for cleansing wounds or burns.
*Caution: follow directions on label*

**Opticlear** a gentle eye wash; follow directions on bottle

**emergency blanket** prevents shock by preserving animal's body heat; can also be used to protect a car's upholstery if the animal is vomiting or bleeding

**gauze rolls** to cover and protect injured areas; can also be used to fashion a temporary muzzle — even the most loving animal may bite if they have been injured or are sick

**Triple Antibiotic ointment** inhibits bacterial growth in cuts and abrasions; promotes wound healing. *Caution: read and follow directions on label*

**tweezers** to gently remove foreign objects from skin and paws

*Left to right* False Solomon's seal, lesser burdock, common milkweed.

*Next page* Great mullein, wild bergamot.

# Plant remedies

You might not have to look further than the cottage garden or the woods and meadows around your camp for some natural age-old cures.

## Medicinal plants

Selfheal is a member of the mint family and has the square stem characteristic of all mints.

**Catnip** has a reputation for curing colds and summer heat stress, for stimulating appetites, as a mild tranquilizer and for inducing ecstasy and aggression in cats. Catnip tea calms the nerves (human, not cat).

Starry **false Solomon's seal** roots can be used in syrups or tea as a cough medicine, while flavorful **selfheal** tea helps cure fevers and digestive upsets, works as a gargle for sore throats, and as an all-purpose salve and wash. Common **silverweed** roots have been used as an astringent in gargles and teas for reducing inflammation and for stopping intestinal bleeding.

The cooked root bulb of **wood lily** was once applied to sores and wounds for its healing properties. Avoid picking the wood lily flowers with their leafy stems because it kills the plant.

## Multipurpose wonder plants

### Lesser burdock

Apart from school bus burr-fights (keep it out of your hair!), burdock has myriad uses. As a medicine it was once used to treat kidney problems, psoriasis, dizziness and rheumatism. The large oval leaves (with a hairy undersurface), were made into a poultice for treating skin problems. The fruits are seeds that can be crushed and applied to bruises, snake bites, and abscesses. Try the taproots of young plants raw or boiled as a vegetable. The pithy stem is also edible raw, steamed, boiled or roasted.

### Common milkweed

As caterpillars, monarch butterflies are totally dependent on milkweed, voraciously consuming the leaves and growing rapidly. The sap of the milkweed they eat protects them from predators, because it contains a chemical that tastes horrible to birds. The milky white sap is poisonous to cattle and sheep but not to many insects. The young milkweed shoots, unopened buds and blossoms can be eaten as a vegetable. All three growth stages need to be parboiled three times, with freshwater for each boil, to get rid of the bitter, sticky sap.

## Great mullein

This giant medicinal herb has leaves so soft that they were once used as diapers and toilet paper (campers take note). The spike is so dense that it can be dipped in gasoline and used as a torch.

## Wild bergamont

This common aromatic mint attracts butterflies and hummingbirds, and has several edible and medicinal uses. The leaves can be dried, crushed to a powder and sprinkled on food for taste and for keeping flies and other insects away. Rub the powder onto hair, skin, clothing and pets as a perfume to discourage insects. Try it as a tea, or as a flavoring for salads, cooked vegetables and stews.

## Heady lettuce

Both the tall blue lettuce and the prickly lettuce have milky sap with narcotic properties. The root of the tall blue lettuce is used by Native peoples in teas as a mild sedative and painkiller, for stopping bleeding and for treating diarrhea and various heart and lung disorders. Prickly lettuce is also known as a "compass plant" because the upper leaves are said to point in a north-south direction.

## Cultivated flax

The species name, *usitatissumum*, means "most useful" and it truly is. The long (12–36-inch / 30–90 cm), tough stems have fibers that are highly valued for making linen thread, rope and cloth. The seeds contain flax oil, used for treating skin irritations, coughs, sore throats and burns. Raw or roasted flax seeds increase the fiber value of breads and cereals.

## Natural alternatives

**Soapwort** is a natural alternative to soap. Also known as bouncing bet, soapwort was introduced from Europe as a source of soap. All parts of the plant produce a soapy lather. Mash 1 cup of leaves in 2 cups of water in a blender and you have a good soap for dishes and laundry.

**Common yarrow** is a natural insect repellant. It is so pungent that it apparently repels insects. The fresh young leaves can be cooked as a vegetable or herb or steeped for tea.

**Pineapple weed** is a natural perfume. The scent of this herb is so strong it will mask any smell, including dead fish. Hang it as an air freshener, rub the leaves over skin or clothing as a perfume or add to hot bath water as an aromatic soak. Toss the flowers into salads or steep in hot water to make a tea.

**Butter-and-eggs** can be used to create a natural insecticide. When the juices of this poisonous plant are boiled with milk, it makes a good insecticide for attracting and killing mosquitoes.

If you find yourself lost at night, the stars that map out the constellation called the Big Dipper (*above*) can help you find Polaris, the north star.

# Lost in the woods

I f you are really lost, standing in the middle of the forest with no compass, no map and absolutely no idea where north is, relax—there is a way out. Stay calm and think rationally. You can survive a long time without food but you will need water in a day or two. The probability of finding water is pretty good as you find your way home. (Only follow the advice below if you are lost in the northern hemisphere.)

## Finding north

### Polaris: the north star

If you are lost in the evening, you can navigate using the stars. However, walking at night can be dangerous so it is better to find your direction using the stars and then travel the next day. In the northern hemisphere, the star Polaris is almost exactly in the north at all times. It is easy to find, at least if the sky is clear and

you know the Big Dipper. The two stars at the end of the Big Dipper's cup will line you up with Polaris. Make an imaginary line upward from the two stars, extend it five times the distance between the two stars and you will see Polaris. That direction is always north. Figure out your east and west directions from the line.

### North by watch

You can also find north with an *analog* wrist watch. Hold the watch up in front of you, and let the hour hand point at the sun. Cut the angle between the hour hand and 12 o'clock in half. (If your watch is set to daylight saving time, use the 1 o'clock mark instead.) This is the north-south line. To determine which direction is north, remember that the sun always rises in the east and sets in the west. If you are wearing a *digital* watch, draw an analog watch face on a piece of paper, then mark an hour hand basing on the time showing on your digital watch.

Using an analog watch to find north at 4 PM. Point the hour hand at the sun (*yellow line*). Divide the angle between 12 o'clock and the hour hand in half (*blue line*). This is north-south.

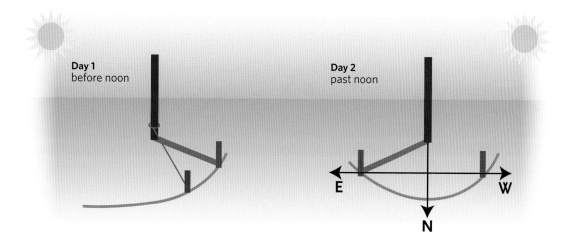

Day 1
before noon

Day 2
past noon

E    W

N

# Finding your way without a compass

Start by climbing a hill to get a look around for traces of human activity. If you see nothing, try another hill, but don't climb more hills than you have to—preserve your energy. If you see nothing, follow the instructions below.

This process requires a lot of time, from before noon one to day to after noon the next. It will only work if you start in the morning, before noon. If it is, try the following method to find north. Then you can decide the direction to travel. You need a fairly clear sky, as well as a straight, 3-foot (1 m) pole, two short (1 foot, or 30 cm) sticks (or rocks), another stick (or rock) with a sharp edge to use as a marker. You will also need something that can act as a string such as a vine. If necessary, improvize by knotting willow branches or another resilient, flexible material together. Find an open area that is flat and relatively level.

- Stick the long pole in the ground, as vertically as possible.
- Place one of the little sticks in the ground *exactly* where the shadow of the pole ends.
- Tie the string to the base of the pole and tie the sharp stick to the other end, so that when the string is stretched it reaches exactly as far as the little stick standing in the soil.

- Scratch half a circle in the soil with your sharp little stick, and wait until the evening (yes, it takes a lot of time!). Make sure what you draw is circular. The shadow will get shorter and shorter, until noon the next day, when it gets longer again.
- At noon, when the shadow is at its shortest, mark the point. The shadow now points north. It is often not very easy to see exactly when this happens, but close is good enough for now.
- Finally, when the shadow reaches the half-circle again, place the other little stick at the spot where the shadow ends. The line from the first stick to the second is west-east. Actually, if you mark points regularly, any two points that have exactly the same distance from the base of the pole will give the west-east line. This is a good idea especially if it is partly cloudy.

## Shortcut to west-east

A short, faster method gives an approximate west-east line, and you won't need the sharp stick and the string. However, the further from the equator you are, the more inaccurate this method is. Wait 20 minutes between placing each of the sticks. The line between the two sticks will be approximately west-east. Often, you won't need anything more accurate.

# How to use a compass

The easiest compass to use is the orienteer's compass. It has a clear *base plate*, which makes it easy to use in conjunction with a map. The base plate is marked with a *travel arrow* and will frequently also be marked with scales found on maps. Some compasses will also have *true north* lines on them; these lines run parallel to the travel arrow.

A turnable *compass housing* is mounted at the rear of the base plate. The compass housing is composed of a *compass needle*, the red end of which always points toward the Earth's magnetic north, as well as a *degree dial* that is marked from 0 to 360 degrees (or azimuth). The four cardinal directions, north, east, south and west, are also clearly marked. You will have to infer intermediate directions; for example, southwest is halfway between S and W and northeast is halfway between N and E. Orienting lines and an orienting arrow are inscribed on the floor of the housing and rotate with it.

Suppose you wish to head northeast. To set your course, follow these instructions:
- Hold the compass level in your hand so the magnetic needle turns freely.
- Turn the compass housing so that northeast (45°) on the housing lines up exactly with the direction of travel arrow on the base plate. This is your *bearing*.

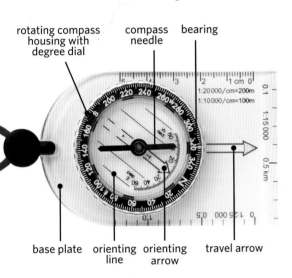

The parts of a standard orienteer's compass.

- Now, turn yourself, your hand or the entire compass (but *not* the compass housing) until the red part of the magnetic needle sits directly over the orienting arrow.
- Walk off in the direction of the travel arrow, checking the compass frequently to make sure you do not go off course. Checking once every 300 feet (100 m) is recommended.
- To double-check, look at the sun; it will always be in the south at noon.

Note that when you head due north or due south something magical happens: compass arrow, orienting arrow *and* travel arrow all line up. This will only happen when you travel in either of these directions.

You may need some time to become comfortable setting your bearing and following your course. Practice for fun, so that you can rely on your skills if you ever find yourself in a survival situation.

> Because the needle is magnetic, never use a compass near metal, like a wristwatch or pen.

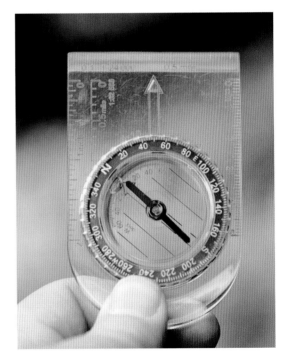

Using a compass to head northeast. When the compass arrow and orienting arrow line up, walk in the direction of the travel arrow.

# Using the compass with a map

To get from A to B, this cottager will be traveling at a bearing of approximately 102 degrees.

The principles are much the same as using a compass on its own, but this time you will use a topographic map to start you in the right direction. Lay the map flat on a flat surface. Suppose you wish to travel from A to B. To take your bearing, that is, to determine the direction in which you will be going, follow these steps:

- Place the compass on the map so that the edge of the compass parallel to the travel arrow is on a line going from A to B.
- Turn the compass housing to align the orienting lines and orienting arrow parallel to the north-south (or meridian) lines on the map. If the map does not have meridian lines, align the orienting lines with the map's north arrow. Make sure the orienting arrow points to the north.
- You can now read your bearing off the degree dial where the housing and the travel direction arrow meet. The bearing is the angle measured *clockwise* from north to point B.

- Take the compass away from the map. Do not turn the housing.
- Holding the compass flat in your hand, turn youself and the entire compass (without turning the housing) until the red end of the compass needle is aligned with the orienting arrow.
- Follow the direction of travel arrow to your destination.

## Get your bearings straight

Bearings can be used to accurately travel to a destination or to describe your position. When using a map, the bearing is called a *map bearing*. If you take a bearing off a distant point with a compass, the angle from magnetic north is called a *magnetic bearing*.

# What is GPS?

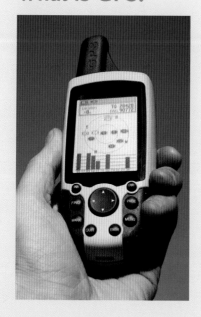

GPS can help you find your destination and return you safely to your cottage, whether you are hiking or biking, canoeing, fishing, or searching for the fabled creature of the lake.

GPS stands for Global Positioning System, a worldwide radio-navigation system of 24 satellites and their ground stations operated by the U.S. Air Force. GPS satellites transmit signals to receivers on the ground. GPS receivers require an unobstructed view of the sky and they often do not perform well in heavily forested areas, so you may have to find a clearing or a high point to get yours to operate if you are in the woods. They do not transmit signals, so if you get lost, don't expect to be tracked by your GPS.

Each GPS satellite transmits data that indicates the current time and its exact location. All the satellites in the system synchronize operations so that their repeating signals are transmitted at the same instant. The different signals arrive at your GPS receiver at slightly different times because some satellites are farther away than others. When your receiver estimates the distance to at least four GPS satellites, it can calculate its position.

Most handheld GPS units can track your location on a map as you move and many can guide you from a starting point to your destination, although that tends to be a more useful feature on the road than in the woods!

# Campfires

**Campfires and forest fires**

Some summers are so dry that the risk of starting a forest fire with your little campfire is real. Make sure that there isn't a campfire ban in your region. Consider the direction the wind is blowing and whether sparks or smoke will cause trouble. And at the end of the evening, douse that fire until it is completely out.

The ingredients: a starry night with a full moon. Bug repellent, sweaters, and lawn chairs, blankets or a nice log to sit on. A guitar or harmonica if you're so inclined. Hot dogs, marshmallows, popcorn, graham crackers, chocolate chips, peanut butter, tortilla shells, apples, bananas, cooking oil and aluminum foil. Chips, party mix, and gorp, if you want. Beer, wine or coolers. Pop for the kids. Oh, and some campfire songs and ghost stories too. Bring flashlights for the walk or boat ride back.

## Campfire rules

No running or roughhousing near the fire! Don't throw plastics or items with toxic materials into the fire, such as white foam, shingles or fiberglass. Don't touch the fireplace or metals that were on the fire pit. If a food catches fire, don't panic—either blow it out or douse with water, or toss it into the fire and start again. Make sure there are enough adults to watch the kids and the fire. One last thing, always heed any "no burning" warnings or alerts issued by forestry officials.

## Campfire foods

Before you crack out the marshmallows, get a roaring campfire going and let a corner burn down to a base of red-hot embers. Cook all the campfire foods slightly above the embers. Have a bottle of water handy to put out those fiery foods you accidentally dip into the coals. A pair of oven mitts is handy too.

## Hot dogs

The standard way to roast hot dogs is to push them on to the end of a long pointed stick or a long-handled fork. Push the weenie lengthwise onto the stick so it won't spin as readily when trying to rotate it in the fire. Forks work better.

The spider variation: Cut two lengthwise slices, about one inch (2.5 cm) deep, in each end of the weenie to make four "legs," eight in total. Put the weenie over the coals and the legs will curl and appear to walk like a spider.

## Marshmallows

Before the mid 1800s, an Egyptian recipe was used to make marshmallow candy from the sap of the marsh-mallow plant. Gelatin replaces the sap in today's marshmallows, along with a mixture of corn syrup or sugar, gum arabic and flavoring. With practice, everyone develops his or her own roasting style. Push a marshmallow onto a stick. Rotate it slowly just above the embers for an even, golden-brown roast.

## S'mores

A campfire classic. These are so good, you'll want s'more. Begin by toasting a large marshmallow over the fire. Place it on a graham cracker. Put some chocolate chips or chunks over the marshmallow, and top it with another graham cracker. Some people put the s'more together first, wrap it in aluminum foil and heat over the fire. Be creative!

## Baked apples

Cut most of the core out of a fresh apple, making sure you leave the bottom intact. Fill the middle with cinnamon, brown sugar, raisins and nuts. Wrap in aluminum foil and heat over the embers. When hot, open up the gooey treat and eat with a spoon.

## Gooey bananas

With the skin on, cut a slit from top to bottom without cutting all the way through. Open the banana slightly to put some chocolate chips inside. Top these with mini marshmallows. Wrap it in aluminum foil and heat over the campfire. Unwrap the banana but but leave it on the foil. Remove the peel, slice the banana or spoon off bite-size pieces and enjoy.

## Choco-Tacos

Spread peanut butter on a tortilla shell, sprinkle chocolate chips and mini marshmallows on top, roll the tortilla up and wrap in aluminum foil. Set it on red-hot embers for about ten minutes. Check periodically to see if everything has melted. If so, enjoy!

## Popcorn

For each person you will need 2 teaspoons vegetable oil, 4 teaspoons popcorn, some salt, and heavy-duty aluminum foil. Tear off an 18-inch (46 cm) piece of foil. Pour the oil and popcorn into the middle. Fold opposite foil corners together at least three times to seal well and keep oil from leaking out. Bring the two remaining foil corners toward the center and roll the edges together to make a tent but leave a small tunnel to push a fork through. Be sure to leave enough room inside for the popcorn to pop. Push the ends of a campfire fork through the last fold of foil at the top of the pack. Set the pack into hot coals until oil sizzles and you hear a few kernels pop. Then pick up the fork and gently shake the pack above the coals until popping is done. Open the pack and add salt to taste.

Okay, so some of us are lazy and just buy Jiffy-pop. Make sure to shake the corn the entire time. Wear an oven mitt, and hold the corn in the hottest part of the fire.

# Closing the cottage: a checklist

One of the saddest times of the year for lake-lovers is closing time. If you have to bring your cottage activities to an end in the fall, properly prepare your summer haven for its winter sleep. Follow the closing checklist carefully, and bring home items that you don't want to freeze, particularly if your cottage or camp is not heated. Even if your cottage is heated, power outages from severe weather such as freezing ice storms, blizzards or furnace breakdowns are not uncommon over a long winter.

## Lake and lakeside equipment

### Water pumps and tanks

❏ Disconnect inflow hose from pump; pull hose and foot valve from lake; drain hose, coil and store.

❏ Bring in anchor, float and any foot valve accessories and store.

❏ Open any valves to drain water tank line and leave open for winter.

❏ Unscrew drain plugs on bottom of pump to drain pump heads; store in a pump accessory bag.

### Motorboats

❏ Add fuel stabilizer to the gas (follow direction on label); mix the tank well, then run the motor until it is warm. Before removing outboard (if light enough to remove), winterize the carburetor and fuel line in the motor following instructions below.

❏ If boat is 14 feet or less, remove boat from water, store upside down on a rack or on blocks, off the ground.

❏ If boat is larger, pull from water and store on a trailer or on rack; if on a trailer, raise and support wheels off the ground.

❏ Drain any water in hull and bait wells.

❏ Clean any mud or dirt off the anchor, neatly coil the rope and store in the boat or in a shed.

❏ Inspect lifejackets, replace in spring if necessary; store neatly in boat or in shed.

❏ Clean boat now or in the spring; store in a shed or cover the boat with a good quality tarp; tie tarp down well so it doesn't flap and tear in the wind.

❏ Disconnect batteries and store on shelf in shed. Batteries should be fully charged before storing. Charge at least once, preferably twice during the winter, so bring it home if you don't plan to return until spring.

### Docks

❏ Remove docks and accessories, store off the ground on racks.

❏ Oil any bolts and hardware and store together in a bucket.

### Minnow traps, minnow buckets and fishing gear

❏ Remove any bread, soils, fish, debris and wipe clean.

❏ Replace any ragged ropes, coil neatly and store in a shed.

❏ Inspect all fishing rods, oil reels if needed, replace any lines now or next spring; take inventory of tackle and replace as needed in the spring.

### Canoes and other watercraft

❏ Remove any removable components (e.g. sail, fins); oil any threaded hardware and store in a shed.

❏ Clean watercraft and store upside down off the ground under shelter.

## Around the cottage

### Barbeques

❏ Clean barbeque. Fire it up for ten minutes to burn off cleansers.

❏ Inspect and clean burners. If rusted, replace next spring.

❏ Disconnect propane tank and store in a dry, protected but open outdoor location.

### Outdoor chairs and tables

❏ Clean and store outdoor chairs in a sheltered place.

❏ Clean and cover or store lawn, deck and picnic tables in a sheltered place.

### Firewood and kindling

❏ Replace any wood and kindling burned over the summer.

❏ Restack any fallen wood.

❏ Pile new wood, leaving room to access old woodpile.

## Locks

- ❑ Oil all locks with 10W30 oil.
- ❑ Cover or recover exposed locks with rubber flaps (old rubber boots work well) to keep water out of locks.

## Hanging outside objects

- ❑ Clean and wash hummingbird feeders, store inside unassembled.
- ❑ Repair any bird houses; store in a sheltered place if house is removable.
- ❑ Lower and remove any flags and hammocks, clean or replace as needed.
- ❑ Remove any wasp nests.

## Laundry room

- ❑ Run washing machine on rinse cycle to drain excess water from machine and hoses.

## Inside the cottage

## Dry cell batteries

- ❑ Test all flashlights, clocks, radios, etc. and dispose of dead batteries in hazardous waste.
- ❑ Remove good batteries from flashlights, clocks, radios, etc. and store in dry place

## Electric devices

- ❑ Reduce risk of electrical fires from lightning strikes by unplugging toasters, radios, TVs, VCRs, etc.

## Stove

- ❑ If wood stove, shake any remaining ashes in stove into ash box. Remove ash box, dispose of ashes, replace ash box.
- ❑ Clean oven and top of stove. If stove is electric or propane, remove grills, clean and reinstall.
- ❑ If wood stove, scrub with steel wool, wipe stove polish or olive oil on surface to prevent rusting.

---

- ❑ Pour plumbing antifreeze into machine and run machine on rinse cycle briefly to mix antifreeze into system.
- ❑ Pull electrical plug and drain any hoses and water tanks that feed the washing machine.

## Sauna

- ❑ Drain any water tanks and lines used for the sauna.
- ❑ Remove ashes from any wood stoves in the sauna or unplug electric stoves.

## Fuel shed

- ❑ Add fuel stabilizer to all cans with gas (follow label instructions).
- ❑ Pack and bring back empty cans for refilling next spring.

## Canned foods

- ❑ Pack and bring home all canned and bottled foods with liquids.
- ❑ Canned dry foods such as coffee, nuts, etc. can stay, but turn cans upside down so mice can't chew through plastic lids.

## Packaged dry foods

- ❑ Pack and bring home crackers, biscuits, cereals, etc.
- ❑ Pastas, sugars, flours, teas, etc., can stay, but are best kept in glass jars with glass or metal lids.

## Refrigerator

- ❑ Remove all goods, pack and bring home all goods that need refrigeration after opening
- ❑ Shut down refrigerator, de-ice and wipe clean freezer and inside of fridge. If propane, you may have to shut down propane tank to shut fridge off, depending on model.
- ❑ Place an open box of baking soda on a shelf and leave door ajar.

---

## Generator

- ❑ Drain gas from tank by removing filter cover below valve; drain into clean can, then filter gas through chamois cloth before putting into gas can. Replace filter cover.
- ❑ Clear remaining gas in line by running generator until engine stops; repeat until generator will not start.
- ❑ Remove and clean spark plug or replace with a new one. Squirt about a teaspoon of high grade synthetic oil into the cylinders then roll the engine over by pulling on the starter cord. Reinstall the plugs.
- ❑ Pull on starter cord until you feel resistance; this stores pistons at top to minimize condensation during storage.
- ❑ Remove all electrical cords from plugs.

## Windows and screens

- ❑ If cottage has shutters or some kind of covering to protect inside from storms, close and lock them.
- ❑ Inspect screens, replace as needed next spring.
- ❑ Pull all blinds (out of sight, out of mind for burglars).

## Sinks and toilets

- ❑ Shut off water supply.
- ❑ Place a bucket under the P-trap of each sink and empty the trap by removing plug on its base. Reinstall plug.
- ❑ Flush toilet. Remove tank lid and soak up remaining water with a rag or sponge. Replace lid.
- ❑ Soak up remaining water in toilet bowl with a rag or sponge.
- ❑ Pour a cup of plumbing antifreeze into bowl. Lower the toilet seat lid.
- ❑ Leave all taps open for the winter.

# Opening the cottage: a checklist

The snow is gone, the birds are back, and the lake is calling — yippee! Cottage opening is much more fun than closing, especially if you arrive to find everything in good order. You'll be glad you spent the extra effort to close things up properly. The opening checklist is basically a reversal of the closing checklist.

## Lake and lakeside equipment

### Water pumps and tanks
(See **Lake and river water** in **Cottage Operations**. For burst pipes, see **Mending pipes** in the same chapter. )
- ❏ Wrap drain plugs with Teflon tape and reinstall them on bottom of pump.
- ❏ If you have water tanks, close any valves that drained the water tank line.
- ❏ Put chest waders on. Place the anchor, float and any accessories used for foot valve out in the lake. Fill the water line by submerging the foot valve end first, then slowly pushing the line, inch by inch, into the water until water exits the open end of the hose. If the foot valve is working properly, and there are no leaks in the hose, the water level should remain at the opening.
- ❏ Connect the hose to the jet pump and clamp in place with a screw clamp.
- ❏ Prime the pump by pouring water into the pump head until water overflows. Wrap Teflon tape on the threads of the plug, reinstall and tighten.
- ❏ Close all valves and taps in the cottage.
- ❏ Turn the pump on and check for leaks. No leaks? Great, you have running water again.

Even if the first visit of the season involves a long list of chores, it still provides a respite from routines at home.

### Boats and motors
- ❏ Remove any tarps, replace drain plugs and return the boat(s) to water.
- ❏ Reinstall any accessories such as anchors, lifejackets, boat emergency kits, fishing rods.
- ❏ If the outboards were winterized properly, they should start with two or three pulls of the starter cord.
- ❏ Fill the gas can with fresh fuel (not stabilized fuel). Later, use stabilized fuel and fresh fuel and all stored, stabilized fuel is used up.
- ❏ If the motors have electric starters, check the charge in the battery, recharge if needed, reconnect the batteries and off you go.

### Docks
- ❏ If you wish to paint the docks, do it before placing the docks in the water.
- ❏ Return the docks to the water.

### Minnow traps, minnow buckets and other bait containers
- ❏ If you cleaned the traps and buckets last fall they should be ready to go.

### Canoes and other watercraft
- ❏ Clean, paint as needed, canoes and kayaks. Repair any sail, fins, accessories (though this is better done in the fall).
- ❏ Return watercraft to shore area and store upside down on racks.

# Around the cottage

### Barbeques
- ❏ Open the lid and check to make sure no animals have settled in over the winter.
- ❏ Connect the propane tank. Test it by starting the barbeque. Let it burn for five minutes to burn off any rust.

### Outdoor chairs and tables
- ❏ Return them to their places.

### Firewood and kindling
- ❏ If you didn't replace any wood and kindling last fall, do it now.
- ❏ Re-stack any fallen wood and pile new wood leaving room to access old woodpile.

### Locks
- ❏ Open all locks. If any are difficult to open or are seized, oil with 10W30 oil.

### Hanging outside objects
- ❏ Fill and return hummingbird feeders.
- ❏ Return bird houses and feeders.
- ❏ Raise any flags.
- ❏ Hang the hammock.

### Laundry room
- ❏ Connect water lines to washing machine; run on rinse cycle to drain any antifreeze in machine.

### Sauna
- ❏ Fill any water tanks used for the sauna.
- ❏ Fill the wood box for the wood-burning heater.

### Fuel shed
- ❏ Use fresh gas to start all motors.
- ❏ For new gas, put dates on all gas cans when refilled and use oldest gas first.

### Generators
- ❏ Start the new season with fresh gas (not stabilized gas). Then use half fresh and half stabilized fuel until all "old" gas is used.
- ❏ Fill oil well with oil recommended in operator's manual.
- ❏ If generator was winterized properly, it should start with two or three pulls of the starter cord.

Another springtime return to cottage country.

# Inside the cottage

### Dry cell batteries
- ❏ Replace all batteries in flashlights, clocks, radios, etc.

### Electric devices
- ❏ Plug in the TVs, VCRs, as needed.

### Stove
- ❏ Follow instructions for lighting wood stove fires in **Cottage Operations** chapter.

### Canned foods
- ❏ Replace all canned and bottled foods.

- ❏ Replace dry foods such as coffee, nuts, as required.

### Packaged dry foods
- ❏ Replace crackers, biscuits, cereals, etc.
- ❏ Replace pastas, sugars, flours, teas, etc. in their protective containers.

### Refrigerator
- ❏ Plug in refrigerator or open propane tank and start propane refrigerator following operator's manual.
- ❏ Leave the open box of baking soda on a shelf.

### Windows and screens
- ❏ If cottage has shutters or some kind of covering to protect inside from vandals, storms, etc., unlock and open.
- ❏ Open all blinds.

### Sinks and toilets
- ❏ Once water is running again, open the taps to release any trapped air in line. Then close.
- ❏ Check for leaks in water lines.
- ❏ Flush toilet to make sure it flushes and the tank refills well.

# Acknowledgments

THIS BOOK WAS MADE POSSIBLE BY THE HELP, SUPPORT AND ENCOURAGEMENT of my former graduate students, my relatives and friends, the editors and designers, my co-author and my family.

I include my graduate students because much of the information in this book comes from the results of their research from 1974 to 2007; thank you (in chronological order) Paul McKee, Peter Seidl, Brian Rooke, Malcolm Stephenson, Bob Bailey, Mark Servos, Robert Young, Margo Shaw, Chris McCall, Bruce Kilgour, Wade Gibbons, Norm Yan, Paul Welsh, Debbie Ming, Patti Gillis, Debbie Dean, Diane Pathy, Evan Dobson, Sheri Hinks, Paul Smilie, Susan Doka, Trevor Claxton, Dave Zanatta, Daelyn Woolnough, Lisa Guenther/ Wren and Kelly McNichols.

Relatives on my wife's side (Balfour, Stuart, Stanley, Marlene and Doug Thomas and their spouses and children) and on my side (sister Sharon and brother George and their spouses and children) provided photos, helped roof my cottage, construct a septic system, build decks and a boathouse, cut trees, chop wood, repair plumbing, build a hillbilly hot tub, and rescue people from CNR tracks. Annual openings and closings would not be possible without the help of my friends; thank you Neil Boone, Cory Bradshaw, Michael Feduzzi, Blair Gemmel, Grant Hicks, Eric Malone, Doug Thomas, Kelly Thomas, and my son Einar and nephew Craig Mackie and his friends.

In such a comprehensive book, one cannot be an expert in everything and I particularly thank my vet, Dr. Nickey Brown of Campus Estates Animal Hospital in Guelph for providing information on quill removal and pet first aid kits. Dr. Ian Martin, a former research associate, is also an expert fly fisherman and provided information on fly fishing techniques. I also would like to thank those whose photos are featured in this book, beginning with Laura Taylor and including many colleagues and others listed in the photo credits. Thanks as well to the artists at Imagineering Media Services, Inc. for their beautiful illustrations created especially for this book. Thanks also to Ryan Price who contributed the line drawings of cottage life found in each chapter.

This book is not only comprehensive but multifarious. Thanks to the editors, Kathy Fraser and Noel Hudson, and to the designer, Kathe Gray and, assisting her, Erin Crickett, as well as designer Christine Gilham. They have made it uncomplicated, intriguing and vibrant. I am particularly grateful to John Denison, publisher of Boston Mills Press, and to Firefly Books for publishing this book.

The first version of this book was quite scientific in nature and contained a lot of line drawings. Laura Taylor was a former student of mine and a talented writer and I asked if she would take my text and convert it into an exciting and interesting read for the layperson. She is also a talented photographer and many of the images in the book are hers.

Finally, I am truly grateful to have such an understanding wife who has put up with my grumpiness, scheduled her life around mine but at the same time has encouraged me to carry on with getting this book on the shelves of bookstores. I also thank my son, Einar, his wife, Kara, my daughter, Carolyn, and her husband, Rob Percival, for constant encouragement and understanding why I had to miss many events for my grandchildren, Katie, Matthew, Ewan and Griffin. —**GM**

**For my wife and family,
faithful cottagers.**

A big thank you to Gerry for being a great teacher and for involving me in this epic undertaking, and to Liz Mackie for her endless patience and cottage hospitality. Thank you to John Denison and Kathy Fraser at the Boston Mills Press for taking on a project of this scope, and to Kathe Gray for her beautiful design work and for her perseverance.

Thank you to Hermann and Erne Kozel for sharing their piece of paradise on Mountain Lake with us all these years. I am grateful, as always, to my mother, Erika, Fred and Oma for all of their support. And to Andrew, faithful photo assistant, cottage enthusiast and love of my life, for endless much-needed encouragement, thank you. —**LET**

# Bibliography

Barron, George. *Mushrooms of Ontario and Eastern Canada*. Edmonton, Alberta: Lone Pine Publishing, 1999

Bennet, Doug and Tim Tiner. *Up North Again: More of Ontario's Wilderness, from Ladybugs to the Pleiades*. Toronto, Ontario: McClelland & Stewart Inc., The Canadian Publishers, 1997

Burns, Max. *Cottage Water Systems: An Out-of-the-City Guide to Pumps, Plumbing, Water Purification, and Privies*. Toronto, Ontario: Cottage Life Books, 1999

Burns, Max. *The Dock Primer: A Cottager's Guide to Waterfront-Friendly Docks*. Toronto, Ontario: Cottage Life and Fisheries and Oceans Canada, 2002

Callan, Kevin. *The Happy Camper: An Essential Guide to Life Outdoors*. Erin, Ontario: Boston Mills Press, 2005

Claudi, Renata and Joseph Leach (eds.). *Non-indigenous Freshwater Organisms: Vectors, Biology and Impacts*. Boca Raton, Florida: Lewis Publishers, 2000

Claudi, Renata and Gerald Mackie. *Practical Manual for Zebra Mussel Monitoring and Control*. Boca Raton, Florida: Lewis Publishers, 1994

Claudi, Renata, Patrick Nantel and Elizabeth Muckle-Jeffs (eds.). *Alien Invaders in Canada's Waters, Wetlands, and Forests*. Ottawa, Ontario: Canadian Forest Service, Natural Resources Canada, 2002

Coad, Brian, Henry Waszczuk and Italo Labignan. *Encyclopedia of Canadian Fishes*. Ottawa, Ontario: Canadian Museum of Nature, 1995

Collins, Henry Hill, *Jr. Harper & Row's Complete Field Guide to North American Wildlife*. New York: Harper & Row Publishers Inc., 1981

Cosgrove, Brian. *Eyewitness Weather*. New York: DK Publishing, 2004

Cudmore, Becky and Nicholas E. Mandrak. *The Baitfish Primer: A Guide to Identifying and Protecting Ontario's Baitfishes*. Peterborough, Ontario: Fisheries and Oceans Canada, 1983

Dickinson, Timothy, Deborah Metsger, Jenny Bull and Richard Dickinson. *The ROM Field Guide to Wildflowers of Ontario*. Toronto, Ontario: McClelland & Stewart Ltd., 2004

Dillard, Gary. *Common Freshwater Algae of the United States: An Illustrated Key to the Genera (Excluding Diatoms)*. Berlin, Germany: Gebrüder Borntraeger, 1999

Evanitski, Cliff. *The Drain Primer: A Guide to Maintaining and Conserving Agricultural Drains and Fish Habitat*. Burlington, Ontario: Drainage Superintendents Association of Ontario, Ontario Federation of Agriculture and Fisheries and Oceans Canada, 2002

Farrar, John Laird. *Trees in Canada*. Markham, Ontario: Fitzhenry & Whiteside and Canadian Forest Service, 1995

Ford, Ray. *The Shore Primer: A Cottager's Guide to a Healthy Waterfront*. Toronto, Ontario: Cottage Life and Fisheries and Oceans Canada, 2000

Forsythe, Robert. *Land Snails of British Columbia*. Royal BC Museum handbook, Victoria, British Columbia: Royal BC Museum, 2004

Hart, Carl W. and Samuel L.H. Fuller. *Pollution Ecology of Freshwater Invertebrates*. New York: Academic Press, 1974

Hartviksen, Connie and Walter Momot. *Fishes of the Thunder Bay Area of Ontario: A Guide for Identifying and Locating the Local Fish Fauna*. Thunder Bay, Ontario: Wildwood Publications, 1988

Hubbs, Carl L. and Karl F. Lagler. Revised by Gerald R. Smith. *Fishes of the Great Lakes Region*. Ann Arbor, Michigan: University of Michigan Press, 2004

Hughes, Janice M. *The ROM Field Guide to Birds of Ontario*. Toronto., Ontario: McClelland & Stewart Ltd., 2001

Kershaw, Linda. *Trees of Ontario*. Edmonton, Alberta: Lone Pine Publishing, 2001

Kershaw, Linda. *Ontario Wildflowers*. Edmonton, Alberta: Lone Pine Publishing, 2002

Kipp, Sarah and Clive Callaway. *On the Living Edge: Your Handbook for Waterfront Living*. Regina, Saskatchewan: Living by Water Project and Nature Saskatchewan, 2003

Lennox, Wayne. *Cottage Essentials: The Everything Guide for Your Cottage, Cabin or Camp*. North Vancouver, British Columbia: Whitecap Books, 2004

Lutz, Frank E. *Field Book of Insects*. New York: G.P. Putnam's Sons, 1948

Lyle, Katie Letcher. *The Complete Guide to Edible Wild Plants, Mushrooms, Fruits, and Nuts. How to Find, Identify and Cook Them*. Guilford, Connecticut: The Lyons Press, 1997

Mackie, Gerald. Chapter 9: "Mollusc Introductions through Aquarium Trade," Chapter 15: "Ballast water introductions of Mollusca," and Chapter 21: Introduction of molluscs through the import for live food." In Claudi, Renata and Joseph Leach (eds.). *Non-indigenous Freshwater Organisms: Vectors, Biology and Impacts*. Boca Raton, Florida: Lewis Publishers, 2000

Mackie, Gerald. "Traits of endangered and invading freshwater molluscs in North America." In Claudi, Renata, Patrick Nantel, Elizabeth Muckle-Jeffs (eds.). *Alien Invaders in Canada's Waters, Wetlands, and Forests*. Ottawa, Ontario: Canadian Forest Service, Natural Resources Canada, 2002

Mackie, Gerald. *Applied Aquatic Ecosystem Concepts*. Dubuque, Iowa: Kendall/Hunt Publishing Company, 2004.

Mackie, Gerald. "Early biological and life history attributes of the zebra mussel, *Dreissena polymorpha* (Bivalvia: Dreissenidae) and impacts on native bivalves in Lake St. Clair." In Tom Nalepa & Donald W. Schloesser (eds.). *Zebra mussels: Biology, Impact and Control*. Boca Raton, Florida: CRC Publications, 1993

Martin, Ian D. and Jayne E. Rutherford. *Fly Fishing the Grand River: The Angler's Vest Pocket Guide*. Elora, Ontario: The Usual Press, 1995

Mason, Cristopher F. *Biology of Freshwater Pollution*. Essex, UK: Longman, 1996

Merritt, Richard W. and Kenneth W. Cummins. *An Introduction to the Aquatic Insects of North America*. Dubuque, Iowa: Kendall Hunt Publishing Company, 1996

Olsen, L-H., J. Sunesen and B.V. Pederson. *Small Freshwater Creatures*. Oxford: Oxford University Press, 1999

Olsen, Oliver Wilford. *Animal Parasites: Their Life Cycles and Ecology.* London: University Park Press, 1974

Pentecost, Allan. *Introduction to Freshwater Algae.* Surrey: Richmond Publishing Company Ltd., 1984

Petrides, George A. *A Field Guide to Trees and Shrubs, Northeastern and North-central United States and Southeastern and South-central Canada.* Peterson Field Guide Series. Boston, Massachusetts: Houghton Mifflin Company, 1986

Robbins, Chandler S., Bertel Bruun and Herbert. S. Zim, revised by Jonathan P. Latimer, Karen Stray Nolting and James Coe. *Birds of North America: A Guide to Field Identification.* St. Martin's Press, New York, 2002

Royer, France and Richard Dickinson. *Weeds of Canada and the Northern United States.* Edmonton, Alberta: The University of Alberta Press and Lone Pine Publishing, 1999

Scott, William B. and Edward J. Crossman. *Freshwater Fishes of Canada.* Oakville, Ontario: Galt House Publications Ltd., 1998

Soper, James H. and Margaret L. Heimburger. *Shrubs of Ontario.* Toronto, Ontario: The Royal Ontario Museum, 1994.

Stephenson, A. *The Safe Boater Manual.* Markham, Ontario: Fitzhenry & Whiteside, 2003

Wetzel, R.G. and G.E. Likens. *Limnological Analyses.* New York: Springer-Verlag, 1991

Whitaker, J.O. *The Audubon Society Field Guide to North American Mammals.* New York: Alfred A. Knopf, 1988

Work Safe Alberta. Workplace Health and Safety Bulletin. Edmonton, Alberta: Government of Alberta, Human Resources and Employment, 2003

# Credits

## Photographs

All photographs by Laura E. Taylor, unless otherwise noted.

Trevor Allen 64
Bruce Amos 45 (bottom right), 69 (bottom), 268
Anyka 191 (left)
Wesley Aston 140
Danny Bailey 225
Maciek Baran 220 (right)
Marilyn Barbone 22 (bottom)
George Barron 208 (bottom left and right), 209, 210, 211, 212, 213 (middle and bottom)
Peter Baxter 56, 155 (right)
Don Bayley 69 (middle)
Ivo Benes 205 (bottom)
Richard C. Bennett 145 (bottom)
Penelope Berger 81 (top)
Ben Blankenburg 47 (top)
Bluestocking 234
Frank Boellman 219
Vera Bogaerts 92 (top), 243
James Boulette 65 (top left)
Ian Bracegirdle 17
Jock Bradley 52
J. Breedlove 45 (top)
Adrian Britton 227
Sascha Burkard 119
Kris Butler 206 (top right)
Elimantas Buzas 263 (bottom)
Caleb 135
Kevin Callan 25 (right), 44, 45 (bottom left), 47 (bottom right), 48 (top left and right), 50 (top)
Melissa Carroll 199
Zygimantas Cepaitis 262 (top)
Yanik Chauvin 11 (bottom), 249
Jeff Chevrier 11 (top)
Sergey Chushkin 259 (second from top)
John Clines 203 (bottom)
Bertie Coetzee 33
Andrew Cribb 112 (right)
John Czenke 153 (top)
Sharon D 160 (left), 196 (top left)
Smaglov D. 250 (left)
Silvia D'Amelio 36 (second and third from top)
Benoit David 218 (bottom)
Christa De Ridder 214
Steve Degenhardt 112 (bottom left)

Sabrina Dei Nobili 207
Jim DeLillo 230, 262 (bottom)
Alexey Demidov 183 (top)
Nikolay Stefanov Dimitrov 115
Lisa Elam 217 (bottom)
Elena Elisseeva 42, 53, 252
Don Enright 198 (right)
EON Decking 82 (top), Robert Faubert 47 (bottom left)
Stephen Firmender 65 (bottom)
Francois Fortin 49
Jackie Foster 81 (bottom)
Kathleen Fraser 10 (top left)
Melissa Garrett 265
Robert Goldberg 247
Jeff Golfarb 63
Michael Gomez 176
Kenneth Graff 55
FhF Greenmedia 195
Ilya D. Gridnev 36 (top)
Tatiana Grozetskaya 16 (bottom)
Jaroslaw Grudzinski 269
Tom Grundy 22 (top)
Jeff Gynane 240 (bottom)
Cindy Haggerty 163
Robert Hambley 164 (left)
Ulrike Hammerich 16 (top)
Paul Hart 216
Michelle Harvey 236
Daneil Hebert 245
Dana Heinemann 256
J. Helgason 130
Steven Hendricks 246 (bottom right)
Greg Henry 85 (top), 86 (bottom)
Rob Hill 239 (bottom)
Nicholas James Homrich 182 (left)
Ronnie Howard 144 (right), 167 (top left)
Benjamin A. Hunter 96 (top right)
Rob Huntley 259 (top left)
Terekhov Igor 235
InStock Photographic Ltd. 68
IRC 22 (middle)
Vladimir Ivanov 106 (top right)
Pekka Jaakkola 99
Javarman (top right) 113
Tomo Jesenicnik 105
Jim Jurica 259 (top row, second from left)
Renars Jurkovskis 120
Chris Kallio 200

James Kamstra 39, 95, 96 (bottom), 159, 160 (left), 161, 171 (left), 173 (bottom)
Denise Kappa 62
Jason Kasumovic 147
John Kirnic 152 (top)
James E. Knopf 114 (top)
Nataly Kochina 198 (bottom left)
Vladimir Korostyshevkiy 10 (top right)
Alex Krapranoff 23 (top)
Kristian 154
Roman Krochuk 128 (top)
Geoffrey Kuchera 146
Emilia Kun 178 (top left)
Robert Kyllo 113 (bottom), 238 (left)
Timothy Large 122
Karin Lau 107
Liga Lauzuma 181
Oleg Lazarenko 72
Chris LeBoutiller 134
Keith Levit 8, 12, 60 (bottom), 61 (bottom)
David P. Lewis 233
Edyta Linek 90, 91 (top)
Nancy Louie 264
Steve Lovegrove 127 (top)
Olga Lyubkina 51
Gerry Mackie 15 (right), 84 (bottom), 231 (bottom), 243 (bottom), 251 (top row)
Robert Manley 251 (bottom)
Milos Markovic 218 (top)
Steve Marshall 35, 36 (bottom), 97, 178 (top right), 182 (right), 183 (bottom), 188, 190 (bottom)
Doug Matthews 149 (bottom)
maxstockphoto 48 (bottom)
Christian McCarthy 113 (top left)
Robert McCaw 38, 138, 141, 142, 143, 144 (top), 145 (left), 152 (bottom), 153 (bottom), 155 (left), 156, 160 (second and third from left), 164 (right), 165, 166, 167 (bottom and top right), 168, 170, 171 (right), 172 (top), 173 (top), 177 (bottom), 196 (top right), 198 (middle left)
Chad McDermott 69 (top)
Sherwin McGehee 194
Stephen McSweeny 169
Steve McWilliam 258 (bottom)

Gita Memmena 74
Craig Mills 71 (bottom)
William Milner 26
Xavier Minguella 185 (bottom)
Mistral 57
Chris Mole 61 (top)
Brian Morrison 77 (bottom)
Stephen O. Muskie 132
mypokcik 180 (left), 240 (top left)
Andre Nantel 92 (bottom)
Sean Nel 54, 129 (top)
Robert Nystrom 114 (bottom)
Nikolay Okhitin 220 (left)
Old Town Canoes 29 (left), 46, 50 (bottom)
Tom Oliveira 238 (right)
Thomas O'Neil 139
Vicki O'Shaughnessy 10 (bottom), 60 (top)
Roman Pavlik 15 (left)
Denis Pepin 240 (second from left)
R. Perreault 58
Olga Petrova 191 (right)
Michael Pettigrew 185 (top), 189 (left)
Anthony Pham 41
Martin Pietak 187
PM Photo 184
Brian Prechtel/USDA Agricultural Research Service 201
Viktor Pryymachuk 204 (bottom)
Pitor Przeszlo 112 (top left), 114 (third from top)
Philip Puleo 177 (top)
Radu Razvan 178 (bottom)
Nicholas Rjabow 100
Robynrg 136
Mike Rogal 137
Richard Sargeant 114 (second from top)
Emily Sartoski 186 (bottom)
Lawrence Sawyer 78
Bonnie Schupp 223
Alistair Scott 260 (top)
Ian Scott 58
Sally Scott 82 (bottom)
Eva Serrabassa 239 (top)
siloto 190 (top)
Warren E. Simpson 150
Deborah Sinclair 30
Brandon Smith 108
Ljupco Smokovski 260 (bottom)
Clint Spencer 96 (top left)
Don Standfield 126
Brandon Stein 65 (top right)

Jacom Stephens 129 (bottom)
Jose Alberto Tejo 157
Greg Thorn 213 (top)
Tihis 127 (bottom)
Wellford Tiller 263 (top)
Andrey Ushakov 106 (top left)
Beth Van Trees 206 (top left)
Stephen VanHorn 40 (bottom)
Ismael Montero Verdu 179 (top), 180 (right), 186 (top)
Amy Walters 189 (right), 241
Clive Watkins 77 (top)
Neil Webster 80
Roger Whiteway 205 (top right)
Sebastien Windal 217 (top)
Shannon Workman 79
Wayne Wurtsbaugh/Utah State University and the American Society of Limnology and Oceanography 75
Paul Yates 124 (left)
Shawn Zhang 231 (top)
Joanna Zopoth-Lipiejko 182 (left)
Tim Zurowski 172 (bottom), 246 (top and bottom left)

## Illustrations

Kathe Gray 29, 37, 261

Imagineering Media Services Inc. 14 (bottom), 18, 20, 21, 24, 30 (bottom), 59, 74, 76, 78, 87, 90, 98, 102, 118, 120, 121, 151, 158, 168, 174, 192 (bottom), 221, 228 (bottom), 229, 248, 254

Ryan Price 1, 5, 6, 7, 9, 13, 14 (top), 19, 25, 30 (top), 41, 43, 57, 89, 93, 105, 109, 110, 117, 133, 149, 175, 192 (top), 215, 228 (top), 266, 268, 271, 272

# Index

Page numbers in *italics* refer to illustrations. Illustrations are not cited if they appear on pages that deal with the subject in the text.